MANUFACTURING POSSIBILITIES

MANUFACTURING POSSIBILITIES

Creative Action and Industrial Recomposition in the United States, Germany, and Japan

GARY HERRIGEL

University of Chicago

OXFORD

UNIVERSITY PRESS

OXFORD

UNIVERSITY PRESS

Great Clarendon Street, Oxford OX2 6DP

Oxford University Press is a department of the University of Oxford.
It furthers the University's objective of excellence in research, scholarship,
and education by publishing worldwide in

Oxford New York

Auckland Cape Town Dar es Salaam Hong Kong Karachi
Kuala Lumpur Madrid Melbourne Mexico City Nairobi
New Delhi Shanghai Taipei Toronto

With offices in

Argentina Austria Brazil Chile Czech Republic France Greece
Guatemala Hungary Italy Japan Poland Portugal Singapore
South Korea Switzerland Thailand Turkey Ukraine Vietnam

Oxford is a registered trade mark of Oxford University Press
in the UK and in certain other countries

Published in the United States
by Oxford University Press Inc., New York

British Library Cataloguing in Publication Data

Data available

Library of Congress Cataloging in Publication Data

Data available

Typeset by SPI Publisher Services, Pondicherry, India
Printed in Great Britain
on acid-free paper by the
MPG Books Group, Bodmin and King's Lynn

ISBN 978-0-19-955773-8

To Carol, Luke, and James

Contents

Acknowledgments

I have received a tremendous amount of support from many quarters during the writing of this book. The following list of people, no doubt incomplete, contributed significant comments and/or provided encouragement to me over the course of writing the various pieces of *Manufacturing Possibilities*: Andy Abbott, Chris Ansell, Ingrid Artus, Lucio Baccaro, Suzanne Berger, Katherina Bluhm, Danny Breznitz, Bruce Carruthers, Steve Casper, Jessica Cattelino, Pepper Culpepper, Emmanuel Didier, Jeffrey Fear, Anthony Ferner, Archon Fung, Dennis Galvan, Christiane Gebhardt, Henrik Glimstedt, Peter Gourevitch, Gernot Grabher, Bob Hancke, Leslie Hannah, Vicky Hattam, Susan Helper, Yoi Herrera, Uli Jürgens, Peter Katzenstein, Christian Kleinschmidt, Bruce Kogut, Hyeong-Ki Kwon, Karl Lauschke, Richard Lester, Tony Levitas, Ken Lipartito, Ricky Locke, Maja Lotz, Dan Luria, John Paul MacDuffie, Gerry McDermott, Jürgen Mandelke, Stan Markus, Glenn Morgan, Karen Orren, John Padgett, Roger Pedersen, Michael Piore, Markus Pohlmann, Amy Poteete, Dan Raff, Jeremiah Riemer, Joel Rogers, Sean Safford, Mari Sako, Dick Samuels, Anno Saxenian, Marc Schneiberg, Andrew Shrank, Steve Skowronek, Jaap Sleifer, Ed Steinfeld, Michael Storper, Tim Sturgeon, Jörg Sydow, Carey Taredo, Mark Thatcher, Kathleen Thelen, Mark Tilton, Matt Vidal, Kazo Wada, Josh Whitford, Richard Whitley, Mira Wilkens, and Nick Ziegler. I also thank Rob Honkonen, Natalia Yarotskaya, Minjae Kim; Nick Kreitman, and Laura Kjeraulf for research assistance.

In the initial phase of this research, I spent a year at the Industrial Performance Center at the Massachusetts Institute of Technology (MIT) on a Sloan Foundation Fellowship. I thank Richard Lester, the IPC's director, for a stimulating environment and generous support of my work. In general, much of this research was supported by various grants from the Alfred P. Sloan Foundation and I thank them for that.

During my research travels to Germany, the SOFI Institute in Göttingen became a second home. I thank Volker Wittke, the Institute's director for his hospitality. Volker is also a dear friend and collaborator. I have traveled all over the world with him following multinational corporations (MNCs) and supply chains. In our travels and joint research, we have had countless discussions about the issues dealt with in this volume. His mark is on *Manufacturing Possibilities* in ways too numerous to count. I also thank the colleagues at SOFI with whom I have discussed many of the matters in this book at great length—and repeatedly: Michael Schumann, Martin Baethge, Hans Joachim Sperling, Uli Voskamp, Michael Faust, Martin Kuhlmann, and Heidi Hanekop.

Also in Germany, I would like to thank Rudolf Luz of the IG Metall Verwaltungsstelle in Neckarsulm and Fritz Janitz of the IG Metall Verwaltungsstelle in Wuppertal. Both generously opened their communities to our research interests over several years. They also proved to be highly reflective and stimulating discussion partners, from whom I have learned an enormous amount.

At the University of Chicago, I would like to thank Dali Yang, who pointed out that making a book out of my ongoing research and writing would not be a bad thing. Dan Slater always followed this project with great interest. He contributed very helpful critical readings of the introduction for which I am very grateful. Moishe Postone never commented directly on this manuscript, but in a different register he and I have argued for twenty years about the issues the volume addresses. His constant skepticism and disagreement, warmly and solidaristically delivered, have made my ideas, such as they are, much better.

One approaches the inner circle. Peer Hull Kristensen and Chuck Sabel have been mentors to me for nearly thirty years. Both have been unquestioningly loyal, unremittingly encouraging, and energetically supportive for that entire time. Anyone with even fleeting familiarity with their work will see their influence all over the arguments in this book. What they will not see are the countless acts of friendship that have sustained me and, significantly, lifted me up when it appeared that few others would. Gerry Berk, old friend, has helped me work through ideas about pragmatism and possibility for decades. I have learned much from his own work and have benefited from his very helpful comments on the material in this book. *Manufacturing Possibilities* is an outgrowth of, and a contribution to, our ongoing conversation.

I need to begin a new paragraph to acknowledge the enormous support I have received from Jonathan Zeitlin. Jonathan has been involved, in one way or another, in all of the research that forms the basis for this book. We have done endless interviews together and have jointly read and discussed all of the literatures upon which the arguments in this book touch. He has read and critically commented upon every word of the manuscript, in most cases several times. We coedited a volume that contains Chapter 1 and we coauthored Chapter 5. The facts clearly show that my work owes a great deal to Jonathan's critical engagement. It is not reasonable in Jonathan's case, however, to be satisfied merely with the acknowledgment of fact. Anyone who knows Jonathan knows that he has extremely high standards, intellectual and otherwise. I have learned a great deal, not only from his engagement with my work, but also, perhaps even more significantly, from his example.

Finally, I thank my family, Carol, Luke, and James, for their wonderful support of my efforts. They really could not care less about automobile components, Minimills, pragmatism, or institutionalism, but they make it clear to me all the time that they care quite a bit about me. Without that there really would not have been any *Manufacturing Possibilities*. I dedicate this book to them.

List of Tables

List of Figures

List of Abbreviations

AISI	American Iron and Steel Institute
AMP	Advanced Manufacturing Project
BOF	Basic Oxygen Furnace Technology
CCSC	Coordinating Committee of Steel Companies
EAF	Electric Arc Furnace
ECSC	European Coal and Steel Community
GmbH	Gesellschaft mit beschränkter Haftung
GMH	Georgsmarienhütte
HGW	Hermann Göring Werke
HKM	Hüttenwerk Krupp-Mannesmann
ID/LPS	Industrial District/Local Production System
ISG	International Steel Group
ITP	Industrial Training Program
ITW	Illinois Tool Works
LP/CSC	Lean Production/Collaborative Supply Chain
M/CM	Modularity/Contract Manufacturing
MITI	Ministry of International Trade and Industry
MNCs	Multinational Corporations
OEM	Original Equipment Manufacturer
OH	Open Hearth
PBGC	Pension Benefit Guaranty Corporation
SCAP	Supreme Command of the Allied Powers
SCC	Sustained Contingent Collaboration
SMA	Steel Manufacturers Association
SMEs	Small- and Medium-Sized Enterprises
USWA	United Steelworkers of America
Vestag	Vereinigte Stahlwerke AG
VIA	Valley Industrial Association
VRAs	Voluntary Restraint Agreements
WMDC	Wisconsin Manufacturers Development Consortium
WMEP	Wisconsin Manufacturing Extension Partnership

Introduction

Manufacturing Possibilities, Creative Action, and Industrial Recomposition

Over the past three decades, tremendous debate has raged about whether or not globalization pressures—market integration, technological diffusion, and multinational company expansion—will cause practices, rules, and governance forms across advanced political economies to become more alike. Those who believe that globalization leads to convergence are united on the claim that global pressures spread market relations and liberal individualism at the expense of nonmarket coordination and solidaristic commitments. They are divided, however, on whether or not such "neoliberalism" is a desirable result (Hansmann and Kraakman 2001; Fourcade-Gourinchas and Babb 2002; Rajan and Zingales 2004; Harvey 2005; Prasad 2006; Mudge 2008; Somers 2008). Those who dispute the idea that global pressures produce convergence point to the continued robustness of indigenous institutions and to the comparative advantages that different institutional arrangements have even in competitive and open markets. Their dilemma, however, is that the theoretical models they use to account for institutional continuity make it difficult for them to capture the many real ways societies, different from one another as they remain, are nonetheless changing in response to global pressures (Hall and Soskice 2001; Amable 2003; Yamamura and Streeck 2003; Pierson 2004; Thelen 2004; Morgan et al. 2005; Streeck and Thelen 2005). Both debates revolve around key conceptual oppositions: convergence versus difference, continuity versus change, market versus coordination, and individual rationality versus solidarity.

This book recasts this debate by insisting that the conceptual oppositions that frame it are not, in practice, mutually exclusive. That is, rather than understanding market and coordination processes as antithetical, it will repeatedly show that actors in the United States, Germany, and Japan are readily combining those principles to solve challenges in their competitive environments. Through these joint creative actions, moreover, actors embrace and initiate change in certain areas even as there is continuity with the past in others. Creative action is making individual rationality work for solidarity. Ultimately, this book argues that global market integration produces both convergence and renewed difference in organizational practices, rules, and governance forms across advanced industrial economies.

This argument is developed through an examination of adjustment dynamics in the steel, automobile, and machinery sectors in Germany, the United States, and Japan since World War II. Crucial organizational forms, business strategies, and institutional systems emerged in these industries that proved to govern industrial practice more broadly in each of the three political economies. Most recently, those industries have been profoundly affected by globalization. As US, German, and Japanese actors try to compete under common global conditions, they recompose the boundaries of firms, industries, producer strategies, stakeholder interests, and governance mechanisms throughout their political economies. Examining adjustment in these important manufacturing sectors over the past six decades thus provides an excellent lens on how global market integration has impacted critical practices and institutional relations governing industry in each country.

The chapters in this book are both historical and contemporary. They analyze industrial change as a bottom-up, socially reflexive process of creative action. Two theoretical claims drive the entire analysis. The first is that action is social, reflexive, and ultimately creative. When their interactive habits are disrupted, actors seek to repair their relations by reconceiving them. Such imaginative interaction causes unforeseen possibilities for action to emerge. The second theoretical claim is that change is recompositional. Creative actors rearrange, modify, reconceive, and reposition inherited organizational forms and governance mechanisms as they experiment with solutions to the challenges that they face. Creativity in the recomposition process makes, among other things, the introduction of entirely new practices and relations possible.

This relational and process-centered view is part of a broader contemporary revival of pragmatism in social theory and political economy (Joas 1996; Emirbayer and Mischke 1998; Sabel and Dorf 1998; Joas and Beckert 2001; Kristensen and Zeitlin 2005; Latour 2005; Sabel 2005*b*; Latour 2007; Unger 2007; Berk and Galvin 2008; Ansell 2009). The revival reflects a feeling of dissatisfaction with neoliberal economism's emphasis on atomized individuals' rational calculations and institutionalism's emphasis on constraining rules and sanctions in shaping industrial change. Though the view here also believes that rules and individual calculations are important, it rejects the separation of actor from context on which both of those traditions rely in conceiving the situation for action. Moreover, rational calculation and constraining rules are only partial aspects of how actors experience, reflect upon, and interact within industrial life. Political, social, and moral commitments also inform industrial action. Too often, failure to acknowledge the role of these latter factors—or, more generally, to appreciate the capaciousness of the reflective dimension of social action—leads analysts to understand the range of industrial adjustment possibilities as unnecessarily limited.

US, German, and Japanese steel industry evolution since World War II is the focus of Part I. All three chapters in Part I show that common global conditions produce similar steel industry strategies. But they do not produce convergence. There are many different ways to do the same (or similar) things. Over time and under pressure from global markets (and, initially in Germany and

Japan, American military pressure), collectively creative players in each national industry embrace similar production technologies (integrated and electric arc processes), strategic industry patterns (bifurcated structures between increasingly specialized Integrated Mills and broadly diversified Minimills), and market control processes (controlled market-supplanting wage and price-setting procedures) while creating and re-creating differences among the societies. Comparative similarities and differences are recurrently created over the course of industry evolution, the chapters argue, because industry players interactively redefine economic rationality and overcome institutional constraint in ways that create paradoxical and counterintuitive possibilities for adjustment in their indigenous contexts.

Part II of the book analyzes the disintegration of production in the automotive and machinery industries in the last thirty years, primarily in Germany and the United States. The story there is also about creativity, possibility, and plasticity in the context of common global conditions. Even as industrial actors pursue similar strategies in increasingly integrated global markets, they do so creatively in ways that produce new relational and institutional governance possibilities in firms, supply chains, and areas of regional, national, and supranational policy. These innovative responses to common competitive challenges are neither hindered nor especially shaped by preexisting national institutional differences. Nor do they lead to convergence between US and German industries. Rather interactively strategizing actors recompose differences between the societies at virtually all levels in an effort to achieve remarkably similar industrial objectives. This is true because the arrangements that emerge from creative action and processes of recomposition are not merely governance solutions to concrete economic challenges. They also express the normative and historical commitments of the creative recomposing actors.

1. WHY MANUFACTURING?

It may seem odd to present a book on comparative political economy which foregrounds manufacturing possibilities in the world's three most advanced economies. For many years, it has been far more usual to eulogize manufacturing than to speak of its possibilities—especially in the United States. Slower growth relative to services (especially the financial and health-care sectors), dramatic trade deficits, repeated structural adjustment crises, social dislocation—all have been woven understandably, but unfortunately, into a folk narrative casting manufacturing as a dying area of our economic life. Indeed, much like the agrarian ideal that it replaced in the twentieth century, manufacturing has lost its prominent place in the social imaginary as a focal point of the political economy and a force that drives us forward. Genetic and bioengineering, mathematical financiers, system analysts, and internet tycoons—the "new economy"—turn our heads to the future. The mechanical world—the "old economy" of complex machinery and components—increasingly becomes outsourced in our minds to locations that are more suited to those kinds of pursuits. They go to societies that we believe look more like we once did, with levels of wealth and development that we have left behind. Manufacturing, it is said, is no longer our comparative advantage because we now occupy a different "level" of development. If anything, design and research are appropriate for us, but actually making things is *naturally* gravitating away. In this view, efforts to attend to genuine adjustment challenges affecting the reproduction of manufacturing use a vocabulary informed by the language of health care and dying bodies: Industries are rescued, jobs are saved. The accent suggests a honorable and heroic effort against ineluctable, almost natural, forces of economic nature and progress (e.g., Packer 2008; Reich 2009).

Despite its prevalence in many editorial board imaginaries, pundit blogs, and political campaign rhetoric, this folk narrative actually rests on tenuous assumptions. These assumptions have become even more tenuous in the wake of the global economic crisis that began in 2008. For example, the distinction between the "new" and "old" economy, and between manufacturing and services upon which it often rests, is rarely very clearly defined. Much of what we call services are in fact either outsourced functions that were formerly conducted by industrial firms, or are functions that continue to be dependent directly on industrial customers. Much modern customized, just-in-time manufacturing in the "old" economy, for example, incorporates services into the product. Further, many producers of "old" technologies very systematically integrate and apply "new" technologies in their products. Finally, the tremendous growth of the financial sectors of the economy (and the high-tech drivers before them), in particular, has been followed by perhaps even more breathless collapse. Manufacturing's comparatively modest but consistent growth in the boom times has been overwhelmed, with everything else, by the collapse of the financial system. But as the enormity of the excesses of the financial boom is revealed, those interested in recovery and greater balance in the future look increasingly to those parts of the "real" economy capable of creating products of tangible and functional value (Bailey and Soyouing 2009; Gomory 2009; Kotkin 2009; McCormack 2009).

Perhaps the strongest reason to reconsider the importance of "old" economy manufacturing in our modern political economy, however, is its obstinate factual refusal to die. As Section 3 will show in more detail, US manufacturing sector production volume, for example, is larger, in absolute terms, than it has ever been. Despite the massive growth of Asian economies, the United States has consistently accounted for approximately 25% of worldwide manufacturing value-added since 1980. Moreover, even as recently as 2005 the United States was the world's second largest exporter and manufacturing accounted for over 60% of total US exports. US producers are among world leaders in a vast array of traditional manufacturing products, ranging from raw steel to fluid dynamic technology and automobiles. In short, Germany (the world's largest exporter in the 2000s), Japan, and the United States remain huge, dynamic, and innovative manufacturing locations. On paper, then, the folk narrative of decay, decline, and death in manufacturing seems, at the very least, overdrawn. Many possibilities still exist for manufacturing in developed economies.

2. MANUFACTURING AND SOCIAL SCIENCE

Beneath the popular "folk" sensibility about manufacturing, of course, a specialized literature exists about how manufacturing has been evolving and changing in the contemporary global economy. This discussion has had two sides, both of which the argument here rejects. One side, associated broadly with neoliberalism, argues that with the opening of trade and financial markets over the last thirty or so years, the logic of competitive efficiency and the superior competitive power of industrial players from "liberal" economies committed to strong market principles is making all advanced industrial economies more and more alike. In a virtuous circle of liberalization, the diffusion of open exchange of goods and services across market areas forces both producers and whole economies to embrace increasingly similar production practices, labor market rules, corporate governance structures, and financial arrangements. This in turn further increases the exchange of goods and services and leads to still more liberalization—ad infinitum. Enduring differences between economies, on this view, have to do either with differences in endowment (more or less land, labor or capital, or specialized agglomerations based on those things) or "barriers to trade" (erected by incumbent monopolies or other opponents of market rationality) or unimportant residuals with little immediate importance for economic performance (Hansmann and Kraakman 2001; Fourcade-Gourinchas and Babb 2002; Rajan and Zingales 2004; Harvey 2005; Prasad 2006; Mudge 2008; Somers 2008).

Against this view has been an institutionalist literature arguing that strong liberalization claims for convergence underestimate the resilience of domestic institutions, for one or both of two reasons. First, institutional arrangements, in production and in the architecture of the economy (labor markets, corporate governance, welfare institutions, and finance) are sticky (path dependent). They are held together by strong political pacts and bargains in societies that have strong feedback dynamics with interrelated institutional systems. Institutions constrain actors from pursuing alternative strategies and provide them with incentives to react to challenges in ways that shore up the existing institutional architecture. As a result, "non-liberal" or "coordinated market" economies resist liberalization's pressures for social transformation in the economy (Streeck 1997; Whitley 1999; Hall and Soskice 2001; Amable 2003; Yamamura and Streeck 2003; Pierson 2004; Hall and Thelen 2009).

Second, resisting liberal (often simply understood as US) practices has a positive, competitive economic logic. The "non-liberal" or "coordinated" institutional arrangements in places like Germany and Japan have comparative advantages that the liberal economies do not have. Indeed, the Varieties of

Capitalism (VoC) school of institutionalism goes so far as to claim that "coordinated" political economies have advantages in gradual innovation and continuous improvement-driven sectors (such as automobiles and machinery), while "liberal" political economies excel in sectors driven by radical innovation (such as electronics, biotechnology, and telecommunications) (Hall and Soskice 2001). Thus, for the institutionalists, differences among advanced industrial countries do not simply block the onset of the virtuous circle of liberalization, as in the neoliberal view. Instead, they constitute viable alternative growth dynamics.

This book engages very extensively with these arguments.[1] In most respects, the chapters chart a course that is quite different from either the liberal or institutionalist accounts. It corroborates the neoliberal view that there are common global pressures, and that successful producers in the same industry pursue similar strategies regardless of where they are located. Against the liberal view, however, the chapters very clearly show that German, US, and Japanese industries continue to have markedly different social relations and forms of institutional governance stretching deeply into their political economies. Indeed, the studies of the steel, automobile, and machinery industries show that new differences are continuously being created in the face of contemporary challenges. The fact that industrial producers in all three economies are competing against one another and are coping with remarkably similar market, organizational, and technological challenges, does not lead to institutional or organizational leveling. There is no virtuous circle of liberalization, even when there is robust growth and change.

Against the institutionalist argument for continuing difference and comparative institutional advantage, the chapters develop two criticisms: They show, first, that differences between societies are not being reproduced because institutions (or underlying political economic power relations) constrain actors to respond to challenges in particular ways. Instead, the chapters show repeatedly that differences are being reproduced because actors in very different contexts are creatively responding to challenges in ways that recompose their identities, relations, interests and, ultimately, institutional forms of governance. Difference begets more difference because creativity trumps constraint. The chapters also show, second, that the strong VoC claim regarding comparative institutional advantages across the political economies is deeply flawed. US, German, and Japanese producers in core manufacturing sectors have all at various times engaged in both radical and gradual forms of innovation. Institutions do not create advantages or disadvantages in this book; instead, creative and reflective actors collectively align and realign roles and rules as they seek to compete in global markets.

---

[1] What follows broadly contrasts the perspective of creative action and recomposition with these two alternative approaches. If the reader is looking for more detailed criticisms, they can be found in Chapters 2, 3, 5, 6, and 7. The Conclusion to this volume, moreover, returns to institutionalist and rationalist theories in a more detailed way, presenting criticisms of those frameworks on the basis of the book's accumulated empirical evidence. The aim of this introduction is to highlight the distinctive contours of the pragmatic view of creative action and recomposition.

Behind these criticisms of neoliberal economism and institutionalism is a distinct pragmatist perspective that contrasts strongly with both traditions' theoretical priors. Section 4 of this introductory chapter will develop the pragmatic perspective more fully. But it is appropriate here to indicate the main differences in relation to the two competing traditions of thought. Most emphatically, pragmatism departs from the neoliberal worldview by abandoning the atomized, rational, individual chooser and the maximizing market logic that is central to that line of thinking about social and economic change. The economistic rational choice framework reduces actors to miraculously pre-formed, passive reactors to external environmental constraints and incentives. The neoliberal image is of a world of self-contained individuals rationally and strategically picking from options that the environment presents to them. Pragmatism also places actors at the center of analysis, but the actors in this book, by contrast, are defined by the social and political relations that they are (always) part of. Most importantly, the actors in this book are vital: they *actively create themselves* and collectively define the context in which they act. Identities and interests are not pre-given. They emerge jointly out of collective interactions about how to understand, define, and resolve challenges posed in a common environment. In this book, action is a vital social and creative process. It is not something initiated by an atomized individual agent with pre-given preferences making discrete choices.

The pragmatist emphasis on creative action in this book also departs from the structuralist theoretical priors of institutionalism, especially as developed in the VoC, Comparative Business Systems, and Historical Institutionalist schools of thought. Those traditions emphasize the way in which institutional arrangements, rules, and norms constrain and enable action and reaction to environmental challenges. The argument here, however, focuses first on the actors themselves, their mutual relations and interactions and the public conversations they have about the pressures they face, and problems that they need to resolve. Action is social, reflective, and creative. Institutions (rules, norms) are markers or expressions of the (always provisional) arrangements that actors have created. Institutions do not constrain or enable actors; actors constrain and enable themselves.

A final contrast involves the relationship between stability and change in social life. Neoliberalism and structuralist institutionalism rigidly divide the flow of social life into periods of equilibrium or reproduction and periods of disequilibrium or crisis. By contrast, the pragmatic view of creative action and recomposition sees stability and change, continuity and breaks, as constantly intertwined features of social life. Changes in industries and their governing arrangements can be provoked by exogenous challenges in the environment (such as the emergence of a global market). They can also be provoked by instability induced endogenously by the simple fact that industry-relevant actors invariably play multiple roles and have multifaceted self-understandings. Industry-related players are constantly engaged in socially reflexive processes that seek both to define the character of the context they find themselves within and to determine what their roles in that context should be: What are our challenges? What are our purposes?

What problems require our collective redress? How are our past practices and understandings in need of reform? Can they be salvaged? Are there alternatives? Do solutions to our problems exist in other contexts?

These highly reflective processes occur at many different levels of manufacturing and industrial life whenever those involved encounter difficulties in their common practice. Disruption produces reflection and creative action that, in turn, changes, modifies, redefines—*recomposes*—relations where arrangements cannot solve the problems that actors jointly confront. These reflective and creative processes do not occur in coordinated or synchronized ways. Change at different levels does not occur simultaneously. Relations that confront no problems are not necessarily placed under pressure to change. Very often, therefore, they do not change. Sometimes they are affected by change elsewhere, and therefore they do change. When change occurs and at what levels is an empirical, not a theoretical question. The bottom line here, however, is not that everything in the social world is changing all the time. It is that where there is change, it is recompositional and creative action drives it.

On one level, this perspective on change and stability mirrors the emerging position of a reformed historical institutionalism that emphasizes gradual, piecemeal institutional change (Streeck and Thelen 2005; Mahoney and Thelen 2008; Thelen 2009; Hall and Thelen 2009). Like the analysis here, that school argues that the source of institutional changes and modifications must be sought outside of institutions in the relations among the actors that utilize them. The reformed historical institutionalists, however, view those "exogenous" social relations in a structural light, as if interests regarding social transformation can be transparently read off underlying positions in the economic structure. The analysis here, by contrast, argues that creativity trumps structural constraint in all dimensions of political, economic, and social life. There is no transparent extra-institutional structure that allows one to predictably determine the interests of historical industrial actors within institutions.

In short, the view in this book is neither rationally individualistic, nor a version of structuralist institutionalism. Actors and action are the drivers of the analysis, and yet it focuses neither on individuals nor their choices. Rather, action is social, interactional, and processual; like a conversation, not a soliloquy. By the same token, the interrelated industrial players in this account live in, give meaning to, and use institutions. Yet they are not guided or constrained by them. Instead, they manipulate, rearrange, discard, and ignore them, as the case may be, as they seek to resolve problems that emerge in their environments. Institutions appear in the chapters that follow as decomposable resources (among a broad array of social, cultural, and political resources) for actors to (re)deploy in the process of social problem solving. Each of the chapters makes clear that the payoff from this alternative perspective is the ability to identify a wider range of practical possibilities for manufacturing practice than is possible within either of the alternative theoretical traditions.

The rest of this introduction elaborates on the two most distinctive elements of the above argument, the continued importance of manufacturing in advanced industrial political economies, and the pragmatist theory of social action emphasizing creativity and recompositional change. Section 3 outlines the somewhat surprising continued importance of manufacturing in the political economies of advanced industrial states. Section 4 elaborates on the ideas of creative action and recomposition that drive the analysis of industrial change throughout this book. Finally, Section 5 details the sequencing of chapters and the flow of argument in the book.

3. THE PERSISTENT IMPORTANCE OF MANUFACTURING IN THE UNITED STATES, GERMANY, AND JAPAN

Manufacturing is frequently underestimated in contemporary characterizations of highly developed political economies. This is particularly true in the United States. It is important for the appreciation of the aims of this book to frame the challenges in manufacturing production in a realistic manner. There are some understandable reasons for the general "folk" underestimation of US manufacturing today. Above all, the relative size of manufacturing in comparison to services within GDP has consistently shrunk over the last half century, falling from approximately 25% in the 1950s to around 14% in 2009 (NAM 2006). The disparity in growth rates between the two sectors has been especially great in the last twenty years, driven in part by astonishing (and as it happens, unsustainable) growth in the financial industries (Krippner 2005; Brenner 2006). The bulk of employment and value generated in the United States is overwhelmingly located in the broad area of services: Manufacturing accounts for just 11% of total employment in the United States, down from 20% in 1979 (a loss of over 5 million jobs) (Deitz and Orr 2006). It is, no doubt, this relative shift in the weight of manufacturing that conjures up narratives of natural courses of development, and produces analogies to the relative shrinkage of agriculture in industrial economies.

The balance between manufacturing and services is slightly more even in Germany and Japan. But services in both economies also account for the vast majority of employment and GDP value. In 2008, in Germany, manufacturing accounted for 25% of total employment and industry as a whole accounted for approximately 30% of GDP by value (CIA 2009). In 2007, in Japan, the manufacturing share of employment was 27.8% (JILPT 2009) while industry accounted for approximately 25% of GDP (CIA 2009). Though manufacturing has continued to be a (slightly) more significant part of employment and total GDP than in the United States, in both countries the sector has shrunk relative to services significantly in recent decades. In 1950 Germany, the extreme case, industry accounted for 43% of total employment (Maddison 1999).[2]

---

[2] Germany is an extreme case because industrial employment was actually larger than service employment in the first part of the twentieth century. Surprisingly, given the prevalence of the analogy to agriculture in the "folk" understanding of development, industry never accounted for more employment than services in either the United States or Japan. See Table 7 in Maddison (1999).

Popular underestimation of manufacturing also stems from the fact that manufacturing has suffered through a difficult series of structural adjustment crises over the last several decades, in among other sectors, textiles, machine tools (above all in the United States), steel, consumer electronics, and automobiles. Large-scale plant closings, layoffs, and portraits of shuttered mills and main streets in "rust belts" and other "old" industrial regions have generated the view that manufacturing is something that highly developed economies can no longer reliably compete in. The technologies are too well known and levels of wages are too high to be able to prevent the migration of production to developing regions of the world (Reich 2009). The persistence of large trade deficits in manufacturing in the United States over several decades only reinforces this sense of demoralization, weakness, and death in the sector.

All of this is heightened still more by the increasingly modest rates of profitability growth that stable manufacturing-based concerns generate relative to the impressively lucrative (and highly volatile) dividends paid in "high-tech" and "new economy" sectors (Krippner 2005; Brenner 2006). Though at least in part they are themselves manufacturing sectors, such highflier elements play into a conceptual framing of industrial adjustment, based in a folk understanding of the laws of comparative advantage, that tends toward the zero sum: Developed high-wage economies can only sustain "new," "high-tech," "cutting-edge" sectors. For other sectors where know-how is broadly diffused across the globe (or at least has existed for quite some time), chances of survival in the developed regions of the world are thought to be small.

There is no reason to dispute the facts about the repositioning of manufacturing relative to services within the economy. I will, however, suggest that the folk narratives that *frame* the above facts seriously overdraw the case against manufacturing in the high-wage regions of developed economies. Even though manufacturing has not grown at the same rate as services within advanced economies, it is still true that even in the paradigmatic case of the United States the absolute level of manufacturing output has continued to grow. Indeed, by the mid-2000s, US manufacturing output was twice as high as it was twenty years earlier (NAM 2006). Indeed, the sector's output is larger now than it has ever been—even with the precipitous drop in production that occurred after the onset of crisis in 2008. Total US manufacturing output is still so large that the National Association of Manufacturers (NAM) points out that if the sector were its own country, it would be the eighth largest economy in the world (NAM 2006). Perhaps more stunning, even with the significant growth of manufacturing in Asian powers such as China, Korea, and Taiwan since the 1980s, the United States has maintained its relative share of total world manufacturing output: accounting for approximately 25% in 1982 and 25% in 2004 (NAM 2006)(Figure 1).

Despite the existence of a chronic and considerable trade deficit, the US economy has continued to be a very prominent player in global export markets. In 2005, the United States was the second largest exporter in the world, behind Germany. Seventy-seven percent of total export trade worldwide

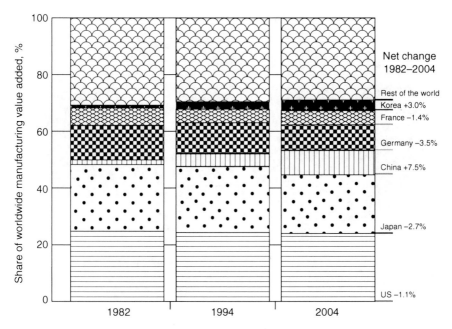

Figure 1. Share of Worldwide Manufacturing Value Added

Source: NAM (2006, p. 6).

is in manufactured goods; 61% of total US exports in 2005 were in manufactured goods (Figure 2). Germany, the United States, China, and Japan are the world's largest exporting nations (in that order) and they account for more than half of all world export trade in manufactures (NAM 2006) (Figure 3).

Further, despite the incontrovertibility of recurrent structural adjustment and job loss in the sector, many large US manufacturing industries have survived structural crises and lived to compete another day. Rates of manufacturing productivity have increased, and innovation, both in products and processes, has continued apace. According to NAM, "between 1987 and 2005, manufacturing productivity grew by 94%, roughly two and a half times faster than the 38% increase in productivity in the rest of the business sector"(NAM 2006, p. 14). Manufacturers, moreover, invest robustly in innovation. By 2009 in the United States, for example, manufacturing firms funded 60% of the $193 billion that the US private sector invests annually in R&D (ETA/Business-Relations-Group 2005).

US producers have been able either to maintain or even extend their leading position in global industrial production tables since the 1960s. Take the main industries that will be the focus of this book: steel, automobiles, and machinery. Steel has been the epitome of a smokestack industry, and it has been beset by repeated periods of crisis and adjustment over the last thirty years (much of which is analyzed in Part I). Nonetheless, global production of steel has

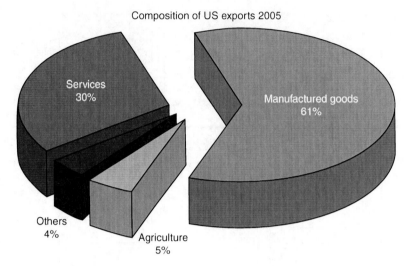

Figure 2. Composition of US Exports, 2005
Source: NAM (2006, p. 39).

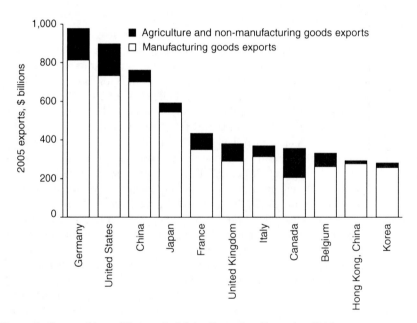

Figure 3. Composition of Exports in Major Exporting Countries, 2005
Source: NAM (2006, p. 41).

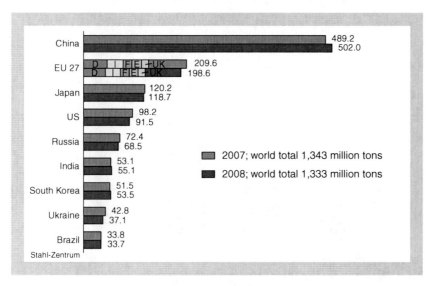

Figure 4. World Crude Production, 2007 and 2008 (in Million Tons)

Source: German Steel Association: http://www.stahl-online.de/english/business_and_politics/economic_and_trade_policy/steel_in_figures/start.asp?highmain=5&highsub=0&highsubsub=0.

continued to grow. Though they all now trail the very rapidly growing steel industry in China, the United States, Japan, and Germany remain on top of the global production tables. Japan is in third place, and the United States in fourth place, behind China and the countries of the EU. If the EU is removed, Germany ranks about seventh in world production, with Japan second and the United States third (see Figure 4).

Steel figures over time show a relative decline of the North American Free Trade Agreement (NAFTA) and EU regional portions of total world steel production, but this is notably not accompanied by a significant absolute decline in production in those regions. In other words, the rest of the world has grown much faster than NAFTA and the EU have grown, but both regions actually produce only slightly less steel now than they did in the 1960s (Figure 5).

Similarly, in automobiles and machinery, the industries in all three countries remain among the world's absolute largest producers (Tables 1 and 2). It is perhaps most surprising to see the United States at the top of world tables in these traditional sectors, not least because of the recent bankruptcy of major US automobile manufacturers, but more generally because the folk feeling is that the manufacturing sector has "lost ground" there more significantly than in the other two economies. Interestingly, in the broad and sprawling category of machinery, the strength of these three economies is expressed not only in the absolute levels of production, but also in the world export tables. Germany and Japan have maintained, even enhanced, their traditional strength in global machinery exports, while

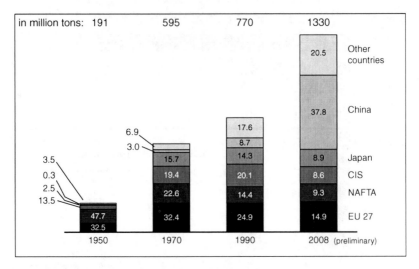

Figure 5. World Crude Steel Production by Regions (Shares in %)

Source: German Steel Association: http://www.stahl-online.de/english/business_and_politics/economic_and_trade_
policy/steel_in_figures/start.asp?highmain=5&highsub=0&highsubsub=0.

Table 1. World Motor Vehicle Production Ranking (Number of Vehicles Produced)

Rank	Country/region	2007	2005	2000
	World	73,101,695	66,482,439	58,374,162
	European Union	19,717,643	18,176,860	17,142,142
1	Japan	11,596,327	10,799,659	10,140,796
2	United States	10,780,729	11,946,653	12,799,857
3	China	8,882,456	5,708,421	2,069,069
4	Germany	6,213,460	5,757,710	5,526,615
5	South Korea	4,086,308	3,699,350	3,114,998
6	France	3,019,144	3,549,008	3,348,361
7	Brazil	2,970,818	2,530,840	1,681,517
8	Spain	2,889,703	2,752,500	3,032,874
9	Canada	2,578,238	2,687,892	2,961,636
10	India	2,306,768	1,638,674	801,360

Source: Organisation Internationale des Constructeurs d'Automobiles (various years).

the United States has continued to be a dominant player in many highly sophisticated, yet slightly prosaic areas (such as air-handling technology and power
systems) that fly under the radar of public attention. In 2006, the United States
was second to Germany in total world exports in machinery (Table 3).

The point of presenting this alternative framing on the experience of
manufacturing is not to celebrate manufacturing or claim that there are not any

Table 2. Estimated World Production in Machinery, by Country, November 2008 (Billions of Euros)

Country	2004	2005	2006	2007	2007/6 (%)	Share 2007 (%)	World ranking
United States	230	258	276	257	−6.87	18.8	1
Germany	155	164	182	207	13.6	15.2	2
China	98	117	154	200	29.9	14.7	3
Japan	170	182	181	170	−5.8	12.5	4
Italy	69	72	77	81	6	5.9	5
France	44	46	49	52	7	3.8	6
South Korea	30	36	41	42	2.4	3.1	7
United Kingdom	32	34	35	38	8.1	2.8	8
Brazil	12	17	20	25	26	1.9	9
Sweden	15	16	18	21	15.1	1.5	10

Source: VDMA: Schätzung Welt-Produktion Maschinenbau, in Mrd. Euro Stand: November 2008.

Table 3. Leading Machinery Exporting Countries, by Machinery Type, 2006

Machinery type	Total world exports (millions of euros)	First rank		Second rank		Third rank	
		country	% share	country	% share	country	% share
Construction machinery	66,038	J	16.6	US	14.8	G	13.8%
Air-handling technology	59,645	US	19.2	CN	11.9	G	11.4
Materials handling	42,196	G	19.6	US	10.4	J	9.3
Power transmission engineering	37,785	G	24.7	J	13.3	US	8.1
Machine tools	36,175	J	20.9	G	19.5	IT	8.8
Valves	32,785	G	14.4	CN	14	IT	13.8
Agricultural equipment	28,579	G	19.9	US	15.2	IT	10.8
Food processing and packaging machinery	24,603	G	26.8	IT	21.4	US	7.2
Precision tools	23,568	G	22.2	J	14.7	CN	6.1
Power systems	23,287	US	23	G	13.7	GB	9.7
Printing and paper technology	22,670	G	31.9	J	8.1	CH	7.2
Fluid pumps	20,835	G	22	US	12.1	IT	10.4
Compressors, compressed air, and vacuum technology	20,660	G	17.6	US	11	IT	10
Mining equipment	19,713	US	40.7	G	9.4	CN	7.6
Process plant and equipment	19,317	G	18.9	US	15.6	J	10.9
Engines and systems	15,805	J	28.5	US	16.3	G	12
Plastic and rubber machinery	14,330	G	25	J	12.9	IT	10.7

(*Continued*)

Table 3. (cont.)

Machinery type	Total world exports (millions of euros)	First rank		Second rank		Third rank	
		country	% share	country	% share	country	% share
Textile machinery (without dryers)	12,985	G	27.1	J	14.2	IT	13
Fluid power engineering	10,879	G	31.1	US	10.3	J	8.8
Woodworking machinery	8,937	G	26.1	IT	16.7	CN	11.2
Clothing and leather technologies	8,785	CN	23.7	G	17.8	KR	11.6
Industrial furnaces/ thermo process technology	7,572	G	21.6	US	13.9	IT	12
Elevators and escalators	5,598	IT	13.9	CN	13.3	G	12.9
Metallurgical plants and rolling mills	5,291	IT	24.7	G	16.1	J	8.8
Testing equipment	2,653	G	26	US	25.6	GB	10.7
Foundry machinery	2,080	J	22.4	IT	11.5	G	10.8
Scales	2,068	G	25.4	CN	21.7	J	7.4
Cleaning systems	1,328	G	33.6	US	22.9	IT	19.7
Firefighting equipment	1,207	US	23.3	CN	17.1	G	12.3
Welding technology (without electric)	770	US	18.1	CN	16.6	G	13.5
Safes and security technology	538	CN	27.2	IT	8.3	PL	7.9
World machinery export total*	641,405	G	19.2	US	12.7	J	11.8

*Total is for all machinery sectors, not only those listed in table.
Source: VDMA: Maschinenbau in Zahl and Bild (2008, p. 21).

significant adjustment pressures or processes of change taking place within the sector in developed economies. Instead, the aim here is to emphasize that it is important to move beyond folk thinking about manufacturing in contemporary developed societies. "Old sectors" continue to be significant generators of value and employ many (increasingly highly trained) people in the most developed economies, particularly in specific regions, such as the American Midwest or the western and southwestern regions of Germany (Deitz and Orr 2006; NAM 2006). Manufacturing is neither dying nor shifting away from the developed regions (even as industrialization takes place in other regions of the world) (see Chapter 5 for an in-depth discussion). Instead of death and retreat, there has been resilience and adjustment in manufacturing. Moreover, if in the aftermath of the current crisis, it becomes true that the developed countries (especially the United States) have to buy less from and sell more to the world while the developing countries (especially China) need to do the reverse (Wolf 2008), manufacturing is in a position to make a significant contribution in such a new world economy.

For these reasons, this book is not concerned with whether manufacturing will go away or how leading manufacturing nations have been able to manage decline. Rather it focuses on the remarkable capacity of manufacturing producers, stakeholders, and regions in the United States, Germany, and Japan to recompose and reproduce themselves over time. In particular, the chapters ask: How did these very different societies organize the formation of large firm-dominated oligopolistic production in the postwar period? How have they managed the breakup of the vertically integrated firm and the global trend toward manufacturing disintegration over the last sixty years? How have the relations and institutions of governance within the manufacturing economy changed in each of these societies since the end of World War II? What do the processes of recomposition have in common, how do they differ and what, if anything, can the societies learn from one another? What possibilities exist for manufacturing in advanced industrial political economies?

4. NEITHER CONVERGENCE NOR RIGIDITY: PRAGMATISM, CREATIVE ACTION, AND RECOMPOSITION

The main theoretical argument in this book is that creative action recomposes industrial life. The theoretical roots of this view are in the orientation toward action and change developed by the tradition of American pragmatism. Main traditions of pragmatic thought include the founding thinkers (James 1897 [1956], 1996 [1912]; Dewey 1922; Mead 1934; Peirce 1991a, 1991b), institutional economists (Veblen 1904 [1978], 1914; Commons 1934), the so-called old institutionalism in sociology (Mills 1964; Hughes 1993; Selznick 1996), symbolic interactionism (Blumer 1986 [1969]; Joas 1996) as well as more recent theorists in the tradition (Joas 1996; Emirbayer and Mischke 1998; Sabel and Dorf 1998; Whitford 2002; Sabel 2005; Berk and Galvin 2008; Ansell 2009).[3] This tradition emphasizes social action, reflexivity, creativity, and change through recomposition. It roundly rejects the conceptions of individualistic rational action and structural constraint that organize the theoretical arguments of neoliberal economism and the various incarnations of modern institutionalism.[4] There are three key moves in this pragmatist position that undergird the orientation of this book: action is social and non-teleological; action is reflective and

---

[3] I will not spend time outlining the tradition in the discussion that follows. Good works that do this very well are Joas (1992), Emirbayer and Mischke (1998), Joas and Knöbl (2004), and Ansell (2009).

[4] The pragmatic turn is paralleled by a homologous critique of structuralist thinking in anthropology and social theory. For representative contributions, see King (1999), Ahearn (2001), Mahmood (2005), Kivinen and Piiroinen (2006), Ortner (2006), Apter (2007), and Depleteau (2008).

creative; action is temporal and recombinatory. This section will first outline each move in the abstract and then subsequently elaborate them more practically regarding industrial transformation.

The first move is to make social action the focus of attention. Following Mead, pragmatists aim to "explain the conduct of the individual in terms of the organized conduct of the social group, rather than to account for the organized conduct of the social group in terms of the conduct of the separate individuals belonging to it" (Mead 1934). Actors are defined by the relations that they are engaged in. Moreover, the outside defines the inside: We know who we are, we have selves, through our socialization. There is no divide between the self and a world out there; the world makes the self possible. That others think of us and have relations with us makes it possible for us to think of ourselves and have relations with others. Crucially, the relations that define actors and the actions actors take are meaningful, communicative (interactive), and dynamic. Blumer (following Dewey and Mead) specifies three core premises in this kind of inter-active action: (*a*) human beings act toward things on the basis of the meaning that the things have for them; (*b*) the meaning of such things is derived from, or arises out of, the social interaction that one has with one's fellows; and (*c*) these meanings are handled in, and modified through, an interpretive process used by the person in dealing with the things he [*sic*] encounters (Blumer 1986 [1969]— cited in Ansell 2009).

Ultimately, pragmatism argues that human beings discover and appropriate the world through their (inter)action (Dewey 1922). There is no divide between thought and action, or even between mind and body in the way that pragmatists think of human conduct (James 1897 [1956]; Dewey 1922, 1940; Phillips 1971). Action is not preceded by thought; rather thought is associated with, engendered, directed, and constituted by action. Thought-in-action, in the pragmatist tradition, is socially interactive, practical, and meaningful. It solves collective problems in the world by organizing and defining the world in which people act.

Pragmatists argue that much of social action is habitual. It involves known, taken for granted, ways of organizing one's actions to reconnoiter transactions in and with the world (Dewey 1922). Pragmatic habit is not routine or rote; it is a kind of learned behavior (Ansell 2009). People reason and ponder how to act habitually, just as a carpenter ponders how to bring tools and materials together to construct the corner of a wooden house. Carpentry is a social trade, a historically accumulated, practically engendered assemblage of (meaning embodying) tools and techniques for construction that are actively applied by practitioners. It is not an individual invention, nor is it invented from whole cloth each time a problem with the manipulation of wood emerges. In most practical cases, moreover, the habits of carpentry are applied interactively, with both other people and objects. Habits are historical, shared, and dynamically enacted. In the pragmatic view, organized human action, in all registers, consists of an infinite (and ever-expanding) array of habitual combinations of thought, meaning, emotion, and action along these lines.

It is important to see here that although actors reason and ponder when enacting habits, the application of a habit is not contingent on the existence of a particular situation, or context: that is, pragmatists do not think there is a divide between the actor and the context in which habitual action takes place such that an actor recognizes a situation outside of herself and then decides to apply a habit. Pragmatic habits are pre-reflective. Action is constituted by the situation. According to Hans Joas (1996, p. 160),

Every habit of action and every rule of action contains assumptions about the type of situations in which it is appropriate to proceed according to the particular habit or rule. In general, our perception of situations already incorporates a judgement of the appropriateness of certain kinds of action. This explains why situations are not merely a neutral field of activity for intentions which were conceived outside of that situation, but appear to call forth, to provoke certain actions already in our perception.

In general, pragmatists understand action to be intentional, yet not teleological (Joas 1996, pp. 148–67). Goals or ends are not external, fixed, or given things that actors strategize to achieve. Rather, they are notions of alternative possibilities, or anticipations that specific outcomes will ensue from specific acts, that actors use to organize their behavior in the present.[5] Action is the experimental working out in the present of possibilities as organized by the idea of an end—or, as Dewey termed it, of an "end-in-view." "A true aim" says Dewey

is thus opposed at every point to an aim which is imposed upon a process of action from without. The latter is fixed and rigid; it is not a stimulus to intelligence in the given situation, but is an externally dictated order to do such and such things. (cited in Joas 1996, p. 154)

Dewey believed that in action goals or ends were interactively, deliberatively, and experimentally derived. An "end-in-view," say for example, the US military government's understanding of pluralist democracy during the occupation of Germany and Japan described in Chapter 1, organizes action in the actors' present. Action in the present, in turn, leads to the modification of goals as actors encounter and experiment with means that alter the context of action and change the range of possibilities. As Chapter 1 will describe, American ideas of democracy for Germany and Japan were repeatedly reconceived in interaction with German and Japanese notions, and given the range of problems the relevant players in the immediate postwar context had to deal with. In this way, "ends-in-view" serve as links in revisable chains of ends–means relations.

The second move is that pragmatic social action is chronically reflective, reconstructive, creative, and self-transforming. Pragmatic actors are vital beings who contribute very actively to the creation of the social world that defines them. For countless reasons, the flow of habitual action can be disrupted or encounter

---

[5] According to Dewey, an end is "the foresight of the alternative consequence attendant upon acting in a given situation in different ways, and the use of what is anticipated to direct observation and experiment [in the present, GH]" (cited in Joas 1996, p. 154). The quote is from Dewey (1916).

unanticipated obstacles: situations can be misjudged, multiple solutions can appear to apply to the same problem, workable solutions for one actor or group can be called into question by actors from another vantage point, etc. Disruption of habit causes disorientation and doubt (Peirce 1991a, 1991b). Unable to enact habitual action, actors do not know how to proceed. In such situations, which are social experiences, actors engage in a collective process of reflection in which they attempt to determine a way to resolve the problem. Reflection involves at once the reconstruction of the situation that gave rise to the problem and a series of abstract projections of solutions that actors imaginatively draw up out of their collective experience (Dewey 1922; Mead 1934). Such projections can involve comparisons of the immediate situation with others that seem to have been similar in order to determine if resolutions there have relevance for the problem they confront. Or they can simply involve creative reimagining of the nature of a habit. In both cases, reflection involves creativity: actors reimagine and redefine the action situation in ways that move beyond or circumvent or avoid the organization of action and context that produced the disruption. This reflective and creative process involves considerable conceptual and real trial and error. Many potential alternative renderings may prove unworkable or impractical. When eventually a serviceable solution is found, the world of action can be substantially transformed, allowing the actors to conceive of an alternative and new range of goals and possibilities in action (Joas 1996, 133ff).

Two further things are remarkable about this reflexive and creative phase of social action. First, actors in disrupted arrangements cannot simply act upon interests to make things aright. They must reconstruct the world in which the interests they had prior to the disruption were possible, and yet do so in ways that avoid the re-creation of the disruption. The players associated with bankrupt steel enterprises in Chapter 3, or the trade unionists coping with the emergence of new forms of stakeholder governance in Chapter 7, for example, do not simply pursue narrow interests. They engage in elaborate reconstructive and reflective debate with their interlocutors about how their situation has changed, what can be reproduced within it, and what must change. Such processes of reconstruction and creative reflection lead actors to reconceive the aims of action, as players reconsider their understanding of the context of action, as well as the range of roles and relations (including their own) which constitute it. And, moreover, since the process is driven by trial and error, aims, identities, and context move through many iterations of experimental modification, revision, and reorientation. In this way, the reflective and creative phase of action is simply a dimension of the general non-teleological understanding of action in pragmatism. Pragmatist actors do not simply maximize means to achieve specific external ends. Rather they continuously modify their ends as they engage with the means to achieve them. Ends do not instigate action; they emerge out of action as a socially interactive, reflective, creative, and experimental process that both discovers and generates possibilities for further action.

Second, processes of reconstruction and creative reflection make it possible for actors to move beyond existing constraints. Relations and rules, such as work rules or stakeholder commitments in industrial relations, that sensibly recommended against courses of action prior to a disruption can be called into question and reconceived in the process of reconstruction and creative reflection. This can be true, as we will see repeatedly in the steel and vertical disintegration examples, because reflection can reveal that rules or older relations contributed to the disruption. But reconstruction and reflection can also recast action in ways that make the old order of rules and constraints irrelevant to the new forms of action.

The third key move in the pragmatic understanding of social action is that creative action is temporal and social change is recombinatory. Actors encounter crises in habitual action in the flow of time. They inevitably draw on their own pasts in the process of reconstruction and creative reflection. Indeed, a dimension of creativity is the capacity not only to reconceive the situation of the present, but to reconceive the character and contours of the past as well. Creative actors reinterpret the relationship of the present to the past and the degree to which the past constitutes a possibility or a constraint on action in the future (Dewey 1920, 1922; Mead 1932).[6]

Crucial in all of this is to see that, for pragmatists, human action is composed of multitudes of habits in all registers of social life: within the self, the family, organizations, society and the economy, nation-states, and epochs of world history. Social arrangements are constellations of habitual social action. There is no inside where social action is endogenous and an exogenous outside upon which it is conditioned. Crises in habits, however, do not occur in all habits in all registers all at once. Pragmatists share with Burke and Tocqueville the view that social life has much continuity, even in times of great upheaval. Very often, crises occur in discrete areas of action, where specific taken-for-granteds, or clusters of habits, are disrupted. In this way, reconstruction and creative reflection involve the reconsideration and ultimate repositioning of the relationship between the realm of disruption and the elements of society and self that continue to be viable modes of progress. Rules and other elements of practice, as a result, can be changed, abandoned or redefined, while other elements remain unchanged. Creative action, fundamentally, is a recompositional social process. As Chapter 6, for example, shows in the case of German and American component suppliers seeking to develop practices that foster innovation and continuously reduce cost, creative social interaction can introduce completely new elements: interests, roles, rules, identities, definitions of context, etc. Yet invariably the new must be reconciled with the serviceable old in the (temporal) flow of life. This iterated, constantly experimental, creative, and reflective process of reconciling refined and recast habits with existing ones is what in this book is meant by recomposition.

These three very abstract elements of the pragmatic theory of creative action—action is social and non-teleological; action is reflective and creative; action is temporal and recombinatory—will be deployed throughout this book to analyze

---

[6] In this way, many pragmatists have emphasized the importance of narrative in industrial action (cf. in particular Sabel and Zeitlin 1997; Kristensen and Zeitlin 2005).

processes of industrial transformation in the United States, Germany, and Japan since the middle of the twentieth century. Each of the chapters deploys these theoretical ideas in a much more concrete way in their renderings of the political economy of industrial development. They also systematically compare the possibilities for understanding generated by the ideas of creative action and recomposition with the explanatory limitations of the alternative middle-range frameworks of neoliberalism and structural and historical institutionalism. To conclude this section, it will be useful to make three elaborations on the abstract points made about action above that illustrate how those theoretical ideas frame and drive processes of industrial transformation.

First, this book portrays manufacturing industries as complex constellations of habitual social action. Steel, automobile, and machinery industries are moving, living, social realms, the components of which—organizations, technologies, governance mechanisms, and market strategies—are always provisionally constituted. Further, the social realm of industry is always interpenetrated with other areas of social, economic, and political life. Actors in the social world of manufacturing—managers, trade unionists, financiers, regional governments, and workers—constantly play multiple roles in continuously changing constellations. As a result, industrial action recurrently overflows (Callon 1998) the arrangements that institutions and rules define as the terrain of industry. Thus with the flow of time and the occurrence of invariable habitual crises, reflective and creative industrial actors perpetually recompose the social relations of manufacturing. They mix together practices and functions that were previously separated, incorporate influences and ideas from other social realms, inaugurate wholly new roles alongside old and familiar ones, abandon roles and practices that lack meaning or utility given present challenges, etc. The range of possible tropes of change within and across the social arrangements of an industry is literally infinite.[7] Viewed in this way, industrial adjustment is a vital, creative, and recompositional process that continuously generates possibilities for new forms of identity and action.

The second elaboration is simply the claim that industries are historical. Industrial actors who create change are themselves the products of their own efforts to make change. Actors know who they are and what they want through collective, interactive problem solving. This is not something that people do on a *tabula rasa*. Identities and resources are inherited. They are the products of previous collective efforts to create serviceable social relations. The past, however, is an endowment for action; it is not a curse. Manufacturing actors jointly apply their imaginations to the resources the past has given them. They interpret the way in which the inherited manufacturing past is being dislodged by processes in the present and create, on that basis, projections of possible manufacturing futures. Such interpretations and projections are vetted publicly, socially,

---

[7] Some have tried to make lists (Streeck and Thelen 2005; Mahoney and Thelen 2008). As creative and provocative for the formation of research questions as these lists are, it is not clear how the authors arrive at their limited number. In the end, the limit seems arbitrary from a theoretical point of view.

and collectively in the form of political and economic debate and struggle over how to cope with the disjunctions in understanding and practice that pressures for change have produced. Industrial development is the product of these processes of reflexive historical sociability. Change occurs when habitual actions and roles are disrupted, dislodged, and become ambiguous; stability exists when this is not (or is no longer) the case. Given the vast complexity of social relations in any industrial context, it follows that both change and stability are always present.

Finally, it follows from the previous two elaborations that narrowly "economic" facts and calculations (about price, cost, market share, or externalities), though important, are always only one dimension of how actors move in, experience, and interpret industrial life. Political, social, and moral orientations also inform the interpretation of fact, shape action, and hence, the recomposition of relations in industry. Failure to acknowledge the role of these latter factors unnecessarily and arbitrarily limits the way in which the range of adjustment possibilities in manufacturing is generated. The cases in this book repeatedly show that there has been surprising plasticity in the arrangements that govern German, Japanese, and US industries since World War II. Industrial actors in all three countries both recompose national and subnational institutions and governance arrangements in response to common global pressures *and* create new relational and institutional differences across the societies. But the processes of industrial change presented in this book are not narrow blinkered stories of rational economic maximization. The book consistently shows that emergent recomposed arrangements express not only governance solutions to concrete (global) economic challenges, but the normative and historical commitments of the actors doing the recomposition as well.

5. THE SEQUENCE OF CHAPTERS
AND FLOW OF ARGUMENT

Manufacturing Possibilities is a series of examinations of creative action and recomposition in US, German, and Japanese manufacturing. The book has two parts. Part I is a historical analysis of the development of the steel industry in the three countries, from the middle of the twentieth century into the present. Part II analyzes processes of vertical disintegration in complex manufacturing sectors, such as automobiles and machinery, over the course of the last thirty years.

Chapter 1 focuses on the reconstitution of the German and Japanese steel industries under US military occupation in the immediate post-World War II period. Chapter 2 traces the organization of the steel industry in the United States, Germany, and Japan during the glory days of the three-decade-long postwar "economic miracle." Subsequently, Chapter 3 showcases the dramatic processes of recomposition that have occurred in these three national steel cases since the mid-1970s. Chapter 3 concludes that the steel industry, often left for dead, is in fact in many ways unfettered by its past. Although their institutional and practical arrangements differ tremendously, firms in each of the three countries are still competing and innovating, creating value, and employing people. And, they are accomplishing this by refusing to view the institutional rules that governed their past behavior as constraints on how they will create their future.

Part II (Chapters 4–7) broadens this analysis of adjustment in manufacturing by examining processes of vertical disintegration in the automobile and machinery industries in Europe and the United States over the past thirty years. Vertical disintegration is understood as a world historical trend affecting producers in all locations, but especially those in advanced industrial economies. It is driven by global competition that creates unremitting pressures to innovate, while at the same time continuously reduce costs. These chapters argue that relations in the disintegrated supply chain are extremely unstable, requiring suppliers and customers to play a broad array of potential roles. Moreover, which role(s) will be played and who will play them is typically unclear to all players *ex ante*. Governance problems, both at the level of production relations and the surrounding institutional context, are generated by this pervasive role ambiguity. Processes of recomposition in manufacturing are in many ways provoking recomposition of the entire architecture of political and economic relations in these societies.

Chapters 4 and 5 set out the general dynamics of vertical disintegration at the firm, industry, and interregional level. They describe emerging modal relations within the supply chain, characteristic firm strategies, and emergent forms of organization and governance that define practice in all of the cases. Chapter 4 argues that role ambiguity and the need for suppliers and customers to continuously innovate and upgrade have given rise to what it calls "sustained contingent collaboration" (SCC) as the modal relation in supply chains. The second part of the chapter outlines the range of product market strategies (specialization versus diversification) that producers adopt given the modality of SCC. Chapter 5 then turns to the way in which the organization of industrial flexibility has been transformed by processes of disintegration. The chapter also examines how disintegration has been accompanied by a process of spatial extension and dispersal—globalization—that poses significant challenges and opportunities for manufacturing actors in both developing and developed political economies.

Chapters 6 and 7 analyze the ways in which the general trends outlined in Chapters 4 and 5 are manifesting themselves in the United States and Germany. Chapter 6 analyzes trends and experiments over the last ten years in firm strategy and corporate and regional governance in the two countries. Chapter 7 is a case study of transformative politics currently underway in the German system of industrial relations. Both chapters show that the experiments in strategic, organizational, and governance recomposition often run in directions completely contrary to historical practice and institutional tradition in both countries, even as that history provides them with the raw material for those experiments.

Throughout, Parts I and II emphasize creative agency and recomposition while critiquing the idea of institutions as structuring frameworks for action. Social transformation within the economy is shown to be a recompositional process driven by collectively reflexive actors. Rules and roles are continuously and reflexively redefined as actors interactively strive to cope with challenges they encounter in their environments. This bottom-up, anti-structural analysis in *Manufacturing Possibilities* points to the critical theoretical importance of identifying opportunities for empowerment and self-governance within and among economic organizations. Not only does the analysis make visible possibilities for change that the alternative frameworks obscure, it also creates a coherent portrait of stability and change in the advanced political economies that elude the more rationalist and structuralist frameworks.

Finally, the conclusion summarizes the empirical findings and reiterates the distinctive theoretical character of the way that the empirical stories are told. In so doing, it rehearses again the limits of the alternative explanatory frameworks, and underlines the significance of pragmatism-informed notions of creative action and recomposition as powerful and coherent tools for understanding processes of political economic development in the modern world.

Part I

Introduction

INDUSTRIAL RECOMPOSITION: THE STEEL INDUSTRY IN POST-WORLD WAR II UNITED STATES, GERMANY, AND JAPAN

The first three chapters use an in-depth historical examination of the evolution of the US, German, and Japanese steel industries to make a variety of theoretical points about creative action, recomposition, and the limits of both neoliberal convergence theory and institutionalist arguments for the reproduction of difference. The chapters generally corroborate the broadly held view (typically associated with neoliberalism) that there are common global pressures, and that successful producers in the same industry pursue similar strategies regardless of where they are located. Chapters 1–3 show, however, that even as producers located in different contexts pursue remarkably similar kinds of strategies, they are doing so in different ways. Globalization does not produce convergence. There are many different ways to do the same (or similar) things.

Chapter 1, for example, demonstrates that while postwar Germany and Japan were strongly constrained to restructure their steel industries according to principles of democratic and market order imposed by their military occupiers, each accomplished this task in its own way. In particular, broadly deliberative processes among military occupiers and domestic stakeholders led to the creative adaptation and interpenetration of foreign political and economic principles with indigenous conceptions of order, exchange, and democracy. The reflective and experimental process ultimately recast the relationship between politics and markets and redefined the identities and boundaries of crucial players within industry in both Germany and Japan.

Similarly, Chapters 2 and 3 show that despite the existence of different institutional systems governing steel production in each country, the producers in the industries pursue remarkably similar steel production strategies. Moreover, the industry structure in each country undergoes a similar bifurcation into traditional integrated producers and newer Minimills deploying a radically new production technology. Paradoxically, even as actors and relations in each industry undergo similar processes of adjustment, they do so in ways that recast or re-create differences between the political economies.

The same stories also criticize strong institutionalist path-dependency arguments that highlight feedback processes induced by institutional complementarities in the functional systems governing industrial practice. The counterargument throughout the chapters is that creative action leads to the circumvention of institutional constraints. Difference is reproduced between (and within) societies as actors' struggles to resolve common problems lead them to break from the constraints of the past. There are differences because the societies have different resources and histories for actors to creatively deploy, not because those resources are constellated in ways that limit the range of possibilities through rigid complementarities and feedback loops. One does not need a path to be different.

Finally, Chapters 2 and 3 also launch a systematic attack on Peter Hall and David Soskice's argument for comparative institutional advantage (Streeck 1997; Hall and Soskice 2001; Hall and Thelen 2009). The core of the Hall and Soskice's "Varieties of Capitalism" (VoC) perspective is that national economies are composed of frameworks of incentives and constraints that shape the strategic behavior and options of producers. In the VoC framework, the United States is a liberal market economy institutionally governed primarily by arm's-length market relations and, therefore, disposed to radical innovation and dramatic social recomposition. Hall and Soskice argue that these same characteristics render US producers incapable of sustaining the kind of collaboration in production between management, labor, and suppliers that produces continuous improvement and sustained international competitiveness in more mature, less technologically dynamic industries (Hall and Soskice 2001; specifically on steel: Vitols 1995). On the same view, Germany and Japan, in different ways, serve as examples of coordinated market economies where institutional arrangements circumvent the market, and foster negotiation. According to Hall and Soskice, this institutionalized stakeholder negotiation causes industrial producers to compete more successfully in industries that reward gradual improvement within technological trajectories. Coordinated market economies foster cooperative adjustment strategies within traditional industries. By the same token, Hall and Soskice argue that the same cooperative arrangements discourage radical innovatory changes and disadvantage producer strategies that involve dramatic social, technological, and industrial recomposition (Hall and Soskice 2001).

Chapters 2 and 3 reject this VoC argument both because it is far too static and rigid and because it links the reproduction of difference to the idea of comparative institutional advantage. The chapters show that most of the analytical oppositions that form the foundation of Hall and Soskice's view—collaboration versus competition, radical innovation versus gradual improvement, coordination versus arm's-length price taking, etc.—turn out neither to be incompatible nor specific to particular sorts of national institutional production regimes. Specifically, the two chapters show that the institutional frameworks that VoC authors claim distribute national styles of innovation do no such thing in the steel industry case.

A remarkable fact about the steel industry is that producers in each society have followed both gradual improvement and radical innovation strategies. US, German, and Japanese integrated mills have all systematically rationalized the traditional integrated steelmaking process, while at the same time Minimills deploying a radically disruptive steelmaking technology have emerged to gain a significant portion of total steel output in each industry. Industries in all three countries have managed both of these developments in distinctive ways. But the chapters show that there is no divide between a case in which market mechanisms determine the process of adjustment and innovation and a case in which cooperation determines that process. All the cases involve distinctive mixtures of coordination and arm's-length market leverage, as well as radical and gradual innovation. The variety of possibilities for recombination in these national institutional environments is greater than the VoC institutionalist theorists believe them to be.

Ultimately, the chapters in Part I cast the problem of the development of the national industries over time into a very different light. Where neoliberals see dramatic convergence and institutionalists such as Hall and Soskice view national frameworks as having striking continuity over time, these chapters show that the arrangements constituting national political economies are in fact continuously modified and changed at various levels. Rather than simply change or simply stable reproduction, creative action and recomposition allow for an analysis that contains both continuity and change in the social relations of the economy. Creative actors do not choose rationally from given incentives (after they have managed to garner the proper amount of information). Nor do they simply follow preexisting rules in path-dependent feedback loops. Instead, in the chapters that follow they continuously redefine themselves and the context in which they act through the reflective process of creating and re-creating roles, rules, and relations.

1

American Occupation, Market Order, and Democracy: Recomposing the Steel Industry in Japan and Germany After World War II

1.1 INTRODUCTION

This chapter analyzes the effect of military occupation on the recomposition of the steel industries in Germany and Japan after World War II. Its point will be that the American occupation dramatically changed both societies by forcing them to grapple with American ideas of social, industrial, and political order. By this I do not mean that the Americans got exactly what they wanted in either case, much less that the two industries (or societies) were "Americanized." Rather, the interaction between occupiers and occupied transformed the way that both understood their own interests and what each understood to be industrial practice consistent with American ideals. In the steel industry, the result was the emergence of genuinely hybrid firms, industrial structures, and market strategies that were all markedly different from their pre-occupation ancestors and far more innovative than the American models that were used to guide their reconstruction.

In making this argument, it is important to emphasize immediately that in my view the terrain upon which contestation occurred between American imposers and German and Japanese receivers/resistors *was not* in the first instance organizational or technological, though ultimately the effects of the encounter were felt in these areas. American military authorities did not insist that Japanese or German industrial actors adopt specifically American internal organizational procedures or implement American production techniques or technologies or industrial relations practices. Indeed, they left considerable latitude for local practice in these areas and allowed substantially different practices and forms of organization within the corporation and in industrial relations to emerge than either existed or were then developing in the United States. In any case, both the Germans and the Japanese had long been familiar with and even implemented a wide variety of American techniques before they ever confronted American military reformers.

Rather, the crucial area of engagement concerned the definition of the political, economic, and social terrain upon which industrial organizational and governance forms and technologies were to be constructed and deployed in each society. Indeed, it was the capacity of the occupying power to establish this as the terrain of conflict that indicates the enormity of the power it wielded over these two vanquished nations. It was certainly the source of its greatest influence. I will emphasize in particular two forms of Allied action on this terrain, one destructive, the other creative. First, the occupation forces systematically deconstructed the central institutions of market and political order in Germany and Japan: Among other things, cartels were outlawed, firms were broken up, leadership structures were attacked, and key associations were either redefined to play a different role or they were simply outlawed. This destructive impulse was defensive: In the political–economic imaginary of the occupying powers, the targeted industrial institutions had contributed directly to authoritarianism and the growth of military aggression in those countries.

Second, the presence and position of the Allies as military occupiers of defeated powers enabled them to structure debate about broad normative guidelines for social, industrial, and political reorganization. American insistence on the ground rules for public deliberation about the reconstruction of each society brought principles of order into debate that diverged markedly from prewar indigenous ideas about the character and interrelationship of social, economic, and political practices and institutions in Germany and Japan. American occupiers believed strongly, for example, that stable democratic societies contained plural, crosscutting organizations, multiple and countervailing instances of social and economic power, a strong middle class, trade unions, market competition and efficient, oligopolistically structured industries. As it turned out, the United States allowed the Germans and the Japanese to create these conditions in their societies in their own way—or in any case to make it seem as if they were. But the source of American power was that deliberating actors were not permitted to deny that a society with such features was desirable.[1]

The two sides of the Allied strategy of occupation in both countries are nicely expressed in a summary memorandum by the Supreme Command of the Allied Powers (SCAP) in Japan: "In the first two years of the Allied Occupation of Japan, SCAP's activities in economic matters [were] directed toward eradicating the old imperialistic, non-democratic economic pattern of life and replacing it with a new framework which would lead Japan into democracy and rightful membership among the community of nations"(Benz 1978, p. 331). In large part, these two factors of US power successfully forced actors in Japan and Germany to engage the categories and logic of the US conception of social order and, as a consequence, get them to establish new rules for market competition and democratic order. Of course, what was actually achieved did not correspond in either case to what the occupying authorities imagined market order, democracy, or their interdependence to be. German and Japanese actors created the mutual limitations between state and economy that the Allies desired, but in ways that were inescapably and

---

[1] I have been influenced in my efforts to describe the character of American power as profoundly shaping and yet accommodating of broad experimentation, creativity, and strategizing by the work of the Comaroffs on the colonial experience in South Africa, as well as by the insightful criticisms of that work offered by Sherry Ortner. The latter in particular has many affinities with the pragmatic orientation of this volume (Comaroff and Comaroff 1991, 2001; Ortner 2001).

insidiously informed by their own peculiar understandings of the categories and relations that the Americans imposed. Enforced, unavoidable confrontation with American ideas of political and market order, in other words, did not force the Germans and Japanese onto entirely virgin terrain. Rather, it forced them to reflect on their traditional practices in light of American ideals and allowed them to recompose elements from both into a strikingly new style of practice.

1.2. PLAN OF THE CHAPTER

In my view, this kind of argument cannot be made by focusing narrowly on the ten-year period following the end of World War II. A bit of historical table setting will be needed in order to persuasively convey the character of the conflicts that emerged as US occupiers set out to restructure the steel industries in the two occupied countries. Thus, Section 1.3 will outline the prewar and wartime structures of the German and Japanese steel industries, highlighting the political boundaries of the industry in each society and the distinctive character both of property forms and of market organization in both industries. Section 1.4 will then turn to the lenses through which the occupying military governments interpreted these industries after the war and to the destructive and creative policies they promulgated to change them. The emphasis here will be on the categories of American economic and political understanding and on the way in which American authorities understood market order to be related to democracy. Section 1.5 will look at the reception of these ideas and policies and their effects on the development of the industries in both countries during the initial period of growth in the first two decades after the war. In this section, German and Japanese understandings of the relationship between market and political order will be contrasted with the Allied conceptions outlined in Section 1.4. The narrative of this section will be how German and Japanese attempts to appropriate American ideas and practices (and American efforts to impose the same) resulted in possibility creating effects that transformed the principles of market and political order within which all the principals defined themselves and their strategies for (inter)action.

1.3. THE STEEL INDUSTRY IN GERMANY AND JAPAN IN THE PERIOD PRIOR TO OCCUPATION

Though the two steel industries differed in size and technological sophistication in this period—the German industry was capable of far larger output than the Japanese industry and was a world leader in technology—there were many similarities between the two in terms of company forms and industry structure. Indeed, by the 1930s in both countries, the steel industry had developed a distinctive bifurcated structure. In each case a large, deeply integrated, diversified producer of relatively high-volume standardized steel goods accounted for nearly half of the total output in the industry, while a larger number of smaller, more specialized companies, which were often part of much larger diversified combines, accounted for the rest of the industries' domestic output. Interestingly, these similarities in industry structure were achieved with dramatically different positions of the government in the industry. The Japanese industry will be described first, the German second.

1.3.1. The Pre-1945 Japanese Steel Industry

There are two distinct yet intertwined strands to the story of the development of the Japanese steel industry up until the end of World War II. The first is a story of relations between private industry and government in the coordination of industrial development and the second involves the development of particular forms of governance and industrial structure in the production of steel. The two strands can be introduced separately, but they then begin to intertwine in a series of cartelization laws beginning in the early 1930s. They then converge almost completely in the wartime innovations in industrial governance known as Control Associations.

1.3.1.1. Government–Business Relations

As was the case with an array of early industries in nineteenth-century Japan, the emergence and early development of the steel industry was strongly shaped by the intervention of the state. This early state involvement, as many have noted, was decidedly *not* because the Japanese government was committed to state-controlled development. Rather, most agree that it was because private actors could not be enticed into carrying the initial startup risks in the industry.[2] Indeed, for nearly two decades at the end of the nineteenth century, the Japanese state tried to encourage private actors, in particular large diversified *Zaibatsu* holding companies, to enter the steel industry because it believed that indigenous Japanese steelmaking capacity was crucial for national development and security. Despite these efforts, the *Zaibatsu* were very reluctant to play along. They believed that the startup costs in steel would be far too high and the profitability and growth

---

[2] For a discussion of the phenomenon of the state creating the initial firm in the industry and then using its position to lure in private actors, see Samuels (1987, esp. ch. 3, pp. 68–134). The Japanese state, particularly in the decade after the Meiji Restoration, pursued this policy of starting and then spinning off or luring in private actors in an array of other industries (beyond coal and steel) as well. On the historical period of industrial promotion and ownership on the part of the Meiji state, see, among many others, Crawcour (1997, pp. 1–49), Yamamura (1997, pp. 294–352), Morris-Suzuki (1994, pp. 71–105), Lockwood (1968).

prospects for the industry too low to justify moving into the industry—even with state support (Morikawa 1982).

Frustrated by this lack of private interest and convinced of the value of indigenous production, in 1901 the Japanese state took the bull by the horns and founded the Yahata Steel Works. The new facilities were state of the art for the time (modeled very closely after German steelmaking technology and practice) and had an initial total production capacity of 90,000 tons of steel a year. In all, the investment totaled over ¥120 million (Morikawa 1982, p. 140, table 1). All of this was very impressive by the standards of the time—but in a way that vindicated the reticence of the *Zaibatsu*, for none of it worked very well. The operation of the blast furnaces and the coke ovens in the new venture suffered continual mechanical problems in the early stages and ultimately had to be shut down for two years to have their German designs adapted to the particular kinds of raw material inputs and skills available in Japan. Further, even when everything was up and running, the Yahata works suffered tremendous operating losses for the first nine years of its existence. When it finally did earn a profit in 1910, it was with state assistance (Morikawa 1982, pp. 141–3). Growth in the domestic market for steel, moreover, was slow, at least until the beginning of World War I, and competition from imports was very intense: As late as 1913, imported steel accounted for 64% of home consumption and 52% of pig iron consumption (Allen 1946, p. 74).

Nonetheless, Yahata did succeed in gradually establishing a position for itself in the domestic market (after all, prior to its establishment, imports accounted for virtually all the consumption of steel and pig iron). This success was used by the government to lure other private domestic firms, many from *Zaibatsu* interests, to enter the industry. On the one hand, the Japanese government used attractive munitions, shipbuilding, or railway contracts to entice *Zaibatsu* investments in steel production. This created a demand for pig iron that lead to further investment, particularly in Japan's colonial possessions in the initial stage of steelmaking (see Table 1.1). And, once private firms had been lured into the industry, the government encouraged and protected them with numerous subsidies, tax incentives, tariffs, and the like (Schumpeter 1940, p. 596ff).

On the other hand, Yahata itself also helped these novice, less-integrated, and much smaller-scale private operations develop. It supplied the private steel units with domestic pig iron and, more significantly, spun off to the private firms specialized steelmaking and rolling technologies that Yahata was not willing itself to develop because they distracted from the large-scale steel production strategy the state firm was pursuing (Yonekura 1994, pp. 57–77). Itself a very significant market actor, for much of the first thirty years of its existence, Yahata nonetheless behaved like an incubator for newer, smaller, and above all private entrants into the industry.

With imported steel as the enemy and the technological development of the Japanese economy as their shared goal, public actors and private producers pursued a cooperative, yet, nonetheless, competitive and market-based strategy of industry expansion. Bureaucrats, bankers, and executives from the *Zaibatsu* holdings and managers from Yahata engaged in continuous discussions

Table 1.1. Overview of Initial Private (Mainly *Zaibatsu*) Moves into Steel Production

Name of enterprise (and affiliation)	Date	Initial capacity	Main product area and market
Yahata (state enterprise)	1901	Crude steel (90,000 t/year) 2 blast furnaces (160 t each) 4 open hearths (25 t each) 2 converters (10 t each)	Pig iron, steel, rolled products
Sumitomo Chukojo (Sumitomo)	1902 (1912)	Crude steel (2,000 t/year)	Cast iron (later: cold drawn steel tube for Imperial Navy)
Kobe Seikojo (Suzuki Shoten)	1905	Open hearth (3.5 t)	Cast and forged steel
Kawasaki Zosen Hyogo (Kawasaki)	1906	2 open hearths (10 t/each)	Cast and forged steel for railway equipment and later shipbuilding
Nihon Seikojo (Mitsui)	1911	2 open hearths (50 t) 4 open hearths (25 t) 2 open hearths (5 t)	Cast and forged steel and weapons for the navy
Nihon Kokan (NKK) (Asano)	1912	2 open hearths (20 t)	Mannesmann seamless steel tube
Hokuton Wanishi (Mitsui)	1913	1 blast furnace (50 t)	Pig iron
Honeiko Baitan Konsu (Okura Gumi and Chinese National Iron Works)	1915	1 blast furnace (130 t)	Pig iron (side business from colonial mining operations)
Mitsubishi Seitetsu Kenjiho (Mitsubishi—Korea)	1918	1 blast furnace (150 t)	Pig iron (side business from colonial mining operations)

Source: Adapted from Hidemasa Morikawa, "The Zaibatsu in the Japanese Iron and Steel Industry," 142, table 1 and accompanying text.

concerning the problems, opportunities, needs, and possibilities of steel production in Japan. One has to be careful to emphasize that this was not planning in any sense. Instead, it was elite dialogue on how to structure market-based economic activity in the interest of the nation's development.[3]

[3] This distinctive kind of close and coordinated relationship between private business (in this case *Zaibatsu*) and government has frequently been noted by scholars of Japanese industrialization—though they disagree about the balance of power between the state and the private economy. A classic account of the Japanese state as a "developmental state" in which the balance of power is placed in the state's favor is given in Johnson (1981). Johnson (1981), Samuels (1987), and Haley (1991) are good examples of scholars who place the balance of power toward the other end.

1.3.1.2. Bifurcated Market of Steel Producers

By the 1920s, these business–government relations had fostered the development of a bifurcated industrial structure in the Japanese steel industry, with a large, state-owned, integrated, high-volume producer on the one side and a number of smaller, more specialized, less-integrated, private producers on the other. In order to understand the strategic and competitive dynamics that produced this bifurcated structure in the industry, the interaction of two sets of relations are important: Relations between the new *Zaibatsu* market entrants and Yahata and relations between *Zaibatsu* steel production and the rest of the *Zaibatsu* operations.

Plainly, in their initial forays into steel production, the *Zaibatsu* were hedging their bets on the growth of the industry. They wanted to have some position in the industry if it finally did begin to grow, but they did not want to carry the burden of large investments on the scale of Yahata. Consequently, the *Zaibatsu* invested in areas of specialized production in which Yahata was not engaged, or in which import competition was weak. Also, as noted above, these investments were encouraged by special state contracts from downstream operations within the *Zaibatsu* themselves such as in shipbuilding and weapons production. On the whole, then, the scale of these private investments was considerably smaller, less integrated, and far more specialized than Yahata. The *Zaibatsu* did not try to take over the steel market either from imports or from the government's firm. Rather, they entered steel production as niche players, gaining experience and know-how technologically, while avoiding direct competition with larger competitors (Morikawa 1982).

Such apparent opportunism was actually in line with what the Japanese government wanted to achieve, for it contributed both to the expansion of indigenous steel production capacity and systematically enhanced the technological sophistication of private firms in areas that the state viewed as progressive. But the strategy was also very congenial to the broader combine-wide strategies of development that the *Zaibatsu* were pursuing during the first decades of the twentieth century. Knowledge of particular steelmaking technologies and markets was beneficial to other firms in related markets for machinery, shipbuilding, engineering, and trade *elsewhere within the conglomerate*. Information circulated in and out of the steel arms of *Zaibatsu* in ways that encouraged learning and innovation in the complex of firms within the *Zaibatsu*'s scope of operations. The cooperative synergy between the steel and/or rolling operations of a *Zaibatsu* steel unit with the particular down-line operations of the conglomerate were the main thing, not vertical technical economies of integration or the lowering of unit costs in the steel unit itself.[4] Often *Zaibatsu* steel units were not integrated (backward

---

[4] *Zaibatsu* were very distinctive horizontal business organizations: Neither hierarchically controlled multidivisional companies nor holding companies of loose ownership ties, they were complex agglomerations of specialties, given boundaries by family property rather than technology, related markets or even contiguous space (cf. Voack 1962; Morikawa 1970).

or forward beyond rolling operations) and purchased pig iron or scrap (and even steel ingots) from third parties (in particular Yahata).

As the industry grew, the bifurcation between the high-volume standardized producer Yahata and the specialized niche players became more entrenched. In a period of (albeit slow) growth like that in the first decades of the century, this was a very stable structure, beneficial to both parties in the industry. It was not a "dualist" or core–periphery structure in which the large core firm was the "most advanced" and the peripheral players less so. The players in the industry were all technologically sophisticated—indeed increasingly so as the new century wore on. They were of different sizes and differently integrated because they were pursuing alternative kinds of profit-making strategies in the same industry.

1.3.1.3. Governance Problems

The stories of business–government cooperation and industrial bifurcation merge when turbulence and market disorder start to affect action in the industry during the late 1920s and 1930s. The stable reproduction of the bifurcated market was challenged during this period due to the following factors: Large investments in new plant and capacity during World War I resulted in overcapacity after the war; the Japanese economy experienced a postwar recession and then later (along with the world economy) a very severe depression by the beginning of the 1930s; finally, during the 1930s militarist forces within the Japanese state began to attempt to accelerate the growth of domestic steel production in order to ensure domestic supplies for military industries.[5] The first two factors (overcapacity and recession/depression) made it extremely difficult for producers to find markets for the steel they were *able* to produce. The third introduced a set of constraints on the range and quantity of steel products they were *allowed* to produce. These pressures gave rise to three different governance solutions: state-enforced private cartelization, merger, and market-supplanting Control Associations.

1.3.1.4. Cartelization

Overcapacity and recession/depression in the immediate post-World War I decade introduced disorder into markets because it encouraged market poaching. In the face of capacity well in excess of the existing demand, firms that had previously left one another's specialized markets alone began not to. Seeking desperately to utilize expensive idle equipment, private specialty producers attempted to enter other specialists markets as well as the standardized markets

---

[5] These factors are generally emphasized in the standard accounts of the move toward cartelization and Control Associations in the interwar and wartime period. Unless otherwise cited, I have relied primarily on the following sources for my information: Hadley (1970, pp. 357–89), Schumpeter (1940, esp. pp. 596–604, 680–740, 789–865), Relations-Secretariat (1941), Bisson (1945), Cohen (1949, chs. 1, 3, 8, 13), Johnson (1981, pp. 116–97), Lockwood (1968), Hirschmeier and Yui (1981, esp. pp. 236–51), MERB (1936, pp. 40–52, 114–30, 195–210), and Lynn and McKeown (1988, pp. 15–28).

dominated by Yahata and imports. Price cutting, special purchase and delivery conditions, and other pernicious competitive devices were the techniques deployed to achieve market entry. Unsurprisingly, with their deployment, market order in the industry deteriorated: Prices became erratic, profits suffered, and employment became unsteady. The classic response to this kind of situation is the formation of a cartel. Producers agree to cooperate with one another on price setting and the fixing of terms and conditions of sale in order to bring stability back to the market.

During the 1920s, the formation of cartels was a completely private matter of agreements between consenting firms on a wide array of elements within their competitive industrial environment. Such agreements were typically satisfactory for short periods to stabilize markets, but proved to be relatively fragile unless they were followed by sustained upturn in demand for product. The Achilles heel of these agreements was that they were never able to cover all producers in particular markets. Without a third party to enforce participation, short-term calculations of advantage tended to outweigh longer-term considerations of stability through cooperation. When the onset of depression at the end of the decade made this irritation in the nature of cartel organization into a serious crisis of market governance, the fragility of these private cartel agreements became a topic of intense debate among both private industrialists and government bureaucrats. Ultimately, debate gave rise to political intervention and, in 1931, the passage of the Major Industries Control Law that brought the authority of the state into the organization of cartels in the industry (MERB 1936, p. 117).

The Major Industries Control Law was significant because it permitted the state to force compliance of non-member producers with the agreements struck by the majority of cartelized producers in a particular product market. This enabled producers in the steel industry to stabilize the specialization relations in the bifurcated structure by establishing cartels that defined the boundaries among product markets as well as the prices in the industry through production and so-called joint sales agreements (i.e., selling quotas, the collection and allotment of orders, etc.). Such agreements eliminated damaging poaching, maintained the integrity of individual producers' specialty niches, and allowed producers to concentrate on innovation rather than covering their costs. Such arrangements were attractive to the *Zaibatsu* because they facilitated productive interaction between their steel interests and the rest of their manufacturing business—something that poaching and competitive chaos in steel markets had made more difficult (Yonekura 1994, pp. 117–18, MERB 1936, p. 118, Lynn and McKeown 1988).

1.3.1.5. Merger

State support of cartels was not enough to introduce stability into the volume sector of the industry. Yahata had been suffering throughout the 1920s and early

1930s from poaching by private firms who sought to unload their surplus production into the volume markets. In addition, several private firms, in particular private independents not part of *Zaibatsu*, had invested in volume capacity during World War I because it seemed at that time that Yahata would not be able to cover all of market demand. Ten years later these producers along with Yahata lived in an unstable merciless market of organized overcapacity, under-production, and low profitability. Cartelization in this market was not enough: Merger was called for. But because Yahata was a state-owned firm, the creation of a merger had to be a political act.

In 1933–4, this is precisely what occurred: The Japan Steel Manufacturing Company Law was promulgated in 1933 and all of the volume producers in the industry, including Yahata, were consolidated into a single firm the following year (MERB 1936, p. 119, Lynn and McKeown 1988). Though the consolidation was encouraged and organized by the Japanese state and it involved a very large state enterprise, the consolidation actually took place through the *privatization* of the Yahata works and the incorporation of the operations of five private iron and steelmaking companies into the newly privatized firm (Yonekura 1994, p. 150). The new industry structure concentrated virtually all of Japan's pig iron production (97%) into the new consolidated firm. Importantly, the market positions of Japan Steel in both the raw steel and finished-product segments of the industry were significantly less: Japan Steel accounted for 56% of steel ingot production and 52% of finished-steel output. The rest of this, more specialized, output was supplied by the remaining non-integrated players in the industry, above all by NKK, Kawasaki, Kobe, Sumitomo, and Asano (Yonekura 1994, p. 150).

As these market-share statistics suggest, this round of industrial stabilization in the early 1930s, driven by coordinated public and private action, successfully stabilized the bifurcated structure of specialists and volume producers. This was a coordinated, market-oriented steel industry. The final set of governance changes introduced during the early years of World War II, however, were of a different character entirely.

1.3.1.6. Control Associations

With the coming of war, the militarists within the Japanese state began to become increasingly concerned that the nation's industrial capacity be able to be used in the service of the nation's military needs. In their view, the structures that were created during the 1930s were unreliable and unwieldy in this regard, especially the cartels. The Major Industries Control Law had stabilized markets, but it also allowed for the continuous fragmentation of markets and proliferation of cartel organizations, all of which made it very difficult for resources to be consolidated and marshaled for state ends (Bisson 1945, p. 25ff). In September of 1941, the government introduced the Major Industries Association Ordinance, whose purpose was to create extra-firm "Control Associations" with the power and authority to direct production and the distribution of products in the industry toward the satisfaction of the state's military needs.[6] If the earlier Major Industries Control Law attempted to bring state authority to bear to help private interests govern themselves in a market context, this later law sought to have state interests completely trump the market interests of private firms (Lynn and McKeown 1988, p. 21–4).

There was considerable debate at the time as to who would staff these associations, with the military and private industry both favoring their own managers (Bisson 1945, Cohen 1949, Johnson 1981). Ultimately, it was decided that staffing would be by members of the industry itself, but in an interesting way: Appointees were taken from among top managers of the operating units of actual steel companies, rather than, for example, from the further removed but more broadly strategically oriented holding companies of the *Zaibatsu*. They were made to resign their positions within their original firms. In effect, this arrangement aimed at ensuring that the decisions of the Control Councils would not be made with the profits of the steel companies (much less the broader technological synergies of parent *Zaibatsu* operations), but rather with the needs of the industry's immediate military customers uppermost in their minds. At the same time, since the designers would have intimate knowledge of the industry and its technology, they would be able to set production targets in ways that would be technologically and organizationally possible to achieve without bankrupting the companies (Yonekura 1994, 1996; Lynn and McKewon 1988).

In the end, however, it seems that the dirigisme of the Control Associations was not very successful. The Control Associations created a coterie of managers with an understanding of the steel industry that was markedly different from the stable bifurcated grouping of specialists and volume producers, which had characterized the development of the industry to that point. Rather than volume production as a specialty among an array of specialties, these actors wanted to create an oligopolistic structure in the industry to increase the total volume output of all producers. We will see that these managers and this conception of the industry proved to be very significant in the reconstitution of Japanese steel after the war.[7]

1.3.2. The Pre-1945 German Steel Industry

The German steel industry was much older and larger than the Japanese industry (Feldenkirchen 1982; Wengenroth 1986; Herrigel 1996, ch. 3). Nonetheless, by

---

[6] Cf. Bisson 1945, Cohen 1949 (pp. 1–48), Yonekura 1996 (pp. 27–51), Johnson 1981 (pp. 153, 162–3). For an entertaining debate on the postwar influence of these initiatives, see, on the one side (lots of influence), Okasaki (Okasaki 1994) and on the other side (not much influence), Hashimoto (Hashimoto 1996). As an outsider, I am largely persuaded by Hashimoto's side, but as will be clear below, the entire debate is a bit orthogonal to my concerns.

[7] Even Okasaki and Hashimoto agree on this (Okasaki 1994; Hashimoto 1996). Note that by "dirigisme" in this context I mean merely the supplanting of market mechanisms by the directives of the Control Associations. I do not mean to suggest with this word that the Control Associations were direct organs of the state. Control Associations were corporatist bodies staffed by private industrialists acting against market mechanisms to organize industry according to state interests.

the middle of the 1930s, it had developed a remarkably similar bifurcated industry structure. Just as in Japan, output in the industry was dominated by one large, integrated, and widely diversified producer, the Vereinigte Stahlwerke AG (hereafter, Vestag). Unlike the Japanese Yahata Steel, however, Vestag was a private concern formed out of companies that traditionally had no ownership participation of public bodies of any kind.[8] The outcome of a merger in 1926 among four of the largest firms in the coal and steel industry, this company accounted for over 50% of all steel and rolled products in Germany soon after it was first established (1927). It continued to be the dominant firm in the industry through the 1930s and into the war, though its output was nearly matched after 1937 by the newly established Nazi state company, the Hermann Göring Werke (HGW, more on which below). Vestag produced a broad range of rolled or finished steel products, but it had only a relatively minimal set of downstream manufacturing subsidiaries (machinery, shipbuilding, etc.), and these were largely holdover properties from the firms that had entered into the Vestag structure.[9]

As in Japan, most of the rest of the interwar output in the German industry was, until the late 1930s, produced by relatively smaller, more specialized operations of broadly diversified conglomerate firms, known in Germany as *Konzerne*. These firms (the majors were Hoesch, Krupp, Klöckner, Mannesmann (after 1932), and the Gutehoffnungshütte) were sprawling combines with far-flung operations throughout the steel-finishing and engineering industries. As in Japan, the output of these firms' steel units tended to be more specialized than the steel operations of the dominant Vestag. Where Vestag concentrated on more standardized fare and larger volumes across finished-steel markets, the steel operations of the *Konzerne* produced specialty and customized finished products. Often, the technical capacity to provide these products was aided by close exchanges of information and expertise with downstream units in the *Konzerne*.

These large conglomerates resembled their Japanese counterpart *Zaibatsu* in that they encouraged intra-*Konzern* exchanges in the interest of furthering the knowledge and innovative capacity of the internal exchanging parties—all to the benefit of the *Konzern* as a whole (Herrigel 1996). Unlike the *Zaibatsu* in Japan, however, the *Konzerne* were not ancient organizations in the country nor did they dominate the German industrial economy: The diversified *Konzern* form only emerged in the first decades of the twentieth century in the steel industry and it stabilized as a form of corporate organization only in the interwar period (Herrigel 1996). Moreover, the *Konzerne* were largely regional entities and had a narrower palette of companies in a more restricted range of sectors than the *Zaibatsu*. Most German *Konzerne* had operations in steel, coalmining, engineering (especially heavy engineering), and shipbuilding. Most also had their own

---

[8] For the most part this was true, though there was brief state participation in the firm in the early 1930s. For detail on the changing and complicated ownership structure of Vestag, see Mollin (1988).

[9] That is, the firm made no effort actively to expand its downstream non-steel operations after its formation. For a more detailed description of Vestag, see Herrigel (1996) and for the company during the Third Reich, see Mollin (1988).

trading companies and several had traditionally significant weapons and military-related operations (e.g., Krupp). Though the so-called *Montankonzerne* had close relationships with major German banks, such as the Deutsche or Dresdner banks, these broadly diversified industrial entities did not have the kind of intimate family-esque relations with a *Konzern*–controlled bank as was the case with their *Zaibatsu* counterparts (Wellhöner 1989). Finally, in the steel segment itself, unlike the *Zaibatsu* steel producers, for the most part the steel producers within German *Konzerne* were integrated producers—that is, they produced their own pig iron, raw steel, and rolled products.

On the level of the governance of market relations, the Germans also had many similarities with the Japanese: Cartels were the mechanism of choice both to maintain market stability and to uphold the integrity of boundaries between specialties. Stable bifurcation in the industry's structure, then, was maintained by a mixture of merger and cartelization in ways that intricately intertwined markets and coordination. Though remarkably similar to the Japanese, the Germans arrived at this governance equilibrium in a very different manner. The key difference was that in Japan, bifurcation in the industry structure was a point of departure in the development of the industry, whereas in Germany it was the outcome of many years of turbulence caused by a midlife crisis in a relatively competitive nineteenth-century industry.

For most of the early decades of the twentieth century, German steel industry markets were extremely volatile, despite the fact that these years were marked on the whole by growth. The problem was that most of the major firms in the industry had emerged during the nineteenth century as suppliers of railroad expansion and the large-scale construction attendant to rapid industrialization. And where in Japan only Yahata Steel was fully integrated, *all* of the major German producers had integrated production facilities, often ranging from coal reserves into finished bar and rail. As demand for rails and structural shapes began to level off toward the end of the century, all the players in the industry simultaneously attempted to diversify into newer and more specialized finished-good markets, giving rise to tremendous and very turbulent competition. Cartels were created continuously, but, though legally binding, were for the most part ineffective: Either new entrants continually entered the market or competition outside the cartel created new finished-goods markets that then attenuated the commitments of customers in existing ones. Merger, on a grand scale to consolidate industrial capacity into a small number of oligopolistic producers (the so-called US Steel Strategy), was also discussed, but was never seriously attempted due to the obstinacy of the primarily family-owned and operated steel corporations in the industry.

Finally, in the general economic turmoil and recession of the early post-World War I decade, a solution that split the difference emerged. Volume production was consolidated into a new firm, the Vestag, through a grand merger of production capacity. The rest of the more specialized steel and rolling capacity was then ceded to newly created *Konzerne* which were able to link their steelmaking operations with extensive recently acquired downstream manufacturing interests.

These moves together both reduced the number of producers in the industry and clarified product–market boundaries among producers. This also transformed the cartel into a durable and effective mechanism for the stabilization of market order in the industry (Herrigel 1996). Indeed, the correspondence between industrial structure and corporate strategy was so harmonious that unlike their Japanese counterparts, German producers never appealed to the state to intervene in the maintenance of commitment or participation in cartels.

This picture of a strong family resemblance between the bifurcated industrial structures in the German and Japanese steel industries must be slightly diluted, however, by two additional aspects of the German case. First, German producers had a very different relationship to the state than their Japanese counterparts. Second, and largely because of that difference, two additional groups of producers existed in the later interwar German industry, both of which grew enormously after 1937 in association with Nazi regime efforts to encourage steel production for war.

German steel producers had a highly ambivalent relationship to the various governments that existed in Germany prior to the end of World War II.[10] On the one hand, large-scale German industrialists, in the steel industry as well as in other sectors, were very firm and articulate advocates of the self-government of industry and of society. This, correspondingly, made them believers in limited state power. They consistently advocated private control over the market (though not market freedom) and limited (though not necessarily democratic) government. Unlike the Japanese case where the government was reconstituted in the mid-nineteenth century in a way that allowed it to be viewed as an agent of the interests of the nation, in Germany the Imperial government after unification and then later the Weimar and Nazi regimes never succeeded in erasing the feeling among non-aristocratic social classes that the government was the affair of a particular social estate. Throughout the pre-1945 period, as a result, large-scale industrialists found their own social and ultimately national legitimacy as a social estate (*Stand*) in the existence of strict limits on the state's capacity to act in the economy in general and in the affairs of private firms and industrial sectors in particular. Modern industry in a powerful nation, German industrialists believed, should organize itself.

That said, German industrialists, particularly in heavy industry, were not beyond engaging in commerce with the state if it proved profitable—as it did with the massive growth of the German military, particularly its navy, before World War I. Nor did they object to the state taking over responsibility for collective-good services that proved to be too cumbersome to maintain cooperatively and privately, such as technical training and other forms of public infrastructure. As long as the State did not insinuate its own designs on the operations of private firms, large corporate private industry appreciated the role that a limited state could play in a market economy. If in Japan industry and govern-

---

[10] Note that this is a story about large firms and the German state, not a general claim about all industry and its relationship to government in Germany. For alternative relations between industry and the state, see Herrigel (1996, chs. 2 and 5).

ment cooperated in the development of a private economy in the interest of the nation, in Germany large industry and government coexisted with mutual respect and dependence, yet without a superordinate purpose or interest to bring them together in sustained cooperation.

Evidence of the salience of this distinction can be seen in the way in which the structure of the steel industry shifted in the late 1930s when the Nazi regime began to attempt to change the rules of the game and become more directive in the affairs of private steel production. The established private enterprises in the industry balked at Nazi efforts to channel their steel output away from their market strategies and toward the satisfaction of state needs. Even the formation of their own Control Associations (*Wirtschaftsgruppen*) in the context of the development of the first Nazi Four-Year Plan in the mid-1930s, staffed very often by trusted former trade association officials, did not attenuate large firms' mistrust of the state or temper their resistance to its projects.[11] The German steel producers were willing to incorporate the state's demand for steel into their output (as they had traditionally done in the past), but they were not willing to turn completely away from their private commercial operations or strategies in the process (Mollin 1988; Overy 1994, pp. 91–174).

This resistance on the part of the industry gave rise to two developments that changed the composition and structure of the industry. On the one hand, a number of private firms emerged that were willing to exploit the resistance of the major producers to the state and cater exclusively to the steel needs of the Nazi government. These new firms cobbled together smaller, non-integrated pig iron, steel, and rolling mills that were broadly dispersed throughout Germany (and after the war began, throughout the expanded Reich). They organized their output completely around the specialized demands of the military or military-related sectors. The largest and most significant firm of this type was the Friedrich Flick AG, which operated as a somewhat loose *Konzern*-like structure, but largely within the steel branch. That is, instead of seeking synergy between sectors (e.g., steel and engineering), Flick encouraged synergy among specialized and non-integrated steel operations.[12]

The other development was the creation by the Nazi regime of its own massive firm, the HGW. Established in 1936, this wholly state-owned firm soon became the second largest producer of steel in the Third Reich (Mollin 1988; Overy 1994, pp. 93–118, 144–74). The HGW was a sprawling agglomeration of cobbled together old firms and new greenfield sites. It was established to disrupt the private power of the *Montankonzerne* in the procurement of raw materials for steel production and in the delivery of steel for the military (and also to enhance

---

[11] Ironically, the Control Associations in Japan were modeled after these *Wirtschaftsgruppen*, though they seemed to have been far more successful in controlling the affairs of the steel industry in Japan than their German counterparts. On the *Wirtschaftsgruppen* as role model for the Control Associations, see Cohen (1949) and Yonekura (1996).

[12] Other producers of this character were the Otto Wolf AG, Röchling (from the Saar region), and Ballestrem (from Silesia). These firms (or their steel holdings) were all spun out of the Vestag after the latter firm's 1932 restructuring.

the bureaucratic power of Herman Göring and his henchmen within the Nazi state apparatus).[13] By garnering a privileged position in the administered distribution system (the *Wirtschaftsgruppen*), the mere presence of the state firm could force the recalcitrant private companies to shift their attentions toward Nazi economic ends. As an actual producer of steel, however, though it had high levels of mostly standardized output primarily for military-related ends, HGW was far less efficient along a whole array of measures than the major privates were, in particular the Vestag (see Table 1.2).

From a comparative point of view, the significance of the HGW and of the newer specialized steel *Konzerne*, such as Flick and Otto Wolff, was to make the German steel sector slightly more fragmented than the Japanese industry on the eve of war, though the general bifurcation between specialists and standard volume producers was maintained. That said, it is remarkable how generically similar the industries were: Both the Japanese and German industries had large centralized steel companies which produced in high volumes, though in the German case there were two such firms, together accounting for market shares comparable to that controlled by Japan Steel alone (at least in steel and finished goods markets). Likewise, both industries had significant portions of market share accounted for by steel-producing subsidiaries of much more broadly diversified industrial combines. These firms, in both countries, were much stronger in specialized and lower-volume markets than was the case with the large dominant firms.

The major disturbance in the analogy between the two industries in the end has to do with the different relationship between steel producers and the state in Germany than in Japan. In Germany, there was greater industrial fragmentation as the economy mobilized for war because the private firms were unwilling to allow their sovereignty to be compromised for state interests. There was no analog in Japan to the upstart catfish-type war production firms such as Flick, which came into being to exploit opportunities for war contracts created by the

Table 1.2. Comparative Data on Vereinigte Stahlwerke (Vestag) and Herman Göring Werke (HGW) in 1942/3

Index	Vestag	HGW (1943)
Ratio of coal to pig iron production	4.7:1	10.5:1
Ratio of coke to pig iron production	0.5:1	2:1
Crude steel production/employee(in t)	25.5	10.1
Percentage foreign workers in total work force	32	58
Sales/employee (Reichs Marks (RM))	11,558	6,333
State credits received (millions of RM in 1945)	0.18	3.2
Depreciation (RM/t of pig iron)	9	22

Source: Mollin (1988, p. 256, table 28).

[13] Mollin (1988) has a very extensive discussion of the political ties and interest of the state bureaucrats involved in the formation and operation of the HGW and their political interests in the *Konzern*.

reluctance of the private sector. In Japan, private firms were more able to reconcile their interests with those of the state (and vice versa) and hence there was no opening for opportunistic profiteering (Mollin 1988, pp. 257–70).

1.4. OCCUPATION AND THE IMPOSITION OF NEW AMERICAN RULES OF POLITICAL–ECONOMIC ORDER, 1945–57

With the defeat of Germany and Japan in World War II by the Allied powers, the steel industries in both defeated countries came under very critical scrutiny. Top executives with close ties to the former enemy regimes were arrested and assets in the industry appropriated by the occupying powers. The personalities in the industry and their culpability in the aims and crimes of the defeated regimes, however, were not the main factor that drove the Allies to seek reform.[14] Rather it was the very structure of the industry itself that became a target: The Allies attacked both the bifurcated structure of the steel producer market and the character of the companies that constituted it as crucial obstacles to democratic order in Japanese and German society.

The attack on the steel industry was consistent with the way in which the Allies dealt with industrial forms that resembled those of the steel industry in all other sectors. The dominant self-understanding of the American and Allied occupying powers in Germany and Japan is easy to detect in the contemporary writings and memoirs of participants in the occupation. One especially concise formulation is given by Eleanor Hadley in her 1970 book which draws extensively on her experiences as an antitrust specialist in Japan during the occupation. I present this lengthy quotation because it underscores the linkage that the victorious powers made between economic organization and political democracy and their sense of legitimacy in intervening in the restructuring of the fundamental rules of economic behavior that structured practice in both societies (Hadley 1970, p. 3):

World War II differed radically from previous wars in the terms imposed by the victors on the defeated. Previously exactions had been limited to territorial changes, restrictions on the military establishment, and reparations. World War II, representing for the first time "total" warfare, extended to the peace conditions "total" peace, with demands for change in the political and economic structure of the defeated powers. In both Germany and Japan

---

[14] For two discussions from the early postwar years of the general belief that German Big Business, especially the steel and chemical industries, helped the Nazis to power and underwrote its war effort, see Stolper (1948, pp. 172–96), Jösten (1948, part 3), and Taylor (1979, pp. 22–39, esp. 27–8). These popular understandings of the implication of German business in Nazism did not, as much other work has shown, correspond to the actual relationship between the two. Stolper makes this point, in a very impatient way, in the book mentioned above. But for the most recent scholarship and the complexities of the relationship, see Schreiber (1978), Neebe (1981), Geary (1983), Turner (1985), Hayes (1987), Stokes (1988), Plumpe (1990), and Gregor (1998).

the victors attempted to revamp the social structure, to establish democracy. In the words of one descriptive title, the Germans and the Japanese were "forced to be free" (Montgomery 1957).... Allied leaders saw the expansionist foreign policy of Germany and Japan as the product of their undemocratic governments, and believed that the future security interests of their own countries required nothing less than the social reconstruction of these two nations. By themselves, proscription of army-navy-airforce, along with territorial adjustments were insufficient. Nothing less than basic social reconstruction was needed if democracy, which would be peaceable, were to take root....

The programs for democratization in Germany and Japan were essentially similar. In both instances they called for a new constitution, new leadership, and change in the structure of the economy. Economic change was demanded for political reasons. The Allies believed that a democratic constitution would be meaningless unless the key pressure groups of the nation supported its ideology. In both Germany and Japan concentrated business was seen as one of the most powerful pressure groups, and because German and Japanese concentrated business was not considered to support democracy but rather oligarchy, it became a target of occupation reform.

Why did the US occupiers consider the structures of the "concentrated" businesses in Germany and Japan to be "oligarchic" as opposed to democratic? It will not do to code this orientation as a simple free-market, antimonopoly position, although advocates of smaller business and "free" markets were important minority voices in both occupation governments.[15] On the contrary, the most influential elements of the occupation governments were quite sympathetic to big business and were not at all opposed to some limits on market competition. They were, in the words of Theodore Cohen, "New Dealers" who believed deeply in the progressive and democratic potential of large-scale, mass production industry (Cohen 1987). But their vision of large-scale industry was one in which the power of large market actors was checked, as they believed it to be in the United States, by other strong and organized actors, both in their own markets and in the society at large: Rather than monopoly, they supported oligopoly; rather than cartelization and cooperation among producers, they favored vertical integration, competitive (oligopolistic) price setting, and the stimulation of stable consumer demand; instead of paternalism and employer discretion in wage setting and labor markets, they favored trade unionism and collective bargaining; instead of

---

[15] In both Germany and Japan, there was a battle within the American camp between radical progressive trust-busters and more conservative so-called "New Deal" advocates of American-style oligopolistic big business and mass production. On these divisions within US policy in Germany, see Berghahn (1985, pp. 84–111) and Taylor (1979, pp. 22–39). For an account of the deconcentration and decartelization process in Germany by a radical trust-buster, see Martin (1950). For debates within the occupation of Japan, see Cohen (1987, pp. 3–48, 154–86, 301–98), Hadley (1970, part 1), and Bisson (1954). New Dealers were more concerned with the consumer than with the size of enterprise: As long as prices could be established competitively, they believed that this would have salutary macroeconomic (and political) effects. For one of the seminal developers of this kind of thinking in the United States, see Arnold (1940). In general, on division in American antitrust thinking during this period, see for example, Peritz (1996, pp. 111–229). For a general overview of New Deal conceptions of the state and democracy in relation to the market see the concise overview article by Brinkley (1989, pp. 85–121).

multi-sectoral private conglomerate empires, they preferred to have corporate actors confine their growth to the vertically related processes of individual industries.[16]

In each instance, the American ideal was to create the economic and social conditions for the emergence of plural sources of power that would have to compete with and respect one another. It was precisely the absence of such conditions, as the Hadley quote above indicates, that the Allies believed made possible the authoritarianism and demagoguery of the two enemy regimes. In the context of industry, this pluralist understanding of a democratic economy was connected to an emerging American conception of industrial mass production and its social and political preconditions. The most significant connection had to do with the possibilities for market restructuring and the achievement of scale economies that would be made possible by the elimination of monopolies and cartels. Inefficient large producers protecting costly specialist production processes and cartels of specialized small producers no longer would be able to survive in an environment that insisted on competition and frowned upon collaboration.[17]

American reformers believed that the creation of this kind of alternative environment in the economy of the occupied societies would have significant positive employment and income effects and, ultimately, social and political ones as well. Traditional middle classes, key villains in the American understanding of the rise of fascism, would decay without the collusive mechanisms they had used to protect their social and economic position.[18] The emergence of efficient, large-scale oligopolistically structured industries would replace the old middle classes with a less differentiated industrial and service middle class. Without cartels and multi-sectoral vertical monopolies to enhance their social, economic, and political positions, "feudal" industrialists would be forced to concentrate their energies and resources on the achievement of efficiency and compete for profits in markets and influence in politics with other firms and associations.[19]

---

[16] Arnold (1940, pp. 14–15) characteristically observed:

The inevitable result of the destruction of competitive domestic markets by private combinations, cartels and trade associations is illustrated by Germany today. . . . Industrial Germany became an army with a place for everyone, and everyone was required to keep his place in a trade association or cartel. Here was arbitrary power without public control and regimentation without public leadership. That power, exercised without public responsibility was constantly squeezing the consumer. *There was only one answer.* Germany was organized to such an extent that it needed a general and Hitler leaped into power. Had it not been Hitler it would have been someone else. When a free market was destroyed, state control of distribution had to follow.

[17] See, for example, the testimony of Paul Hoffmann, head of the Economic Cooperation Administration, before the Senate Foreign Relations Committee (1949–50, p.184 and passim).

[18] For the linkage between traditional middle classes and fascism, see Lipset (1963).

[19] In addition to the above references, this characterization of American views is drawn from a reading of Montgomery (1957), Hadley (1970), Cohen (1987), Pells (1989), and Berghahn (1995). On feudal elements in industry, see Ranis (1955), Bendix (1956), Dahrendorf (1964), Hirschmeier (1964), and Landes (1965).

1.4.1. Destructive and Creative Policies

In order to achieve these goals in the occupied political economies, the Allies developed a strategy that involved both destructive and creative elements. The most notable destructive strategy involved the direct intervention into the property rights structure of industrial holdings in order to "deconcentrate" industries deemed by the Allies to have "unhealthy" or "undemocratic" monopoly structures. The same logic was also applied to cartels: Allied powers immediately advocated the elimination of all cartels in both the economies (Stolper 1948, pp. 264–72, Bisson 1954, Iyori, 1967).[20] The creative element of occupation strategy came with efforts to create rules for practice in the economy that would prevent the reemergence of the structures that the Allied governments destroyed and which would encourage instead the development of strong, countervailing organizations in markets and in society. In both occupied countries, this resulted in a very aggressive emphasis on antitrust legislation as well as a positive disposition toward the emergence of an organized labor movement (Gordon 1985, p. 331). Both kinds of shifts, American reformers believed, would foster the democratization of the occupied economies. Significantly, though the American occupiers viewed the formation of trade unions and employers organizations favorably and understood their competition and cooperation to be constitutive of stable democratic order, they disapproved of direct joint governance by these groups: Bargaining over wages among independent organizations was acceptable and democratic; parity management of single organizations to determine and set wages and prices was not. The United States wanted plural sources of social, economic, and political power (Prowe 1993).[21]

In both occupied countries, the steel industry became a primary target of both the destructive and creative aspects of Allied occupation reform. The huge market positions of Japan Steel and Vestag and HGW were considered by the occupiers to

[20] According to Article 12, Economic Section (Section B) *Potsdam Agreement. Joint Report on Results of the Anglo-Soviet-American Conference*, Berlin, 1945, released August 2, 1945: "At the earliest practicable date, the German economy shall be decentralized for the purpose of eliminating the present excessive concentration of economic power as exemplified in particular by cartels, syndicates, trusts and other monopolistic arrangements" (excerpts reprinted as Appendix B in Stolper (1948)). Similarly, in Japan, as early as September 6, 1945, the president of the United States issued to the SCAP an executive order, Number 244 for the Liquidation of Holding Companies. This edict charged the SCAP with 1. breaking up existing *Zaibatsu* companies and other holding company arrangements; 2. elimination of various mechanisms for the creation of private monopolies; and 3. the foundation of a system of free competition. The first two measures were understood to be transitional measures; the third was to be a fundamental principle of order in the new Japan. See Bisson (1954), and Iyori (1967).

[21] Prowe, however, suggests that American authorities opposed more corporatist arrangements because they involved a different kind of democratic representation than the Americans wanted. He opposes these corporatist groups to political parties. I do not believe that this is the appropriate distinction to make: Americans did not approve of the corporate arrangements Germans proposed because they preferred representative parties. They disapproved of those groups because they thought these would be monopolistic groups which would undermine social competition and pluralism. US occupiers did not have a conception of democracy narrowly confined to party competition and elections.

be excessive: They were concentrations of economic power that circumvented efficiency-inducing competition and gave producers the potential to hold society hostage to their interests. Likewise, the companies that were part of diversified combines (*Konzerne* and *Zaibatsu*) were attacked as unreasonable concentrations of power. Cooperation was viewed as collusion that undermined developments toward greater efficiency and larger scale within individual market segments. Both types of firms, and the bifurcated market structures that they created in the steel industry, became the targets for dismantling by military authorities in both Germany and Japan. Naturally, there was resistance in both societies to these reforms. The remainder of this section will detail the reforms that were both pursued and implemented in both countries. Section 1.5 will address the reality of resistance and the transformation of indigenous and American ideals it ultimately produced.

1.4.2. Allied Policies for the Deconcentration, Decartelization, and Democratization of German Steel

The American occupiers believed that the extreme integration and cartelization that had traditionally characterized the structure of the German steel industry both blocked the diffusion of efficient technologies and industrial practices in this industry and created dangerous monopoly power in the economy. Outsiders viewed the relatively large numbers of small and flexible rolling mills attached to individual companies as a sign of steel mill monopoly power and its inefficiency, rather than as an explicit strategy on the part of producers to expand their range of products. The Allies agreed that the industry needed to be deconstructed and rearranged in a way that would allow more "modern" and "healthy"—that is, larger-scale and less horizontally diversified—forms of industrial production to take root.[22]

To this end, all of the assets of the iron and steel industry were seized by the military governments in 1946 and early 1947 (Warner 1989, 1996). All six of the major Ruhr steel producers (Vestag, Krupp, Hoesch, Klöckner, GHH, and Mannesmann), which alone during the 1930s (before the formation of HGW) had controlled over 78% of German crude steel production, were completely broken up, as were the sprawling HGW and Flick operations (though in these cases there was the additional factor of capacity and units lost in liberated non-German territories). Bargaining between the Allies, the German government, and the iron and steel industry throughout the end of the 1940s resulted in a constant game of strategic recombination in the industry. Properties and plants

---

[22] Lucius Clay, ultimately only a moderate enthusiast for deconcentration, was very clear on the unacceptability of the traditional organization of the iron and steel industry. Clay was confident that the breakup of the industry would lead in an efficient direction because it would follow a plan drawn up by a committee lead by George Wolf of the United States Steel Corporation, see Clay (1950, pp. 329–30).

were torn apart and repositioned both on paper and in fact (Warner 1989). Ultimately, twenty-three new companies were created, thirteen from the old Vestag alone (Table 1.3).[23]

The new structure of the industry was organized around steel works: each new company was dominated by one facility. But, significantly, the degree of diversification in the finished rolling-mill product palettes in each of the newly created steel firms was disrupted. Though the Deconcentration Authority for the Steel Industry (*Stahltreuhändervereinigung*) attempted to retain as much integration between existing steel and rolling mills as "was technically necessary," much capacity was deemed inessential and allocated to other steel production units. In this way, parts of the industry's rolling-mill capacity was spread across the industry, rather than within firms. This kind of distribution of plant linkages was often extremely awkward: In some cases, rolling mills were realigned with steel works that could not supply them with the proper kind of steel and separated from ones that previously had (Stahltreuhändervereinigung 1954, pp. 129ff, 301–4).[24] But this kind of allocation of capacity was desirable from the point of view of the reformers both because it was difficult otherwise to achieve the goal of creating more companies to enlarge the arena of competition and because it raised the costs of diversification and created an incentive for firms to grow by increasing the scale of rolling mills they possessed. A political conception of the proper relationship between market order and democratic order, in other words, trumped narrower concerns of technical and economic efficiency (Stahltreuhändervereinigung 1954, pp. 129–31, 191–3).[25]

This intentional reallocation of finishing capacity among steel works was most dramatic in the Vestag successor companies, but a narrowing of rolling-mill capacity occurred within the steelmaking operations of the old *Konzerne* as well. Often this was less the result of explicit deconcentration efforts than it was the outcome of war damage or dismantling losses in rolling-mill plant that the deconcentration authorities did not attempt to redress. But, whatever the cause, the key outcome of the deconcentration for all firms' steel operations was the need to seriously rethink their strategy in rolled production. In particular, the old pre-war strategy of the *Konzerne* steel units that emphasized product proliferation, specialty production, and broad horizontal synergy and diversification was now seriously undermined, both physically and technologically. Moreover, it became only one of a number of alternative strategies available to producers as they set about reconstructing themselves.

---

[23] See Schröder (1952), Herchenröder et al. (1953), Stahltreuhändervereinigung (1954), Lammert (1960), Baare (1965), and Weil (1970). The Stahltreuhandervereinigung, Schroeder article and Herchenroeder et al. volume all have charts outlining lineages of firms.

[24] For complaints about disruptions to rolling mills, see Schröder (1952). Schroeder lists nine newly created companies with uneconomic combinations of steelmaking and rolling capacity.

[25] Norman Pounds (1952, p. 259) noted that the recomposition of the industry had not followed the guidelines that technical efficiency would have dictated: "It is too early to suggest the shape which the future organization of the heavy industry of the Ruhr is likely to take. It is clear, however, that the unwisdom of too great a fragmentation has been realized."

Table 1.3. The Twenty-Three "New" German Steel Enterprises Created After World War II[a]

New enterprise	Old parent
Deutsche Edelstahlwerke AG, Krefeld	Vestag
Rheinisch-Westfälische Eisen- und Stahlwerke AG, Mülheim/Ruhr	Vestag
Bergbau- und Industriewerte GmbH, Düsseldorf	Vestag
Hüttenwerke Phönix AG, Duisburg	Vestag
Dortmund-Hörder Hüttenunion AG, Dortmund	Vestag
Gußtahlwerk Bochumer Verein AG, Bochum	Vestag
August Thyssen-Hütte AG, Duisberg-Hamborn	Vestag
Hüttenwerke Siegerland AG, Siegen	Vestag
Gußtahlwerk Witten AG, Witten	Vestag
Rheinische Röhrenwerke AG, Mülheim	Vestag
Niederrheinische Hütte AG, Duisburg	Vestag
Stahlwerke Südwestfalen AG, Geisweid	Vestag
Ruhrstahl AG, Hattingen	Vestag
Mannesmann AG, Düsseldorf	Mannesmanröhren-Werke
Hansche Werke AG, Duisburg-Großenbaum	Mannesmanröhren-Werke
Stahl- und Walzwerke Rasselstein/Andernach AG, Neuweid	Otto Wolf
Stahlwerke Bochum, AG, Bochum	Otto Wolf
Nordwestdeutscher Hütten- und Bergwerksverien	Klöckner
Hoesch-Werke AG, Dortmund(Hoesch)	Hoesch
Hüttenwerk Rheinhausen AG, Rheinhausen (Krupp)	Krupp
Eisenwerk-Gesellschaft Maximilianshütte AG, Sulzbach-Rosenberg-Hütte (Friedrich Flick KG)	Friedrich Flick KG
Luitpoldhütte AG, Amberg	Reichswerke AG für Erzbergbau und Eisenhütten
Hüttenwerk Oberhausen AG (HOAG), Oberhausen	Gutehoffnungshütte Aktienverein für Bergbau und Hüttenbetrieb

[a] Ilseder Hütte, the twenty-fourth enterprise, was left unchanged by the rearrangements.
Source: Stahltreuhändervereinigung (1954).

In addition to this specialization of core steel production units (blast furnaces, steel mills, rolling mills), deconcentration also aimed at severing all but the most essential non-steel ties within the old *Konzerne* enterprises (Stahltreuhändervereinigung 1954, pp. 129–31, 133–41). The logic here was the same as within steel more narrowly defined. The broad cross-sectoral diversification of the *Montankonzerne* was viewed both as inefficient and monopolistic. Such enterprise structures were undesirable from an Allied point of view in two ways: They allowed steel operations to run inefficiently by providing them with guaranteed markets, while at the same time effectively subsidizing the downstream operations that perpetuated inefficiency and market fragmentation there as well. The Allies did not view the *Konzerne* as dynamic entities pursuing strategies of continuous innovation and product proliferation. They understood them instead to be archaic and pernicious economic forms that constituted obstacles to efficiency, democracy, and progress (Borkin and Welsh 1943; Pritzkoleit 1960; Manchester 1968). The effect of breaking up cross-sectoral linkages, however, was nonetheless to undermine the dynamic economies of technological variety that had sustained the *Konzerne* in the prewar period.

All of Vestag's machinery and manufacturing interests were collected together in the Rheinische Stahlwerke AG, its coal holdings into three independent companies and its trading businesses into the Handelsunion AG (Herchenröder et al. 1953; Pritzkoleit 1960, 1960, pp. 57–118, 131–41). The same vertical deconstruction occurred in most of the *Konzerne*. Mannesmann, Klöckner, and Hoesch, for example were stripped of crucial steel plants, all but their most-needed coal mines and most of their downstream engineering interests (Herchenröder et al. 1953, pp. 171–94, 199–218, 230–41). The GHH had its networks of coal mines and steel mills expropriated but retained its extensive holdings in manufacturing, primarily in heavy engineering and shipbuilding. Its sizable former steel operations in Oberhausen were constituted as a fully independent steel company, the Hüttenwerk Oberhausen AG (HOAG) (Herchenröder et al. 1953, pp. 119–40; Menges 1976). Krupp was forced to sign a commitment to separate legally all of the family's steelmaking facilities (concentrated primarily in the work at Rheinhausen) and attendant coal mines from the rest of its business, collect them into a holding company, and sell them off. The major non-steel lines of Krupp's business included some trading companies and a wide variety of specialized heavy engineering workshops located around Essen and in the Ruhr Valley more generally.[26]

Deconcentration thus significantly reorganized and decentralized both the production of steel and rolled products and the broad cross-sectorally diversified companies that produced them. The bifurcated industry structure of giant mass producers surrounded by smaller specialist producers was eliminated. Individual producers were smaller, less-integrated (especially with forward non-steel sectors), and less-diversified producers of rolled steel products. These developments totally destroyed the coherence of both the industry and the companies in it as they had existed prior to the war.

---

[26] For complicated reasons, the steelmaking facilities were never, in fact, sold off but were kept in a separate holding, apart from the rest of its business in the manner dictated by the Allied settlement, until the late 1960s—when the firm went bankrupt and had to be completely reorganized. Descriptions of the reconstitution and development of the Krupp empire are given in Klass (1954, pp. 431–3), Herchenröder et al. (1953, pp. 145–70), Weder (1968), Wirtschaftswoche (1972, pp. 323, 62–3), Manager Magazine (1973, 1975, pp. 27–34).

The strategic intent behind all of these deconcentration efforts (i.e., to create the economic conditions for the formation of oligopolies and integrated mass producers and the social conditions for pluralist democratic order) was reinforced through the simultaneous implementation of very strict decartelization measures in the industry. An outright ban on all cartelization in the German economy was announced by all three Allied governments in the West in 1947 (Günther 1951).[27] The ban was enforced by the Allied occupying governments until 1955 and continued to be enforced by the Germans thereafter until it was replaced by a new law governing competition in 1957. This ban on cartels was complemented on a European level in the coal and steel industry where the European Coal and Steel Community Treaty and Organization (ECSC) made the rejection of all forms of cartel a condition of membership (Lammert 1960, pp. 201–4; Burn 1961, pp. 407–16).

The intention of this rule-change regarding cartels was to alter the environment in which producers in the steel industry competed. In the prewar industry structure, concentration, specialty production, horizontal diversification, and cartelization were integrally related. Volume production of standard products was concentrated in the large Vestag and HGW combines, while production of lower-volume and more specialized products was taken by the smaller, horizontally diversified *Konzerne*. The large volume producers strove for scale economies, while the *Konzerne* looked for horizontal synergies and economies of scope across their many manufacturing businesses. The curiosity of this structure is that it gave the smaller *Konzern*-based specialist producers an interest in the formation of cartels to stabilize competition. With a wide variety of smaller-sized rolling units, oriented toward specialization, yet with high fixed costs despite their small size, the threat of ruinous price and terms-based competition during downturns in the business cycle was very real to these producers. By forming cartels, they could stabilize the structure of specialization (Herrigel 1996, chs. 2 and 5).

The Allied and ECSC reform measures undermined the integral logic of this industry structure. In effect, the reforms discouraged strategies of specialization and customization in finished products by taking away the governance mechanisms and business forms that made them stable and profitable. At the same time, they created the possibility for the radically fragmented pieces of the industry to be recombined, both within firms and across the industry as a whole, in ways that would facilitate larger-scale, more "efficient," production. Through specialized investment in select finished-product markets, greater capacity in each product-market segment could be spread across a more limited number of firms than had been possible in the past. Bifurcation would be replaced by oligopoly, monopoly and specialization by mass production. In any case, with the absence of *Konzerne* strategies of scope and synergy across sectors and the stabilization mechanism of the cartel, the possibility of making profits in a

---

[27] British Zone Law Number 56; American Zone Law Number 78; and French Zone Law Number 96.

broad variety of rolled products with only a modest scale commitment in each was significantly reduced.

Finally, the occupying powers were extremely active on the labor side in the industry. The prewar German steel industry was notably hostile to trade unionism. This was not only true of the industry during the Third Reich but had actually characterized the industry's outlook from its very inception. While, by 1913, Germany had the largest social democratic movement and one of the world's largest trade union movements, there was no union representation in the steel industry at that time (Domansky-Davidsohn 1980). The High Commissioner for Germany within the occupying government created an Office of Labor Affairs that attempted, systematically, to encourage the rejuvenation of the German labor movement after its period of enforced dormancy within the Third Reich (Kelly 1949; Fichter 1993). According to a US Policy Directive for the High Commissioner issued in November 1949, cited by Michael Fichter (1993, p. 260), the goal of the United States in the labor and industrial relations field was "to encourage the development of free, democratic trade unions and the negotiation of agreements and cooperative settlement of problems between them and employer associations." The Office of Labor affairs sponsored hundreds of trips by trade unionists to the United States to learn about "the American way of life." It also sponsored a Training Within Industry (TWI) Program which established educational committees on the shop floor level designed to undermine what were viewed as the "authoritarian or paternalistic" shop floor relations in German firms and impart more democratic "American" habits. Production units in the steel industry figured very prominently in these programs. Unions began to assert themselves very aggressively in the industry almost immediately after the occupation began (Fichter 1993, p. 262).

1.4.3. Deconcentration, *Zaibatsu* Dissolution, and Allied Efforts to Create a Democratic Economy in Japan

The Allied occupying force in Japan, Strategic Command of the Allied Powers (SCAP), attacked the bifurcated structure of the Japanese steel industry and the diversified multi-sectoral *Zaibatsu* holding companies with at least as much alacrity as they had the analogous structures in Germany. The procedure, timing of the reforms, and official position of the authorities differed significantly in Japan, however. In particular, unlike Germany, there was not actually a military government in Japan. Because there was always a clear divide between the government and the military in Japan, and because the government did not collapse as it had in Germany (and perhaps because there were not enough people knowledgeable about the place and capable of speaking the language), the occupation forces dissolved only the military and its institutions. They decided to run all of their reforms through the existing civilian government structure, even as that structure was to be changed. All reforms in politics were formally legislated by the Japanese government and carried out by the bureaucracy—though always at the bidding of the SCAP (Kawai 1960; Ward and Sakamoto 1987; Cohen 1987, Hadley 1970, Finn 1992). Such reforms ranged from making a new constitution, reconstituting parties, and changing the suffrage laws to industrial deconcentration policies and the promulgation of new rules regarding market behavior. Allied antipathy toward "monopoly" power and multi-sectoral conglomerates came through very clearly in the policies that were ultimately put in place. As in Germany, SCAP pursued policies that were both destructive and creative.

The earliest and most economically significant targets of SCAP destructive policy were the *Zaibatsu* firms.[28] These were attacked in a number of ways, all of which effectively destroyed the coherent, centrally controlled, and diversified *Zaibatsu* as a governance structure in the Japanese economy.[29] First, a Holding Company Liquidation Commission (HCLC) was established that designated eighty-three holding companies for immediate dissolution. This list included all of the major *Zaibatsu* property interests (Mitsui, Mitsubishi, Sumitomo, Yasuda, Asano, etc.) and all of those who had significant interests in the steel industry. Then, in 1947, the ten major families who controlled these eighty-three designated companies and other companies were declared to be *"Zaibatsu"* families. The ownership shares of both the families and the holding companies were transferred to the HCLC. Further, a 1947 Antimonopoly law, also designed by the SCAP but implemented by the Japanese government, completely outlawed holding companies (among other things). Then, the resale of the assets of the dissolved holdings were limited in crucial ways: In particular, no one was permitted to purchase more than 1% of the shares of any given company (Acino 1958; Iyori 1967; Hadley 1970; Aoki 1987; Iyori 1990). Taken together these policies effectively eliminated the traditional structure of family control through holdings of broadly diversified multi-sectoral operations.

Next, there was a purge of leading managers in the largest companies (not only *Zaibatsu*): The SCAP mandated the removal of all the wartime chief officers of 200 important companies in the economy. Moreover, participation in the new management of the restructured companies by *Zaibatsu* family members or any of the high-ranking directors of 240 *Zaibatsu*-related companies was banned for a period of ten years. There are disagreements in the literature as to how many

---

[28] Cohen (1987, p. 427) quotes Edwin Pauley as representative of SCAP feelings regarding the *Zaibatsu*: "Japan's *Zaibatsu* . . . are the comparatively small group of persons, closely integrated both as families and in their corporate organizations, who throughout the modern history of Japan have controlled not only finance, industry and commerce, but also the government. They are the greatest war potential of Japan. It was they who made possible all Japan's conquests and aggressions. Not only were the *Zaibatsu* as responsible for Japan's militarism as the militarists themselves, but they profited immensely by it. Even now, in defeat, they have actually strengthened their monopoly position . . . Unless the *Zaibatsu* are broken up, the Japanese have little prospect of ever being able to govern themselves as free men. As long as the *Zaibatsu* survive, Japan will be their Japan."

[29] Excellent comparisons of the pre- and post-*Zaibatsu* dissolution character of large Japanese corporations can be found in Hadley (1970, pp. 205–315) and Yamamura (1967).

managers were actually purged as a result of these measures: Hadley (1970) estimates around 2,500 while Aoki (1987, pp. 268–9) places the figure at 3,500. In any case, it seems fairly clear that an entire generation of top leadership in firms was wiped away by SCAP efforts to cleanse the positions of power in the economy of "militarists and ultra-nationalists."

So much for the diversified, multi-sectoral combines. These reforms undermined the old system of central coordination of diversified operating units and created essentially autonomous and isolated units, weakly related by interpenetrated property ties (and, crucially, without any controlling property interest). In the context of the steel industry, as in the German case, this had the consequence of cutting loose the individual producers from the security and technological and market resources provided by their association with up- and downstream conglomerate units. The most dramatic example of this was the case of Kawasaki Steel, which, due to the personnel and property changes in the Kawasaki Group, severed itself completely from its long-time parent, Kawasaki Heavy Industries. As in the German case, this new autonomy would profoundly affect the strategies that individual producers believed that they could then pursue (particularly after the breakup of Japan Steel as will be discussed below).

A final destructive intervention was the abolition of the Control Association infrastructure that had been created during the war at the bidding of the military. These organizations were viewed as monopolistic, market-hostile forces and as sources of cartelization. In the reformer's view, they undermined the emergence of a plurality of organizational forms in the economy. The Iron and Steel Control Association was among the first to be abolished (in February of 1946 by SCAP decree) but by the end of the year all remaining Control Associations were slated to be abolished (Cohen 1949, p. 431). The United States was hostile to the control function exercised by the Control Associations: that is, the central control and allocation of investment resources within an industry. SCAP, however, was not opposed per se to the existence of trade associations in an industry. In the Trade Association Act of July 1948, while banning all control functions and all other activities that were or could lead to cartel, monopolistic, or unfair trade practices, the law explicitly allowed trade associations to "receive voluntary submissions of statistical data and to publish such data in summary form without disclosing business information or conditions of any particular entrepreneur" (Yamamura 1967, p. 25). The law also allowed the dissemination of technical information and cooperation in research. In other words, as long as trade associations acted like trade associations in the United States, representing the interests of their members and providing non-market-related services and publicity, they were acceptable and fully compatible with a pluralist economic order (Lynn and McKeown 1988, pp. 24–32 and *passim*).

As in Germany, SCAP's actions were not all destructive. The military authority also made an effort to create a set of rules in the industry that would foster the development of a pluralist political and economic order. American-style antitrust legislation was passed on April 14, 1947 by the not yet newly constituted Japanese Parliament. As in Germany, it completely outlawed all forms of cartel arrangements and severely curtailed the possibilities for merger and holding company arrangements as well. In the spring of 1948, US authorities allowed the law to be reformed to reduce the severity of obstacles to the merger. They also established at that time a Deconcentration Review Board, staffed by American business and government officials, to review each individual market arrangement to determine precisely whether or not it constituted unfair competition. This innovation slowed the initial hell-bent antimonopolist fervor of US deconcentration policy, but it established an effective mechanism to ensure that only organizations consistent with American pluralist conceptions of market order would find the space to reconstitute themselves (Hwang 1968, p. 10f; Cohen 1987, pp. 353–77; Iyori 1990).

The central achievement of this new system was the breakup of Japan Steel. Like the Vestag (and the HGW), this large firm was taken to be an "unreasonable" concentration of economic power by the Allied authorities. Unlike Vestag, Japan Steel was not fragmented into as many pieces: Instead of the thirteen that came out of the Vestag, Japan Steel was broken into two new and independent firms: Yahata Steel and Fuji Steel (Scheppach 1972; Yonekura 1991, 1994, pp. 189–211).[30] This move had a significant impact on the industry, in two ways. First, it increased the number of integrated producers in the industry from two to three (in addition to Yahata and Fuji, NKK was also integrated). Second, and more significantly, by making the formerly state-controlled Yahata and Fuji private firms with a responsibility to sell their production on the market at competitive prices, the breakup of the firm introduced significant uncertainty in the supply of pig iron to non-integrated producers. In the past, non-integrated firms such as Kawasaki, Sumitomo, and Kobe had been content to purchase pig iron from Japan Steel at subsidized prices. Now this was no longer possible. Moreover, since Fuji and Yahata had to be competitive in finished-product markets as well, they posed a significant competitive threat to the non-integrated steel producers (Yonekura 1993). SCAP's hope was that by introducing greater competition into the integrated steel sector, this would ultimately foster the adoption of more efficient, vertically integrated structures by all remaining producers and ideally, in the emergence of a new, stable oligopolistic market structure.

Indeed, taken together, it is clear that the combination of destructive and creative policies completely ruined the set of institutions and practices that had created the distinctive bifurcated structure in the pre-war steel industry. Instead of one, there were several integrated volume producers. The specialty producers no longer had dynamic relations with conglomerate partners nor the ability to arrange and stabilize the boundaries of their specialties in the market through cartelization. The new environment that the SCAP reforms created, moreover, structured

---

[30] Yahata Steel took over the Yahata Works while Fuji took over the Hirohata, Kamaishi, Wanishi, and Fuji Works.

incentives in such a way as to make the pursuit of volume and integration more attractive than attempting to recast the strategy of specialization.

Finally, again as in Germany, moves were made to foster the emergence of an organized labor presence both in Japanese industry generally and in the steel industry in particular. As in Germany, during the entire period of industrialization, labor organizations had suffered from considerable repression in the steel industry (though, unlike Germany, in Japan they had made few inroads elsewhere).[31] In October 1945, General Douglas MacArthur (the head of SCAP) instructed the Japanese Diet to enact labor legislation that would protect the rights of labor, including the right to organize. Ultimately, three crucial laws were enacted in the ensuing year that established a very favorable environment for the formation of trade unions and collective bargaining (Gordon 1985; Gordon 1998, pp. 330–9). The first law, the Labor Union Law, guaranteed workers the right to organize, collectively bargain, and strike. Discrimination by employers for union activity was also outlawed. This law further established a national Central Labor Relations Commission as well as regional commissions in each prefecture. The second law, The Labor Relations Adjustment Act, explicated more precisely the role and purview of these boards. Essentially, they were constituted as arbitration boards in which representatives from labor, employers, and government sat in deliberation. Finally, a third piece of legislation, the Labor Standards Law, set minimum hours, wages, insurance, injury compensation, and unemployment benefits for all workers, unionized and non-unionized (Gordon 1985, pp. 330–9).

The American authorities conceived of these moves as essential for the creation of a social infrastructure in Japan capable of sustaining democracy. Crucially, however, though supporters of union organization in markets for political reasons, the US authorities were strong opponents of political activism on the part of unions. Of the view of the Occupation labor department that he headed, Cohen (1987, p. 204) says: "To the Americans, political unionism, that is unions as partners of a party, was an anti-democratic and un-American concept." Japanese unions and workers did not agree with this idea, as we shall see. Indeed, in Section 1.5, we will see that many of the framework interventions undertaken by the occupying governments encountered resistance from the occupied societies, giving rise to significant social, economic, and political recomposition in each society.

---

[31] This is not to say that there were not efforts to organize or that there were no union-like organizations prior to the occupation. There were. But they were very embattled and persecuted by both the state and employers. See the outstanding account of pre-war developments in heavy industry in Gordon (1985, pp. 1–326). Cohen (1987, p. 191) notes that the Japanese labor movement reached its pre-war high for union organization in 1936 with 420,000 members—approximately 7% of the non-agricultural workforce.

1.5. THE APPROPRIATION AND RECOMPOSITION
OF AMERICAN IDEALS IN GERMANY AND JAPAN

Most treatments of the American occupation of Japan and Germany have narratives that begin, as this one has, with aggressive American efforts to reform the indigenous systems. But typically the narratives then turn to internal conflicts or incoherence within the occupation governments, intransigence on the part of powerful local leaders, and finally to a weakening of American resolve for reform, especially in the economy, with the onset of the Cold War and in particular the outbreak of the Korean War. All of these factors are held to undermine American reform ideals and lead to a "reverse course" in policy or the reconstitution of central institutions and actors from the prewar societies (Müller 1987, 1991).

Without in any way wanting to cast doubt upon the *existence* of factors disrupting American resolve and distracting attention, the discussion here will depart significantly from this traditional narrative of American failure. Its claim, as indicated at the outset, is both that American occupation profoundly altered the German and the Japanese political economies and that indigenous institutions, actors, and ideas recomposed the American ideas in the process of appropriating them. This mutual transformation of the occupied and the occupiers occurred not by the allies imposing particular institutional forms on the occupied lands and the occupied populations blocking some and not blocking others and/ or deconstructing those imposed structures. Rather, recomposition occurred because of the way in which contestation itself was constituted. American power successfully established a range of normative social, economic, and political background ground rules according to which deliberation about the construction of new institutions had to take place. Yet, these background rules (pluralism, crosscutting power, antimonopolism, limited state power, etc.) were neither unambiguous nor directly reducible to a finite set of clearly "American" organizational forms or practices. The deliberative process of identifying a practice or institution that could be legitimately recognized as consistent with higher normative goals resulted in the mutual transformation of all participants, understanding of the object of deliberation. We will look at the German case first and the Japanese second.

1.5.1. Engagement with American Reform Efforts in Germany

The defeat of the Nazis and occupation by foreign anti-National-Socialist powers utterly delegitimized the understandings of market order and state power that the Nazis had attempted to institutionalize during the Third Reich. At the same time, a space was created by the occupation for the reassertion of ideas about social and economic order that had been suppressed by the Nazis. Holders of these latter views, however, were forced by the situation to articulate their positions anew.[32] In particular, in putting forth their own political and economic goals they were compelled to address the Allied critique of the authoritarian elements within the German political economy and the Allied desire for a pluralist democratic order in the economy and the polity. This joint, interpenetrated, recomposition of imposed and traditional categories occurred in three areas in the context of the steel industry debate: (*a*) in the area of property rights in industry and the sovereignty of private property ownership; (*b*) in the area of codetermination, workplace democracy, and the scope of trade unionism; and (*c*) regarding the reconstitution of market competition, antitrust, and cartelization.

1.5.1.1. Property in Industry

The property issue was central to all discussions of industrial restructuring in the occupation period and it was of decisive importance for recomposition in the steel industry (Warner 1996). While the US government and German industrialists both opposed the elimination of private control of the steel industry (unlike the British) (Schmidt 1970; Turner 1989, pp. 37–154), the two did not share the same conception of the political significance of private property or of its role in political order. In the American view, private property was, at its most basic level, a constitutive feature of a market economy, without which there could be no exchange. By protecting its sovereignty in market competition, and yet at the same time opposing monopoly, Americans believed that an ensuing healthy competition among private capital would drive innovation in the economy, expand the spectrum of opportunity for individual private actors, and create the social power of organization to limit the unhealthy growth of state power. This view of property assumed an equality among property holders and understood social order to be a competitive equilibrium among plural sources of social and political power. Private property was constitutive of the American conception of liberal–democratic pluralism.

German industrialists had a conception of private property that had little to do with equality, liberal freedoms, democracy, or competitively constructed social order. For them, private industrial property entailed both a particular status in society and a whole range of mutual obligations with other social groups, the nation, and the state. Whether as individual private property holder or as managerial representative of diffused joint-stock capital, the status associated with private industry came from an idea that society was divided into specialized roles—skilled workers, farmers, artisans, shopkeepers, bankers, lawyers, etc. Private industrialists played the esteemed role of steering industrial production, providing employment and income, housing, education, and social provision for their employees, and driving industrial progress. It was significant for the private industrialists that their ownership of property entailed authority. If they were

---

[32] It was, in other words, a moment of Deweyan "reconstruction."

obligated to provide their employees with the benefits just noted, they fully believed that their employees owed them unconditional respect for their authority, and all matters relating to it, both within and outside of the factory walls (Berghahn 1985; Turner 1985; Overy 1994).

German private industrialists, in other words, understood themselves to be playing a crucial role, *as a corporate group*, in the maintenance of the traditional German social and political order. As mentioned in part 1.3.2 of this chapter, this role was to be performed in support of and in conjunction with, but always independently of the state. Large industrialists understood their role as contributing to the greatness of the nation, not to the greatness of the state. For them, the state, as a higher authority, had complementary ends and reciprocal obligations to its citizenry to maintain public order, respect the order of status and entitlements in society, and provide for the developmental needs of the nation. Industrialists believed that the power of the state should be limited vis-à-vis the rights of property, just as they believed their own power over their workers was tempered by obligations. Such mutual recognition and limitation contributed to good order. Though perhaps obvious, it is important to underscore that there is nothing in this view of the rights and status of private property that held that the state should be democratic or even equally limited in its power relative to all social groups—hence German industrialists' tolerance of Nazi labor measures and labor repression but resistance to Nazi efforts to influence managerial decision making (Turner 1985; Overy 1994).

In the context of Allied occupation and debates about the deconcentration of the steel industry, then, private property was not private property. And, in the face of Allied power (all steel assets were held by the Allied government in trust), German steel industrialists found it prudent in the struggles over restructuring to formulate their arguments for the social and political value of private property in industry in a way that was consistent with American understanding. Crucially, they did this in a way that did not involve the simple appropriation of the American view. Rather they highlighted elements within their traditional view that resonated with the American one. In particular, an important industrial argument regarding private property throughout the occupation period (and well into the mature Federal Republic) involved the important role that private capital and its organizations could play in the limitation of state power and as a bulwark against the return of authoritarianism. Weak property rights and poorly organized industrial associations, they argued, made society vulnerable to unjust incursions of state power and prey for demagogic political actors. Further, this idea of the central significance of sovereign private power being capable of limiting state power was linked to the traditional idea of self-government (*Selbstverwaltung*) in which private industry as well as its associations were understood to have the social obligation and privilege of being able to govern its own affairs without outside interference (Berg 1966). These very traditional ideas about the significance and rights of property could be made to appear consistent with American desires to establish a regime of private property that would foster social pluralism, limited government, and economic progress.

What the new German positions did not do, however, was abandon the idea of society being composed of deeply entrenched functional groups, whose location and identity involved complex notions of status, entitlement, and mutual obligation. By emphasizing the key limiting role of private property on the growth of state power, German industrialists were simply highlighting the part of their understanding of property that was compatible with the American notion of property. There was nothing manipulative or dishonest about this: This was simply a way in which the American discourse could be understood within the traditional frames of German understanding. Indeed, the American insistence on democratic pluralism encouraged this kind of recomposition in the German view.

By the same token, it is important to insist on the idea that this was not a process of the Americans being somehow duped. When the military authority decided to make the restructured steel assets exchangeable for shares in the *Altkonzerne* in May of 1951, the Americans did so because they understood German arguments as acceptance of their own understanding of private property as a vehicle for social and political pluralism. According to James Martin (1950, p. 91), who did not believe this, the view was, "They were not Nazis; they are businessmen."[33] The American occupiers understood the category of "businessman" or private industrialist to have a transparent meaning—as did the Germans. Yet, in both cases the Germans and Americans were nodding their heads in agreement when the content of what they agreed upon differed quite radically.

For the German actors, their own position merely involved a recalibration of the kinds of entitlements and mutual obligations that were to be publicly associated with private property. Private property in industry was still understood to be crucial for the maintenance of social order and hence deserving of respect and recognition. The American view denied that distinctions of status and entitlement could be politically drawn among private actors, while the adapted German view assumed this to be a foundational dimension of what was meant by private control of industry. In both forms of understanding, however, private property constituted a countervailing power against the authority of the state— and this was crucial for Allied approval.

An additional arena in which a recalibration of indigenous understandings of social categories and political status took place in confrontation with American ideas was in the context of the governance of the workplace and the labor market. As in the case of property in industry, German and American understandings of markets, social order, and democracy diverged despite formal harmonies and the appearance of consistency in social and political understanding. The interesting

---

[33] The reference to Nazis in this quote may distract: The view conveyed is that the Americans were persuaded that a businessman was a businessman, while I am pointing out that this was not the case. Where Martin would probably associate the corporate dimensions of the German industrialists understanding of property immediately with Nazism, I would not. The corporate idea of private property is much older and industrialists were forced to recompose the idea to accommodate the Nazi regime as well.

aspect of this process of recomposition is that it occurred in interaction with the developments in the reconstitution of property just outlined.

1.5.1.2. Codetermination, Workplace Democracy, and the Scope of Trade Unionism

As noted earlier, the Allied government was favorably disposed to the formation of trade unionism in occupied Germany and very much encouraged the development of collective bargaining practices. This was in line with their idea of pluralist democracy as a system of countervailing powers. German workers embraced this idea enthusiastically. But they also extended it in a way that went far beyond the American understanding of a trade union or of the proper boundaries of countervailing power in the labor market. The reason for this stems from the fact that, unlike the American occupiers, the German workers understood the traditional roots of the social and political lines that German industrialists were drawing around their property. In response, the labor movement sought to apply American notions of the limitation of power (or at least that language) to what it viewed as unwarranted concentration of corporate social power in the form of independent managerial control over industrial enterprises. In the German labor movement's view, the only way to get countervailing power was to have it inside industrial enterprises (Müller 1991; Streeck 1992, pp. 137–68).

To be sure, this idea had a wide variety of indigenous precursors: Social Catholics and Social Democrats had both advocated variants of industrial democracy during the Weimar Republic (and even before). Syndicalist ideas had informed the spontaneous takeovers of factories after both World Wars I and II (Teuteberg 1961). But the particular variant that emerged after World War II in the context of occupation and restructuring in the steel industry was distinguished from these by the way in which its defenders indicated its consistency with American understandings of pluralist democratic order. Previously, codetermination had been argued for very much in corporate social terms, that is, as an argument for the social entitlement of the working class to be able to co-influence the organization of work and the direction of the production unit's investment. In the postwar variant, the language was not about social entitlement for the working class, but about the need to limit concentrations of private power with countervailing social organizational power in order to create secure democratic order.

Though they were wary of the threat to their own understanding of private property that codetermination seemed to pose, the American governors, and other American observers seemed to be persuaded that, though unconventional, codetermination was at least consistent with their own democratic concerns. Clark Kerr, an early observer of the German labor movement from the United States, made sense of the codetermination in this revealing way:

The program defies labeling for it is not social democracy, nor catholic corporatism, nor socialism, nor capitalism, nor syndicalism, nor voluntarism, although it bears some similarity to each. It might, perhaps, be termed "joint economic pluralism." "Pluralism" because it envisages many loci of power, "economic" because it emphasizes the role of functional interest groups; "joint" because power is shared by capital and labor. It is a sort of meeting ground between liberalism and socialism, for it has elements of both private enterprise and social control. It is also a meeting ground for capital and organized labor since each, in Germany, favors a privately controlled economy. The battle between them is not an ideological one of capitalism versus socialism; rather it is more a practical but nonetheless quite intense one over how joint shall self-administration be. (Kerr 1954, pp. 553–4)

The German unions sold codetermination as an institution for the limitation of private industrial power and the American occupiers understood it that way. Yet codetermination was not only that. It was also clearly understood by both trade unionists and employers in Germany as an institutional move to secure and improve the social and political status of the working class. It challenged the social and political entitlements involved in the industrialists' understanding of their social position and asserted the rights and entitlements of workers. This latter dimension of the struggle over codetermination was very far removed from the liberal pluralist concerns of the Americans. It involved the recomposition of corporate social rights. Or, as the eminent legal theorist Ernst-Joachim Mestmäcker criticized in the 1970s when revision of the law was being widely debated, the legal justification of codetermination by the trade unions has a liberal pluralist heritage, but this heritage has always paradoxically supported a system of political entitlement for the participating social groups (Mestmäcker 1978, pp. 135–54).

The system of codetermination was, thus, neither the direct product of Allied occupation nor thinkable in its precise form without it. Consistent enough with American pluralist ideals to lead the American authorities to keep arms length over the German debate over the passage of the law, calling it a "German affair," the system of codetermination was also an arrangement that never spawned any imitators in the United States. By all accounts, however, the system was a tremendous advantage for the steel producers during the great postwar economic boom. It fostered cooperation between labor and management in the labor market and on the shop floor and thereby gave steel producers remarkable flexibility in work and production (Thelen 1991; Streeck 1992; Herrigel 1996, ch. 6).

1.5.1.3. Reconstitution of Market Competition, Antitrust, and Cartelization

As we saw in Section 1.4, Allied intervention into the order of markets in the steel industry was extremely aggressive: Firms were broken up and reconstituted as much more specialized units, downstream linkages to machinery and other product markets were severed, and all manner of cartelization was banned. It was plain to the steel managers that the Allies were attempting to block the reconstitution of the old prewar industrial structure and encourage a more mass production-oriented, oligopolistic industrial structure to develop.

German steel managers were divided on the attractiveness of this situation. Some, such as Hermann Reusch of the GHH *Konzern*, found the entire Allied program unacceptable and abandoned their commitment to the steel industry and concentrated their business in the machinery sector. Others, however, recognized the kind of strategy the Allies were encouraging as reminiscent of a strategy that earlier actors in the industry, such as August Thyssen, had advocated, unsuccessfully, earlier in the century (Chandler 1990, p. 493; Herrigel 1996, ch. 3). Thyssen and his allies failed in the earlier period both because the intransigence of existing property relations in the industry blocked consolidation efforts and because the bifurcated industrial structure of a large volume producer and numerous more specialized *Konzerne* proved to be a profitable alternative strategy (Chandler 1990; Kleinschmidt 1993). With the old firms physically and technologically broken up into distinct property units and Allied hostility toward the *Konzerne* strategy, however, the mass production and oligopoly strategy appeared both attractive and possible. Here, producers found that a strategy for development was being made available to them that was both consistent with a dimension of their past and in line with the American understanding of "modern" industrial structure.

Seen in this light, it should be of little surprise that the industry developed in precisely this way during the 1950s and 1960s: In response to strong demand during the Korean War and then subsequently with the growth of the automobile and other consumer goods industries, producers invested heavily in new, larger-scale, modern rolling-mill equipment, in particular wide strip mills, that enabled them to achieve greater production efficiencies at higher volumes. At the same time, a process of concentration occurred in the industry over the course of the 1950s as the smaller units created by the Allied deconcentration reforms were recombined to consolidate industry capacity and accommodate the large-scale technologies.

This process of recomposition in the industry can be clearly seen in the way that the companies of the old Vestag were recombined during the initial period of expansion. Of the thirteen steel companies originally created out of the breakup of the Vestag in 1953, only four were left by the beginning of the 1960s: the August Thyssen Hütte AG (ATH), the Phönix-Rheinrohr AG, Rheinische Stahlwerk AG (Rheinstahl), and the Dortmund-Hörde Hütten Union (DHHU).[34] For the most part, the consolidation and expansion of these companies did not result in direct competition between them. Instead, each expanded and consolidated its capacity

---

[34] The attentive reader will note that three of these companies—ATH, Phönix, and Rheinstahl—correspond, at least in name, to companies that existed prior to the formation of the Vestag, and which were instrumental in its creation. DHHU, as noted above, was a creation of the allies, brought about by the merger of two plants from the old Vestag. Prior to the creation of the Vestag, the Dortmund plant of the DHHU was part of Hugo Stinnes' giant Rhein-Elbe Union, while the Hörder plant belonged to the Phönix group. The two plants were formally linked together by the Vestag during the 1930s, but both continued to operate independently. All of these companies, especially the former three, differed substantially, in holdings and specializations, from these earlier incarnations.

in areas that the others ignored. The vast majority of the steelmaking capacity of the old Vestag was reincorporated within the operations of either ATH or Phönix-Rheinrohr. Their product offerings and specializations in rolled-product markets were for the most part not overlapping. ATH specialized in the production of lighter, semifinished and finished rolled sheet and coils, and wire and specialty steels, whereas the Phönix-Rheinrohr specialized in the production of steel pipe, heavy plate, semifinished steels, and raw iron (Lammert 1960, pp. 207–8; Huffschmid 1965, pp. 110–15; Müller 1991, pp. 300–3). The coordinated growth and reconsolidation of these two companies were facilitated by the fact that both enterprises were controlled by different members of the Thyssen family.

Rheinstahl, which had very broad ownership, was less interested in getting involved in the reintegration of Vestag steelmaking interests. This company received all of the non-steel manufacturing interests of the old Vestag as a result of deconcentration. It held an interest in only a small number of relatively small and specialized steel works from the old Vestag, and, though it continued to produce steel during the 1950s, it was a very minor player in the industry (Lammert 1960, pp. 206–7; Huffschmid 1965, pp. 185–91; Müller 1991, pp. 304–5). The DHHU, for its part, was an important producer of crude steel. But unlike its larger Vestag cousins, the company was not as broadly diversified across steel industry markets. By the beginning of the 1960s, the company was concentrated on two general areas: It was the Federal Republic's largest producer of heavy plate and an important producer of steel bars and structural steel (Huffschmid 1965, pp. 147–55).

Together, these four firms, with their coordinated capacities, accounted for nearly 35% of west German crude steel output in 1960/1. ATH and Phönix-Rheinrohr together accounted for 20.91%. Another 41% of total industry output was taken up by the steel operations of the former *Konzerne* Hoesch, Klöckner, Mannesmann, HOAG,[35] and Krupp.[36] On the whole, these producers followed the DHHU pattern of specialization, each attempting to organize its steel and rolled-product output in a way that would give the company a strong position in a limited number of markets. Thus, for example, Mannesmann concentrated its production on steel pipe and a variety of high-quality fine and zinc-treated plate steels; Krupp on specialty steels, structural steels, bar, and semis; Hoesch on sheet steels and fine plate; HOAG on heavy plate, structural steels, and specialty wire; and Klöckner on sheet steels, fine plates, wire, and bar (Huffschmid 1965, pp. 122–46, 156–84, 192–7). The producers accounting for the remaining 15% of the industry's output in 1960, who were located both inside and outside of the Ruhr, followed a similar pattern of specialization.

The emergence of oligopolized submarkets and more specialized firms oriented toward mass rather than specialty production ultimately resulted in a distinctly

---

[35] Hüttenwerk Oberhausen AG belonged to GHH until 1945.

[36] Krupp's steel interests were grouped in a separate holding which included the Hütten- und Bergwerke Rheinhausen AG.

different industry structure than had existed prior to World War II. Before the war, only six companies controlled nearly three-quarters of the industry's total output, whereas by 1961 that same share was divided among nine enterprises. More significantly, the successor companies of the old Vestag did not recapture the same dominant share of industry output that had belonged to their ancestor: Vestag had accounted for roughly half the industry's total output during the 1930s, whereas the successor companies were only able to achieve 35% by 1961. Decartelization and deconcentration in the 1940s and early 1950s had succeeded in creating a more internally specialized and more competitive German steel industry— much as the Allies had intended when they busted up the old structure at the end of the war.

Nonetheless, it would be misleading to characterize this newly structured German steel industry as a complete triumph of Americanization. Its new structure and practices differed in significant ways from the American pluralist conception of mass production and oligopoly. First, as indicated above, the actors in the industry, both in management and labor, understood themselves to be corporate groups with social and political status in the broader society and with an understanding of mutual obligation and responsibility. By all accounts, this mutually accepting, and through codetermination, codified, arrangement created significant flexibility within high-volume production. Labor and management were able to cooperate in ways that allowed firms to take on special orders, produce in varied lot sizes, and reallocate labor and materials within plants in ways that the more rigid, bargained out arrangements of equal contracting citizens in American plants did not allow.

Indeed, secondly, this reserve of flexibility within the new industry and its structure led the actors in the industry to favor a modified rather than the strongly American version of Cartel Law in the debates over the reform of German antitrust law that raged during the 1950s (Bethusy-Huc 1962; Robert 1976; Berghahn 1985). This modified version accepted, in principle, the general American injunction against cartels and monopoly of any kind. It insisted, however, on a concession to flexibility. The new law rejected the proposal for a strict ban on cartels in favor of negotiated and constructive solutions to problems of market order among the industry players and the Cartel Office of the Federal government. Moreover, several forms of cartels, in particular rationalization cartels, were permitted under the antitrust law that was accepted by the parliament in 1957. Both of these characteristics of the new rules of market order were sympathetically received (if not enthusiastically lobbied for) by the steel industry because it created space among firms for the flexible orientation to the market that the situation inside the plants was making possible. These provisions in the law proved to be significant for the industry in the late 1960s when overcapacity became a problem and producers avoided ruthless and destructive competition by forming distribution syndicates for the allocation of their finished steel. These syndicates both removed pricing from competition and facilitated the recombination of capacity and specialization within the industry (Röper 1974).

In conclusion, it is clear that though the German steel industry adopted or was forced to adopt American principles of market order and production and was profoundly changed by this encounter, this in no way resulted in an erasure of distinctively German features in the production of steel. Indeed, German producers embraced the vocabulary and practices of Americanism and pluralism, but in doing so creatively recomposed them in ways that either were consistent with their own prior understandings and practices or extended the received principles in ways that were not in evidence in the United States nor foreseen by the Allied reformers. We will now see that, on this level, the case was very similar in Japan.

1.5.2. Engaging Allied Reforms in Occupied Japan

Allied reforms engendered debate and recomposition in different areas in Japan than they did in Germany, in part because the character of the occupation was different, and in part because the two were very different political economies in different geopolitical locations. In Japan, for example, the centrality of private property for stable political order was never debated in the same way as it was in Germany: This is not necessarily because Americans and Japanese held the same political understanding of private property in a democratic market order. More likely it was because there were neither British socialists nor threatening communist neighbors to push the alternative case in Japan.[37] Nonetheless, at a different level, there were many similarities between German and Japanese experiences. In particular, in Japan, as in Germany, defeat and reform created spaces in the debate for the rearticulation of abandoned, defeated, or unrealized conceptions of social and industrial order from the past that the wartime regime had suppressed. Moreover, as in Germany, those advancing such ideas, though liberated, were also engaged by American insistence on the creation of a pluralistic democratic economy. The central areas of contestation relevant to the reform of the Japanese steel industry were (*a*) the reconstitution of mutually limiting relations between the state and industry; (*b*) the recomposition of firms, associations, and industrial structure; and (*c*) the recasting of authority in production. The outcome of these encounters was a completely new way of understanding the identity, boundaries, and organization of the steel industry.

1.5.2.1. Government–Business Relations

American reformers took it as their goal to establish a system of countervailing powers between the Japanese state and economy in order to prevent actors in either realm from gaining unchecked monopoly power. The abolition of the Japanese military, the breakup of the *Zaibatsu* holding companies, and the dissolution of the old Control Associations, for example, were all guided by

---

[37] And SCAP simply refused to allow the minority Communist views in Japan to push the issue onto the agenda.

the conviction that these institutions had been either monopolistic or unaccountable (or both) and in their basic structures were incapable of being reformed in a way that would allow them to be checked. As noted earlier, however, the central institutions of the civil bureaucracy were not targeted by SCAP either for dissolution or even serious reform (Cohen 1987, pp. 378–97). Unlike the other institutions, SCAP believed that it was possible to check the power of the existing state bureaucracy through the construction of countervailing forces and institutions in both the state and in society. The creation of parliamentary institutions that monitored the bureaucracy, the creation of conditions that favored the formation of strong oligopolies in the economy, and the construction of a trade association law that both forbade monopolization and encouraged the formation of interest groups, for example, all were directed at the construction of a set of rules and a population of social organizations that could fragment social, economic, and political power (Haley 1991, pp. 139–68). Rather than destroy the bureaucracy as it did the other "authoritarian" institutions, SCAP attempted to make it one organization among many in a plural system of social and political power. Though it is possible to say that this is what the reforms did indeed achieve, the self-understanding of the Japanese actors in the change and the quality of state relations with industry differed very significantly from what the Americans had in mind.

Some Japan scholars view the above strategy on the part of SCAP with great irony. They point out that by removing the *Zaibatsu* and the military from the field of play, the occupiers actually enhanced the power of the civil bureaucracy in the postwar environment by removing the traditional indigenous checks on its power without introducing effective countervailing institutional forces.[38] This view, however, significantly underestimates the constraints the new reforms placed on bureaucratic power and overestimates the power of the elements within the Japanese bureaucracy that believed in unilateral state control over resource allocation. After the reforms, bureaucratic ministries were newly constrained by the constellation of power in the parliamentary arena and by the competing interests and agendas of other ministries (Haley 1991, ch. 7). Moreover, Bai Gao argues that with the coming of the market-oriented Dodge Plan and the foundation of Ministry of International Trade and Industry (MITI), the elements within the bureaucracy that favored a heavily *dirigiste*-planned economy lost influence in the construction of state intervention to those who favored a more cooperative and "managed" approach to private actors (Gao 1994, 1997).[39] In other words,

---

[38] Chalmers Johnson acidly observes about this: "Ironically, it was during the Occupation that one of the fondest dreams of the wartime 'control bureaucrats' were finally realized. With the militarists gone, the *Zaibatsu* facing dissolution and SCAP's decision to try to set the economy on its feet, the bureaucracy found itself working for the *tenno* [MacArthur] who really possessed the attributes of 'absolutism'." See Johnson (1975, p. 16), also quoted in Haley (1991, p. 141).

[39] The key shift that occurred with the Dodge Plan and the foundation of MITI, according to Gao (1997, p. 150), was that "from then on state intervention in the Japanese economy changed from control over resource allocation to control over credit."

the civil bureaucracy that led Japan through its postwar miracle had an interest in limiting itself as an organizational actor in the economy and encouraging the development of private organizations and markets.

Even though seen in this way the reformed bureaucracy contains features that are compatible with American concerns for the limitation of power, it seems clear that the bureaucrats themselves understood their role and relation to private industry to be consistent with the long-standing developmentalist traditions of the Japanese state. But for the brief period of the ascension of the military in the 1930s and early 1940s, the bureaucracy was never interested in directly controlling the allocation of resources in the economy and preferred instead to assist private firms and to use the market to achieve goals that all agreed were significant for the nation. SCAP believed it had modified the structural location of the bureaucracy in a way that made it compatible with its own New Deal-informed conception of a market-friendly interventionist state. The Japanese believed that they were returning to more traditional mechanisms for the pursuit of national economic greatness. Neither was entirely wrong.

Thus, even in the immediate aftermath of the reforms, when it was in fact the case that the traditional checks on the bureaucracy had been removed, there were clear limits on its capacity and interest in intervening in the economy—some of which were unknown to and unanticipated by the reformers themselves. The subsequent development of the private economy and the associations that engaged it created the kind of societal checks against bureaucratic power for which the Americans hoped. But as is clear from the steel industry example, this new development resulted in a new constellation of relations between the three relevant actors (state, firms, and associations) which produced not only mutual limitation, but also a cooperative orientation toward industrial improvement and technological transformation that ultimately far surpassed the competitive capacity of the American industry, embedded in its own less-cooperative system of countervailing power.

1.5.2.2. Business, Associations, and the State

The dissolution of the Iron and Steel Control Association, the breakup of Japan Steel, and of the *Zaibatsu* destabilized the steel industry in a whole variety of ways. The smaller and more specialized steel producers were simultaneously confronted with direct competition from larger integrated firms and deprived of the dynamic and nurturing downstream exchanges with diverse *Zaibatsu* units that had previously sustained their strategies of specialization. The large volume producer Japan Steel was broken up into two new units that found themselves in the unaccustomed position of having to compete with one another. The top leadership of all the major firms in the industry was purged and the central association linking firms and fostering intra-industry informational exchange was banned. Neither the structure of the industry, nor the identity of the firms that would constitute it, nor the identity or interests of the managers that governed the firms could be taken for granted nor their strategies for reconstitution clearly defined.

The only aspect of the situation that was very clearly defined for all the actors was that the Americans found the old bifurcated structure of volume producers and specialists to be unacceptable and that they wanted to encourage instead the formation of a competitive oligopoly structure with some number of volume-producing integrated firms. If clarity in the midst of disarray grabs the attention, it should not be surprising that the actors in the industry attempted to recompose themselves along the American lines. There was no debate about reconstituting the old structure of bifurcation because the conditions that had made it possible no longer existed.[40] Ex-*Zaibatsu* firms such as Kawasaki, Kobe, and Sumitomo found that they either had to abandon steel production entirely, or commit themselves to strategies of higher-volume production and integration. In the end, the latter option was the one that they took (Scheppach 1972, pp. 27–31; Yonekura 1994).

This compelling structuralism belies a great deal of local innovation on the part of Japanese actors as they attempted to define precisely what the American constraints actually allowed and how much of their own knowledge of steelmaking and organization could be utilized in the pursuit of the new kind of strategy in production. Destabilization and constraint forced actors to draw on their knowledge of steel manufacture and organization in new ways and thereby led them to possibilities in the organization of integrated volume production and in the nature of oligopolistic competition that were not part of the American program. At the same time, their success in doing so dramatically changed the face of the industrial structure of steel production in Japan. Creativity trumped constraint.

The move toward integration and volume production was very explicitly conceived of as an effort to adopt an American strategy and move away from the old strategy of specialization. Kawasaki led the way in the integration of the non-integrated works with the construction of its dramatic Chiba Works in 1953. The firm's new chairman, Nishiyama Yataro, decided to construct this plant because he was convinced that the only way for his firm, and for the entire industry to survive, was to adopt an American approach to production:

The Japanese iron and steel industry must cut costs and develop the ability to compete internationally by switching to the American mode of production and away from the European mode of small-lot production. It is necessary to construct an integrated works with a blast furnace. (Yonekura 1993, p. 221)

---

[40] It may strike some readers that I am overestimating the difference in the conditions facing the steel producers because the reconstitution of Japanese corporations formerly affiliated with *Zaibatsu* into *Keiretsu* was in the end simply the recreation of the old *Zaibatsu* conditions under a new name. I disagree with this view—and moreover, so does much of the historical literature. Rather, from the perspective of interest here, the recasting of groups as *Keiretsu* is, in fact, a further indication of the way in which the steel firms were cut off in the new structure. Though *Keiretsu* involved extensive interunit cross-holdings and cooperation, the centralized control of the *Zaibatsu Honsha* (central holding office) was eliminated. The salience of inward coordination and cooperation by steel units with filial downstream consumers relative to non-filial downstream consumers was weakened, while the pressure to reorganize along mass production lines was considerably strengthened, as we shall see. On the crucial differences between prewar *Zaibatsu* and postwar *Keiretsu*, see, among others, Yamamura (1967, pp. 110–28).

Rather than purchase or build upstream operations to complement Kawasaki's existing facilities, Nishiyama sought to gain a competitive advantage by constructing a giant new integrated facility on a greenfield site located on the sea coast to facilitate easy and massive in-and-out transport through deep harbors. The construction of the Chiba Works was announced in late 1950 and was completed in 1953. According to Yonekura, at the time its construction was announced, it was forecast to have a capacity equal to nearly a fifth of Japan's entire 1950 iron and steel output. The plant had "two 500 tons per charge (tpc) blast furnaces, six 100 tpc open-hearth furnaces, matching slab mills and hot and cold strip mills with annual capacities of 350,00 tons of pig iron and 500,000 tons of crude steel" (Yonekura 1994, p. 213). The Chiba Works also had an extremely efficient and consolidated plant layout: The plant had only 60 km of railroad track linking its various operations. This was 440 km less than the Yahata works at the time (Scheppach 1972, p. 88ff; Yonekura 1994, p. 213ff). In this and other ways, the Chiba Works took American principles of large-scale production and the technologies to achieve it and constructed them in ways that outstripped its domestic competitors' best forms of organization. Moreover, in the efficiency of organization and completeness and newness of its conception, the works exceeded the ambition of most American producers of the time as well. In many ways, Chiba took Americanism and perfected it beyond what American producers themselves had achieved.[41]

The success of the Chiba Works emboldened the other significant nonintegrated producers to follow suit. Soon after the construction of the Chiba Works, both Sumitomo and Kobe decided to integrate their blast furnace operations, first in 1953 and 1954, by buying smaller integrated works and then, like Kawasaki, by building their own greenfield plants near deep harbors. Others followed these firms like dominos. By 1961, there were ten fully integrated steel producers in Japan: Yahata, Fuji, NKK, Kawasaki, Sumitomo, Kobe, Amagasaki, Nakayama, Osaka, and Nisshin (Scheppach 1972, p. 88ff). The top six firms (Yahata, Fuji, NKK, Kawasaki, Sumitomo, and Kobe) accounted for about 90% of pig iron production and 80% of crude steel, but the market structure of producers was much more oligopolistic (i.e., evenly distributed among all producers)(see Table 1.4).

As in the German case, the effect of the Allied interventions in Japan was to create a set of competitive conditions in industry that gave rise to a very different, less monopolistic, more pluralistic industrial structure of high-volume producers. Indeed, if you compare the industry structures of the Japanese, German, and US steel industries by the beginning of the 1960s, they all look very similar (see Table 1.5). The difference, of course, was that the Japanese (and the Germans) by this time were using forms of organization (and as we shall see shortly, technologies

---

[41] Indeed, it was only in the 1960s that the balance of US production began to shift toward facilities located near deep harbor ports and even then significant portions of capacity were still located inland in the Pittsburgh-Youngstown area. See the discussion in Burn (1961, pp. 518–36, esp. 528–31).

Table 1.4. Concentration in Pig Iron and Rolled Steel, 1950–67 (Percent of Total Production)

	Number of Firms	1950	1955	1960	1965	1966	1967
Pig iron	3	89	81	69	58	57	60
	6	91	94	87	89	88	93
	8	92	97	94	95	96	98
	10	93	98	95	98	98	99
Hot-rolled steel	3	50	51	51	45	46	49
	6	68	69	69	70	70	76
	8	74	75	75	75	77	81
	10	77	77	79	78	80	83

Source: Scheppach (1972, p. 94, No. 48).

Table 1.5. Comparison of Market Shares of the Largest Firms in the United States, United Kingdom, West Germany, and Japan, 1965 (Percentage of Total Industry Output)

USA (%)	UK (%)	FRG (%)	JAPAN (%)
US Steel 25	US 12.5	ATH 23.3	Yahata 18.6
Bethlehem 16	RTB 12.2	Hoesch 15.6	Fuji 17.4
Republic 7.5	Wales 10.1	Krupp 10.5	Kokan 10.4
National 6.5	Colvilles 9.8	Klöckner 8.3	Kawatetsu 10.4
Armco 5.9	S&L 7.4	Mannesmann 7.1	Sumikin 10.1
J&L 5.6	GKN 7.3	Oberhausen 6.1	Kobe 6
Inland 4.9	Dorman 7.2	Salzgitter 5.1	Nisshin 2.2
Youngstown 4.6	John 6.2	Röchling 3.4	Nakayama 2
Kaiser 2.1	S. Durham 5.5	Dilinger 3.3	Otani 1.5
Wheeling 1.6	Consett 3.7	Ilseder 2.9	Daido 1.4

Source: Adapted from Scheppach (1972, p. 94, Nr 48).

as well) in production that were superior to those in place in the American industry. The imitators had taken American principles and made them better by making them their own. What made oligopolistic competition in Japan so much more dynamic than the same form of competitive industry structure in the United States?

The answer is that in embracing competitive oligopoly, the Japanese reinterpreted and recomposed the American understanding of oligopolistic competition in a way that produced both extremely rapid growth and striking leaps in technology and innovation. The key was the union of competition and cooperation among actors in the industry. Actors in the industry did not abandon the cooperative exchanges among firms and between firms and the bureaucracy that had been a hallmark of development in the old prewar structures. Instead, they recast the method of cooperation within the industry away from the old model of cooperation between a state monopoly and broadly diversified holding companies to cooperation among relatively equal rival steel firms. This was a strategy, as we saw earlier, foreshadowed by the industry reform efforts of steel managers who had been active in the Control Associations during the war.

The advocates of cooperative oligopoly within the industry were eagerly encouraged and guided by bureaucrats within MITI and by players within the newly reconstituted trade associations (many of whom had previously been members of the Control Association as well). Both saw it as their mission to foster the reconstruction and modernization of private industry in the interest of the recovery of the nation. These bureaucrats and trade association figures, we saw, abandoned their market-supplanting or *dirigiste* orientation toward industrial coordination and turned toward an older market-preserving approach of discussion, collective priority setting, and problem solving with private operating units in the industry. Under the new conditions of pluralistic oligopoly and competing institutional actors, this new system was congenial (if not identical) to the original political–economic norms established by the Americans for democratic industrial practice.[42]

This dynamic three-way interaction between MITI bureaucrats, trade associations, and newly competitive firms led to the development of two sequential "Rationalization Plans" for the steel industry which drove its rapid technological development in the 1950s (and then, with subsequent plans, beyond) (Japanese Iron and Steel Industry Federation 1952; Vestal 1993). In the development and execution of these plans, MITI engaged steel producers in constant discussions and exchanges about their capacity requirements and technological needs. The trade associations played a crucial role in bringing managers from the various firms together to discuss mutual technological, production, and market concerns with one another and with representatives from the bureaucracy (in particular MITI). All of the discussions involved the identification of competitive organization and technology from abroad and developing strategies for the adaptation and appropriation of those practices in Japan (Lynn and McKeown 1988; O'Brien 1992; Vestal 1993; O'Brien 1994; Yamamura 1995; Yonekura 1996). MITI used its resources to affirm and coordinate decisions on capacity expansion that the three-way discussion produced and it also subsidized cooperative research efforts,

---

[42] And in part, as Lynn and McKeown (1988, pp. 55–119) emphasize throughout their account, this was facilitated by the fact that the bureaucrats and association leaders had personal experience within steel companies or had dealt with the *Zaibatsu* holdings directly. Chalmers Johnson (1981, ch. 7 and passim) also emphasizes the centrality of personal contacts between bureaucrats, upper-level steel managers, trade association officials and their revolving affiliations, as central for facilitating tripartite coordination in steel—and also, paradoxically, for maintaining the autonomy of each: "All of the big six [steel producers] had high-ranking former MITI officials on their boards of directors. . . . But even so it was hard to give direct orders to the industry because so many of its executives were top leaders in business organizations such as Keidanren and Keisai Doyukai" (p. 268). This emphasis on Johnson's part is ironic because after pointing out the autonomy of the actors, he suggests that "From the era of priority production just after the war down to approximately 1960, MITI had exercised detailed control over investments in the steel industry. . . ." (p. 269). On his own evidence, it seems more accurate to conclude that MITI engaged in extensive dialogue over the direction of investment with the other two interlocutors.

coordinated by the trade associations and involving all the major firms, on the development of key technologies that had been identified as crucial for the industry's competitive evolution: Most crucial in this regard were, of course, basic oxygen furnace (BOF) technology, the development of high-quality domestic refractory brick for use in blast furnaces, and, later, continuous casting technology.[43]

These new technologies, of course, were systematically incorporated into the physical plant in virtually all of the new greenfield facilities built alongside deep harbor ports following the opening of the Chiba works noted above. In fact, the decision to integrate production and to adopt the BOF were linked. Japan's steel producers were plagued by extremely high materials costs—especially due to the high cost of imported scrap—and sought integration and BOF because they minimized these costs. Integration backward into pig iron production radically reduced producers' need for scrap inputs. BOF was an attractive technology because it could make high-quality steel with little or no scrap (Gordon 1998, p. 63).[44] Crucially, MITI and the Japan Iron and Steel Federation worked hard in the mid-1950s to ensure that the technologies necessary for this lower-cost production strategy would diffuse among all the producers in the industry (Gordon 1998, pp. 62–3).

This cooperative investment strategy was enormously successful. Already, at the beginning of the 1960s, Japanese steel producers had more BOF capacity than any other steel-producing nation in the world. By the beginning of the 1970s, the same was true of continuous casting. The enormity of these achievements should not go unappreciated. In effect, cooperation among the state, associations, and leading firms, recomposed and reconstituted through engagement with American reforms, produced a radical revolution in the mass production of steel. The American model had been appropriated and transformed in a way that ultimately led the industry to surpass US producers in technological sophistication, plant layout, organization, capacity, and quality of output (Gordon 1998, pp. 60–1).

So, there you have it: The Japanese industry was dramatically recomposed by the SCAP reforms and the direction of that recomposition was, on the level of industrial structure (oligopolistic competition) and in the strategy of production (high-volume mass production), very consistent with what the Americans wanted and attempted to encourage. Nonetheless, the outcome diverged markedly from what Americans understood to be pluralist oligopoly or integrated steel production. Rather than applying the American understanding of pluralist

---

[43] The first rationalization plan, which ran from 1950 to 1954, focused on the replacement of capacity and modernization of technologies, while the second rationalization plan (1955–60) targeted capacity expansion and the dramatic adoption of new technology—eleven new blast furnaces for the production of pig iron were constructed in the period and a phenomenal thirteen BOF for steel production were introduced. See Vestal (1993, pp. 122ff) and Lynn and McKeown (1988, pp. 90–119, 140–71).

[44] The problem of high scrap costs had actually shaped the way that numerous producers adopted technology in the prewar period as well: see, for example, the interesting article by Kobayakawa (1996, pp. 53–71).

competition and the limitation of power through the construction of comparable adversaries, the Japanese organized oligopoly, with the eager involvement
of the state and of newly reconstituted trade associations, as a process of
collaborative discussion and cooperative learning. Rather than attempting to
replicate the organization of American integrated steel production, the Japanese
took American principles and applied them in a way that was more efficient
and elegant. Developments in the workplace, as Section 1.5.2.3 will show, which
were also profoundly influenced by American intervention and example, only
enhanced the dynamism of Japanese steel firms.

1.5.2.3. Recasting Authority in Production: Pluralism and Status

As in the German case, Japanese workers seized the opportunity presented to
them by Allied support of trade unionism and worker organization. Only in
Japan, where the extent of trade union organization prior to occupation had
always been relatively muted and suppressed, the encouragement of organization
had the effect of opening a flood gate of pent-up interest in worker organization.
In October 1945, there were only 5,000 people in trade unions in Japan. By
December of 1946, that number had increased astronomically to nearly 5 million
(Gordon 1993, p. 378). Workers took the American political values of democracy
and the need for countervailing organizational power in society very seriously.
Like their German counterparts, however, they interpreted these political values
through the lens of their own traditions and their understanding of the social and
political position of workers in Japanese society. The result was a profoundly
different set of industrial relations institutions than Americans typically associated with voluntary labor organization.

As in Germany, the structures of authority at the level of the enterprise
emerged immediately as a constitutive arena in the Japanese worker's conception
of democratic order. For the Japanese worker, the creation of a countervailing
organization in the labor market was not sufficient, by itself, to check the power
of management in society at large, or within the enterprise. This was because the
enterprises themselves were structured in ways that presupposed a hierarchy of
status in society in which managers enjoyed ascribed social privilege and workers
suffered a caste-like social denigration. The creation of organizational power for
labor without explicitly attacking these traditional differences in status would not
have created equality or plural power. It merely would have created a social
organization for a subordinate estate in society.[45]

Thus, in the initial years of the occupation when the expansion of worker
organization was most dramatic, organized workers in numerous industries,
including steel, repeatedly called the role of managerial authority into question

---

[45] On the significance of social status in working class action in prewar Japan, see Smith (1988,
pp. 236–71); for a discussion of how these sentiments played out at the NKK steel mill in the early
postwar years, see Gordon (1998, ch. 2).

and attacked status distinctions in plants between blue-collar and white-collar workers—all in the name of democracy.[46] In response to worker demands labor-management councils were formed which gave workers joint control with management over the workplace, personnel management, and corporate strategy (Gordon 1985, pp. 339–49, 1998, pp. 59–67, chs. 1–3, wap 36ff; Hideo 1987; Kume 1998). And, according to Andrew Gordon, this made possible a whole cascade of profound firm-level reforms:

through council deliberations or collective bargaining, workers eliminated many petty and substantive status divisions between white-collar staff and blue-collar staff that they found pervasive and repugnant throughout the prewar era. Under union pressure managers did away with separate gates, dining halls, and toilets as well as distinctions in dress and terminology (some companies replaced the terms *worker* and *staff* with the single term *employee*). Workers also gained a new equality in wages and bonuses. Some enterprises replaced a distinction between workers, who were paid by the day, and staff, who were paid by the month, with a common calculation in terms of monthly wages and paid bonuses to all employees as multiples of this monthly amount. (Gordon 1993, p. 379)[47]

These targets of democratic struggle were not anticipated by the Americans when they advocated labor organization as a key component of democratization. Yet, American encouragement made the struggles possible. Moreover, American advocacy of democratic order also provided them with a vocabulary (democratization) in which to acceptably express traditional desires about status change against the claims of other positions (in particular, management) in the social order. Moreover, (initial) SCAP toleration of the gains won, allowed them to become institutionalized in Japanese factories (Cohen 1987, p. 206). It is also true that many of these early gains were possible because management itself was extremely weakened, both economically and ideologically, by the defeat, occupation, purges, etc. and could not but cede to labor's transformative demands.

All of this naturally was very short-lived in the occupation. SCAP's enthusiasm for labor power shifted abruptly when labor began to cross the line into politics in January 1947 and threatened to topple the government with a General Strike. As in the German case, the American conception of democratic order did not include "politicized" labor organizations, only countervailing organizations in the labor market. American resistance to labor's moves into politics emboldened the Japanese employers to counterattack and roll back many of the reforms that the workers had won in the initial years (Gordon 1998; Kume 1998; Moore 1983). But the rollback, though significant, was not by any means a return to the social order in the factory or in society that ante-dated the initial years of labor mobilization. The early postwar achievements created a new balance of power and new poles in debate in the struggle between labor and capital. In future struggles,

[46] Otake Hideo writes: "The term 'democratization' thus acquired in some quarters an extremely radical content, quite contrary to the intentions of the Occupation. Especially with respect to the economic order, it was variously used to legitimize 'enterprise democratization', management participation by labor, and even management exclusively by labor . . . " (Hideo 1987, pp. 366–91, quotation 366).

[47] Gordon (1998, chs. 1–3) for discussion of these events at NKK.

employers argued away from the gains workers had made, but they could not and did not argue for the complete abandonment of the workplace and status change that the early gains had implemented. To that extent, mobilization under American encouragement and in the name of democracy brought lasting change to working life in Japan.

There was, however, significant rollback. Struggle over authority and power in the workplace continued for another fifteen years or so in Japan before a stable equilibrium was reached. Much of this struggle ultimately produced outcomes favorable to employers and against the most aggressive factions within the unions. Of the early enterprise-level gains, unions were forced to compromise most significantly on the degree of their formal influence on labor-management councils. Their role was shifted from direct participation in decision making with management to the lesser one of a body to be consulted by management in its decisions and planning. This was a setback, to be sure, but not a defeat. According to Kume, "management regained the power to control the management system in the company, but labor maintained its right to be consulted in the case of personnel as well as managerial decision making . . . Labor continued to be a legitimate participant within the company rather than devolve into a mere production factor" (Kume 1998, p. 61).

Gains in the form of wage payment and production control were also rolled back over the course of the 1950s and 1960s. In these cases, the rollback was driven by management's desire to implement what they considered to be more advanced American practices. The result, however, was not more Americanism or even familiar forms of managerial control. Rather, given the organizational strength of labor on the shop floor, managers were forced to recompose the American techniques in the interest of achieving their desired goals in production. The result in both cases was the creation of the very distinctive Japanese hybrid systems of combined seniority and merit-based wages and decentralized, shop floor-based, cross-functional quality control.

The homogeneous seniority-based payment system actually began to diffuse in Japanese industry during the final years of the war before it spread widely during the period of worker radicalism in the initial postwar years (Gordon 1985, pp. 257–98, 374–86). Employers disliked the pure seniority system, calling it "evil egalitarianism" (Gordon 1998, p. 66), because it offered them no way to link pay to performance on the job. They began to attack it as soon as the balance of power shifted in their favor during the course of the 1950s. In the steel industry, an effort was made to introduce American "job wages" in which different jobs would be compensated at different rates. The idea was not to supplant seniority completely as a method of payment (the newly mobilized workers had far too much invested in the old system for that), but to factor in the differential contribution of different jobs to the overall value output of the company.

Though it made some initial headway, the solution soon proved inadequate. First, the technological changes in the steel industry over the course of the 1950s created a more automated industry. This undermined the rough correspondence that had existed between seniority and the level of skill in the early postwar years.

Increasingly, young and old were engaged in comparable production tasks. This fact made younger workers resentful of the seniority principle. Second, management itself became dissatisfied with the job-wage system. When combined with the seniority principle it allowed workers within a given category to have their wages increased over time regardless of performance. These problems led in the beginning of the 1960s to a shift away from seniority and job wages to pay based on a combination of seniority and merit. This satisfied both older workers and younger workers, as well as managers interested in maintaining a tight relationship between pay and performance. In this case, an American idea introduced by management (linking payment to the contribution of the specific job) was modified beyond recognition (pay for individual performance) in an effort to adapt it to Japanese circumstances (Gordon 1998, pp. 66–70, 164–7).

This was similarly the case with the emergence of quality control circles. Here the American idea was the creation of centralized bureau for production engineers responsible, in good Taylorist fashion, for instructing shop-floor workers how best to maintain quality in production. Centralized quality control engineering bureaus were thus established in numerous steel production facilities during the early 1950s. But it soon became apparent that the production engineers from the quality control bureaus were greeted with significant distrust on the shop floor from both production workers and foreman. Both regarded their own knowledge of production as far superior to that of the distant and elite engineering interlopers. Given this resistance, steel management began to reverse the centralizing impulse in the quality control initiative. Instead of separating engineering from the shop floor, they began to create committees—or "circles"— that systematically brought them together. As Gordon notes, these reversals of the Taylorist American logic of separating engineering and planning from production and execution marked "the first stirrings of quality control as a system of widespread small group activities, foreshadowing a shift in the meaning of the abbreviation QC from 'quality control' to 'quality circles'. This was the start of a crucial breakthrough to "total quality control" (TQC) involving technicians, foreman and the rank and file" (Gordon 1998, p. 71).

Once again, in the context of a new balance of power between management and labor, American techniques were modified and transformed in improbable ways. The recomposed institutional forms that emerged in this case as well as in that of the wage payment system, however, were hailed as cornerstones of Japanese competitive advantage in international manufacturing markets during much of the postwar period.[48]

Though very significant for the long-term competitiveness of Japanese production, these workplace-level conflicts were at the time dwarfed in intensity by industry-level conflicts over the role and position of organized labor in the Japanese political economy. Literally epochal struggles during the 1950s focused

---

[48] The two most notable authors bringing this dimension of Japanese success to the forefront are, of course, Abegglen (1958, 1973) and Dore (1973).

on the issue of the scope of collective bargaining and the extent to which labor would be able to act as a countervailing power in postwar Japanese society. Should collective bargaining concentrate on the level of the enterprise or should it be extended to the level of the entire industry: that is, enterprise versus industrial unionism? This was a matter of particularly intense conflict in the steel industry throughout the 1950s. The leadership factions within the unions at all the major producers solidaristically fought for industry-wide bargaining and the employers at these firms just as solidaristically opposed this.

The conflict resulted in three major strikes in 1956, 1957, and 1959. Had the unions been able to win one of these strikes and force the employers into accepting industrial unionism, it would have positioned them as sovereign rivals of capital in debates on the distribution of the social surplus. It would have also placed them in a position to re-enhance their power within the enterprises.[49] But this was not to be: In the heat of each of the strikes, the employers were able to get one or more enterprise unions to break from the national coalition (frequently the more conservative Yahata union) and thereby insist on local rather than industrial wage deals. After the defeat in 1959, factionalism within the unions, already a source of instability during the 1950s, intensified. Eventually, those elements within the unions that did not want to further jeopardize their enterprise-level gains by continued conflict at the industry level gained control. They abandoned the idea of industrial union- ism and refocused union energy on the enterprise level (Gordon 1996, 1998; Suzuki 1997, ch. 2; Kume 1998).

A victory in the struggle for industrial unions might have launched the trade union movement in Japan onto a European trajectory, where strong centralized unions bargained with peak-level employers' associations over the distribution of much of society's surplus. So these losses at the end of the 1950s were significant for Japanese labor. But they did not by any means erase the significant gains in organizational, economic, and social power *relative to their prewar position* that the unions had gained in the early postwar years. With American encouragement and support, Japanese workers were able to redefine their status within enter- prises, and in the society at large. Symbolic markers of difference were abolished, and reforms that insisted upon equal treatment (and equitable and just reward) among employees within the enterprise, and respectful and informed relations between all employees and management were asserted. Here again, a very dis- tinctively Japanese reality was created with the vocabulary and at crucial mo- ments encouragement of American occupiers.

---

[49] And hence block entirely the Americanization efforts noted above in favor of internationally unprecedented labor control in production. The Japan of today could have been dramatically different than what it became and this possibility existed until at least as late as 1959. Gordon and others, in emphasizing the significance of the pivotal decade of the 1950s, have rightly criticized those who try to portray the Japanese system as somehow entrenched in transhistorical institutional and cultural features of the Japanese people. See Gordon (1998, *passim*).

1.6. CONCLUSION

This chapter has attempted to show the way in which political ideas about the proper relationship between democracy and market order were constitutive in the reconstruction of core institutions and practices in both the German and Japanese political economies after World War II. The power of the American occupation was its ability to establish the discursive and conceptual terrain upon which debate and struggle for the reconstruction of industrial institutions and governance mechanisms would take place. My claim here is neither that the US occupiers had a unitary conception of the kind of economy they wanted to see emerge in Germany and Japan, nor that they had specific institutional arrangements or governance practices that they viewed as indispensable for the construction of a pluralist economy. Indeed, both cases of steel-industry reconstruction have shown in a very rich way how the occupation tolerated and even encouraged institutional forms that corresponded neither to their original conceptions nor to the institutional arrangements that then existed in the United States itself. Rather, the occupation first destroyed those institutional arrangements in the economy that it deemed morally and politically incompatible with a pluralist democratic economy and then established normative guidelines and pressures intended to encourage the creation of countervailing institutional powers within the economy that German and Japanese actors were compelled to take into account. This was a profound form of domination—a sort of supra end-in-view—and the chapter makes plain that it led to dramatic recomposition of both societies.

The irony in the story, of course, is that the recomposition of the German and Japanese steel industries created forms of practice and relational governance in production and at the level of the industry as a whole that were far more competitive than their American rivals for much of the postwar period. Destabilization and political constraint imposed by the occupation gave rise to a remarkable process of collective and creative reflection among actors in both societies about the plasticity and recomposability of their own practices and institutions. As we saw in both cases, experimentation with technologies and organizational practices from elsewhere (especially America) as well as struggles for control were part and parcel of this process of collective reflexivity and redefinition. The new structures that emerged and became so competitive in many cases combined traditional indigenous practices with American ideas in ways that resembled neither but which often established entirely new international standards of performance.

2

Contrasting Forms of Coordination in the Steel Industry: Germany, Japan, and the United States (1950–74)

2.1. CONTRASTING FORMS OF COORDINATION IN THE GOLDEN AGE

This chapter acts as a pivot between the previous chapter and the one that follows. It engages in a kind of stocktaking, while at the same time making a critical theoretical point about institutions and competitiveness. On the stock-taking side, the chapter answers the following questions: What became of the three national industries once the turbulence and creative recomposition of the occupation period was finished? How did the three industries compare to one another during the halcyon days of postwar steel production prior to the profound crisis that beset all global steel producers beginning in 1974? What kinds of distinct institutional resources did producers possess as they entered what has become a permanent process of adjustment and consolidation in the industry after 1974?

On the theoretical side, the chapter points out that despite significant institutional differences in the way in which firms were organized and embedded in their societies, producers in the steel industry in each society pursued remarkably similar production strategies. Comparative institutional advantage (Hall and Soskice 2001) plays very little role here. Apparently, different institutional arrangements can be adapted in different ways to do remarkably similar things. Further, the story here suggests that the Varieties of Capitalism (VoC) character-izations of the United States as a liberal market economy and Germany and Japan as coordinated market economies are also overdrawn, at least for this period. We will see that the United States was a very coordinated economy, though it deployed quite distinctive coordination mechanisms. Similarly, the cases of Germany and Japan suggest that coordination and the limitation of the market in itself is not a barrier to radical innovation in industry.

In any case, as a historical matter, the 1950s and 1960s in steelmaking is an interesting period to recall. The steel industry used to be a big deal in an industrial society. The material it produced was a central input to a whole series of rapidly growing downstream sectors in the history of industrialization: railroads, shipbuilding, weapons production, automobiles, aircraft, electrification, home automation, food processing, civil engineering—to name only the major consumers (e.g., Parrish 1956). By the mid-twentieth century, the industry had become a symbol for both the good and the bad in the power of private industry in capitalist societies. Steel industrialists became known as "Barons" or "Titans." Belching smokestacks symbolized productivity and power before they ever became signifiers of dreck and industrial excess. Organized workers became "big labor."[1]

In 1965, in the United States, the steel industry employed over half a million (overwhelmingly unionized) workers. In the same year the German industry employed nearly 350,000 workers, while in 1968 in Japan there were over 356,000 workers employed in the industry. Moreover, the trend there was increasing (workers employed in the Japanese steel industry would exceed 400,000 by the mid-1970s). Though there were other industrial sectors by this time that employed more, the imposing thing about the steel figures is that most of the steelworkers in each of these countries worked in a handful of massive production facilities. The centrality of the product and the concentration of power in large plants made wage negotiations in the industry the focus of attention with both central bankers and heads of state (not to mention stock markets). Steel managers and workers in each of the countries, with some justification, considered their industry to be the bedrock of the success, prosperity, and greatness of their national societies. There was nothing modest or marginal about the steel industry in its postwar heyday. The Japanese referred to steel as the rice of industry (Kawahito 1972; Scheppach 1972; Warren 1973; Barnett and Schorsch 1983; Gold et al. 1984; Eckart 1988; Tiffany 1988).

Section 2.2 presents the similarities in organization among the three industries between the end of World War II and 1974. Section 2.3 then turns to an elaboration of the differences. The conclusion reflects on the theoretical implications of the comparative evidence presented here for the business system side of the VoC literature.

2.2. STEEL SIMILARITIES

Between 1950 and 1974, producers in the United States, Japan, and Germany all made steel in an integrated fashion, all participated in industry-wide procedures for coordinating the setting of base prices in the steel market, all had fairly diversified product palettes, and all confronted organized workers with whose

---

[1] For the monikers, images, and rhetoric, see for example Brooks (1940), Hessen (1975), Clark et al. (1987) and Misa (1995); for Germany, see Feldman (1977) and Kleinschmidt (1993); on Japan, see Yonekura (1994).

formal organizations it was necessary to negotiate to get anything at all done in the factory. This section looks at each of these areas of similarity in turn.

2.2.1. Integration

There are five discrete parts to the steelmaking process: (*a*) the mining of ores, (*b*) the production of pig iron (actually three giant facilities: the sinter plant, coke ovens, and blast furnace), (*c*) the transformation of pig iron into steel (in open-hearth (OH), basic oxygen, and then later electric arc furnaces), (*d*) the rolling of crude steel into discrete forms (bar, wire, sheet, shapes, and plate), and (*e*) the distribution and sale of finished products to the customer. "Integrated Steel" as a category generally refers to the interlinkage of some or all of these five areas (Hall 1997, pp. 1–35).

By the beginning of the postwar period, the mining of ores was a separate business from steel in most places. Few companies in any of the countries here integrated backward to capture their supplies. The Japanese did not have very much on their island to begin with and the Germans had very low-quality ores. But even in the United States, where high-quality ore was plentiful, producers purchased ore on the open market, and/or from mining companies jointly owned with their competitors (Fusfeld 1958). It was more economical to have ores shipped in by boat and train to steel mills located in the neighborhood of major purchasing industries than it was to locate their mills by raw materials sources and ship finished product out to distant users.

The production of pig iron, steel, and finished shapes (*b*, *c*, and *d* above) is the heart of the integrated steelmaking process. All of the major producers in Japan, Germany, and the United States operated plants that linked these processes together (indeed, many still do). The core economics of steelmaking is in the size and efficiency of the various heating devices that are deployed and in the number of times that material has to be cooled and reheated on its way to final form. The larger and hotter the former and the fewer number of the latter, the more efficient the production process.

There was also considerable similarity on the distribution and sales end of the steel industry. Up to the 1960s, the major steel manufacturers in each country controlled the distribution and sale of their product through their own distribution divisions, subsidiaries, or otherwise affiliated companies. In Japan, steel companies tended to be part of larger, more diversified conglomerate arrangements, *Keiretsu*, which had large trading operations that sold all of the varied products of the filial operations. Thus, a large portion (80% in Japan) of their sales was mediated by large, indirectly affiliated wholesalers (Kawahito 1972, pp. 97–101). The United States and German producers were more specialized, but nonetheless operated steel distribution companies that controlled the steel market, at least for the most part. Unlike Japan, however, in the United States and Germany there were also independent, small-scale distributors of steel who customers could turn to when the major suppliers were backed up or crippled by strike. In the United States, these small, mostly regionally based suppliers emerged after World War II in response to the broad availability of salable scrap afforded by the shift to a peacetime economy. These independent producers then were able to survive, and ultimately grow and prosper, by supplying steel that was not manufactured by the major US integrated producers (Hirsch 1962; Schmidt 1968; Beckers 1969; Reutersberg 1985; Hall 1997, pp. 28–35).

2.2.2. The Control of Prices

The ebb and flow of supply and demand guided by the transparent signals of a free unfettered price system has never been the modus vivendi in anybody's steel industry. Giant integrated producers with hugely expensive technologies and wage bills have always sought security of return by placing a floor on the price of steel that would insure that the product would sell above cost (Dennison 1939). Different steel industries achieved this in different ways.

In Japan, after an initial ten-year period of price instability, coordination in price setting and maintenance was established by convening a monthly meeting of major steel producers, their distributors, representatives of major consumers, and the Ministry of International Trade and Industry (MITI). Through open, face-to-face, negotiation among relevant players, prices were established in all major product markets. There was no contract and technically prices were the decision of each company individually. This system was not formally a cartel. Indeed, it worked best when the market was growing and stable. In the event of a recession or dramatic or unforeseen change in the level of demand, the coordination tended to break down. In such cases, the MITI inevitably stepped in to provide "administrative guidance" on industry pricing policy (Kawahito 1972, pp. 101–14). On the whole, however, this system of price setting proved to be very enduring. The steel companies established long-term relations with individual large buyers who exchanged higher prices for reliability of supply and quality. Because the steel producers could rely on long-term sales at a slightly higher than world market price for a significant percentage of their steel output, they sold the rest of their output in world markets at impressive discounts (Tilton 1996, pp. 169–89).

In the United States, the system, though more informal, was also highly coordinated and organized. The price-setting process was more hierarchical within the industry and unilateral with respect to customers than in Japan. Essentially, for most of the first three decades of the postwar period, the US Steel company and the United Steelworkers Union (USWA) effectively set American steel prices. US Steel controlled approximately 30% of total American steel production, while labor costs for all producers in the industry accounted for approximately 40% of steelmaking costs during that period. Starting in 1956, every three years representatives of the entire steel industry and USWA entered into collective bargaining and (ultimately) agreed on a wage bill. Once an agreement was reached, US Steel established a price level for its palette of products. The other producers in the industry followed suit on both the wage agreement and the price change. Essentially, prices increased systematically thereafter with cost of living adjustment (COLA) increases in labor costs.[2] As in Japan, when recessions and unforeseen shifts in demand threatened to destabilize the system, the government intervened to stabilize prices in the industry. The most dramatic intervention was Harry Truman's takeover of the steel industry in the early 1950s during the Korean War (Marcus 1994). But presidents regularly intervened in collective bargaining in the industry to encourage agreements or avert strikes (McConnell 1963). They also then insisted that pricing policies by all industry firms follow agreed upon guidelines (Gold et al. 1984, pp. 617–20).[3]

The control of German steel prices was more formal than either the Japanese or the American systems due to German producers' membership in the European Coal and Steel Community (ECSC). The ECSC was and is a government-sanctioned cartel that establishes price lists, conditions of sale, and capacity limits in the steel industry throughout Europe. Typically, the list prices were set too high, given the amount of capacity available in the industry, so individual firms competed by offering customers rebates that effectively reduced the commission set price. This system protected the consumers of steel while encouraging firms to make money by lowering their costs to improve efficiency and quality. Obviously, such a system could also lead to a collapse of cost-covering revenues in a recession as customers allowed competing steel suppliers to beat each other's rebates down. This happened at the end of the 1960s in Germany and industry responded by forming so-called "Rolled Steel Offices" (*Walzstahlkontoren*). These collective regional selling consortia allocated and limited capacity among members while establishing minimum prices. These organizations, which existed into the mid-1970s, also helped to foster a rationalization of capacity in virtually all rolled product markets in the German market area (Wulff 1958; Lammert 1960; Köhler 1969; Köhler 1971; Eckart 1988; Lee 1990).

2.2.3. Diversified Product Palettes

Integrated producers wanted to produce as much steel as they could in their steelmaking furnaces, be they open hearth (OH) or basic oxygen furnaces (BOF). "More tonnage" was the mantra for steel producers of this generation, in part

---

[2] When one says "thereafter," it could mean the very next day. In 1956, for example, after a brief strike, the industry accepted a settlement that increased hourly employment costs by 30% for three years, including a COLA; on the day after the contract was signed, US Steel announced a general price increase of $8.50 a ton (Hall 1997, p. 46).

[3] John Kennedy had a famous run in with US Steel in 1962 in which US Steel raised prices by 6% after Kennedy had coaxed the company and the USWA into a wage agreement that presupposed no price increases and a smaller COLA increase. Enraged, Kennedy established congressional hearings on illegal steel pricing practices and allowed himself to be quoted to the effect "My father always told me that businessmen were sons of bitches, but I never believed him until now" (Hall 1997, p. 47). US Steel reversed itself and the other steel producers all fell into line.

because there was tremendous world demand, but also because throughput was key to efficiency on the huge furnaces. In order to achieve this, firms tried to produce as many different kinds of steel product at a single facility as possible. Steel would be cast into semifinished ingots or billets and then ferried around a plant or between plants to different reheating rolling mills to be shaped into strip or wire or rebar or plate or sheet. If there was a lot of demand for wide strip steel for the automobile industry (which there often was) more capacity could be directed that way and less to wire or plate production. The strategic logic was to always be able to form and sell something with the steel that the furnaces churned out. In this, US producers were no different than their Japanese or German counterparts. On balance, the Germans tended to be slightly more specialized than the producers in the other countries. The introduction of continuous casting by the Japanese did not change this basic logic. Continuous casters had the flexibility to change the size of the semifinished steel they produced to make it suitable for different rolling requirements in the same way that traditional ingot/billet casting could. It just made quicker changeover possible (Burn 1961; Eckart 1988; Yonekura 1994).

2.2.4. Contending and Cooperating with Labor

Finally, all three industries confronted highly organized labor interests that they could not only not ignore, but with whom they jointly established firm and even industry-wide policies and strategies. The most spectacular example of this, of course, was the West German one, where firms were legally forced to establish joint labor–management oversight institutions (works councils) all the way from the shop floor to the executive meeting rooms. This inserted labor input and power into all manner of work reorganization, wage payment, and investment decisions. Due to the vicissitudes of labor power in the early postwar period, the system of codetermination in the steel industry is much more extensive than in the rest of German industry. In steel, there is full-parity representation on the board of supervisors of the companies, whereas elsewhere ownership has the legal majority. Relations within the firms and in the industry as a whole are as a result of this joint participation extremely cooperative. Labor feels a commitment to the competitiveness of the firm and management feels a commitment to the preservation of jobs (if not their creation) (Müller 1987; Thelen 1991; Streeck 1992).

The USWA held no legal claim to the oversight of property rights like their German counterparts. Nonetheless, they wielded considerable influence in the industry during its postwar heyday. As we saw above, they were integral to pricing politics in the industry. This role in wage compensation was undergirded by an equally powerful position in the way in which working conditions, training, seniority, and job definitions were defined within firms themselves. Through collectively bargained steel industry contracts, organized management and steel labor jointly created a very specific, horizontally and vertically delineated structure of labor markets within firms. Boundaries between skill classifications were boldly spelled out and aggressively defended. Levels of qualification and seniority within a particular skill category were also clearly specified. Contracts always had so-called "right to manage" clauses within them giving management the ultimate authority over decisions about production. The basic contours of who and what was managed were collectively determined by associations in the industry (Herling 1972; Gold et al. 1984; Rose 1998).

The Japanese situation had a bit of both of the above, without actually resembling either. By the end of the 1950s, Japanese trade unions had lost their battle for industry-wide collective bargaining (see Chapter 1). Wage bargaining occurred primarily within individual firms between the management and company-specific union representatives. There was some informal coordination among steel industry unions in the character of their bargaining through an industry-wide union federation. But essentially, each individual union was on its own with its employer.[4] Nonetheless, the power of Japanese steel unions should not be underestimated. For one, they typically represented upward of 75% of all employees (blue and white collar) in any given firm. Second, most employees in large Japanese steel companies had virtual lifetime employment guarantees. Thus, if the companies could not get rid of their workers, it was convenient to have an organization that enabled management to. bargain with labor as a group. Ultimately, like the American union, Japanese steel unions controlled the structure of internal labor markets and seniority systems within the companies. Like the German unions, moreover, Japanese union representatives tended to be included in all aspects of decision making in the firm and frequently had access to their company's financial information and plans for investment (Kawahito 1972; Yonekura 1994; Sako 1997; Suzuki 1997; Gordon 1998; Kume 1998).

There are admittedly many differences within this outline of what I am claiming are similarities. The point of framing these things in this way, however, is to emphasize the coordinated character of each of the industries. Steel production in advanced industrial states in the postwar period was deeply embedded in non-market practices and institutions that structured the allocation of resources and the manufacture of product. In the four areas mentioned above, the US, Japanese, and German steel industries were similar in that they established extensive systems of coordination (both inter- and intra-firm) for the governance of their practices in the integration of facilities, the setting of prices, the organization of the product palette, and in the organization of the labor market within firms. Seen in this way, the distinction introduced by Hall and Soskice (2001) between Liberal Market Economies (the United States) and Coordinated Market Economies (Germany and Japan) is very misleading. All the economies coordinated industrial behavior, and confined the operation of the market to a very narrow and highly regulated sphere.

---

[4] Though its employer, as we saw, typically coordinated its actions with other unions' employers.

2.3. STEEL DIFFERENCES

That said, there were a number of differences between the industries that would prove to be salient, especially for the way in which each of the industries fell into crisis and then responded to it after 1974. Five factors in particular turned out to be key: (*a*) relative capacity to innovate, (*b*) work practices and governance, (*c*) industrial concentration, (*d*) the legality of cartels in crisis situations, and (*e*) the location of the industry in the body politic. Along these five dimensions, the United States, in particular, was markedly different from the Germans and the Japanese.

2.3.1. Relative Capacity to Innovate

The situation here is very surprising when viewed through the lens of the VoC comparative institutional advantage framework. During the initial postwar decades, the Japanese and Germans demonstrated a remarkable capacity for radical innovation, while US producers were more oriented toward piecemeal and gradual improvements in existing technology. Until the 1960s, the United States was the most productive producer of steel with the largest plants in the world. Most US plants used a (now nearly defunct) OH furnace technology for the middle, steelmaking, operation (Hall 1997; Rose 1998, p. 447). The Germans and especially the Japanese, however, spent much of the 1950s and early 1960s replacing their old OHs, often building new greenfield sites in the process, with a new, larger, and more productive BOF technology. In addition, the Germans and again especially the Japanese were able to cut down on the reheating costs between the production of crude steel and the rolling of finished shapes through the implementation of continuous casting technology. This allowed molten crude to be immediately cast into easily manipulable shapes (slabs, blooms, and billets) that could be rolled with minimal reheating.

For its part, US producers eschewed such large-scale greenfield investment and focused on a process of modernization through "rounding out": According to Hall (1997, p. 38), this was

in part because rapid wartime expansion had left a number of plants with unbalanced facilities (such as more steelmaking capacity than rolling capacity, or vice versa); in part because some facilities were obsolete or worn out by wartime production levels and needed replacing; but chiefly because incremental expansion was far cheaper than the greenfield route. . . .

US steel producers added nearly 40 million annual net tons of OH furnace capacity during the 1950s and introduced a wide array of incremental changes (Hall 1997).[5] Indeed, according to Hall, the United States had developed the old

---

[5] Hall (p. 40) notes that OH production accounted for 126 million of the 139 million ton total steelmaking capacity in the United States by 1959: "The amount of OH capacity was larger than the entire steel industry of Germany or Japan at the time."

OH technology to "the most efficient level of which the process was capable" (Hall 1997, p. 41). Furnace size had grown to a minimum of 250 tons per heat. Advanced oxygen blowing increased OH heat times and better refractory linings were introduced that increased the longevity of the furnaces. Finally, such efficient furnaces could be run with a wide array of inputs—ranging from 100% pig iron to 100% scrap (Hall 1997, p. 41).

The problem was, of course, that the radically new technology introduced by the Germans and Japanese provided production advantages and savings that were an order of magnitude greater than the OH. Capital costs of the BOF were estimated to be half those of the OH because the increased speed of refining made fewer furnaces necessary. Hall (1997, p. 41) again explains as follows:

By the time that 300 ton BOFs were developed in the 1960s, it was accepted that two such BOFs could replace a battery of eight or more similar sized OHs, given average tap to tap times of forty five minutes for the BOF versus between six and twelve hours [for the OH]. Savings of between 5 and 15 percent of raw steel costs were common, depending on the age of the OH units being replaced.

US producers realized that they had bet on the wrong horse by the beginning of the 1960s and began implementing the new technology on a large scale throughout the decade. But even then they were hampered by their tremendous existing investments in OH. Changing to the new equipment would have to take time, which the rapidly advancing Japanese and Germans placed in short supply.[6] By the beginning of the 1970s, the US industry had fallen behind in the productivity race in steel (Barnett and Schorsch 1983, pp. 13–76; Gold et al. 1984).

2.3.2. Work Practices and Governance

In both German and Japanese steel factories, management and labor collaborated locally (i.e., on the shop floor) on the specific allocation of work roles in production. Boundaries between specific tasks were frequently blurred. It was often possible to reallocate manpower in relatively rapid response to changes in technology or the market (or both). Indeed, contra the Hall and Soskice view, it is precisely this cooperative flexibility that enabled the industries to incorporate the dramatic technological changes of the 1950s and 1960s.[7]

In Japan, cooperation on the shop floor was possible because there were essentially no clearly defined and rigid role positions in production. From the late 1950s onward, workers were recruited into companies and trained in a wide range of different tasks that they then were regularly forced to utilize in

---

[6] Some contemporary takes on the varying rates of diffusion are Adams and Dirlam (1967), Maddala and Knight (1967), McAdams (1967), and Gold et al. (1970). The definitive study of the difference between the Japanese and the United States in BOF technology is Lynn (1982).

[7] Hart (1994) makes this point—in a way quite different than I do here.

the context of work teams in the factory (Dore 1973; Gordon 1998). In Germany, there were fixed role positions: Specialized skill is the foundation of the German trade union movement and a cornerstone of worker status in German society. But the particular activities of individual skilled workers were not ever specified completely. Consequently, there was considerable latitude for the allocation and the recombination of production workers in German steel companies in response to changes in the market (Lutz 1975).[8] In both Germany and Japan, arrangements for systematic labor management communication on the organization of work and training existed: works councils in the former and team representatives and enterprise unions in the later.

In the United States, by contrast, there was neither any shop-floor-level institution for labor–management communication, nor were work roles loosely defined or easily rearranged. The right-to-manage clause in the steelworkers' contracts meant that once the contract was set, management had the authority to allocate work and technology in the way that it wished, as long as it respected the job structures and work rules contained in the contract.[9] And, unlike the Germans and way unlike the Japanese, American work rules were very precise and specialized. Workers were not trained to be flexible in American integrated steel factories. This proved to be a very salient difference between the United States and its German and Japanese competitors not only during the 1950s and 1960s, but also (and more profoundly so) when the world steel industry fell into crisis in the mid-1970s (Hall 1997).

2.3.3. Industrial Organization

Another important difference between the US industry on the one hand and the German and Japanese industries on the other was in the area of industrial organization. Relative to the other two, the American steel industry was fragmented. The Coordinating Committee of Steel Companies (CCSC), the collective bargaining organ of steel employers during the industry's heyday, had representatives from eight companies on it. These eight companies were selected to be representative of an industry which by 1974 had twenty-one independent integrated producers in it (producing in that year 125 million tons of steel). The United States had twelve companies among the world's top fifty producers in 1966 (Hall 1997; Tiffany 1988). In Japan, the industrial structure could not have

[8] The trajectory of legal reform in Germany has only tended to enhance this flexibility by reducing the number of skill categories and leaving the remaining ones more general and vaguely bounded.

[9] And this often proved to be a significant barrier to change. Article 2B of the standard collective agreement between the USWA and the steel producers, which was in place for a great deal of the postwar period, effectively barred management from reorganizing work or making significant changes in manning in all cases where there was no introduction of new technology. This was an extremely awkward clause for an industry opting for gradual improvement over radical innovation. See the discussion in Rose (1998).

been more different: By 1960, eleven integrated producers controlled over 90% of the industry's crude steel output and by 1970, the top five companies accounted for over 90%. Japan had six companies in the world top fifty in 1966. By this time, the Japanese industry was producing similar quantities of output to the United States (Yonekura 1994). The German industry was less concentrated than the Japanese and more concentrated than the US industry. By the end of the 1960s, the industry was dominated by eight major producers (seven of whom were on the top fifty list in 1966) (Herrigel 1996, ch. 6). Lack of concentration and many firms meant that the US industry tended to be spatially more dispersed than either of the other two. This left many individual companies and their workers isolated when crisis hit. Dispersal and fragmentation also made it difficult to construct industry-wide plans or coordinate systematic reductions in capacity in the industry.

2.3.4. Competition Policy Differences

Added to this was a fourth important difference between the United States and its major competitors: antipathy to cartelization in any form. American antitrust law is very hostile to cartels and has consistently prohibited their formation since the beginning of the twentieth century. Traditionally, the American monitoring authorities have preferred stable oligopolies with tacit cooperation to explicit agreements on price and production movements. Competition policy in America, at least since the New Deal, has been based remarkably strongly on negotiation between the Justice Department (and to a lesser extent the Federal Trade Commission) and industrial actors. This has allowed for great flexibility in the rules that both define the boundaries of an industry as well as those that govern acceptable competition within it over time. Industrial producers and state-monitoring agents (primarily in the Justice Department) constantly redefine the terrain in which competitive order must be maintained as technology and competition change over time (Waller 1998).[10] Despite this remarkable flexibility in other areas, the US government has been uncompromising in its opposition to all forms of cartelization (Hovenkamp 1991; Peritz 1996). As we will see, this imposes strong parameters for legitimate industrial adjustment strategies in the United States and generally starkly distinguishes US industrial culture from its competitors in Europe and Japan.

Indeed, though both countries have strong traditions of continual dialogue and negotiation between industry and government as in the United States, Germany and Japan never fully shared the Americans' aversion to cartelization. In Japan, the law outright encouraged the formation of cartels prior to the end of World War II, viewing them as vehicles for the organization of growth. After the war, Japanese antitrust law was for a short while given a patina of American

---

[10] Waller makes the point that the emphasis on negotiation in US antitrust enforcement, while characteristic of practice since the New Deal, has intensified in the last twenty years.

hostility toward cartelization. Ultimately, the reforms imposed by the occupying powers were amended to allow for cartels in a wide range of circumstances, including crucially in this case, in times of crisis and to foster rationalization (Hadley 1970).

Likewise, German law has traditionally had a friendly disposition toward cartels, though not as friendly as the Japanese. Antitrust aficionados characterize the difference between the German and Japanese orientations in the following way: The Japanese state encourages cartelization, while the German state seeks to prevent the abuse of cartels by those who create them (Iyori 1967; Hwang 1968; Iyori 1990). German toleration of non-abusive cartelization survived American meddling in the 1950s as well. Both rationalization and crisis cartels are perfectly legal under German competition law (Herrigel 1996, ch. 5). This legal variation refers to differences between the three countries regarding formal collusion in the market. All countries, as we saw, tolerated (even encouraged) considerable informal collusion. Nonetheless, as Chapter 3 will show, the possibility of formal deals in two countries would prove significant in shaping the pace and character of adjustment during the crisis period.

2.3.5. Industry in the Body Politic

The relationships of governance and power within each of the steel industries described above were deeply involved with broader principles of governance and strategies for power within the larger body politic in all three societies. Historically specific conceptions of the political and legal status of corporations and trade unions delimited the terrain upon which battles over institutional order and change took place in each of the countries (see Chapter 1). Coalitions both in parliament/congress and among peak associations in the economy emerged on this terrain and established broad rules that sanctioned the practices of both managerial and labor camps within the steel industry. The public construction, status, and strategic behavior of corporate industry and organized labor in each of the societies differed quite significantly.

In the United States, two factors were central in this area. First, until the beginning of the 1980s, in the words of James Willard Hurst "corporate status had no social relevance save as a device legitimized by its utility to promote business" (Hurst 1970, p. 70). That is, the corporation was defined as an explicitly and decidedly private entity, radically separate from the public and yet neither a kind of organic person, nor the representative of individual property claims.[11]

---

[11] There was a significant period of time in which the notion of corporate personality played a very important role in the public understanding of corporations—or at least there is great debate about whether or not it did. But this understanding seems to have collapsed in the 1920s and 1930s and was replaced by the managerialist conception being outlined in the text. On the Corporate Personality in American law, see Horowitz (1992, arguing for its salience) and Dewey (1988, arguing against the coherence of this idea in American law). For an excellent overview of the debate, see Mark (1987).

Instead, the courts and even much of economic theory constructed corporations as hierarchical entities of private property and economic power which facilitated economic undertaking and which were legitimately controlled by managers. Such entities were free to conduct their affairs in the economy in any way they saw fit, so long as the interests of the public were in no way jeopardized (Hurst 1970, pp. 58–111; Bratton 1989; Peritz 1996, pp. 111–264). Similarly, after the Wagner Act in 1935, trade unions were understood to be legitimate associations representing the interests of working people in the labor market, free to press their interest within the bounds of good public order (Barenberg 1993). Much of both antitrust and industrial relations conflict in the United States between the New Deal and the onset of the Reagan Presidency in the 1980s took place on the terrain that these conceptions of industrial actors defined. Predictably, such conflicts involved arguments about what the public interest was and how it might be jeopardized by the actions of these industrial entities.

Second, and following from this conception of the identity of actors and of their boundaries with the public, both labor unions and industrial managers related to the US government as representatives not of institutions, but of constituencies in the body politic. They were producers of steel and steelworkers. They did not conceive of themselves as bearers of public status or responsibility. Instead they acted as pressure groups vying for state attention, seeking to influence the construction of the public and its interests in ways that would be beneficial to those they claimed to represent. The degree to which they received political attention depended on their capacity to influence the polycratic political process in the United States.

In this regard, the crucial contour of the terrain of industrial politics relevant to the steel industry in the postwar period was a very strong alliance between organized labor and Democratic Party-dominated governments. The rise of the USWA was encouraged by the political reforms instituted by Roosevelt's New Deal Administration.[12] During the 1950s and 1960s, organized labor became increasingly a crucial part of the "New Deal Coalition" and a prime vote collector for the Democratic Party. The party in congress and Democratic presidents frequently rewarded the unions that supported them with sympathetic appointments to national labor boards as well as to ad hoc committees appointed to reach closure in collective bargaining with employers.[13] Further, Democratic congresspersons from steel districts were able to exercise influence, especially during the 1960s and 1970s, on US tariff policies and other governmental strategies to curb the influx of imported steel.

---

[12] In particular, the passage of the pro-union Wagner Act.

[13] Indeed, collective agreements between the USWA and the Steel Companies in 1947, 1949, 1952, 1955, and 1959 were invariably resolved by the intervention of presidentially appointed labor negotiators very sympathetic to labor's cause. Speaking of the period in the 1950s and 1960s, Mark Perlman writes that "industry became saddled with governmental wage intervention for reasons that had nothing to do with the manufacture of steel. Rather it had much to do with discipline within the Democratic party" (Gold et al. 1984, p. 619). See also the discussion in Hall (1997) and Tiffany (1988).

For their part, steel managers were repeatedly recognized by the courts as the legitimate controllers of corporate property. They also very routinely engaged with the Justice Department about the consequences of their merger plans. In other ways, however, managers had ambivalent ties to politics: public opinion (as well as congressional and presidential opinion) was often arrayed against steel producers for passing wage increases on into price increases. Republican Party interests during the period were on the whole hostile to both protection and to the oligarchic, big steel–big labor collaboration that defined the industry (Tiffany 1988; Hall 1997, pp. 45–55; Stein 1998). Steel managers were nonetheless significant personages in the body politic. Their investment and pricing decisions had consequences and as a result political actors from all quarters solicited their attention and sought to influence their opinions. In the end, as we shall see in Chapter 3, the relations between labor, management, and government were recomposed and repositioned as the onset of economic crisis gave rise to efforts to redefine the identity of corporations in the body politic and consequently of the terrain of conflict and distributional order within it.

In Germany and Japan, the identity of industrial actors and their position in the body politic was very differently constituted. Linkages between the industry and government were much more formal, centered on institutions. The boundaries between private power and public responsibility were more fluid. In Germany, corporations were constitutionally defined in the postwar West German "Basic Law" as instruments of private property with very explicit responsibilities for the public welfare and good health of the economy (Chapter 1). In the same vein, trade unions and business associations were imbued with political status that was far more profound than a "mere" pressure group alliance with a political party. They were established as core social pillars of democratic political order in the country. The postwar Federal Republic of Germany understood itself to be a "Social Market Economy" in which the government was enjoined to protect the integrity of private property and market competition, while at the same time acting in ways that ensured that the negative consequences of the market would be tempered (Nicholls 1994). All the major political parties as well as the major organizations representing labor and capital committed themselves to this ideal. Associations and corporate enterprises were not only explicitly identified with the political order by the political parties and the public. They understood themselves to be crucial social preconditions for the survival of democratic capitalism in Germany (Pirker 1979; Markovits 1986; Katzenstein 1987).

As a result, and for example, collective bargaining in industry was always viewed with political interest. Negotiations were enacted in a language of responsibility, national loyalty, and partnership. In the high-growth period of the 1950s and 1960s, the government never intervened in the autonomous affairs of industry, beyond the appropriate regulation of the boundary rules for fair market competition. Instead, it preferred to leave the development of industry to the outcomes of negotiations among the social partners. This circle of mutually reliant and accepting organizations, moreover, proved to be utterly bipartisan. The conservative Adenauer government accorded respect to trade unions as pillars of democratic order just as the social democratic Brandt government accorded that honor to business associations (Esser and Väth 1986; Markovits 1986).

If in the United States the ties between industry and politics were significant but informal, while in Germany they amounted to a corporatist marriage of political commitment, in Japan industry was tied to the state through bonds of national ambition and the melding of private prestige with political authority. The Japanese state in many ways created private industry. Throughout the industrialization process, it cultivated the development of private empires through selective and highly favorable contracting practices. The steel industry was a particularly interesting example of state efforts to foster the development of private industry. As we saw in Chapter 1, the Japanese state created the first steel producer, Yahata steel, and used the firm to cultivate the development of other private producers around it.

The earlier paternal role of the Japanese state in fostering the development of a corporate business class over time gave way (with much political battling between business and bureaucracy) to a relationship of mutual support, common purpose, and continual negotiation (Calder 1986, pp. 137–55). In the steel industry, the major firms consulted directly with the MITI during the 1950s to coordinate investment in modernized technologies and larger scale. The state was like a consultancy for the firms. It encouraged them to reform, and arbitrated disputes among them and between them and their customers. All of this was in the interest of the common goal of industrialization and growth of the industry and economy as a whole (Vestal 1993, pp. 115–44; Tilton 1996, pp. 169–89; Gordon 1998). Like the consociational character of the relations between business and government in the German case, these intimate ties between industry and bureaucracy in Japan had a corporate or estate-like character. Industries and corporations interacted with government as meaningful social groupings with great prestige and quasi-public authority. Unlike the German case, however, organized labor did not hold the same kind of public authority and prestige as business. It did not participate directly in negotiations with the state on the trajectory of industrial policy. Labor had power within the enterprise, but its public authority was overshadowed by that of the corporation (Calder 1986, pp. 137–55).

2.4. CONCLUSION: LOTS OF COORDINATION, IN DIFFERENT WAYS

Each of these five areas of difference points to significant variation among the three steel-producing economies, despite the many commonalities that characterized steel production noted in Section 2.2. The similarities and differences pointed to here amount to a very different portrait of the three economies than that provided by the VoC school. On this portrait, the United States was not a liberal market economy. That is, relations among stakeholders within the political economy were not primarily governed by arm's-length market principles. Rather, relations in the political economy were highly coordinated and negotiated. Coordination in the United States, however, was quite different than coordination in either the German or Japanese political economies. As in Germany and Japan, there was cooperation and negotiation in the United States between industry and government (competition policy), between industrial actors (stable oligopoly), and between industry and labor (collective bargaining). Unlike Germany and Japan, US producers were attributed little public status and were accorded even less public responsibility. They were forced to eschew cartels, chose gradual improvement over radical innovation, and contended with a highly institutionalized workplace environment in which the limits of managerial authority were clearly specified. Actors in each of the national steel industries ultimately had quite distinct identities and the relational conversations that players had about the industry and its problems differed substantially, despite the fact that all involved some manner of coordination.

Chapter 3 will show that the differences between the societies at these various levels provided the conditions for the course of future adjustment in each society. These different conditions, however, did not inhibit the steel industry's adoption of remarkably similar practices and technologies in each country during the postwar glory days. Moreover, as Chapter 3 will show, the differences would also not stand in the way of the development of remarkable similarities in the postcrisis period. National industries in different social, economic, and political contexts engaged in strikingly different processes of recomposition to arrive at remarkably similar competitive positions in the production of steel.

It has been possible to arrive at this point because the chapter has proceeded in a very bottom-up manner. It focused on the social, technological, and economic problems that actors in the steel industry had to resolve, rather than focusing on the institutional rules that defined the industry and "constrained" actors. Moreover, this portrait of the postwar steel industry emphasizes similarities and differences in ways that actors conceived of themselves within the industry and of how they conceived of industry's boundaries with other areas of social and political life. In this way, attention has been given to legal rules and definitions, but neither the industry nor the players within it have been entirely defined by those rules. On the contrary, roles in the industry (management and labor) are defined and enacted out of interaction and mutual understanding. Rules reflect understanding about roles. As we will see in Chapter 3, roles change in response to challenges in practice. Changes in roles give rise to creative action and recomposition of rules, and ultimately, to the recomposition of industry and institutions.

3

Left for Dead? The Recomposition of the Steel Industries in Germany, Japan, and the United States Since 1974

This chapter continues the story of the evolution of the post-World War II steel industry in the United States, Germany, and Japan. It begins the narrative with the onset of what has become a period of permanent instability and recomposition in the industry since 1974. Section 3.1 lays out the global conditions for disruption in the industry as well as the general trajectory of transformation that has been followed. This is then followed by a discussion of the specific experiences in the three case countries. The chapter claims that all three national industries followed remarkably similar trajectories, but in decidedly different ways. The cases are presented in a way that highlights the limits of conventional institutional analysis as well as the centrality of creative action and the recomposition of industrial practice.

Interestingly, despite sometimes radical consolidation and rationalization in all of the industries over the period, each national steel industry remains quite robust as a generator of value and supplier of crucial inputs in their respective manufacturing economies. Largely due to the consolidation and significant job losses, these industries have often been left for dead in both the public imagination and the scholarly literature. They are coded as rust belt, smokestack industries that will slowly succumb to the inevitable logic of comparative advantage and migrate away from high-wage environments. A substantive implication of this chapter is that such conclusions are excessive. They overlook enduring steel industry dynamism in each political economy.

3.1. GLOBAL CRISIS AND ADJUSTMENT

The steel industries portrayed in Chapter 2 are ancient history. 1974 was the peak boom year in the steel trade of the postwar period. Since then it has been an exceedingly rough and profoundly transformative ride among the major country industries, though world output has continued to grow. The turbulence and recomposition has been induced by a range of fundamental changes in the character of both the supply and demand for steel. Five changes have been most important:

- There has been continuous entry of new producers worldwide. International markets have become very competitive due to the emergence of lots of comparably competitive producers. Younger producers tend to have better technology. World capacity has gained considerably, but largely at the expense of producers in the United States, Japan, and Europe. Overcapacity has become a chronic source of adjustment pressure on national industries (D'Costa 1999).

- Consumers of steel are themselves under competitive pressure and increasingly demand higher quality product, with more precise characteristics, at lower cost. They require enormous flexibility from their steel suppliers. Cooperation between producers and consumers is increasingly encouraged and sought after. At the same time, larger consumers in the automobile and consumer products sectors are reducing the number of steel suppliers they deal with. Quality is becoming less and less of a refuge from demands for continuous cost reduction (Orr 1990; Kalagnanam et al. 1998; Ranieri and Aylen 1998; Nill 2003).

- There has been significant development and growth of substitutes for steel in main consumer markets: plastics and aluminum in particular are crucial substitutes in flat-rolled product markets (Ranieri and Aylen 1998; Nill 2003).

- Changes in steelmaking technology have been occurring continuously. The electric arc furnace (EAF) has rapidly diffused and there has been a continual upgrading of its capabilities—in particular movement into strip and sheet production. There have also been great strides made in plant automation, integration of transfer operations in steel transformation, continuous casting, etc. (Ranieri and Aylen 1998).

- Environmental concerns across the advanced industrial countries have placed great pressure on steel producers to clean up their act, making expensive capital investments in environmental technology, greater heating/melting efficiencies, more emphasis on recycling, etc., become part and parcel of the strategic calculations of steel production (Ranieri and Aylen 1998; Nill 2003).

Each one of these changes by itself is a disruption. Taken together they have pushed the industry into a permanent state of disequilibrium for nearly four decades. Broadly, this has created three apparently irreversible trends in the industry.

The first is a general reduction in employment levels. From a peak of 583,851 in 1965, employment in the US industry fell to 151,000 in the year 2000 and 121,000 by the year 2003. The Japanese decline has also been tremendous: From a 1974 figure of 459,000, the total number of workers in the iron and steel industry fell to 197,000 by 2000 and 171,000 by 2003. In fact, between 1992 and 2000 alone the big five Japanese integrated producers cut 60,000 jobs (38% of their total employment) (Tylecote and Cho 1998; Iwase 2000). Not to be outdone, the

Table 3.1. Employment in the Steel Industry 1974, 1990, 1996–2000, and 2003 (in Thousands at the End of the Year, Selected Countries)

Country	1974	1990	1996	1997	1998	1999	2000	2003
Belgium	64	26	23	21	20	20	20	18
France	158	46	39	38	38	38	37	37
FR Germany	232	125	86	82	80	78	77	72
Italy	96	56	39	37	39	39	39	39
Spain	89	36	24	23	23	22	22	23
Sweden	50	26	14	14	14	13	13	19
United Kingdom	197	51	37	36	34	31	29	22
European Union	996	434	306	293	290	280	278	
United States	521	204	167	163	160	153	151	121
Canada	77	53	53	53	55	57	56	58
Brazil	118	115	79	74	63	59	63	68
Japan	459	305	240	230	221	208	197	170
South Korea	n/a	67	66	64	59	58	57	57

Notes: FR Germany data includes former German Democratic Republic, 1996–2000. Totals are rounded. United States figures are averages for twelve months. Various other differences in coverage and definition exist.

Source: www.worldsteel.org; The same information can be found at http://www.explorepahistory.com/odocument. php?docId=310

German numbers are also sobering: from 232,000 in 1974 (and over 350,000 in 1965), total employment fell to 72,000 in 2003 (see Table 3.1).

The second general trend has been toward bifurcation in national industry structures: fewer and fewer and larger and larger integrated mills on the one hand and more numerous Minimill producers and EAF operations on the other. In different ways, overcapacity, market turbulence, and technological change have created possibilities for newer and smaller producers to enter the industry. Indeed, as increasingly large integrated producers in the advanced economies have shifted into high-quality specialized areas—flat-rolled steel and other higher value-added markets—seeking more (global) pricing leverage and stable competitive conditions, they abandon many product markets to smaller Minimill (or Minimill-like) production units. Increasingly, the more flexible producers competitively manufacture all but the highest value and highest volume variants of steel. As a result, all steel markets have become more competitive (Barnett and Schorsch 1983; Hogan 1987; Scherrer 1988; Hogan 1994; Weinert 1995, 1997; Nill 2003).

Third, the pressures that have led to such dramatic reductions in manpower and repatternings of market structure have also pushed all producers (large and small) in the advanced industrial states to enhance their productive flexibility, become more innovative, and lower costs. Producers in all three industries have been trying to develop longer wearing, lighter, stronger, more adaptable steels that can be used in a broader array of areas of application. Production processes have been highly automated and increasingly staffed by highly educated workers. Hierarchy within firms has been reduced and functional division between sections of companies has been softened and integrated, particularly on the shop floor.

The general narrative is the same. Integrated mills have consolidated their operations, radically reorganized internally to lower costs, and specialized on higher quality steels. At the same time, smaller producers, so-called Minimills, employing radically new, lower cost, and more flexible production technologies, have aggressively moved into remaining markets. Indeed, in many cases they are now even threatening to move into the core markets of the integrated producers. In the three country cases, this bifurcation has been extremely awkwardly accommodated by the arrangements of coordination and governance among integrated producers outlined in Chapter 2. Large collective conversations among relevant players have emerged in each country to define the challenges they face and devise solutions. As we shall see below, in this process creative foreign and domestic actors in all the cases have initiated change by either breaking or ignoring the institutional rules that governed the old industry.

Indeed, a key point about Minimills in the German, US, and Japanese industries is that they are, for the most part, renegades. This is true even in cases where they emerge within the old integrated firms themselves. By renegade, I mean that the Minimills have emerged as production units either by breaking or ignoring the rules of coordination that traditionally governed integrated steel production. The Minimills selectively acknowledge practices and rules that are articles of faith for the integrateds, while also developing alternative rules and organizations to govern practice in their part of the industry. Their intervention in the steel industry's collective conversation about the challenges it faces has been both disruptive and possibility creating. It has made it possible for traditional actors to redefine themselves as they engage in struggles over the redefinition of the steelmaking context in which they are acting. In each of the industries, the trajectories of industrial adjustment are similar, though the precise weights between integrated and Minimills differ slightly. The particular stories of recomposition in each of the three countries, however, are quite different.

Finally, it is important to emphasize that from the point of view of the institutionalist claims of comparative institutional advantage, all of the stories are a wash. Despite different institutional starting points, the US, German, and Japanese industries have moved in remarkably similar directions. And, rather than a story of radical innovation in one country and gradual improvement within a mature technological trajectory in others, the stories below involve interesting and unique mixtures of both. The following sections show how creative agency, rule breaking, and experimentation led to the recomposition of the industries in each of the cases. It is not a story about how preexisting institutional constraints shaped strategies for adjustment in these places.

3.2. THE US STORY

Developments in the United States follow the above general scenario to the letter. Minimills have grown from accounting for around 10% of total steel output in the mid-1960s to 55% of total output by 2005 (see Table 3.2). Correspondingly, integrated mill production *capacity* fell by over half between 1979 (139 million tons capacity) and 1993 (66 million tons capacity). In the mid-1990s, integrated mills began abandoning production of most steel products outside of flat-rolled strip and plate steels. Integrated producers sought to recast themselves as specialists by hiving off and consolidating assets and capacity. At the same time, they had to learn how to respond more quickly and effectively to customer requests. This was not an adjustment that the old arrangements in the industry could easily and painlessly manage. Bankruptcy, merger, capacity consolidation, layoffs, and rationalization of work have been the most outstanding features of nearly forty years of integrated industry dynamics. Players have repeatedly sought to find the

Table 3.2. Minimill Production of Raw Steel, and as a Percent of Steel Production in the United States 1965, 1970–93, 1998–2000, 2004–5

	Minimill production (million tons)	Minimill percentage of total output
1965	13.8	10.5
1970	20.2	15.3
1971	20.9	17.4
1972	23.7	17.8
1973	27.8	18.4
1974	28.7	19.7
1975	22.7	19.4
1976	24.6	19.2
1977	27.9	22.2
1978	32.2	23.5
1979	33.9	24.9
1980	31.2	27.9
1981	34.2	28.3
1982	23.2	31.1
1983	26.6	26.6
1984	31.4	31.4
1985	29.9	29.9
1986	30.4	30.4
1987	34	34
1988	36.9	36.8
1989	35.2	35.2
1990	36.9	36.9
1991	33.2	33.8
1992	33.6	36.9
1993	36.7	38.2
1998[a]	49.067	45.1
1999[a]	49.673	46.2
2000[a]	52.756	47.0
2004	52.6	52.2
2005	57.5	55.1

[a] Electric arc furnace (EAF) production in general, not exclusively Minimill.

Source: Chimerine et al. (1994, p. 94) and AISI 1998–2000, own calculations, 2004 and 2005: USGS.

right combination of production capability, product mix, and capacity to remain competitive and profitable.

We will deal with the rise of Minimills first and the recomposition of the integrated producers second. Along the way, it will be made clear that the transformation of the industry did not simply involve the rational restructuring of firms within a stable governing framework of institutions. Rather, it involved a remarkable recomposition of both firms and the governing framework within which those firms acted.

3.2.1. The Rise of Minimills

The key to the rise of Minimills in the US story is the vulnerability of the industry to imports during the 1960s. This vulnerability can be attributed to the interaction of two factors: The unreliability of the central price-setting mechanism in the industry and the lack of complete control over the distribution of steel on the part of the integrated steel producers. Together, these factors made it possible for new entrants to establish a base in the industry and gave them an incentive to reject the rules of coordination that governed integrated production.

The problem with the price-setting mechanism in the United States was that the major principals in the process, the United Steelworkers of America (USWA) and the Coordinating Committee of Steel Companies (CCSC), could not cooperate well enough to avoid long disruptive strikes. Or if they could avoid a strike, they were bad at convincing the major consumers of steel prior to the agreement that this would be the case. Long strikes in 1956 and 1959 disrupted steel supplies in the United States and placed major strains on significant steel-consuming industries such as the automobile and construction industries. During the 1950s—indeed, for the entire twentieth century up until that point—when production of steel in the United States took place, US consumers generally turned to US suppliers. Imports of steel traditionally were insignificant and well below (themselves relatively small) export figures. Imports serviced the very variable sections of steel consumption in periods of high demand.

With the disruption caused by the strikes, however, this began to change. Major consumers turned to imported steel to tide them over the strike period. During the 1960s, they began to diversify their purchases among domestic and foreign steel to insure against disruption. And, as the quality of foreign steel began to improve while relative prices remained below domestic steel prices, domestic US steel users began to buy more and more foreign steel. By the middle of the 1970s (despite an array of protectionist measures), foreign steel accounted for approximately 20% of US consumption.

None of this displacement of US output by imports would have occurred, however, if there had not been actors in the United States willing to purchase and sell foreign steel. As noted in Chapter 2, during the first part of the twentieth century domestic steel producers sold most of the steel consumed in the United States through their own sales divisions. If these divisions had been able to control the steel distribution market, it is unlikely that imports would ever have become a major factor in the US market. Why undermine your own company by selling steel made elsewhere?[1] But these divisions did not control the market entirely. There was a small steel distribution sector, composed largely of small regional firms who traditionally focused on the sale of scrap and secondary market steel. When steel supplies were disrupted by strikes in the 1950s, importers and domestic consumers encouraged these distributors to increase their business with imports. The situation also gave entrepreneurs an incentive to enter the steel distribution business. As the 1960s progressed, these distributors began to account for a larger share of all steel sales in the United States. Integrated producers, in other words, lost control of their markets due to a quirk in the composition of relations that coordinated steel production in the US market (Hall 1997, pp. 33–65, 105–77).

The headline story about the emergence of a robust sector of independent steel distributors in the United States, however, is not that this created opportunities for foreign steel industries to expand at the expense of US integrated producers (though that might count as a bold internal heading). Rather, the big story is that the emergence of this sector made possible the complete recomposition of the steel industry. An opening was created for new specialized domestic producers who could pick at the market shares of the integrated producers by producing more cheaply and selling through the independent distributors. This is what the Minimills did. The rise of the Minimills and the rise of an independent steel distribution sector went hand in hand. Over the course of nearly forty years, the consequence was the complete recomposition of actors, and the rules that govern practice in the industry.

Minimills have many advantages over integrated producers, when both can produce the same kind of product at the same level of quality. The central advantage is that they use a type of steel furnace, an EAF, that is capable of producing steel entirely from scrap and is efficient at significantly lower levels of output. Recall from Chapter 2 that one key dimension in the economics of steelmaking is the reduction of the number of times that raw materials have to be reheated on the way to a finished product. The EAF eliminates an entire stage in the steelmaking process (stage (*b*) in the list in Section 2.2.1 in Chapter 2—pig iron production), thus producing very considerable cost savings. Added to this, Minimills from the beginning used continuous casting technology to create efficiencies on the transition from steel brewing to rolling. Minimills could thus profitably produce less steel per heat, allowing them to react quickly to the needs of consumers without increasing costs. A further advantage, following from the relative small size and low capital costs of the plants, is that Minimills can locate close to regional markets. They are not tied to specific locations as the deeply embedded integrateds are. Even the largest Minimill producer, Nucor, which for a period in the early 2000s was the largest steel producer in the United

---

[1] If you doubt this claim, look at the level of imports in Japan where steel producers control either directly or indirectly all the distribution of steel.

States, does not have a single production facility remotely as large as US Steel's or Mittal's (the two largest integrated producers in the United States) largest plants. Rather, Nucor serves myriad regional markets from myriad small EAF plants (Scherrer 1988).

These significant cost savings and gains in flexibility stemming from the technology were made even more significant by changes on the labor side of the equation. Minimills generally have avoided the USWA and have refused to organize their workplaces according to big steel contract guidelines (Arthur 1992; Kuster 1995). Firms shifted overwhelmingly to team-based production in which the old USWA job ladders were completely abolished (Konzelmann-Smith 1995; Berg 1999; Konzelmann and Barnes 1999). Rates of automation were dramatically increased allowing firms to rely increasingly on higher-skilled technical workers. Services and maintenance were subcontracted out to reduce costs and enhance flexibility. Most Minimills, until very recently, paid their workers at levels below what comparable unionized workers in the integrateds made.[2] These workers, however, were compensated with stock options and ownership shares in the companies that increased their wages to roughly integrated firm levels—if not higher.[3]

In these ways, Minimills have completely revamped what it is to be a steel company in the United States. The companies use remarkably fewer people and make them all stakeholders. They level managerial hierarchies, and rely on team-based negotiation to produce steel very efficiently. Minimills produce with lower cost and more flexible technology than their integrated rivals. At the same time, they reject all of the governance institutions of the integrated system. They do not collectively bargain with the USWA. They do not informally follow integrated steel price-setting practices. And they are not vertically integrated. Minimill producers have also created their own trade association, the Steel Manufacturers Association (SMA), though they continue to participate in the traditional association for the industry, the American Iron and Steel Institute (AISI) (Hall 1997, pp. 145–78, 235–66; Hogan 1987, 1994; Konzelmann-Smith 1995; Konzelmann and Barnes 1999). Finally, Minimills style themselves as new economy entrepreneurs. They are ideologically hostile to the hierarchical, management-dominated old culture of the integrated mills. They understand their success to be dependent upon collaboration on multiple levels—with stakeholders in the firm, with suppliers, and with customers. This entirely new kind of steel enterprise produces steel that is much cheaper than the output of integrated mills.[4]

---

[2] Bankruptcy and crisis since 2000 have forced the USWA into strong concessions in this area that have brought their wages more into alignment with the Minimill sector, see Bruno (2005).

[3] And here the Minimills are actually now more generous than the integrateds, as the concessions made in the latter sector have not been compensated for by profit-sharing arrangements.

[4] Information on the self-understanding of Minimill producers can be gleaned from readings of the regular "Roundtables" sponsored by the journal *NewSteel/Iron Age* during the 1980s and 1990s on various subjects (McManus 1985; Berry 1994a, 1994b, 1995, 1998, 1999, 2000; Berry and Ninneman 1997; see also Dimicco 2005).

Initially, Minimill producers were only able to produce a limited range of products: the simplest commodity shapes, such as reinforcing bar for the construction industry and certain structural steels and crude plate. Over time, the technology has been refined. Minimill producers have moved into more and more areas of the steel market. Indeed, by the beginning of the 1990s, Minimills could produce everything that integrated mills could produce, except for certain kinds of high-quality flat-rolled steel used in the automobile industry (a very big market). With the growth of Minimill capacity (both in the number of plants owned by particular companies and in the number of Minimill producers), the improvement and expansion of the range of the technology, and the inherent cost advantages in the use of scrap, the Minimills have beaten back both imports and integrated producers. They hold dominant market shares in all American steel product markets except flat-rolled steel for the automobile industry (Hall 1997, pp. 235–66).[5] By the mid-1990s, they had become so efficient that "the total labor cost per ton of most US Minimills was lower than the freight cost per ton of bringing steel from Korea" (Hall 1997, p. 307).

3.2.2. Recomposition of integrated mills

Understandably, these developments have been a nightmare for the integrated producers, their employees, and the USWA. As we shall see shortly, it was possible from the 1960s through the 2000s to use the political clout of both the industry and especially the Union to get the government to place pressure on importers to limit the amount of competition the integrateds faced from outside (Bruno 2005). But it has not been possible to limit the growth and expansion of the Minimill sector. The integrateds, unlike their counterparts in Japan, never completely controlled the sale of steel in the domestic market. Since the absolute size of the US market for steel has not increased significantly since the mid-1970s, the consequences of Minimill expansion have been absolute integrated decline. The number of integrated firms, plants, number of workers employed in them, variety and array of products they produce, and level of absolute output generated by integrated producers have all declined absolutely. As we shall see below, this has not been an entirely negative result for the integrateds. But, in effect, integrated producers have become entirely different types of firms from what they were in the 1960s.

Quantitative evidence of the shift in the industry shows the significance of the transformation (see Table 3.2). By 1974, roughly fifteen years after the introduction of the EAF into the United States, approximately 29 million of the 150 million tons of raw steel produced in that year came from EAFs (19.7% of total output) and 48% of those 29 million tons were produced by EAFs in major

---

[5] See also the excellent monograph on Nucor in Crawfordsville, Indiana, in the late 1980s and early 1990s (Preston 1991) and the case studies by the Pittsburgh group (Giarrantani et al. 2005, 2006).

integrated works. By 1993, total raw steel production had declined to 97.9 million tons, but the percentage of total output accounted for by EAF production had increased to nearly 39% of total. In that year, Hall (1997, p. 269) notes that

integrated companies raw steel capacity was limited to 66 million tons from BOFs and 4 million tons from electric furnaces. Of their actual 1993 production of 62 million tons . . . all but about 3.5 million tons went to feed plate and strip mills.

In other words, by 1993, integrated works had abandoned to Minimill producers production of nearly all steel products except sheet and plate. In 2000, total raw steel output in the United States was 112.242 million tons and EAFs produced 52.756 or 47% of that total. By 2005, Minimill output as a percentage of total raw steel output was slightly over 55% (Table 3.2). By this time, in addition to all non-sheet and plate segments of the steel market, significant portions of Minimill output could be found in the core integrated markets as well.

Though integrated mills have ceded capacity in the industry to their Minimill competitors, they have done so through a long process of restructuring that has aimed to increase the efficiency and profitability of remaining operations. This process, still on-going, has involved broad reflection and struggle over what the scope, function, and character of integrated steel production should be, how it should be governed, and what the distribution of ownership and authority in the industry should be. This broad dynamic of creative action has been shaped on three different, yet constantly intertwined levels: the level of the industry, the level of the corporation or firm, and the level of industry stakeholders.

3.2.3. Industry

A crucial step in the reorganization of the integrated sector was to insulate all the firms in the industry from price competition in the international market. Very continuously, from the onset of the growth of a significant share of imported steel in the American market, the steel producers and the USWA pressed for the US government to provide relief in the form of protection from foreign competition. Foreign producers were, at various times, accused of dumping and of otherwise competing unfairly (e.g., by accepting subsidies from their governments or by organizing themselves into cartels, etc.). Such unfair competition, it was argued, was both hurting the steel-producing community in the United States and making it difficult for producers to restructure in a way that would make them more competitive and efficient. In the face of such arguments, and with the industry under genuine duress, the government implemented a series of home market protection measures—voluntary import curbs, trigger price mechanisms, etc.—designed to protect the industry and make restructuring possible. Such protectionist measures began in the late 1960s, persisted throughout the 1970s and 1980s, and were reinstituted by the Bush administration at the beginning of the twenty-first century (2003 onward) (Hall 1997; Tiffany 1988; Bruno 2005).

Significantly, protection facilitated internal restructuring within American integrated firms. Indeed, this has been an explicit purpose of protection, in framing and implementation, since the 1980s. On the one hand, the arguments for protection were characteristically American: Both affected parties (labor and the steel firms) sought to bolster the legitimacy of their arguments by emphasizing the importance of their constituencies for the maintenance of public welfare. Likewise, the government indulged the demands for protection in the name of the constituent communities' right to compete in fair markets. Protection was to provide relief, in the last analysis, to communities and citizens, not to firms or trade unions.

On the other hand, it is clear that, beginning in the 1980s, protection was an alternative to cartelization as a mechanism for the organization of industrial restructuring. As we saw in Chapter 2, when the Germans and Japanese were confronted with similar overcapacities that disrupted pricing strategies and created competitive imbalances, they formed cartels in the industry to organize adjustment. Americans were deprived of this mechanism for legal and constitutional reasons. Deprivation is not necessarily a constraint, however. Indeed, the US industry players sought creatively to influence the level of steel prices using other means, such as protectionist instruments. In both American and non-American cases, the aim is the same—price relief to facilitate the redirection of investment productively. Moreover, in both cases, the government plays a crucial role as an interlocutor in the construction of these non-market price altering strategies. It is just that mechanisms for achieving the alteration of prices are different.

The protectionist measures that were put in place during the 1980s, and the early 2000s, very explicitly linked domestic restructuring to protection (Seebald 1992). In 1984, the Steel Import Stabilization Act was passed, authorizing the United States Trade Representative to negotiate wide-ranging voluntary restraint agreements (VRAs) with twenty importing countries to radically curb steel imports to the United States. With the additional revenues generated by the VRAs, however, the steel producers agreed to reinvest that money back into their own plants and to worker retraining. According to the Economic Strategy Institute:

Under the . . . VRA's, steel imports fell from their peak of 26 per cent market penetration in 1984 to 18 percent (17 million tons) in 1989. Just as important, the Act established a compact between the American steelmakers and the American people: Additional revenues generated by the VRAs *had to be plowed back into capital investment and training.* The additional $7.8 billion invested under the Act's auspices between 1984 and 1989 played a pivotal role in the industry's remarkable comeback. (emphasis mine, Chimerine et al. 1994, p. 64)

A similar logic was at work when the Bush administration reimposed tariffs in 2003. The construction of (very high) tariffs to protect domestic sheet and plate producers (overwhelmingly an integrated part of the industry) was clearly linked by both government and the industry to processes of radical restructuring (Bruno 2005). Most notably, the sheltering tariffs (which created minimum prices) allowed the private equity entrepreneur Wilbur Ross to cobble together many of the largest integrated steel firms in the entire US industry (in particular Bethlehem Steel and LTV Steel—both in bankruptcy at the time) and create a new, and radically streamlined integrated company, International Steel Group (ISG).[6]

Note that this is not a "liberal market" restructuring process in which market relations remain sovereign and actors engage with one another at arm's length. Instead, it is negotiated industrial restructuring. A political deal at the level of the industry as a whole among producers, the USWA, and relevant parts of the executive branch (commerce, judiciary, and state) used protection to create a space for adjustment in the industry. In addition, in the case of the formation of ISG, parties negotiated the rearrangement of assets and obligations not on a market, but within the state-mediated forum created by Chapter 11 bankruptcy (Clark 1991; Carruthers and Haliday 1998; Bruno 2005; Porter 2005).[7] Plant and company recomposition in the US steel industry was a negotiated process. The negotiated character of adjustment in the industry appears even more pronounced when one views recomposition at the level of the corporation.

3.2.4. Corporation

Recomposition at the level of the individual steel corporation after the onset of deep crisis in the industry in 1974 was decisively shaped by a watershed transformation in the way in which financial markets conceived of and valued joint-stock enterprises. By its very nature, the crisis produced firm failure and the desire to restructure assets in the industry on the part of managers and investors. As both groupings began to engage with and collectively reflect on this process, it became clear that the actors in financial markets held a very different conception of the corporation than the managers did. Much of this had to do with secular developments in the financial markets themselves, away from a very fragmented and decentralized set of players toward more concentrated institutional investors with more leverage vis-à-vis the corporations.[8] These players were attracted to new ideas on the nature of the firm coming out of the academy and certain courts that rejected the fiduciary manager and stakeholder conceptions of the corporation discussed in Chapter 2. The new views, instead, favored a "contract" or "shareholder value" conception that reduced corporations to nothing more than a constellation of discrete contracts (Kaufman and Zacharias 1992; O'Sullivan

---

[6] ISG was itself later sold to the Indo-British Mittal Steel, which in turn later became Arcelor-Mittal—currently the world's largest steel producer (Schorsch 2005). As Section 3.2.4 will show, continual recomposition of firm boundaries is a defining feature of the recomposition process in the industry. Nucor was able to engage in similar capacity consolidation in the Minimill sector—purchasing over ten other Minimills in the period, see Dimicco (2005).

[7] More generally on the politics of Chapter 11 in the United States, see Carruthers and Haliday (1998, ch. 6).

[8] Groups whose strength, among other things, rested in the growth of pension plans (O'Sullivan 2000; Krippner 2005).

2000, chs. 5 and 6). Neither unitary, nor clearly or legitimately controlled by managers, the new view held the enterprise to be a multitude of discrete agreements that were expected to generate rents efficiently for investors. If they did not do so, the view held that investors could legitimately demand better performance at the cost of shifting their investments elsewhere (Bratton 1989; Kaufman and Zacharias 1992; Kaufman and Englander 1993; Peritz 1996; Roe 1996; O'Sullivan 2000). Institutional investors embraced the new theoretical view of the corporation and began pressing corporate managers to pay attention to investors performance targets (O'Sullivan 2000, ch. 5).

This alternative conception of the corporation among financiers did not replace the older stakeholder, managers-as-holders-of-fiduciary-trust view of the corporation in US public understanding more generally. It did, however, destabilize it and introduce considerable complexity in the strategic and conceptual negotiations among corporate managers, stakeholders, courts, and financial players regarding how to recompose steel production. Many twists and turns ensued in this public, collective, process of reflection on what a corporation was.

Hostile takeovers and merger mania in the 1980s (largely outside the steel industry), given voice by the contract notion of the firm, led to successful stakeholder counter-mobilization (by communities, trade unions, and managers). These actors tried to persuade state legislatures and courts to strengthen the hand of managers (and stakeholders) against the stock market. Toward the end of the 1990s, this led in turn to notorious (e.g., ENRON) managerial abuses and self-dealing, which ultimately produced national legislation (Sarbanes–Oxley) that strengthened the governance structures of corporations. This, in turn, forced better and more independent monitoring of managerial conduct and the creation of more reliable information for stock markets (Carruthers and Haliday 1998; O'Sullivan 2000; Armour and Skeel 2006).[9]

Even with the return of the pendulum in Sarbanes–Oxley, however, the aim ultimately was to create honest managers who would perform their capacious roles honestly rather than simply to bring the monitoring eye of the stock market directly into the firm. The law of the land continues to regard corporations as entities run by managers whose responsibilities are not exclusively, and certainly not narrowly, to protect shareholder interests. Whether or not managers continue to have a fiduciary obligation to stakeholders is less clear, though the history of recent recomposition in the steel industry suggests that at least there the stakeholder claim continues to carry some weight. Financial pressures and interests press managers with the contract conception and the rights of shareholders, while local courts, state governments, and trade unions press them with community and stakeholder claims (Kaufman and Zacharias 1992; Kaufman and Englander 1993; Mark 1998).

---

[9] Carruthers and Haliday note that US bankruptcy law places much more emphasis on the responsibilities of managers and the importance of continuity of the firm than is the case in the much more shareholder-, investor-, and creditor-friendly United Kingdom.

At the level of the steel corporation, all of this macro-level turbulence around roles and rules among managers, financiers, courts, and labor and community stakeholders meant that all players were (and are) forced to creatively negotiate among these competing definitions of their roles. Multiple kinds of alliances and alignments of interests proved possible over the course of forty years of restructuring. Players in the restructuring process were not structurally given or legally provided for. Depending on the local context and its history, a wide variety of interests were brought to bear in restructuring negotiations. Thus, at different points and in different contexts and situations, managers allied with stakeholders against shareholders and financial interests, or they allied with finance against the stakeholders. Stakeholders and shareholders, likewise, pursued their own strategies with and against one another and managers to manipulate the boundaries and future course of development of steel firms.[10]

The setting for this process of recomposition, of course, has been the existence of three chronic problems facing integrated firms since 1974. First, overcapacity has been a scourge. Due to the emergence of Minimills, to improvements in integrated mill productivity, and to the growth of overseas capacity that enters into the US market as imports, integrated producers repeatedly found that they had more capacity than they could ever hope to profitably utilize. Consolidation of plant and capacity, in this way, has been an unending process. Second, technological change both in the integrated and Minimill sectors has repeatedly made capacity obsolete and left producers trying to compete in markets with products that could be made at better quality and greater efficiency by other forms of technology. Third, integrated producers have constantly struggled with high costs due to bulky bureaucratic management structures, overly high inventories, dramatic and unnecessary levels of vertical integration, and rigid wage agreements and work practices with the USWA.

Individual integrated producers, many operating multiple plants, responded to these adjustment pressures in a variety of ways. Three of the main strategies were

1. liquidation of "underperforming assets,"
2. sale of assets (i.e., sale of pieces of their operations, grouped together in various ways, at and across all levels of the operation), and
3. rationalization of plants and lowering of employment levels, largely through negotiated early retirement agreements.

These strategies could be pursued either discretely or in combination. Capacity reduction, for example, could be achieved in two ways. First, it could be reduced

---

[10] There are many excellent case studies and overviews of steel politics in the United States, which together sketch out the broad range of alignments that have been possible in the industry, ranging from worker buyouts (management–labor alliances against shareholders) to pure financial domination and gutting of the firm (as occurred, for example, in the case of Youngstown Sheet and Tube). My point is that these are poles, not modal cases, and there is great heterogeneity over time in the array of alliances that produced the restructuring of the US integrated sector. See Hoerr (1988), Beamer and Lewis (2003), Beamer (2007), Safford (2009).

through flat-out closure of individual plants. The underperforming assets were simply written off as loss against current balances. US integrated steel producers incurred nearly $15 billion of such liquidation losses between 1980 and 1994 (Hall 1997, p. 212). Of forty-seven functioning integrated plants in 1975, Hogan estimates that twenty-four had been taken out of operation by 1986 (Hogan 1987, p. 45). Such radical action was not always either desirable or possible, however. There were considerable barriers to exit with large-scale steelmaking operations. The most important obstacles involved liability for environmental cleanup, outstanding debt, pension, and healthcare obligations for employees, and resistance by communities to job losses and downsizing (Bensman and Lynch 1987; High 2003).

These obstacles to closure encouraged integrated producers to follow a second route to capacity reduction: selling off unwanted or underperforming facilities. Buyers ranged from the employees and managers of the individual unwanted plant, to interested outsiders, such as foreign corporations looking to enter the US market, or groups of entrepreneurs, or private equity players (Florida and Kenney 1993; Treado 2004).[11] Often to make the sale attractive, managers and unions within the selling firms divided the organization to be sold into a group of discrete salable pieces and exempted buyers from having to deal with certain costs, such as environmental cleanup charges or pension charges. Or, buyers agreed to assume such liabilities in lieu of cash payment. In some cases, such things could be sold to other private buyers or government entities. The government-owned Pension Benefits Guarantee Corporation, for example, assumed much of the industry's pension obligations as firms restructured, often while they were in Chapter 11 bankruptcy (Tiffany 1988; Hall 1997; Carruthers and Halliday 1998; Wypijewski 2002; Bruno 2005).

Individual firm solutions, however, did not always immediately solve the problem of overcapacity. Holders of remaining capacity, or the buyers of spun-off capacity thus further applied the same deconstructive logic to those assets. Remaining actors negotiated out how to redefine roles and processes within the plant to run them more efficiently, generate value, and consolidate cost. In the process, further pieces of the firm or processes within it could be sold, contracted out, or simply shut down. Those pieces capable of generating value at acceptable cost could be retained and those that were not would be either liquidated or sold to outsiders who could make them profitable. Efficient plants, but with unattractive capacity, could be victimized by the need to consolidate capacity in larger integrated units, while less-efficient larger units could benefit (for a short time) from the same logic. Pieces were in play at all levels: in the plant, in the firm, and

---

[11] Initially, Japanese steel companies, above all others, moved aggressively into the US market and became key forces of restructuring in the industry. In the 1990s, producers from other global regions entered the industry, in particular from Europe (Arcelor and ThyssenKrupp). Another important foreign entrant in the industry is Mittal Steel, a truly global company, that purchased Inland Steel in the late 1990s and then ISG in 2004, making the company one of the largest steel producers in the United States (and making the company the largest single steel producer in the world).

in the industry. Reconstruction followed deconstruction, reconsolidation followed de-consolidation, over and over again.[12]

A crucial dimension of this process was that, with every iteration, workforce levels were reduced and remaining production organization made more productive. Seeking to avoid layoffs, the USWA and management favored early retirement schemes. Thousands of steelworkers were shifted out of production in this way. In 1980, there were still roughly 400,000 steelworkers in the American steel industry. By the year 2005, that number fell to roughly 120,000. Productivity increased enormously through this process. In 1980, it took nine man-hours to produce a ton of steel, while in 2005, with nearly a quarter of the number of workers, a ton of steel could be produced in about two hours (Bruno 2005; Porter 2005).

By the 1990s, this recombinatory process created very successful and lean integrated steel companies in the United States (Chimerine et al. 1994; Hall 1997; Nair 1997; Mueller 1999*a*, 1999*b*, 2000, 2002; Arndt 2003; Aston et al. 2004; Robertson 2007). Recomposition also generated extremely high secondary cost burdens on the companies in the form of legacy costs, that is, health and pension obligations to all of the workers who had been negotiated into early retirement. By the end of the 1990s, one estimate suggested that there were about three retirees for every active worker in the steel industry (Porter 2005). For a while, it was possible to pay for these obligations through more efficient capacity utilization, higher rates of productivity, and successful management of pension fund investments. But when the Asian crisis at the end of the 1990s undermined global steel prices, while financial markets in the United States fell into crisis with the collapse of the high-tech bubble, favorable conditions for the support of steel company pension obligations collapsed. Steel could not be sold at favorable prices, and pension funds lost tremendous amounts of value. Between 1999 and 2002, for example, Bethlehem Steel's pension plan shrank to $3.7 billion from $6.1 billion. The pension plan's obligations on the other hand, grew to $6.6 billion (Porter 2005). Under such conditions, steel producers were overwhelmed. Between 1997 and 2002, over forty steel corporations in the United States filed for Chapter 11 bankruptcy protection.

As it turns out, pervasive bankruptcy did not disrupt the ongoing process of recomposition in the industry. On the contrary, it seems to have allowed for it to occur in a very orderly and deliberative manner. In Chapter 11 bankruptcy, the courts directly mediated negotiations between stakeholders, managers, creditors, and financial interests. Ultimately, these multiple, simultaneous court-mediated processes of negotiation pushed even further the already dramatic redefinition and rationalization of the industry and its key actors. Perhaps the most dramatic change came when Wilbur Ross, a private equity investor, allied with the USWA

---

[12] See Hall (1997, ch. 7) for an extensive discussion of this logic with three case studies—of LTV's bankruptcy reorganization, the sale of the Geneva Steel plant by US Steel to a group of local Utah investors, and the reorganization of the spun-off CF&I works in Pueblo, Colorado. See also the *Business Week* descriptions of the turnaround maestro investor Wilbur Ross's efforts to reorganize the ISG group, a company he assembled out of the most productive assets of several major bankrupt steel works, including LTV and Bethlehem Steel (Byrnes et al. 2003; Aston et al. 2004).

to convince the courts and creditors to allow Bethlehem Steel, LTV, Republic Steel, Acme Steel, Weirton Steel, and Georgetown Steel to consolidate their most productive operations into the ISG. The new firm was not held responsible for either the outstanding debts of the member companies, or their pension obligations. While collaborating with Ross in the consolidation of a large part of the industry within ISG, the USWA also worked with US Steel to push for analogous consolidation moves. Initially, USWA pushed US Steel to take over Bethlehem (the trade union even tried to get Federal Guarantees for Bethlehem pension obligations). But US Steel balked and ISG moved in. US Steel did, however, turn and take over National Steel. When the Indo-British firm Mittal took over ISG in 2005, the US steel industry was dominated by three very large corporations: Mittal, Nucor, and US Steel (Bruno 2005; Porter 2005; Wysocki et al. 2007).[13]

So it went. Since 1974, US steel industry recomposition has been a more or less continuous process of negotiation, conflict, deconstruction, reconsolidation, and cost cutting, interrupted periodically by smaller and larger upturns in the global demand for steel (especially in the mid-1990s and the mid-2000s). Two aspects of this general historical process of US steel corporation recomposition since the 1970s are important to highlight.

The first is that this was not an arm's-length "liberal market"-driven process. Salable pieces of firms and their value did not imminently emerge as transparent "sub-particles" in a larger aggregate. On the contrary, they were created through bargaining and negotiation among struggling participants within and outside the firm in the heat of the recomposition process. The identity of salable pieces varied with the conceptions of the firm that each of the participants brought with them to the negotiation process. In virtually all cases of deconstruction, the USWA, suppliers, and, significantly, various government actors negotiated with managers and investors either in the context of bankruptcy negotiations or with the justice department regarding the sale of productive assets in the industry to new entrants (or both) (Bruno 2005). Corporate reorganization (and by extension industrial recomposition) in the US steel industry was not a "return to the market" or an unleashing of the market in the industry. It was a process of negotiation among constantly shifting (self-redefining) groups of stakeholders, their representatives, and government actors that recomposed the rules of practice and the relationship between institution and market in the integrated sector.

This unprecedented consolidation in the industry in turn was facilitated by the cooperation of the Justice Department and, in the 2000s, the Bush administration. The government recognized that the industry was under significant global pressure and that fragmentation was a disadvantage for producers against larger and more efficient foreign rivals. As a result, in the context of bankruptcy negotiations the justice department agreed to suspend antitrust concerns regarding consolidation moves (Arndt 2003; Bruno 2005).

---

[13] Ultimately, the pensions from nearly two dozen companies—nearly a quarter of a million workers and retirees—were moved to the US government-operated Pension Benefit Guaranty Corporation by 2005, while assets and capacity in the industry were massively recombined.

The second general aspect of this recompositional process is that it had consequences for the way in which the boundaries of the firm were drawn. In many cases, bankruptcy negotiations and then new owners ultimately dis-integrated firms. At Cr&I Steel, for example, new owners stripped the old plant of much of its integrated operations (as well as its debts and pension obligations) and recast the location as a Minimill specialized on a narrow range of steels (Hall 1997). In other cases, the development, implementation, and/or maintenance of individual processes in the steelmaking process were contracted to specialists and groups of investors. In the 1990s, for example, Bethlehem Steel agreed to have a group of outside investors pay for and develop gigantic continuous casters for its Burns Harbor, Indiana and Sparrows Point, Maryland Plants. According to the Economic Strategy Institute, "the group—consisting of various US and Austrian Banks, an Austrian [Equipment] Supplier and the Austrian Government—in-vested $540 million in the facilities which it leases to Bethlehem for a rent based on steel tonnage produced" (Chimerine et al. 1994, pp. 73–4). Other examples include virtually all services previously conducted by the firms themselves, such as finishing operations on cast steel, maintenance, mill services, and sometimes sales and marketing representation (Hall 1997, pp. 232–3).

Both of these aspects of corporate-level recomposition—public–firm–union negotiation and systematic deconstruction through licensing and outsourcing—ultimately redefined what a steel firm was in the United States. The former unitary, hierarchical, and private integrity of the integrated steel corporation was abandoned and replaced by explicit reliance on negotiation, collaboration, and contract to produce steel in a coordinated way. Adjustment was a profound process of institutional recomposition in which the identity of the players did not follow from existing rules or underlying positions within the socioeconomic structure. Rather, they emerged through the redefinition of what the specific behavioral rules for the production of steel would be. Contemporary integrated steel producers are the products of long-standing role definition conflicts in which a broad array of players—unions, communities, courts, states, share-holders, investors, etc.—were constitutively involved.[14]

3.2.5. Stakeholder Recomposition: The Case of the USWA

As the above account suggests, the industry and the steel firm were not the only actors to be redefined in this process. The role and identity of the stakeholders were also recomposed in the process. This section illustrates the character of stakeholder recomposition with the case of the USWA. All of the above integrated sector recomposition forced both the integrated firms and the USWA to abandon the set of arrangements that had defined their relationship during the postwar

---

[14] For a suggestive discussion of how the broadly political dynamics described here in the recomposition of the steel industry apply more generally to corporate development in the American economy, see Davis and McAdam (2000).

period. The growth of imports, rise of Minimills, and protracted crisis of overcapacity in the world steel market that began in 1974, undermined both the organized form of price setting in the oligopolistic industry as well as the industry-wide system of collective bargaining that had characterized wage setting in the industry since World War II (Kuster 1995). Since 1985 individual integrated producers have been setting their prices on their own and negotiating wage deals with the USWA on a firm-by-firm and plant-by-plant basis (Hoerr 1988; Mangum and McNabb 1997).

Unlike the Minimills, however, integrated mills did not seek to abandon or circumvent the USWA as a bargaining partner (Arthur 1992). Instead, each individual firm used the crisis situation as leverage to negotiate profound changes in work rules, production staffing, and wages that by the middle of the 1990s produced an incredibly flexible and, in a good market, profitable set of work relations. The USWA proved willing to cooperate in these changes, largely because it had little choice: Firms could not compete within the old structure and had either to radically reform or be liquidated. For much of the 1980s and 1990s, the USWA largely adopted the strategy of exchanging work rule and wage concessions for early retirements and pension commitments. But, as we saw above, with the tremendous wave of bankruptcies (over twenty-five) that came after the 1997 Asian-crisis-induced import surge, the USWA was forced even to abandon its line on pensions. When Wilbur Ross negotiated the formation of ISG in 2003, the union (reluctantly) agreed not only to significant job losses in exchange for Ross's restarting the dormant and bankrupt LTV mills, but also to the transfer of all retiree pension coverage to the Pension Benefit Guaranty Corporation (PBGC). When Ross took over Bethlehem Steel soon afterwards, the Union agreed to similar concessions on pensions. Keeping some version of the company running became more important to the union than fighting, literally to its death, for the preservation of legacy obligations (Beamer and Lewis 2003; Bruno 2005; Beamer 2007).

A final unlikely aspect of this recomposition of the Union role, which grew out of the intense financial dilemmas in the industry, is the development of genuine financial and managerial expertise within the union. With so many of its members in bankrupt firms, so many jobs and pension beneficiaries teetering on the precipice of ruin, the Union developed its own ability to analyze the financial health of employers. Just as importantly, the USWA developed the capacity to evaluate competing proposals for asset combination that came into play in takeover bids and bankruptcy negotiations. In this way, the Union leveraged its stakeholder position to identify desirable investors interested in pursuing consolidation and rationalization strategies most beneficial to the company and its employees. According to an excellent *Wall Street Journal* article describing the new Union tactic:

[The USWA's new] strategy, rather than simply to pound the table for higher pay or threaten strikes, is to block takeovers, take sides in bidding wars and fight for board seats.... The union also muscles its way to the negotiating table in bankruptcies, billing itself as a "creditor" whose claims are workers' lost wages and benefits. In its most sophisticated tactic, it cuts deals with private-equity players and other financiers. 'If you are not in the game, you're really going to get screwed', says Leo Gerard, president of the 850,000 member Union. (Wysocki 2007)

The process of recomposition in the industry, thus, has not only redefined what an integrated firm is; it has also profoundly redrawn the role of stakeholder players like the USWA within the firm and in the industry.

3.2.6. Summary

The period since 1974 has been an extremely turbulent one in the US steel industry. The industry today looks very little like it did in 1974. The industrial structure has become bifurcated between two different sorts of technological processes and styles of firm. Industrial concentration has increased. Corporations have been transformed. The managerial role has been recomposed and key stakeholder actors, in particular the USWA, play an enormously different role now in the industry than they did forty years ago.

In many ways left for dead in the public imagination, the industry obstinately kept on living. Indeed, as of 2007 the United States remained the world's third largest steel producer, behind China and Japan, measured in millions of metric tons of crude steel production (see Introduction). All of the restructuring and recomposition has had efficiency-enhancing effects. Bruno (2005) notes, for example, that between 1980 and 2000, the hours worked per ton produced in the US steel industry improved by over 174%. By the year 2000, many individual North American facilities were producing a ton of finished steel in less than two man-hours (Mueller 2000). This remarkable case of adjustment must be characterized as a highly negotiated process of recomposition among managers, stakeholders, financial interests, courts, and governments. It was not a liberal market process of adjustment in which managers and investors interacted exclusively on the basis of market signals and arm's-length market calculation. Nor was it a process shaped by a background institutional framework. Indeed, the process itself redefined the rules that governed roles in the industry.

3.3. GERMANY AND JAPAN: ALTERNATIVE RECOMPOSITION

Neither Japanese nor German integrated producers confronted the kind of home market competition that American integrated producers did. Until the 1990s, imports were not especially significant in either market. Nonetheless, decline and consolidation have been the defining features of integrated steel industry experience in both economies. Integrated firm adjustment in both places has been brought on by the shrinkage of export markets (largely through the growth of developing country producers) and the stagnation/transformation of home demand for steel due to the reasons enumerated at the outset of this chapter. Despite this processes of consolidation, however, neither German nor Japanese integrated producers experienced anywhere near the same degree of radical recomposition as their counterparts in the United States. Moreover, the governance regimes described in Chapter 2 that guided the postwar success of both industries have also remained comparatively robust.

Given this remarkable continuity of arrangements in the integrated sector, it is perhaps all the more surprising that Minimill producers in both countries successfully implanted themselves alongside the integrated system. Larger integrated producers in each case have been forced to cede significant market share to the upstart producers using alternative technologies. The process through which this has occurred in each country is different. The character of integrated producer coordination in Japan and Germany has different sorts of vulnerabilities and limits. But, in both countries, the end result—as in the United States—has been a growing bifurcation in the industry structure. In each country today, there is significant concentration of integrated mill production, increasing specialization of integrated production on a narrower range of steel product, and the rise of a new Minimill sector. Interestingly, as in the United States, Minimills created an alternative system of governance alongside the stable and traditional system that has governed integrated production in the postwar period. Thus, we see that while the older institutional system governing integrated steel production did not change significantly over the period, the framework of rules and relations governing the steel industry as a whole changed dramatically. Indeed, we shall see that in each case, the systems of coordination governing integrated steel production were ultimately modified to accommodate a new style of producer with alternative relations and rules governing steel production.

Again, notice that these outcomes are inconsistent with the Varieties of Capitalism (VoC) notion of comparative institutional advantage. The institutional systems governing the steel industry in Japan and Germany did not inhibit the development of radically new technologies and players in the sector. Nor did the institutional systems in either industry produce a significantly different market strategy by either integrated producers or Minimills from the sort that US producers developed. The central point is that both German and Japanese coordinated institutional systems proved to have limits. Institutional arrangements did not entirely shape industry evolution in either country. New entrants exploited these limits and in the process recomposed the overall governance of steel production in each society.

The process through which these similar strategies and industrial structures were achieved differed significantly in each of the countries, as did the recomposition of the institutional systems that governed them. I will outline the German process first and the Japanese second. In each case, consolidation in the integrated sector will be presented first. A second section outlining the emergence of the Minimill sector then follows.

3.4. GERMANY: ORGANIZED SHRINKAGE OF INTEGRATED STEEL PRODUCTION

The shrinkage of the integrated sector in Germany has been very significant. In 1962, there were thirteen integrated producers in Germany (Herrigel 1996, p. 237). By the beginning of 2008, there were only two large integrated wholly German-owned producers left in the industry—ThyssenKrupp and Salzgitter. Six other integrated plants continue to exist in Germany—Dillinger Hütte, Saarstahl, Arcelor-Mittal Eisenhüttenstadt, Arcelor-Mittal Bremen, Arcelor-Mittal Ruhrort, and the tube producer Hüttenwerk Krupp-Mannesmann (HKM). All of these, however, are owned wholly or in part by foreign firms (or, in the case of HKM, by ThyssenKrupp and Salzgitter). Arcelor-Mittal is a global company controlled by an Indian family based in Britain.[15] In addition to the three companies bearing its name, it also has a 51% stake in the Dillinger Hütte, which in turn, has a 25.1% stake in Saarstahl. Some of the most revered and distinguished firms in German industrial history—Hoesch, Mannesmann, and Klöckner—fell victim to the consolidation process.[16]

Of the firms that remained, ThyssenKrupp is by far the largest. It produced 15 million tons of steel in 2008 (almost two-thirds of total basic oxygen furnace (BOF) raw steel output in Germany in 2000). The next largest German producers, Salzgitter AG and Arcelor-Mittal AG, produced 7.2 million tons and 7.1 million tons, respectively, in 2008, while Dillinger Hütte and Saarstahl produced 2.6 million tons and 2.5 million tons, respectively. Figures 3.1 and 3.2 outline current steel locations, by type of process, and output by firm, also with output by type of process indicated.

The process of arriving at this small group of integrated producers followed a more or less orderly and responsible trajectory in which capacity, workforce reductions, and company mergers were amicably negotiated between producers, trade unions, and ownership/financial interests (for the most part).[17] Unlike the situation in the United States, the postwar rules that guided the interaction between the stakeholding parties during the postwar expansion of the industry also proved suitable for the negotiation of the integrated industry's shrinkage.

---

[15] This is the same company that took over ISG in the United States.

[16] Though Mannesmann continues to exist, it is now owned by the British telecommunications concern, Vodafone. All of Mannesmann's steelmaking and machinery assets have been sold off. Much of the steelmaking plant of Mannesmann was devoted to pipe and tube production and has been part of a joint venture with ThyssenKrupp since 1990 (first as Krupp, then Krupp Hoesch and then finally as ThyssenKrupp).

[17] The merger between Thyssen and Krupp was very turbulent, as Krupp initiated the marriage as a hostile takeover. This was defeated, however, and then Thyssen purchased Krupp through a process of negotiation involving all the major stakeholders in each of the firms. See the account in English by Ziegler (2000).

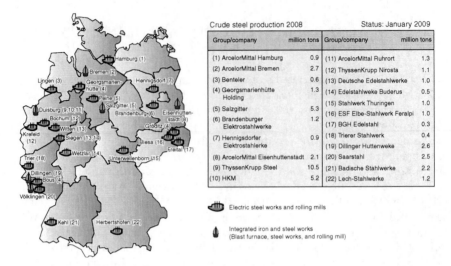

Crude steel production 2008   Status: January 2009

Group/company	million tons	Group/company	million tons
(1) ArcelorMittal Hamburg	0.9	(11) ArcelorMittal Ruhrort	1.3
(2) ArcelorMittal Bremen	2.7	(12) ThyssenKrupp Nirosta	1.1
(3) Benteler	0.6	(13) Deutsche Edelstahlwerke	1.0
(4) Georgsmarienhütte Holding	1.3	(14) Edelstahlweke Buderus	0.5
(5) Salzgitter	5.3	(15) Stahlwerk Thuringen	1.0
(6) Brandenburger Elektrostahlwerke	1.2	(16) ESF Elbe-Stahlwerk Feralpi	1.0
(7) Hennigsdorfer Elektrostahlerke	0.9	(17) BGH Edelstahl	0.3
(8) ArcelorMittal Eisenhuttenstadt	2.1	(18) Trierer Stahlwerk	0.4
(9) ThyssenKrupp Steel	10.5	(19) Dillinger Huttenweke	2.6
(10) HKM	5.2	(20) Saarstahl	2.5
		(21) Badische Stahlwerke	2.2
		(22) Lech-Stahlwerke	1.2

⛩ Electric steel works and rolling mills

⚓ Integrated iron and steel works
(Blast furnace, steel works, and rolling mill)

Figure 3.1. Steel Production in Germany and Most Important Locations, by Type of Process, 2008

Source: http://www.stahl-online.de/english/business_and_politics/economic_and_trade_policy/steel_in_figures/start.asp?highmain=5&highsub=0&highsubsub=0

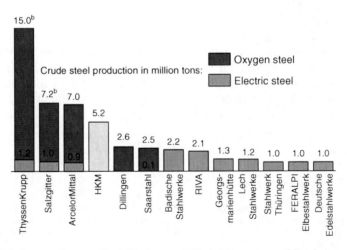

Figure 3.2. Largest German Steel Producers, 2008, by Percentage of Total German Raw Steel Production (45.8 million tons)

Source: http://www.stahl-online.de/english/business_and_politics/economic_and_trade_policy/steel_in_figures/start.asp?highmain=5&highsub=0&highsubsub=0

At certain key moments, the structure was shored up through government participation in tripartite negotiations, most frequently to organize significant layoffs and capacity reductions in the midst of crisis and European Union (EU)-mandated cuts. In two cases, Salzgitter and Saarstahl, regional governments intervened to take property stakes in the companies to keep them going (and to keep them out of foreign hands). The best documented corporatist crisis negotiations are the cases of Saarland and North Rhine-Westfalia in the west and EKO Stahl (now Arcelor-Mittal Eisenhüttenstadt) in the east (Esser and Väth 1986; Czada 1998). The EU also intervened with subsidy money in special cases to assist firms with restructuring, though this came with an obligation to repay.

On the whole, the industry reduced steel production capacity through merger and consolidation processes. Redundant plant was shuttered after the union of competing firms. Although there were few outright closures and write-offs as in the US case, there was not none. Krupp was forced to close its Recklinghausen plant in the mid-1990s. In some cases, tragedy struck and a firm went into bankruptcy, as with the large and venerable Klöckner AG and the smaller Neue Max Hütte in Bavaria. But even in these cases, managers, relevant bankers, the trade union, and government bodies negotiated an acceptable denouement for the assets.

All of the surviving integrated firms, both German and foreign owned, have, much like their American counterparts, increasingly specialized on particular sorts of higher value-added steel product. The difference between American and German integrated strategies of specialization is that German integrateds have adopted a broader array of specialization strategies. Only ThyssenKrupp, Arcelor-Mittal Eisenhüttenstadt, and Arcelor-Mittal Bremen have concentrated most of their capacity in sophisticated flat steels, primarily for automobile industry customers (ThyssenKrupp).[18] The other integrateds have adopted other specialties: Dillinger Hütte primarily produces heavy plate and pipe; Salzgitter makes heavy plate, cold, and strip; Saarstahl makes wire rod, sectional steel, and forgings; and HKM continues to focus on its traditional specialty of steel pipes and tubes. ThyssenKrupp also maintains a very strong position in stainless steel production through the cultivation of its independent subsidiary, ThyssenKrupp Nirosta AG (American-Embassy-Bonn 1993; Anon 2001). Figures 3.3 and 3.4 reflect these specialization trends. They also show that as in the United States consolidation of production has resulted in greater efficiency and impressive productivity gains, despite massive losses of employment in the industry.

---

[18] This accounted for 18 million tons of output in 2000—well over half of all the integrated mill output. For a self description of ThyssenKrupp's strategy, see the straightforward discussion of steel specialization at http://www.thyssenkrupp.com.

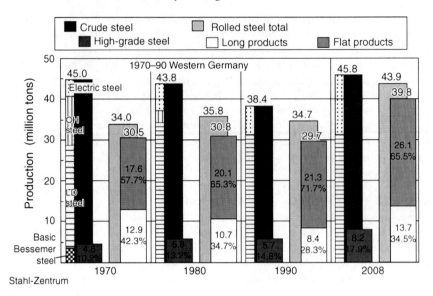

Figure 3.3. Steel Production in Germany, by Type of Product

Source: http://www.stahl-online.de/english/business_and_politics/economic_and_trade_policy/steel_in_figures/start.asp?
highmain=5&highsub=0&highsubsub=0

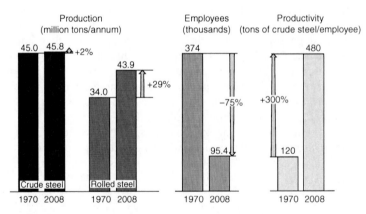

Figure 3.4. Production, Employment, and Productivity in Germany (Share of Iron and Steel Industry)

Source: http://www.stahl-online.de/english/business_and_politics/economic_and_trade_policy/steel_in_figures/start.asp?
highmain=5&highsub=0&highsubsub=0

3.4.1. German Minimills

The rise of Minimills in Germany is extremely interesting—and very improbable from the point of view of institutionalist claims about comparative institutional advantage. The technology was a radical innovation in the industry. To different degrees at different times, Minimill proponents engaged in direct conflict and partial accommodation with the reigning practices of coordination in the industry. At other times, Minimill players simply did not participate in the existing steel industry governance arrangements. Embattled by overcapacity and shrinking demand, integrated firms were initially not enthusiastic (to say the least) about the entry of smaller, flexible, and more efficient EAF producers in the lower value-added sections of their market.[19] For many years, the integrated producers and their bank and trade union allies tried very vigorously to block the emergence of Minimills. I will use the case of Willy Korf and Korf Stahl below to illustrate the dynamics of this period.

But over time the integrateds could not successfully block the entry of Minimills into the market. In part, this had to do with creative product market adjustments on the part of the emergent Minimill producers. Minimills waltzed with integrated producers over the course of thirty years, from the mid-1970s to the first decade of the twenty-first century. After the initial direct confrontation in the lower value rebar and structural markets, new Minimill entrants avoided competing in markets where integrated losses would be greatest. Instead, they captured market share in more specialized areas where integrated scale was not an advantage or where integrated commitments were weakening or fragile. Moreover, in many cases the new Minimill players came forward with different self-understandings. They saw themselves not as traditional "Montan-industrie" steel firms, but as specialists out of the industrial "Mittelstand." Most of the new Minimills were either established by firms diversifying into steel from other related areas (e.g., auto parts supply or foundries) or by entrepreneurs who were quick to diversify their interests into other related industrial sectors (industrial forging and casting, plant building, and recycling). In so doing, such firms were often able to acquire exemptions from many of the rules that governed integrated steel production. The case of Georgsmarienhütte (GMH) outlined below will show that that this even included parity codetermination rules.

As the newer Minimills were achieving success on these fronts, integrated producer struggles with overcapacity and changing market demand resulted in moves to specialize on high-value, high-volume steels. This created the possibility for new Minimill entrants in the lower rebar and structural markets or in bar and wire markets with small volumes. To a certain extent, European (especially Italian and French) Minimill imports filled this space. But Arcelor-Mittal Hamburg also established a German beachhead in this market. The firm produces specialized kinds of bar and wire from a former Korf Stahl facility in Hamburg (see below).

---

[19] Rebar and structural steels for the construction industry.

Three stories illustrate each of these dimensions of Minimill sector growth. The direct conflict phase is captured by the story of Willy Korf, the founder of Korf Stahl, one of the first Minimills established anywhere in the world. I will use the case of GMH as an illustration of direct conflict avoidance, though there are several other producers who pursued similarly specialized, identity recasting strategies (e.g., Benteler and Bruderus). The belated reentry of Minimills into rebar and structural markets is illustrated by Arcelor-Mittal Hamburg.[20] Each of the stories is interesting for the way in which they show producers systematically circumventing and/or adapting for their own ends the institutions and rules of coordination that govern integrated steel production in Germany.

3.4.1.1. Willy Korf

The grandfather hero of the Minimill sector in Germany is the pugnacious Willy Korf who engaged in direct conflict with the integrated sector for nearly twenty years from the mid-1960s to the beginning of the 1980s. In fact, Korf was one of the first Minimill entrepreneurs in the entire world.[21] Korf started out as a steel distributor in the Siegerland, taking over his father's family business after World War II. The company's primary market was the construction industry. Korf realized that the wire mesh supplied by integrated mills to builders and contractors was both overpriced and not meeting their needs. Seeing an opening, he started an extremely small steelmaking operation specialized exclusively on wire mesh production. Korf sold his output to his customer network all over middle and southern Germany, well below integrated mill prices. This infuriated the integrated mills. They colluded to undercut his prices and encouraged their banking allies to refuse him financing. Korf persisted nonetheless, and with some success, until the integrateds finally bought him out and paid him to stay out of the steel industry. He took the money, but could not keep himself from trying once again to enter the industry.

The second time he entered, in the mid-1960s, he did so as a Minimill, using electric arc technology. The facility produced 100% of its output (primarily rebar for the construction industry) from very cheap south German scrap. Not surprisingly, Korf's move once again completely infuriated the established steel powers. Producers sought to undercut his prices and banks refused him reasonable financing. Though the new technology proved to be highly competitive, despite the aggressive competition, the refusal of financing proved to be a major problem. Korf responded to this, in the late 1960s and throughout the 1970s, by widely

[20] Prior to the Arcelor Mittal merger, the Hamburg work was a Mittal-owned operation known as ISPAT Hamburg.

[21] This portrait of Korf is assembled from many articles on the person and his firm collected in the HWWA Firm Clippings archive (Anon 1967a+b, 1968, 1970, 1974, 1976, 1977, 1980a+b, 1981a+b, 1982a+b+c, 1983a,b,c,d,e,f,g,h, 1986, 1991a+b+c; Schumann 1969; Eglau 1973; Gehlhoff 1977, 1981, 1983; Spies 1978, 1980; Duffy 1981; Ringleb 1982, 1983; Uebbing 1982, 1983; Fleming 1983; Schäfer 1983; Sturm 1983; Radzio 1991). See also Ondracek and Bauerschmidt (1998).

diversifying in order to spread his costs and gain access to alternative sources of financing. The company opened new EAF Minimills in the United States, Brazil, and in Africa. Korf also sought and received significant financing from the Government of Kuwait during the 1970s. By the end of the 1970s, Korf had a very global company of Minimills, all producing with the most advanced EAF technologies. On an even playing field, Korf, an outsider, was the most efficient producer of rebar in Germany.

The trouble was the playing field was never even. When the world industry fell into crisis in the mid-1970s and the German and European industry formed into a cartel that regulated prices and managed capacity reduction, Korf was excluded. Suddenly, his competition was being subsidized to produce at a given price while Korf had to make the price on his own. As the steel market became bleaker and bleaker at the beginning of the 1980s, the cartelized price became more and more unrealistic. Korf Stahl's financial situation began to become dire. Korf called for relief from the German government and was refused. His company went bankrupt in 1982.

Korf lost his personal battle with the integrated industry, but the facilities in Germany that he established continue to exist as independent companies today (not as subsidiaries of any of the integrated mills). One company is known as Badische Stahlwerke (originally Sudweststahl) (BSW), located in Kehl in Baden. The other operating unit of Korf enterprises was in Hamburg and existed for nearly fifteen years as the Hamburger Stahlwerke until it was bought out by Ispat (Mittal) in the mid-1990s. Badische Stahlwerke produces a specialized palette of wire, bar, and mesh products very profitably for the European construction market (see Figure 3.3 and 3.4). For a discussion of the Hamburger Stahlwerke, see below.

3.4.1.2. GMH: Avoiding Conflict with the Integrated Mills

The broadly diversified metalworking companies Benteler and Buderus pioneered the conflict avoidance, identity recasting, low volume, high value strategy in Germany. Both established electric arc Minimills in the 1970s to complement their automobile parts, machinery, forging, and casting businesses.[22] Those cases are interesting because they confirm the point about Minimill production developing outside the traditional integrated steel institutional complex. Both family-run corporations were known to be significant players in other more specialized downstream industries, but were never regarded as central players in steel production.

---

[22] Benteler is a very successful automobile supplier. Its steel output is concentrated primarily on the production of very specialized tubes and pipes for machinery, automobiles, and other technical apparatii. See http://www.benteler.de. Buderus is a producer of highly specialized forged, cast, and rolled-steel products for a broad array of end-user industries—http://www.ag.buderus.de.

The most dynamic pure steel player currently pursuing the high value, low volume strategy in Germany, however, is GMH. This company has also been driven by a charismatic entrepreneur. GMH's emergence as a significant steel-maker in Germany involved a considerable amount of creative rule breaking (or at least rule stretching) in an effort to create the conditions needed for efficient Minimill production within the German institutional environment.[23] Interestingly, the company has also pursued a diversification strategy into neighboring industrial sectors, such as the foundry and forging businesses. The company represents itself not as a traditional steel producer, but as a flexible, small-scale specialist metal industry firm. This is a very different category in the spectrum of available German industrial identities.[24]

In the GMH story, the rule breaker started out as a member of the integrated fraternity and took advantage of bankruptcy to create space in the market for the new technology. GMH's current owner (75% of equity), Jürgen Grossman, was a former executive at Klöckner steel. Grossman purchased the entire plant at Klöckner's Georgsmarienhütte Works outside of Osnabruck for 1.50 DM (about $1.00) in 1993. He promptly gathered financing for a new EAF and offered jobs to younger and willing segments of the bankrupt Klöckner's workforce. He also offered these employees capital stakes in the newly formed company. Interestingly, Grossman received the full cooperation of the local metalworkers union in this, even though such arrangements were not allowable under parity codetermination law. After a year of construction, the new facility began production. Symbolically, the initial scrap starter feed for the furnace was the remnants of the blast furnace and BOF from the old bankrupt plant. GMH produces high value-added steels for the automobile and other industries. It has pursued an aggressive strategy of expansion, not only into diversified steel niches but into forging and casting areas as well, throughout the 1990s. By 2002, nearly thirty small independent Minimills and foundries were part of the GMH holding.[25]

GMH does not compete directly with the integrateds in many of its markets. Instead, it has focused on market segments that can potentially provide high return for a steel producer capable of efficiency at low volume. By eliminating layers of hierarchy in the company and relying on the flexibility and high skill of their remaining workforce, GMH has increased its operating efficiency and productivity in its main steelmaking facilities. At the same time, total workforce size has been significantly reduced (mostly through natural attrition). Still technically large enough to fall under the codetermination laws (over 1,000 employees

---

[23] By rule breaking, I do not mean illegality. Nothing that GMH has done has in anyway been against German law. When the company does not do things that other companies are legally required to do, it is either because they have been able to negotiate an exception for their case or because they have noticed that the existing rules do not apply to the area in which they are acting.

[24] In addition to interview data at GMH, the following portrait of the company is based on these HWWA press clipping archive material (Anon 1991*a*+*b*+*c*, 1993*a*+*b*, 1994, 1995, 1997*b*, 1998*a*+*b*; Hennes 1993; Stumpfeldt 1995; Helmer 1996; Jaspert 1996; Ninneman 1997; Petersen 1997; Wintermann 1998).

[25] http://www.georgsmarienhuette-holding.de

in the Osnabruck Minimill), the company expects the number to fall below 1,000 eventually, making the firm truly independent of the older integrated institutional system.

3.4.1.3. Arcelor-Mittal Hamburg: Niche Specialists

The Arcelor-Mittal Hamburg story is an ironic one in that it involves the purchase by Indian steelmaking entrepreneurs of a bankrupt Hamburg Minimill, originally established by Willy Korf.[26] The Indo-British company restructured the firm to produce specialty grades of wire and rod (e.g., piano wire and aircraft cables). The Hamburger Stahlwerke (HSW) was originally established by Korf in the early 1970s as a wire- and rod-producing Minimill. It was the only Minimill in Europe to deploy the direct reduction process, which allows EAFs to operate without scrap. HSW continued to be part of BSW after the Korf concern went bankrupt, but the firm itself fell into bankruptcy in the mid-1990s. HSW had an overly broad palette of mostly lower value steels for which there was great overcapacity in the European market. Ispat (the then name of the international steel operations of the Mittal group), a world leader in direct reduction processes, purchased the firm in 1995 for an extremely modest sum. At the time of purchase, the Mittal company promised the Hamburg Senat that it would save a maximum of jobs by repositioning the company as a specialty producer within a non-specialty market.

Since 1995, the company has done just that, shutting down unprofitable product lines and building up the company's position in specialty wire and bar. Crucial about the Ispat/Arcelor-Mittal move here is that it also entered the industry as an outsider. Ispat came with its own financing and negotiated a special arrangement with the Hamburg Senat for the takeover of the bankrupt HSW. Success was achieved by creatively redefining the rules governing German steel production and focusing the plant's output in product areas that are unattractive to, or neglected by, larger integrated producers.

The three case studies show that despite the relative robustness and health of the traditional governance arrangements in integrated steel, the German steel industry proved capable of growing the radically new Minimill technology. Growth of the alternative technology goes back to the 1960s, but there has been a very significant increase in the 1990s. German Minimills expanded essentially by creating a new industrial space in the industry outside of the traditional governance mechanisms and institutions of the integrated steel industry. While the EAF producers do not today have as large a market share as comparable producers in the United States do, their 31% market share in 2006 represents a near doubling of EAF capacity since the middle of the 1980s (Figure 3.5).

---

[26] This portrait is based on the following: American-Embassy-Bonn (1993), Anon (1993, 1999, 2001), and Burgert (1998).

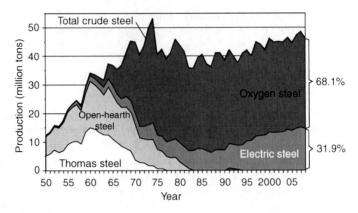

Figure 3.5. German Raw Steel Production, by Process Technology

Source: http://www.stahl-online.de/english/business_and_politics/economic_and_trade_policy/steel_in_figures/start.asp?highmain=5&highsub=0&highsubsub=0

3.5. JAPAN

The story of Japanese integrated mill adjustment is a middle case between the dramatic recomposition of the US industry and the relatively stable reproduction of the system of governance within the German integrated steel sector. Between 1974 and 2007, Japanese integrated producers consolidated operations, and reduced capacity significantly. Much as in the German case, this process of consolidation took place within the industrial coordination mechanisms that had emerged over the course of the twentieth century. Somewhat more intensively than the Germans, however, the process of integrated sector consolidation placed the traditional institutional structure under stress, forcing producers into extensive use of "exceptional" measures.

In the event, producer firm consolidation in Japan was more radical than the process in either the United States or Germany. During the first several years of the twenty-first century, the five integrated producers that dominated the industry throughout the postwar period consolidated into two very large groups. One consolidation among Nippon Steel, Sumitomo, and Kobe Steel was technically not a merger. Rather it was an extremely close cooperative agreement to coordinate capacity and production strategies. In this context, the firms created several jointly held companies that consolidate their combined capacity for plate fusion cutting, specialty steels, and cast steel rolling operations—as well as some other related diversified businesses. At the same time, the companies increased stock crossholdings to cement their cooperation.[27] The second group that was created

---

[27] Nippon Steel outlines the extent of cooperation among the three firms on its Web site: http://www0.nsc.co.jp/shinnihon_english/company_profile/product_sales/index.html. See also Shimamura (2005). More generally on the strategies of Japanese steel groups in this period, see Nair (1997).

was in fact a merger between NKK and Kawasaki Steel to form JFE Holdings (Iwase 2001).

A number of major changes in the Japanese political economy stimulated these radical consolidation moves. Large customers in the automobile industry, for example, announced plans to dramatically reduce the number of steel suppliers they purchased from.[28] Large mergers and consolidation took place in the Japanese financial system, combining banks that previously had acted as "main banks" for each of the steel producers. This made financing more uncertain for individual companies and acted as a stimulus for firms to combine. Finally, changes in the structure of the steel producer market outside Japan also encouraged consolidation. The growth of giant producers in China, Korea, and Europe, all capable of presenting strong competition for customers in important markets for the Japanese producers, encouraged the integrated mills to increase their capacity and strengthen their global presence. The traditional club of five Japanese integrated mills discussed in Chapter 2 could not reproduce itself in the face of these changes in their environment (Anon 1997a; Tilton 1998; Tylecote and Cho 1998; Shishido 2000; Hoshi and Kashyap 2001; Jackson 2003; Vitols 2003; Tilton 2005; Vogel 2006).

Thus, much like their counterparts in the United States and Germany, Japanese integrated producers became larger, leaner, and more specialized. Also as in the other two countries, Minimill producers have taken up larger portions of production as integrated capacity has been reduced. Moreover, Minimill production has upgraded, moving into a wider array of rolled steel products. As in the other two cases, Japanese Minimill producers recomposed the governing arrangements, roles, and rules for steel production as they grew. We will look more in depth at the development of the "integrated sector" first and the Minimill sector second.

3.5.1. Transformation of the Integrated Sector

Japanese integrated mills have followed two paths of restructuring since 1974. The first, very significant during the 1980s, was diversification away from steel. In part, this strategy is similar to ones pursued by the German firm ThyssenKrupp, which systematically built up business in related areas, such as machinery and automobile parts supply.[29] This strategy was initially very successful. Over the course of the 1990s, however, some of the new spin-off operations floundered and weighed down the parent steel companies. This was particularly true in semiconductors and non-manufacturing investments (e.g., amusement parks). Firms ultimately abandoned the investments. Nippon Steel, for example, established a

---

[28] Nissan was the first to make this announcement in 1998 (Tilton 2005).

[29] The German practice, however, dates back to the early twentieth century (Herrigel 1996, ch. 3).

semiconductor division in 1993 and abolished it in 1999. It created a Silicon Wafer division in 1999 and abolished it in 2004.[30]

The second integrated producer strategy was to dramatically cut back capacity, concentrate production in fewer, larger, and more efficient plants, and increasingly focus production on higher value-added and especially flat-rolled steels. Indeed, much like American producers, firms such as Nippon Steel developed "lean" strategies offering customized solutions to their customers on a just-in-time basis (Rapp 1999, p. 23). This involves significant consolidation of operations. Nippon Steel, for example, consolidated its capacity between 1988 and 2007 from twelve down to eight blast furnaces, closing (or selling) four plants entirely, reducing capacity in a further plant (Yawata) and expanding capacity from two to three blast furnaces in its Kimitsu plant.[31] As in Germany and the United States, large Japanese integrated producers increasingly focus production on lucrative high-volume, high-quality, and rapidly changing demand from the automobile industry.

As in the past, these strategies unfolded in a broadly cooperative manner. Guidelines for consolidation within and across firms were established in negotiation with government ministries, competitors, important distributors, and even in many cases customer representatives (Tilton 2005). Integrated steel producers, with the support of the Japanese government, also cooperatively developed new technologies crucial for high-quality flat-rolled production, such as continuous casting and improvements in BOF technology (O'Brien 1992, 1994; Vestal 1993). Finally, except for a brief period at the end of the 1990s when Nissan disrupted the pricing mechanism in the steel industry by insisting on competitive bidding among producers, the steel producers cooperated in domestic steel price setting (Tilton 2005). All of this is consistent with the Japanese system described in Chapter 2. Despite massive adjustment pressures and changes in their environment, Japanese integrated mills continued to understand themselves as coherent hierarchical firms with responsibilities to stake holders and to the nation.

Some cooperative commitments and practices, however, were weakened over the time period. Though the mergers in the industry were amicable, and worked out with the relevant ministries and accompanying bank interests, merger, as such, is a move away from cooperation. Nippon's intensifying alliance with Sumitomo and Kobe is a hybrid between cooperation and merger, in which joint property holdings have substituted the coordination of capacity in independent units. The most significant departure from the postwar system of steel industry cooperation, however, was in the way labor stakeholders were dealt with in the process of consolidation. Constant pressure from customers to reduce costs

---

[30] The company remains tightly diversified, with operations in all sectors closely related to steel production or consumption: Steelmaking and Steel Fabrication, Engineering and Construction (Plant Building); Urban Development, Chemicals, New Materials; and System Solutions. See http://www.nsc. co.jp/shinnihon_english/company_profile/product_sales/index.html

[31] Again, this is all available on the Nippon Steel Web site: http://www.nsc.co.jp/shinnihon_english/company_profile/product_sales/index.html

and changes in the system of corporate governance that weaken ties between producers and main banks made steel producers pay much closer attention to their balance sheets, and in particular to labor costs. During the 1990s, commitments to lifetime employment at the Japanese integrated mills (always informal to begin with) began to be significantly truncated, if not outright abandoned. Traditional diversification and subsidiary creation strategies to fulfill commitments to employment or sending un-needed employees to suppliers were checked (Schorsch and Ueyama 1993; Rapp 1999; Kato 2000; Thelen and Kume 2003).

Cost pressures eroded traditional mechanisms for paying attention to stakeholder interests, without clearly replacing them with something else. All layoffs and violations of long-term employment commitments are negotiated out with stakeholders. But each instance is understood to be an exceptional measure. As the exceptions continue to accumulate, it is possible that a new rule will emerge. Though the Japanese, like the Germans, continued to organize integrated mill steel production throughout the long period of adjustment along lines essentially consistent with arrangements that emerged after World War II, the Japanese integrated mill system experienced more stress than the German one.

3.5.2. Minimills: Outside looking in

Japanese Minimill producers exist outside the integrated system, in two different ways. First, many are active in markets that integrateds have abandoned, such as long products and rebar for the construction industry. Second, many others are owned and operated by entrepreneurs who have no connection to the integrateds or to the institutions that support them (main banks, etc.). For some firms, both things are true. Minimills first emerged in the 1960s. It was a relatively cheap technology that could be operated at a small scale and run on scrap, though electricity inputs were more expensive in Japan than elsewhere. Early Minimills focused exclusively on rebar for the construction industry. Many firms were established and growth in the sector was robust in that early period (Uriu 1989, 1996).

Most of the initial firms were founded either by the integrated mills themselves, by banks or trading companies that were directly or indirectly affiliated with the large mills. By 1980, companies tied either directly or indirectly to the steel majors accounted for 38% of Minimill output in Japan (Uriu 1996, p. 117). Trading company-related firms were also significant players by 1980. Independent company growth followed the growth of these dependent sectors.

Once it began, Minimill sector growth was robust, growing from effectively no percent of total output at the beginning of the 1960s to nearly 20% by 1978. The alternative producers avoided conflict with the integrated mills through an agreement within the state organized "administered guidance" regime where the integrateds gradually abandoned rebar to the Minimills. The same thing happened in the United States through the disintegration of the integrated mill regime and in Germany first through conflict and then through a process of mutual accommodation with the integrated mill regime. The Japanese regime organized the allocation of demand across production technologies. The Americans were too tied into their labor agreements with the USWA to painlessly give up rebar capacity to Minimills (or imports). The Germans walked a line somewhere in between.

Over time, the flurry of new firm groundings produced overcapacity in the Minimill sector. The Japanese dealt with this problem through various forms of cartelization (price, trade associational, etc.) that focused on the limitation of growth and the consolidation of capacity. A state ministry, the Ministry of International Trade and Industry (MITI), enforced and helped coordinate cartelization. MITI focused on the limitation of capacity expansion and the slow concentration of firms and production plant (Uriu 1989, 1996; Tilton 1996, 1998).

A substantial minority of producers gradually moved into additional steel product markets by adopting new technologies, especially in the interface with rolling. These moves, however, initially remained more limited in Japan than elsewhere by the powerful presence of the integrated mills and their trading houses in the steel market in general and in the distribution system in particular. Integrated mills were loathe to give up capacity to their own Minimills when they were committed to employing steelworkers in the integrated mills. Integrated majors constantly had to balance Minimill expansion with their own shrinkage. On the whole, since Japanese integrated mills had significant scale and ran efficiently, they were able to retain integrated capacity against Minimill challenge in many markets.

Through the control of their own Minimill production, and with help from allied trading houses who controlled steel distribution, for many years the integrated mills effectively shut independent Minimills out of markets in which integrated steel was dominant. This was especially so in markets with concentrated buyer markets structures, such as automobiles and consumer appliances. There is evidence that the most prominent independent Minimill, Tokyo Steel, was shut out of automobile markets by Nippon Steel and its affiliated trading houses (Uriu 1989, 1996; Rapp 1999; Furukawa 2001).

Despite the strong presence of dependent Minimills and impressive resistance by the integrated mill sector, the trend over time nevertheless steadily favored independent Minimills. While integrated mill-owned Minimill operations have stagnated, independent Minimill share of total Japanese steel output is now nearly 30%. Minimill flexibility and cost advantages put even the relatively flexible Japanese integrated producers at a disadvantage in many product markets. Minimills can run efficiently at smaller scale and can change over very rapidly. Like their counterparts in Germany and the United States, Japanese integrated steel producers have consolidated, focused, and streamlined capacity for the production of a smaller array of final higher value-added steel product (flat-rolled steel). Increasingly, other types of producers supply demand for other sorts of steel.

Indeed, the most dynamic, innovative, and efficient Japanese Minimills, such as Tokyo Steel, have been doggedly nipping at the heels of the integrated majors, successfully gaining market share in more higher value product markets. Tokyo Steel moved into H-beams in the early 1980s (it became the leading producer in that market by the end of the decade) and then flat-rolled products such as hot-coil and stripping in 1992. The company built a new H-beam and sheet-piling facility in 1995 and introduced cold rolled galvanizing in 1997 (Rapp 1999, p. 18). Ironically, Tokyo Steel's hard fought advance seems to have impressed the integrateds and fostered efforts on their part to create internal imitations (Furukawa 2001; Iwase 2002).

At the end of the day, Tokyo Steel is a bit like the story of Willy Korf in the German context, without the defeat at the end. The firm fought head on against the integrateds, suffered tremendous price and market access pressures, enjoyed no easy access to Main Bank finance or to MITI technological interest—and nonetheless gained market share. The firm produces with dramatically lower *total* costs than the integrateds. In large part, this comes from the extraordinarily lean structure of the firm. There are very few levels of management and the cost of fixed capital in a Minimill is miniscule in comparison to a gigantic integrated work. Minimills produce with a wage structure that is similar to that of the integrated mills. Most work practices are also comparable between the two sectors. Nonetheless, the flexibility and low capital cost of the Minimill has a significant impact on productivity and productivity measured by tons per worker is over four times higher than the most efficient integrated (Nippon): Tokyo Steel's tons per worker from 1993 to 1997 was 2,858 while Nippon's was 697 for same time period (Rapp 1999, pp. 21–2, appendix II). Tokyo Steel and other dynamic Japanese Minimills, in other words, have introduced a disruptive technology into the steel industry that led them to dramatically recompose the relations and practices that traditionally organized steel production in Japan.

Table 3.3 shows the direction of development in Japanese steel production and the relative division of capacity between various processes.

The division here is much like the German case. EAF producers account for roughly a third of output, compared to nearly half in the United States. Expansion of the sector has been significant since the 1980s. The process of adjusting to the challenges of the international market for steel, however, as in the United States and the German cases, has resulted in significant recomposition in the Japanese industry. Much like the Germans, the Japanese have been able to adjust in ways that do not radically recast the macrostructures that governed the integrated mill portion of the industry throughout the postwar period. But alongside of that integrated realm, the emergence of Minimill steel production has produced relatively radical recomposition of steel production at all levels.

Japanese steel producers have contours today that they did not have thirty years ago. The industry structure has become both more highly concentrated and significantly bifurcated between essentially two large integrated steel-producing groups on the one hand and a more competitive population of smaller Minimill producers, on the other. The remarkable element in this transformation is that

Table 3.3. Japanese Crude Steel Production 1950–2007, by process (in thousand tons)

Year	Basic oxygen furnace (BOF)	Electric arc furnace (EAF)	Other	Total
1950	194.9	752.5	3,891.1	947.4
1960	2,628.6	4,464.4	15,045.4	7093.0
1970	73,847.0	15,619.9	3,854.6	89,466.9
1975	84,427.7	16,782.2	1,103.0	101,209.9
1980	84,150.2	27,244.9		111,395.1
1985	74,775.6	30,503.1		105,278.7
1990	75,640.4	34.698.5		110,338.9
1994	67,224.3	31,070.3		98,294.6
1995	68,841.8	32,797.7		101,639.6
1996	65,852.7	32,948.0		98,800.7
1997	70,295.4	34,249.4		104,544.8
1998	70,869	32,449		102,800
1999	62,512	28,467		90,979
2000	69,193	28,809		98,002
2001	77,095	29,806		106,901
2002	74,264	27,800		102,064
2003	79,771	30,018		109,789
2004	81,401	29,596		110,997
2005	82,734	30,161		112,896
2006	82,939	29,779		112,718
2007	86,453	31,291		117,744

Source: Japan's Iron and Steel Industry (1998, p. 149) and Nippon Steel from http://www0.nsc.co.jp/shinnihon_engl-ish/company_profile/product_sales/index.html (under steelmaking operations—production). Numbers are rounded and do not sum to total.

much of the change, especially that involving the Minimills, has involved very explicit creativity around industrial rules. Initially, Minimills were experiments driven by integrated firms and their growth was organized and coordinated in the traditional negotiated manner. Gradually, the balance in the new sector between insiders and outsiders shifted and new entrants refused to be constrained by the existing institutional order. They decided to combat and in many cases simply ignore the existing rules in the pursuit of new product market possibilities. They developed organizations and market strategies that creatively recomposed the roles and rules defining traditional steel industry practice in ways that ultimately created a new and dynamic sector within the industry.

3.6. CONCLUSION

This case study makes two points about change in the United States, German, and Japanese steel industries. The first is that the three national processes of steel industry recomposition call into question the VoC school's argument for comparative institutional advantage. The institutional systems governing the steel industry in Japan and Germany did not inhibit the development of radically new technologies and players in the sector. Just as in the United States, though to a slightly lesser extent, outsiders and renegades entered the industry in Germany and Japan and created an entirely new form of steel producer. In each case, the new-style producers accounted for more than a third of total domestic steel production. At the same time, despite the existence of different institutional arrangements in each case, integrated producers in all three countries followed strategies of specialization and consolidation that focused on high-value products, quality improvement, and cost reduction. It seems that, contra the comparative institutional advantage claim, radical innovation as well as gradual improvement proved to be characteristic of the recomposition process in all three cases.

The second point that this case study makes is that creative action produces industrial recomposition. Creative actors (entrepreneurs, unions, managers, financiers, government ministries, courts, and communities) looking to solve chronic problems in the industry, reconceived roles and rules in ways that ultimately recomposed what the industry was. Again and again, creativity trumped constraint in the United States, Germany, and Japan. Actors creatively recombining available resources to solve common problems created both convergent strategies and striking organizational and institutional differences across the three cases. Finally, it is important to notice that recomposition does not mean that there is no continuity. Many dimensions of the steelmaking process and the way that it was governed, particularly in Germany and Japan, remained relatively stable. New elements were added, old elements repositioned. Change occurs with continuity in social life.

The stories in this chapter interestingly invert the story told in Chapter 1. In Chapter 1, it was the Germans and the Japanese who underwent processes of recomposition at all levels of industrial governance—the plant, the corporation, the industry as well as the background macro-institutional context. At that time, the United States acted as a focal point and governor of the process. In this chapter, by contrast, the German and Japanese systems accommodated radical recomposition at the level of the firm and in the plant more readily than the US system did. Since 1974, steel production has been so radically recast in the United States, that its current incarnation barely resembles its former self. Even so, a central point in each case is that the coordinated institutional systems governing integrated production had limits. They proved incapable of entirely shaping the evolution of the industry. New entrants creatively exploited these limits. In the process, they significantly recomposed the organization and governance of steel production in each society.

Part II

Introduction

CONTEMPORARY RECOMPOSITION IN THE UNITED STATES AND GERMANY: COPING WITH VERTICAL DISINTEGRATION ON A GLOBAL SCALE

Chapters 4–7 shift our attention from a historical narrative about the evolution of a single industry since the middle of the last century, to a more contemporary focus. These chapters all focus on a single industrial phenomenon: a global trend within manufacturing toward vertical disintegration. Chapters 4 and 5 lay out the general characteristics of the contemporary global trend: its distinctive impact on the organization of production, on the location of production, on supply chain relations, and on producer strategies in product markets. These chapters are broadly comparative and seek to illustrate the dynamics of vertical disintegration—or what Chapter 5 calls *disintegrated production*—with examples from across the developed and developing world. Chapters 6 and 7 invert the focus of Chapters 4 and 5. That is, rather than looking at the general characteristics of disintegrated production, the chapters examine the way in which those general trends are working themselves out in the specific (and different) relational and institutional contexts of the US and German political economies. Chapter 6 shows how producers in both the United States and Germany are adopting similar strategies and organizational techniques in the supply chain. Yet, they are doing so in ways that reflect the distinctive practical and resource inheritance of each location. Chapter 7 then turns to a case study of industrial relations reform in Germany in an effort to explore how trends toward disintegration are provoking reform of basic governing arrangements in advanced political economies.

These four chapters stem from research conducted in conjunction with several collaborative research consortia that I have been involved with since the year 2000. The first consortium, the Advanced Manufacturing Project (AMP), ran from 2000 to 2006. It was funded by the Alfred P. Sloan Foundation and included Dan Luria of the Michigan Manufacturing Technical Institute, Susan Helper of Case Western Reserve University, Joel Rogers and Jonathan Zeitlin of the

University of Wisconsin, and myself. AMP's focus was on the restructuring of supply chain relations in the United States and its consequences for regional policy.

The second collaborative project, run jointly with Volker Wittke of the University of Göttingen in Germany and funded by the Alexander Humboldt Stiftung's *TransCoop* program, ran parallel to AMP. It had an explicitly similar analytical focus, but with an emphasis on the restructuring of supply chains in German manufacturing.

Finally, a third research consortium, the Global Components Project, followed immediately on the AMP project and was also funded by the Alfred P. Sloan Foundation. It ran through 2009. The focus of the Global Components Project was on the globalization of manufacturing supply chains and the possibilities that this created for high-wage regions in Europe and the United States. The Global Components Project included Peer Hull Kristensen of the Copenhagen Business School, Volker Wittke of the University of Göttingen, Josh Whitford and Charles Sabel of Columbia University, Edward Steinfeld of Massachusetts Institute of Technology (MIT), Jonathan Zeitlin of the University of Wisconsin, and myself.

All of these research undertakings relied very heavily on qualitative interviewing. Collectively, across the three projects, more than 300 interviews were conducted (and transcribed) with representatives of all the relevant players in manufacturing supply chains in the United States, Denmark, Germany, Italy, Hungary, Slovakia, Poland, the Czech Republic, and China. Relevant players include large multinational corporations (MNCs), end product producers, suppliers in all positions within the supply chain (first, second, third, and fourth tier), small- and medium-sized enterprises, trade unions, business associations, and regional governments. Target sectors for all the research projects were automobiles and machinery. In addition to the qualitative interviewing, the AMP project (under the direction of Dan Luria and Susan Helper) conducted surveys within the target population in the United States. Unless otherwise indicated, the evidence presented in what follows stems from this database of interviews and survey material.

4

Coping with Vertical Disintegration: Customer–Supplier Relations and Producer Strategies in Complex Manufacturing Supply Chains

This chapter[1] has three aims. First, Section 4.1 introduces the idea that there has been a secular trend toward vertical disintegration in global manufacturing. The conditions that have given rise to this are outlined and reasons for the continued existence of considerable heterogeneity in the practices of both original equipment manufacturers (OEMs) and suppliers are suggested. Second, Section 4.2 constructs a typology of customer–supplier relations, all of which can be found in some guise in the current environment. The section also suggests that one form of customer–supplier relation, what it calls "sustained contingent collaboration" (SCC) is rapidly becoming the modal form of relation across producers in old-line manufacturing sectors and supply chains. Third, Section 4.3 outlines the range of strategies that supplier firms appear to be adopting to cope with the environmental conditions that Sections 4.1 and 4.2 outline. The section argues that suppliers need to constantly find a balance between specialization and diversification in their product palettes.

4.1. VERTICAL DISINTEGRATION AND THE HETEROGENEITY OF CONTEMPORARY MANUFACTURING PRACTICE

For over a decade now, the literatures on the automobile and electronics industries have been preoccupied with the process of vertical disintegration in production (Womack et al. 1990; Clark and Fujimoto 1991; Borrus and Zysman 1997;

[1] Portions of this chapter were written with Volker Wittke and appeared in Herrigel and Wittke (2005). Thanks to Jörg Sydow for very helpful suggestions on the diversification literature.

Liker et al. 1999; McKendrick et al. 2000; Sturgeon 2002). Recently, observers of lower volume sectors of manufacturing, such as the production of agricultural equipment, construction machinery, and other forms of industrial machinery have also been describing this phenomenon (Mesquita and Brush 2002; Whitford 2006). The contemporary logic of vertical disintegration is the following. Due to intensifying global competition, rapid technological change, shortening product life cycles, and greatly variegated consumer demand for product customization, the spatial, financial, manpower, and organizational resources of firms become overtaxed and cannot respond efficiently. In order to save time and resources, diversify exposure to risk, and enhance flexibility, OEMs concentrate their activities on so-called "core competence" areas—that is, on particular functions, such as marketing or overall styling and product design, and/or on particular aspects of the manufacturing process in which they for one reason or another hold a competitive advantage or have valuable, difficult to replicate, expertise (Prahalad and Hamel 1990). In all other areas outside core competences, OEMs rely on suppliers to contribute essential components, systems, and aspects of product development.

This change in the purchasing strategies of OEM firms has had enormous consequences for suppliers. On the one hand, it has increased the amount of business available to component suppliers and other specialists. On the other hand, it has also dramatically changed the kinds of demands that OEMs place on them. Suppliers are now expected to

- provide their customers with significant know-how (in the form of product design and/or manufacturing expertise),
- produce at extraordinarily high levels of quality (fewer than 100 defective parts per million is increasingly standard),
- provide a variety of services for the customer (in the shape of logistics and subassembly), and
- all the while continuously reducing the cost at which they provide these things.

Moreover, customers do not simply trust that their suppliers are doing these things. Even longtime customers are now subjecting their traditional suppliers to constant benchmarking procedures, which place their performance in comparison to "best practice" in their market. Importantly, this is not simply a disciplining tactic on the part of newly dependent OEMs to protect against potential supplier opportunism (though it can have that effect). Rather, even in cases where there is extensive collaboration and mutual dependence between customer and supplier, constant benchmarking and comparison of supplier performance and capabilities stems from the OEM's urgent need for information about new developments in technology and manufacturing practice. Because they are increasingly dependent on outside knowledge, and because their future technological and manufacturing needs are uncertain and always subject to change, the process of surveying suppliers has become a crucial mechanism for learning for the customer firm (Sabel 1994; Helper et al. 2000; Sabel 2005*b*).

In the same direction, with a slightly different accent: When OEMs are increasingly dependent on the capabilities of their supply base, it becomes crucial for them to be vigilant in surveying the ways in which this external pool of capabilities is changing. It is not simply a matter of determining, in the narrow sense of "benchmarking," how much better one supplier is at doing something than another. Instead, OEMs seek to systematically survey the supply base in order to determine, in general, what can be expected or gained from available pools of expertise.

As a result of all of this surveying, benchmarking, and comparison on the part of OEMs, suppliers, as we shall see below, must learn to live with the paradoxical reality of customers becoming both more reliant on them for know-how and manufacturing input, while simultaneously becoming more demanding. Customers actively survey (and contract with) their supplier's competitors for newer, better, and lower-cost alternatives.

Finally, even though the trends toward vertical disintegration just described are unmistakable, the practices of OEMs in manufacturing are far from uniform. There are at least three significant aspects of the situation in which OEMs find themselves that produce broad heterogeneity in their practices in production and in relationship to suppliers (Herrigel 2004).

First, many OEMs are very large multinational corporations with far-flung operations involving multiple plants and production facilities in many locations. Moreover, such firms produce a broad and wide array of products and models across those far-flung plants. Companies of this scale and complexity do not vertically disintegrate massively, all at once, and in toto. Instead, they seek to do it piecemeal in locations where it is very easy to do, or where it is most urgently needed. Or they introduce new models as "experiments" with disintegrated production in locations where there will be no entrenched in-house opposition. In other production locations, or with respect to a particular product model, where internal resistance to disintegration is great or where in-house production continues to be profitable or where suitable suppliers are unavailable, vertical disintegration does not occur.

This reality creates great complexity in customer–supplier relations. Neither internal engineers and purchasers nor outside suppliers are ever completely sure what the internal capacities of the OEM are. For example, certain plants of a large automobile producer may abandon stamping, while one or two others maintain it because they have productive machinery that is not yet amortized or that is running at full capacity due to the success of a particular product model. In such a situation, an outside stamping supplier may find that it is drawn into intimate design and product development discussions on one project and yet is then completely shut out of discussions on another with the same customer because the latter development team regards stamping as a core competence! The same customer is not always the same customer.

Second, even in cases where it is clear that an OEM does not view a particular aspect of production as possessing special long-term competitive advantage for the firm, it may nonetheless retain some internal production capacity in that area simply to retain in-house know-how. This enhances its ability to engage in knowledgeable collaboration with (and evaluation of) outside suppliers. In-house production facilities can be made to bid on projects against outsiders to facilitate this. In some cases, the supplier could win the bid and be brought intimately into the development process of a model, while in other cases the in-house unit is the victor. This kind of competition between in-house and external suppliers can exist for extended periods of time, with the outcomes continuously changing and unpredictable (Bradach and Eccles 1989).

Third, heterogeneity in practice with respect to suppliers arises out of the sheer complexity of the contracting that vertical disintegration in production produces for any given model or product—and the content of heterogeneity changes over time. OEMs seek to gain cost savings and know-how from their suppliers. But it is not necessarily true that the OEM seeks to maximize both of those goals in every contract with every supplier every time. For example, a buyer for an OEM may need to achieve certain aggregate cost-reduction targets on a particular model and she can achieve those targets by using leverage with one or two suppliers (or helping them achieve leverage). Or, still further, she can bid out a relatively standard or mature component or subassembly that had been designed and until then produced by a particular specialized supplier.

This move to push a supplier further away, however, can be undertaken to create space for OEM engineers to engage in a valuable but relatively expensive collaboration with another supplier of a different component or subassembly for the same product. Thus, the same OEM on the same product model may be engaging in a variety of different sorts of relations with suppliers simultaneously. And, as the product is redesigned, OEM behavior toward suppliers may change. Those pushed away may be offered greater intimacy (and better margins), while the intimate partners of the past suddenly find themselves having to bid on their own designs against competitors. As we will see, good suppliers learn to participate in this kind of waltz with their customers, often agreeing to (or offering) a cost reduction that ruins the margin of profit on one contract in exchange for future business with the customer, at a better rate.

All of these examples are intended to show that although the evidence is incontrovertible that there is a secular trend toward vertical disintegration in manufacturing across industries worldwide, this has in no way produced uniformity in the practices of OEMs across industries, within industries, or even within single firms and plants. There are multiple and changing strategic calculations in play. In the following sections, we will attempt to outline the range of relationships that seem to be emerging and the characteristic strategies that small- and medium-sized supplier firms are developing to maintain their position in the extended division of labor ecology in old-line manufacturing.

4.2. TYPOLOGY OF EMERGING OEM–SUPPLIER RELATIONS

All of this change in the kinds of demands that are being placed on suppliers as well as the variety of practices that OEMs pursue have given rise to a great deal of turbulence in the way in which relationships between OEMs and suppliers are constituted. Indeed, vertical disintegration can produce (at least) five ideal typical forms of customer–supplier relations in manufacturing:[2]

1. Arm's length/spot market relation
2. Autocratic or captive supplier relation
3. Contract manufacturing
4. Relational contracting
5. Sustained Contingent Collaboration

The concern here is with the division of labor between design and production on the one hand and in the roles that customers and suppliers play in the relationship over time. The first four types all involve supplier production, and all have clear role divisions between customer and supplier over time. But they vary in the amount of design the supplier engages in and production the customer engages in.[3] The fifth type has neither a stable division between design and production, nor a clear role division between customer and supplier over time. The contemporary environment is such that it is possible to find each of these relationships in practice today, but types 3, 4, and 5 are the most historically distinctive. Type 5 in particular is rapidly emerging as the most stable and modal relation.

4.2.1. Arm's Length/Spot Market Relation

For a core part of the twentieth century in many of the most developed industrial economies, vertical integration was a dominant strategy in manufacturing across many sectors. In this context, the typical supplier relationship was an arm's-length one in which the price mechanism in the market governed the logic of exchange. In this kind of relationship, suppliers either constructed complex parts according to designs made by the OEM, or they sold commodity or standardized products to the OEM. In both cases, the relationship was characterized by a strict division between product development and production and by a strong emphasis on price. Contracts went to the lowest bidder.

---

[2] This typology was jointly worked out with Volker Wittke.

[3] Our first four types are consistent with those developed in Gereffi et al. (2005). They use a scale of market hierarchy and suggest that degrees of explicit coordination and power asymmetry between lead firms and suppliers map to this scale. This is fine, but such a scale does not generate our fifth type, which combines coordination and price competition and parity and imbalance in power relations.

These relationships continue to exist in the current environment of increasing vertical disintegration, though now they exist as one of several different kinds of ties between suppliers and customers, and tend to appear under relatively specific and quite constrained conditions. In all cases of spot market subcontracting, the competences between customer and supplier are very clearly defined and the contours of the desired component are very precisely specified. In particular, no customized design input from the supplier is needed. There is neither ambiguity nor competition between customer and supplier on their respective roles in the process of developing and producing the customer's product.

Under these conditions, there are two ways in which arm's-length relationships come into being. First, normed or standard parts, typically purchased in high volume, are classic components in which price is the central determinant of the exchange. In such cases, the contours of the product are well known so that product designers can build the components into their own designs and suppliers make no design contribution to the customer's product. Further, the manufacture of the component does not belong to the designated manufacturing core competences of the customer firm, so that the outside supplier does not compete with in-house production units. The second manner in which arm's-length contracting emerges is in the classic case of "capacity subcontracting" or "verlängerte Werkbank" subcontracting (Whitford and Zeitlin 2004). Here the component part is well defined by the customer, no design input is needed from the supplier, but the manufacture of the component counts as a core competence of the customer firm. Under such conditions, arm's-length contracting takes place when in-house operations at the customer run into capacity bottlenecks. Firms then solicit bids from supplier firms on their own in-house component blueprints. The lowest bidder gets the work.

This is not a historically novel relationship nor is it an especially problematic one for either customer or supplier. There is no loyalty, no informal trust, no obligation between the parties beyond that specified in the contract. In a sense, there is no history in the relationship—gaining repeated contracts with a customer is an indication of a supplier firm's efficiency and does not in any way lessen the likelihood that the customer will turn to an alternative supplier with a lower price in a subsequent round of contracting. At the margin, components that can be produced within this kind of relationship have a great potential to migrate to low-cost production locations. But there are also many countervailing trends such that one still finds significant amounts of this kind of contracting taking place among customers and suppliers in high-wage regions.

4.2.2. Autocratic or Captive Supplier Relations

This kind of relationship exists in only very specific contexts, most quintessentially within Japanese Keiretsu networks. Here, the competences in design and production of the supplier and customer are complementary, but the relationship is extremely hierarchical. The supplier is typically utterly dependent on a single customer, and follows the lead of the customer in design and production. The contours of the product can be uncertain at the beginning of the relationship, but the solution to design and manufacture problems follow the lead of the customer and there is no ambiguity on the distribution of returns. In the Japanese case, such relationships are possible because suppliers are integrated in a larger Keiretsu network that structures the flow of resources among a large end assembler and its suppliers (finance, technology, skilled labor, etc.). Cooperation and flexibility among the players within this context is high and improves over time as the constancy of the tie (neither supplier nor OEM has alternatives) allows for learning and continuous improvement in the joint undertaking. Moreover, the moral hazard risks typically associated with bilateral mutual dependence are significantly mitigated due to mutual embedding of the supplier and customer in the Keiretsu network (Smitka 1991; Nishiguchi 1994; Nishiguchi and Brookfield 1997; Sako 2004, 2006).

In many ways, these relationships resemble vertically integrated relations, and as a consequence it is not surprising that they seem to be under significant stress in the contemporary environment (Dyer et al. 1998). One very important limitation in the captive relation is that its practical business ties to specialists and bearers of know-how outside the network of dependent producers, much less outside the industry, are limited. While learning occurs through the process of joint problem solving among the dependent parties, neither party seeks analogous relations with competing specialists nor customers in order to survey the terrain of technology and practice.

4.2.3. Contract Manufacturing

The distinctive feature of the customer–supplier relation here is a clear and unambiguous separation between processes of product design and product manufacture. OEMs (or "lead firms") do the design (and also marketing and distribution) and award production contracts to sophisticated suppliers who conduct and coordinate all of the production and assembly of the item. There is virtually no supplier input into the design of a product, but there can be interaction and negotiation between supplier and customer in the process of applying designs to manufacturing processes. Customers undertake no production.

As such, there is a strong mutual dependence between customer and supplier within this type and relationships can be long term and grow stronger over time. On the whole, this clean separation is made possible by a far-reaching standardization and modularization in the base technology of the sector. Products are composed out of modules with distinctive content, interlinked by standard interfaces. Indeed, nearly all of the hardware components manufactured by suppliers are in some way standardized—volumes are very high and supplier competitiveness hinges strongly on its capacity to achieve leverage. The quintessential realm for contract manufacture in the contemporary manufacturing environment is product-level electronics (computers, consumer electronics, etc.) (Lüthje 2002; Lüthje et al. 2002; Sturgeon 2002, 2006).

The tie between OEM and supplier in this relation is very close, but limited. In some ways, the limitation allows for the deepening of the relationship over time. Because suppliers have no ambition to design and customers have no ambition to produce, both have an incentive to work together to exploit one another's strengths. History strengthens the tie and improves the character and efficiency of limited collaboration. Because the roles and boundaries between customer and supplier are in this way so clear, contract manufacturing relations, at least as an ideal type, are less plagued by the kinds of heterogeneous OEM sourcing strategies and behaviors described in Section 4.1. OEMs are never competitors of their suppliers.

This is not to say that such pressures for heterogeneity do not exist—indeed, they could even be intensifying (Sturgeon and Lee 2001; Chesborough 2003; Leachman and Leachman 2004). Unpredictability and instability in this relationship is introduced by two factors: The desire on the part of OEMs to avoid capture by powerful contract suppliers and the need on the part of both parties to seek alternative customers and suppliers as a way to survey the relevant terrain in their sector for emergent technological and organizational possibilities. Both of these factors push OEMs to limit their commitments to a single supplier or even to a stable pool of suppliers in the interest of gaining technological and cost-reduction leverage. For their part, contract suppliers search the terrain for additional technological and organizational possibilities as well, causing them (opportunity cost) to bound their commitments even to their most trusted and reliable customers.

In the long run, this search process is not only valuable to the individual development of customers and suppliers, it can also strengthen the ongoing relationship between the parties. What each learns from its relations with others allows them to contribute more creatively to mutual projects. In the short run, however, such mutual searching creates difficulties as finite quantities of work have to be parceled between traditional and new suppliers (customers). Compromises and concessions on all sides must be made and this can produce considerable heterogeneity in the quality of relationships. For example, customers may give existing suppliers less lucrative work, while it expands production with another contractor in a more attractive area—with a promise that in another product round the old supplier will be back in the queue for the high-margin business. Such suppliers accept the business to preserve the long-term relation, but at the same time seek to compensate for the lost business by expanding their business with other OEMs.

Such creeping heterogeneity in the character and quality of relations destabilizes, or at least complicates, the contract manufacturing type and pushes it in the direction of what below will be called "SCC." It deserves to be its own type, though, due to the strict division of labor between customer and supplier. If the role boundary between development and production is never crossed, then there is contract manufacturing.

4.2.4. Relational Contracting

If you map the first four types on a power/coordination scale (Gereffi et al. 2005), then relational contracting is the limit case in the global trend toward vertical disintegration. The relationship differs from the captive supplier relationship in that there is near parity in the power balance between customer and supplier: Each depends on the other for the definition and production of the desired part, and both bring know-how to the relationship that neither could nor would be interested in acquiring on its own. Thus, competences are fully complementary and leverage is counterbalancing. Relational contracting also differs from the contract manufacturing relationship in that the competence and capacities of both parties are jointly indispensable not only for the production of a desired component, but for its design and development as well. In this limiting case, collaboration begins as a joint exploration of the possibilities for the definition of a product between customer and supplier. Neither party has a clear idea ex ante what the precise contours of the final product of the collaboration will be nor of its specific articulation or interface with the overall design of the end product. But both parties recognize that they require the competences of the other and their collaboration defines the content of both design and production. As a result, the collaborating parties view the outcome of their collaboration as a joint product from which equal rents should be drawn.

As a type of relation between customer and supplier, relational contracting is defined by the systematic integration of development and manufacture between the parties. Both bring competence in both to the joint project. This distinctive characteristic of the relation, however, is also what makes relational contracting a limiting case in the typology. While it is possible to imagine stable relational contracting for the life of a particular joint product, it is extremely difficult to identify conditions under which relations between customers and suppliers could be characterized by full integration of production and development capability over multiple contracts over time. In part, the explanation for this is the same one that contributed to creeping heterogeneity within the contract manufacturing relation: The need to enlarge the pool of ties in search of new possibilities is in tension with the reality of a finite amount of work and capacity at any given time. Through their efforts to learn, in other words, customers and producers are forced into trade-offs and compromises in an effort to preserve old ties while developing new ones (Sabel 2001, 2004; Whitford 2001; Whitford and Potter 2007). This invariably leads to the separation of development and manufacture between customer and supplier. Customers vary the quality of the contracts they establish with a single customer, some involving full-blown collaboration, others involving only manufacture or more limited collaboration on design, in order to expand the number of potential suppliers it has available for collaboration. As such, over time and multiple contracts, relational contracting as a type has a very strong tendency to degenerate into the fifth and final type, SCC.

4.2.5. Sustained Contingent Collaboration (SCC)

If the relational contract is the limit case in the current environment, SCC is the modal one. This relationship can only be understood as a tie that exists between customer and supplier over time. It emerges under conditions where both customer and supplier have important capabilities in both design and production. This makes role definition a central point of negotiation between the contracting parties. As we saw above, collaboration is one limiting—and reproducible—moment within an SCC. But the definition of roles turns out to be much more heterogeneous within a relationship of SCC due to two factors (both already mentioned) in the current global competitive environment:

1. The tendency of both customers and suppliers in the process of searching their environments for new technological and organizational capacities to vary the quality and character of their relations with even their most valued partners in the interest of expanding the size of their pool of ties/partners.
2. The fact that the volatile, complex, and non-simultaneous character of product change in the current environment leads OEM firms to separate their aggregate goals for the outside acquisition of know-how and cost reduction from the particular relationship that they establish with individual suppliers.

The mutual desire for access to outside capability results in variation in the intensity of the tie between customer and supplier over time and across projects. Because customer and supplier each has development and manufacturing capabilities, the parties can negotiate on the definition of the roles they will play in each contract round. A customer and supplier involved in intense and intimate collaboration on one project may opt for a more limited relation (perhaps the supplier manufactures a component according to someone else's designs) for a different project on a different product. The variation allows each party to seek rewarding ties to others without exhausting their own capacities, while also avoiding the possibility that their relations will be entirely severed once the older very intimately collaborative project runs out. The more flexibly partners can vary the roles they play, the greater is their capacity to search their environment for innovation and the more enduring can their relations with any particular partner be over time.

Thus, the first factor above explains how a relationship between a single customer and supplier that is variously constituted over time can nonetheless be thought of as a sustained collaboration. The second factor helps to elaborate how such collaboration can also be contingent. OEMs maximize the know-how gains and cost-reduction contributions they receive from suppliers at an aggregate level, rather than at the level of each individual supplier relation, because it gives them more flexibility. In many cases, they attempt to realize both cost reductions and know-how gains in the same relationship through collaboration with the supplier. But in other cases, circumstances may be such that the OEM would like to lure an attractive specialist into its pool of suppliers, so it will be willing to pay a premium for that specialist's know-how. In order to meet aggregate cost targets for the whole product, however, such a move will have to be compensated by significant cost reductions from other suppliers in the pool. The OEM can use its market power, leverage, or very frequently the promise of more lucrative work in a subsequent round to extract extra cost concessions from suppliers.

This kind of multiple goal contracting with suppliers engenders significant role ambiguity and hence contingency and even conflict in the character of relations between suppliers and customers. Suppliers are never sure what role they will play, or even are playing, at any moment in time—will they be courted for their know-how, integrated into a collaborative process of combined development and cost reduction, or will they simply be pressed for cost concessions on components that were once understood to be one of the previous two categories? OEMs foster this ambiguity because it is in their interest to have a supply base with broad capacities. Good suppliers should have both technological know-how and a skilled understanding of how cost can be eliminated from their role in the supply chain. Suppliers, naturally, resent providing cost reductions because it threatens their margins. Hence, they continually resist OEM pressures by attempting to define their role as a know-how providing, premium-deserving, collaborator. It is in the OEM's interest to allow the supplier to succeed sometimes in their counter-arguments regarding their role (otherwise they risk losing the supplier and its know-how). It is also in the supplier's interest to develop the skill of being able to supply cost reduction when demanded without such reductions irreparably damaging the supplier's margins. If it cannot do this, the OEM is likely to regard the supplier as unskilled and too costly to keep within the pool of suppliers. Strategic interest in the present and concern for future business make customer–supplier relations into an SCC.

Strictly speaking, the logic of the first factor causing heterogeneity in customer–supplier relations is distinct from that of the second. The search for know-how in a world of finite contracts is different than endemic conflict over role definition. In practice, however, the two logics blend into one another and produce powerful systematic pressures for the production and reproduction of heterogeneity in customer–supplier relations (O'Sullivan 2006).

This is especially obvious in the case of cost reduction. Supplier firms have an incentive to seek contracts with a range of customers so that they have access to new forms of both technological and organizational know-how. This increases their competence and enhances their case vis-à-vis a particular customer that they be defined as a premium supplier of know-how. But since all customers seek both know-how and cost reduction in equal measure (and in similarly flexible ways), suppliers find that they must have the ability to produce cost reductions wherever they go. Skill at providing givebacks without sacrificing either margins or production quality, it turns out, is just as attractive to customers as is special technological know-how. The more experience one accumulates through multiple contracts with multiple customers, the better one becomes at being able to accommodate customer demands—and in being able to bargain with the customer about the role that the supplier firm should be playing. But then, the more adroit a supplier becomes at adopting multiple roles with a customer, the more the customer will exploit this flexibility on the part of suppliers. There is an in-built escalation in the process of increasing intimacy and enforcing arm's length on both sides of the relation. Suppliers and customers who learn how to thrive in this environment, succeed; those who cannot learn, fall out. In this way, SCC is fundamentally a learning-based process. Through many iterations of trial-and-error dealings with intimacy and distance in their relations, producers learn how to more smoothly alter the roles they play and maximize the benefit they receive out of each.

4.3. EMERGING SUPPLIER STRATEGIES IN THE CONTEXT OF SCC

This section considers the range of strategic responses that supplier firms have been developing in an environment in which SCC is the modal form of customer–supplier tie. Most fundamentally, successful SCC suppliers need the capacity to design and develop products with their customers; they need the organizational capacity to play a variety of roles; and they need to be able to spread a variety of kinds of work through their organizations in order to accommodate their need to search the terrain for innovation. Given those requirements, suppliers have the following three general strategic options:[4]

- specialize on a particular area within the supply chain;
- diversify across a number of locations within a supply chain (vertical diversification);
- diversify across supply chains (horizontal diversification).

Each of these strategies has advantages and disadvantages and firms typically experiment with mixtures and variants of each of them, seeking an optimal balance of their own capacities with the risks that those capacities and the market expose them to. The interesting feature of the current competitive situation is that firms are rewarded and punished both by specialization *and* by diversification. As a result, strategies, much like the relationships within SCC supply chains, are multifaceted, or driven by multiple goals. Firms need to constantly find a balance between deepening their knowledge in a single area on the one hand, and leveraging that knowledge (and spreading their risks) to other areas on the other.[5] This will become clear through the discussion of the various strategies.

---

[4] See Whitford and Zeitlin (2004) for a parallel discussion.

[5] Put another way: specialization narrowly defined (i.e., dedication of resources on only one product or process) is perhaps the least common strategy. Knowledge and risk push firms toward diversification. Yet the virtues of specialization are ones that all firms want to embrace and cultivate.

4.3.1. Specialization

Specialization has the advantage of focus. Firms can become better and better at developing and delivering a single product (or product type) of value within the supply chain. By excelling in this area, they become an indispensable partner for their customers. The better they become at the specialty, the more the customer is going to devolve work to them, and the less likely the customer will be to retain the capacity to make that specialty themselves, in-house. Moreover, as Adam Smith indicated very long ago, specialization often leads to innovation as the depth of concentration on a particular range of problems induces the specialist to devise improvements.

For all its attractions, there are at least four problems with a pure specialization strategy. First, in the current environment, the pure specialization strategy can remain profitable only if a firm continuously grows and acquires new customers. If the firm reaches a plateau and a stable set of customers, the pressures of cost reduction will drive the firm's margins down to nearly zero (Whitford and Zeitlin 2004). Second, and in a related way, if the firm specializes so narrowly that its customer base becomes too circumscribed, the firm runs the risk of technological myopia and can miss opportunities to develop its specialty in new directions. Third, specialized firms, even those that have paid attention to technological evolution in the specialty, run the risk of demand for the specialty going away. This can occur either in a short-term way because there is a downturn in the business cycle, or (more seriously and enduringly) because the specialty has been replaced by a more superior technology. Fourth, specialization strategies that involve considerable design and development competence on the part of the specialist often result in the under-utilization of the know-how that firms have been enhancing in an effort to participate in the supply chain.[6] For all of these reasons, specialization as a pure strategy is often very unstable and short-lived in the current environment. Firms seek to compensate for the risks that attend greater specialization by diversifying.

4.3.2. Vertical Diversification

Vertical diversification within a given supply chain or related sets of supply chains has a number of attractive features. By developing the capacity to produce related parts, firms can leverage their development know-how across contracts and production processes. It also gives them the capacity to integrate products for their customers; that is, provide subassemblies and, in special cases, even modules. Although diversified suppliers can supply integration for their customers,

---

[6] This is a reason often given for diversification strategies more generally in the resource-based management literature. See Rumelt (1974), Teece (1980), Panzar and Willig (1981), Rumelt (1982), Hill and Hoskisson (1987), Hoskisson (1987), Chandler (1990), and Argyres (1996).

they do not have to. Diversification allows them to be specialists in several markets and customers can know them primarily as specialists, rather than subassembly suppliers. In the context of SCC, the capacity to mix and match, bundle specialties, and supply specialties individually, gives the supplier firm the capability of expanding the range of customers that it encounters. This fosters learning, staves off myopia, and diversifies risk.[7]

The downside of vertical diversification within a supply chain is that it is expensive. Firms must invest in more production equipment, and if they supply subassemblies or modules, they have to invest in more assembly workers and engineers with integrated knowledge of their own product portfolio. Since diversifying firms are creating a menu of possible ways to service their customer, they can spread the risk associated with the development of diversified capacity across a broad array of different kinds of contracts. Yet since the products in the firm's palette tend to be related and often are in the same industrial sector, their fortunes can rise and fall in tandem as demand in the customer industry rises and falls.

Greater investment creates the possibility for greater rents, but it also increases the risk. Firms must calibrate risks, costs, and rewards in the way that they negotiate efforts to diversify along a supply chain. For small firms, this negotiation process can constrain diversification quite significantly. For large firms, the negotiation often leads to continual recomposition of the group of products that they have in their palette.

4.3.3. Horizontal Diversification

Horizontal diversification makes it possible to avoid the risk that vertical diversification creates. That is, by developing the capacity to produce products with customers in a variety of industrial sectors, the firm can avoid being completely dependent on the cyclic fortunes of customers in a single sector. Very often, firms attempt to achieve this sort of sectoral diversification with a single kind of specialty. For example, a manufacturer of springs or bevel gears lives by thinking of as many possible applications for their specialty as they can. Such creativity inevitably drives producers to look for customers in a broad array of sectors. A bevel gear, for example, can be used in a highly sophisticated jet fighter, in a Formula One race car, or on roller coaster at an amusement park. Springs can be

---

[7] This description represents a development away from the diversification form developed at the end of the 1990s where firms sought to diversify along the value chain in order to be able to supply customers with subassemblies and modules. This strategy led to many bankruptcies as customers were less interested in modules than they were in components. Vertically diversified firms these days do not lose touch with their identities as specialists in each area, nor with their ability to supply individual specialties. They have the ability to supply systems or modules; but that is not what earns them money. On the earlier strategy and its limits in this sector, see Herrigel (2004), Sabel and Zeitlin (2004), and MacDuffie (2007).

used in virtually any application where there is variable tension or shock absorption required.

Though there are many interesting kinds of specialty products of this kind that allow for horizontal diversification among component producers in manufacturing supply chains, not all allow for horizontal diversification as extensive as springs and bevel gears. Pistons, for example, can be made in different sizes and adapted for engines of different fuel types and as a result sold in an array of end user sectors—automobiles, heavy trucks, and defense, construction, and agricultural equipment industries.

Horizontal diversification can also be achieved when firms develop a related product—perhaps something based on the same machine park used to make their original specialty, or something based on the physical or mechanical properties of their original product—which can be used by customers in a different sector. For example, one German firm interviewed diversified away from its original exclusive specialization on the production of high-quality hand tools (screwdrivers), into the production of customized precision machine goods in the automobile industry. The move leveraged the firm's knowledge of machining as well as its familiarity with pressure and coupling functions.

The disadvantage of horizontal diversification is that scope economies can become unwieldy. It is not possible to keep track of the production and delivery of an infinite number of different applications, and a firm can often extend itself beyond its managerial or production capacities. Similarly, the creative energy being extended to invent a way to apply your specialty to a new area is so much energy not spent attempting to improve the way in which the application performs in the original area of specialty. Some, even quite a bit, of such creative effort can pay off with deeper knowledge of the specialty in general and improvement in the way the firm is able to solve customer solutions. But too much can have decreasing returns on all of the firm's capacities.

4.4. BALANCING SPECIALIZATION AND DIVERSIFICATION

Each of these three types of strategic orientation can be found currently among firms attempting to position themselves within supply chains marked by SCC. Interestingly, these strategic considerations appear to govern the actions of both very large and quite small supplier firms. The pressures on firms to provide design and development to their customers play a variety of roles and accommodate search processes across production are general ones and are not affected by scale. Component suppliers come in all shapes and sizes, yet in all cases, they are seeking to balance specialization and diversification. At one extreme, there are giant grocery store supplier firms, such as Magna in the automobile industry, that produce the complete range of components needed to produce an entire automobile. At the other extreme, there are thousands of small- and medium-sized specialist firms who have diversified a step up or down the supply chain in order to capture the value that their newly acquired development and design capabilities have created. In between these extremes are firms of all sizes, more and less broadly diversified, all seeking to gain rents from specialization, while diversifying to spread risk, attract customers, and take advantage of the added know-how that participation in SCC supply chains has generated.

Saying that both large and small suppliers need to find a balance between specialization and diversification is not the same as saying that there are no differences between large and small firms in the way that they have pursued these things. On the whole, large firms look to create synergies within themselves through the construction of internal mechanisms for the circulation of technological, organizational, market, and even customer information. Firms do this in a variety of ways.

One creative way to achieve a balance between the benefits of specialization and diversification is the serial niche defining method of the Illinois Tool Works (ITW). ITW is a holding company with a technology center attached to it. There are two layers of management between the head of the entire company and the General Manager of an operating unit. ITW owns 600 companies (about twenty-five in the automobile components sector) and expands by forty companies a year. Not all of the new companies are acquisitions; many are spin-offs that result from the breakup into smaller specialized units of previous ITW entities. Each of the units of ITW is independent—they make their decisions about product, technology, labor, whether or not to buy another company or to spin off a part of themselves (which they do all the time) entirely locally.

The central management of the company imposes a single order on the operating units in the guise of a formal principle of self-analysis: the so-called 80/20 analysis. This idea, which says that 80% of revenue and business will always come from 20% of operations, is not entirely arbitrary. It traces its origins back to an argument made by Vilfried Pareto in the nineteenth century. Yet the point of the rule is that it requires all member firms to go through a rigorous process of self-analysis on a regular basis. Moreover, the analysis must not only take place; it must have consequences. Firms should focus on the 20% and get rid of the other 80% of their operations. Doing this analysis constantly leads to splits in operating companies, the creation of new focused factories for specialized products where there was but one unit before. The pursuit of the benefits of specialization, in other words, leads to the diversification of the firm.

The advantage of pursuing specialization in this way—the aim is always to find a particular component product with a very competitive functionality in the products of the end user—is that it drives efficiency in production to very extreme levels. At the same time, in Smithian fashion, ITW believes that specialization focuses the mind and fosters innovation. The very extreme risk that comes with the specialized focus is also an incentive for continuous improvement and technological innovation. Member firms are constantly embracing specialization and greater risk, but they can rely on horizontal information and tech exchange among the independent units (most of the general managers and engineers have worked together in the past at some historically common ancestral ITW company). Also, each ITW member company pays an annual fee for unlimited access to the corporate tech center. Most use it on a regular basis. So, like an industrial district, ITW companies are very flexible and specialized, and endure a lot of risk that comes from extreme specialization. But they also rely on an exoskeleton of open exchange and corporate tech support within the corporate holding that makes it easier to deal with the risk.

An alternative pattern of large firm balancing of specialization and diversification is pursued by Emerson Electric. In this case, the radical autonomy and specialization of the ITW operating units does not exist. Instead, products are divided into various special, but vertically and horizontally related, divisions. Performance of the individual specialties is reviewed on a regular basis by management teams composed of elements from within the specialized unit and superordinate managers responsible for the division. These regular joint review sessions evaluate current performance, identify future goals for the division, and specify ways for the local unit to access the resources (technological, organizational, and financial) that it will need to achieve the goals. In the process, resources within and across the company are identified, as are potential resources outside the company. The evaluation teams need to systematically benchmark unit and divisional competitors to ensure that goal setting realistically locates Emerson units as market leaders. Through this process of regular joint review and goal setting, the interests and value-creating capacities of the specialized unit are identified and honed while at the same time those capacities are aligned with strengths and potential elsewhere in the corporation (Knight and Dyer 2005).

Thus, in contrast to ITW's formalized 80/20 procedure performed within an individual operating unit, Emerson encourages transparency and improvement through the confrontation of levels of corporate expertise and responsibility in the form of strategic evaluation teams. Both companies share, however, a concern for the value of specialization and the need to use diversification as a risk-balancing and knowledge-leveraging mechanism within the company and across the supply chain.

Smaller specialized companies also diversify to balance risk and leverage knowledge. The German high-quality hand tool manufacturer mentioned above did both in moving into precision machining. Mechanisms for balancing specialization and diversification in small firms are frequently much less formal than those in larger organizations. Rather than impose upon themselves a formal review, as in the case of ITW or Emerson, smaller firms are more likely to structure their organizations in ways that create confrontations among functions that engender collective reflection on firm strategy. Family owners, for example, involve themselves in the daily activities of production and order fulfillment at the same time that they devolve accountability for the success of projects to teams of engineers and skilled workers. Boundaries between engineering and production and between management and shop-floor worker are blurred through the creation of multifunctional design teams and through the devolution of cost-accounting responsibilities into production teams. By blending functions and responsibilities in this way, stakeholders are created who not only have an interest in the success of the firm, but also have repeated occasion to collectively reflect on the firm's fortunes: How well are the projects working out? Are orders being renewed? What opportunities appear to be within the firm's reach, technically? What kinds of capacities could be acquired?

Successful small supplier firms have been able to create these kinds of internal conversations among functions and stakeholders in ways that effectively balance specialization and diversification. Frequently, the creation of such arrangements involves the invention of new roles within the firm. One deep stamping firm in western Michigan (where there is cluster of family-owned stamping firms) created a special category of toolmaker that involved the integration of toolmakers into both design and production teams. Becoming an information broker and monitor within the firm could in this way become a career goal. Another German manufacturer of conveyer chains for machinery encouraged its works council to become more familiar with the firm's overall budget so that it could participate more effectively in internal discussions of cost reduction and organizational optimization. In both cases, the idea behind the idea was to create a range of actors with cross-functional knowledge of the firm who could participate in strategic discussion about firm performance with management. In small firms with little hierarchy, cross-functional role definitions can facilitate processes of monitoring and learning that are crucial to managing a balance between specialization and diversification.

Though the creation of internal self-evaluation arrangements within small firms are often informal, it is interesting to note that they often emerge in response to the imposition by customers of formal auditing procedures, or through a firm's effort to become certified within the more deliberative and self-revising ISO series of quality standards (e.g., ISO 9000). Audit's by (often larger) customers push suppliers to have answers to questions about where their costs come from and how the company intends to solve specific technical or organizational problems that the contract with the customer generates. Companies create the new roles and fashion cross-functional exchanges, at least in part, in order to be able to effectively respond to such questions. Similarly, in order to achieve ISO accreditation, firms must create procedures to attend to quality issues throughout the entire production process. Roles on the shop floor must be altered in ways that specifically involve the generation of information that will be shared across the firm. The point here is that the imposition or diffusion of certain forms of formalized evaluation procedures originating outside the firm has stimulated the rearrangement of relations within small firms in ways that systematically foster cross-functional self-examination.

Finally, the need to balance specialization and diversification under the conditions of SCC has also led smaller companies into interesting forms of cross-firm collaboration and coordination. This has been especially true in Europe. In Germany, for example, many smaller specialist producers of component products, and even industrial machines, have entered into formal arrangements with closely aligned competitors to both gain leverage in design and development areas and develop the capacities to take advantage of the gains that increasing development capability produces. A group of independent, family-owned, specialized

German precision spring and stamped metal manufacturers, for example, have formed a holding company that creates an architecture above the member firms that both rationalizes the relations among the member specialties (eliminating redundancy in capacity within the group and consolidating strengths in individually specialized members) while at the same time providing for know-how transfer within the group. Much like Emerson Electric, member firms systematically dialogue with representatives of the holding (managers from other member firms) to discuss individual strengths and identify future goals for the unit in the context of the overall capabilities within the group. Specialties are in this way refined and improved and possibilities for innovation are quickly identified. Generalizable discoveries, moreover, are quickly diffused across group members.[8]

Interestingly, in Germany it is possible, in the form of a Gesellschaft mit beschränkter Haftung (GmbH), for small family-owned specialized producers to unite within a property structure that creates a single governing entity that preserves claims to assets and returns of each of the individual participating entities. Thus, these internally specialized GmbH holdings have the character of a small property alliance—more cohesive and unified than a specialization cartel, but less unitary than a proper merger of companies and assets. Homologous developments have been identified in Italian industrial districts, where large groups of small specialist producers have begun to form to balance the demands of specialization and diversification in the current context (see Chapter 5). Such arrangements are more difficult, apparently, to construct in the American context. As a result, small firms either limit the extent to which they diversify, or they seek to become part of larger more diversified groups (if not always groups as large as ITW or Emerson). But in the latter case, the firm owner often loses its autonomy as an actor within the process. Ownership is dissolved into unit management.

4.5. CONCLUSION

This chapter has outlined the way that the general global trend toward vertical disintegration in manufacturing has affected customer–supplier relations on the one hand, and the strategic behavior of supplier firms, on the other. With respect to customer–supplier relations, the aim was to outline the range of typical relations that can be found in supply chains and to identify one type, SCC, that is emerging as the modal form of relation. The section on firm strategies emphasized the need for firms to balance the advantages and disadvantages of specialization and diversification in the current highly dynamic environment of SCC. Chapter 5 will turn to the internal and spatial governance challenges that these developments pose to firms and regions. It will, in particular, explore the implications that the emergence and diffusion of formal mechanisms for self-evaluation have for firm and organizational flexibility and governance.

---

[8] Such arrangements also facilitate the globalization of such specialized firms (see Chapter 5).

5

Interfirm Relations in Global Manufacturing: Disintegrated Production and Its Globalization

This chapter[1] extends and contextualizes the examination of the trend toward vertical disintegration outlined in Chapter 4. On the one hand, it locates the problem of vertical disintegration historically and outlines the way in which scholarly analysis of disintegrated production systems has evolved. On the other hand, the chapter also places the trend toward vertical disintegration in a global context, examining the dispersal of value chains and the impact of spatial dispersal on firm and regional strategies in developed and developing countries. The analysis is divided into three parts. Section 5.1 discusses the historical emergence of clustered, flexible, and/or vertically disintegrated production (hereafter: disintegrated production) since the 1980s. It contrasts disintegrated production with production within hierarchical, vertically integrated Fordist/Chandlerian firms, arguing that the former has undermined the latter over the past thirty years, both in scholarly discussion and to a large extent in the practical orientations of the actors themselves. Two related but distinct variants of disintegrated production are presented: the industrial district/local production system (ID/LPS) model and the lean production/collaborative supply chain (LP/CSC) model.

Section 5.2 addresses the globalization of disintegrated production. It examines the strengths and weaknesses of the modularity/contract manufacturing (M/CM) approach to transnational supply chains, and then goes on to contrast these with alternative forms of internationalization by multinational customer and supplier firms. Just as the disintegration of production was seen to undermine hierarchy within and between firms in Section 5.1, here the global dispersal of production appears to be gradually undermining old hierarchies between developed and developing regions. Recomposable hierarchy, collaboration, and mutual exchange increasingly shape interactions between the two types of manufacturing regions.

[1] This chapter was written jointly with Jonathan Zeitlin. In slightly altered form, it is forthcoming in Morgan et al. (2010). I thank Jonathan for allowing me to use our joint written work here.

The subjects of Sections 5.1 and 5.2 can usefully be thought of as historically sequential: Vertical disintegration and regionalization occurred prior to extensive globalization of production. Today, however, the analytical distinction between the two has become less sharp as different systems of decentralized producer relations increasingly interact and interpenetrate in ways that generate their own distinctive dynamic. This is particularly true of small- and medium-sized firms (SMEs). Section 5.3 analyzes interactions between production in developed and developing regions, together with the evolution of SME strategies in high-wage regions in response to the resulting challenges and opportunities.

5.1. MANUFACTURING DISINTEGRATION: PERMANENT VOLATILITY, THE CRISIS OF FORDIST/ CHANDLERIAN ORGANIZATION, INDUSTRIAL DISTRICTS, AND LEAN PRODUCTION

Much of the recent literature on interfirm relations and disintegrated production in manufacturing dates back to discussions that began in the 1980s about the crisis of the vertically integrated firm (Piore and Sabel 1984; Lipietz 1987; Harvey 1989; Harrison 1994; Storper 1997). At that time, both actors and observers perceived that the environment in core sectors of manufacturing in advanced industrial economies had become distinctly more volatile and uncertain. Many factors were advanced to account for this qualitative transformation: macroeconomic destabilization, shortening product cycles, accelerating technological change, the differentiation of consumer taste, the intensification of competition, and the globalization of product markets. There is no consensus on what separates symptom from the cause in this transformation. But all arrows point in the same direction: toward the conclusion that producers confront a permanent and ineradicable challenge of increased environmental volatility and uncertainty.

These new environmental conditions have had organizational and strategic consequences for producers. At the most abstract level, debate since the 1980s points to a shift between two opposed ideal types: from the vertically integrated "Fordist" or "Chandlerian" firm to decentralized, clustered, networked, lean, flexibly specialized, and/or recombinatory producers. The former characterizes the dominant model of organization and practice prior to the onset of new environmental conditions; the latter the organizational forms and practices that have proved most successful in the new environment. Pervasive environmental volatility and uncertainty rewards continuous innovation. Competition elevates production quality and cost-reduction capability to the fore. Flexible and specialized (disintegrated) producers, engaged in ever-shifting collaborative and market exchanges, flourish under these conditions while hierarchical and vertically integrated producers flounder. Put in a more evolutionary idiom, competition from recombinant coalitions of independent specialists gradually drives out firms seeking to integrate those specialties within their own operations.

Disintegrated production emerged along two main pathways during this historical transition. First, vertically integrated producers disintegrated their operations, focusing on core competences and shifting production operations and component design processes out to suppliers (Sabel 1989; Helper 1991*a*, 1991*b*; Storper 1997). Second, disintegrated districts and clusters of specialized, cooperative small- and medium-sized producers, both old (the Third Italy, Baden-Württemberg, Jutland) and new (Silicon Valley), became strikingly competitive in world markets (Saxenian 1994; Herrigel 1996; Kristensen and Sabel 1997; Kenney 2000; Lüthje 2001; Zeitlin 2007).

Before proceeding further with this analysis, however, a few methodological observations are in order. First, this "transition" narrative cannot be taken as a reliable empirical guide to understanding historical developments (though it is remarkably prevalent as a meme in the literature). Practices, strategies, and organizational forms supposedly characteristic of the "new" environment could be found well before that environment emerged. The same is true of elements of the "older" practices and organizational forms in the present (Sabel and Zeitlin 1985, 1997, 2004; Herrigel 2009). The movement in the last thirty years is much clearer in the analytical literature than in practice. There is much empirical evidence showing that large manufacturing firms across a wide range of sectors have disintegrated since the 1970s (Helper 1991; Abraham and Taylor 1996; Lorenzoni and Lipparini 1999; Essletzbichler 2003). There is even more evidence that conglomerate forms have broken themselves up during the same time period (Davis et al. 1994; Zenger and Hesterly 1997; Budros 2002; Rajan and Wulf 2003). But there is also significant variation within sectors. For example, large Japanese and Korean consumer electronics companies are much more vertically integrated than their American or European counterparts (Berger 2005; Sturgeon 2006). Conglomerate forms continue to prosper in the developing world where financial systems are less developed, as for example in the case of the Indian Tata Group (Acemoglu et al. 2007). Many regions of specialized producers continue to flourish, such as Silicon Valley, or a variety of Italian industrial districts. But other specialized regions such Prato, Route 128, or the Ruhr have struggled or declined (Grabher 1993*a*; Saxenian 1994; Ottati 1996). Moreover, none of these regions emerged out of whole cloth, and many have histories that go back well into the eighteenth or nineteenth centuries (Herrigel 1996; Sabel and Zeitlin 1997; Zeitlin 2007). Finally, even though there is nothing about any particular national institutional system that prevents the emergence of successful disintegrated or Fordist production, both polar organizational forms allow for significant variation, both by sector and by national economy (Chandler 1990; Herrigel 1996; Storper and Salais 1997; Zeitlin 2007; Herrigel 2009).

Thus, the analytical types presented in this section are stylizations. They highlight the distinctive features of contemporary disintegrated interfirm practices. But they are by no means fictitious or imaginary, since much ethnographic evidence suggests that they inform the dominant orientations of firms and other economic actors about the nature of the environment and the organizational forms regarded as normal or paradigmatic.[2] But such orientations should not be confused with the actual array of practices "on the ground." The Fordist/Chandlerian firm and the contrasting model of disintegrated production should be understood as orientations guiding (but not determining) the actions of firms and other actors. Practice itself is much more diverse, because actors themselves are frequently aware of both the complex dependence of forms of economic organization on multiple background conditions, and the possibility of sudden, unanticipated shifts in those conditions. Hence, they often seek to avoid definitive choices between polar alternatives and/or to anticipate in their forms of economic organization the need for future reconstruction in the face of changed circumstances. Actual disintegrated production is thus dramatically heterogeneous, both institutionally and strategically. Moreover, all the various configurations of disintegrated firms must reproduce themselves over time. They encounter challenges, suffer from internal disputes, and many are not able to reproduce their success. The contingency of success and the significance of appropriate governance structures for enduring reproduction should be a core focus of any analysis of disintegrated production (Zeitlin 2007).

With these caveats in mind, the aim of this section is, first, to present the basic *orienting* contrast between the Fordist/Chandlerian and disintegrated types of manufacturing organization. The primary focus will be on the shifting boundaries of the division of labor in production: the organizational location of design, development, component manufacturing, and assembly. Having established this basic contrast, we then go on to outline the two most common variants of disintegrated production: the ID/LPS model and the LP/CSC model. As we will see in Section 5.3, these two variants increasingly overlap in actual manufacturing practice. But the two forms remain distinct ways of conceptualizing disintegrated flexibility in production. It is thus useful to draw out the contrast between the two at the outset.

5.1.1. Fordist/Chandlerian Versus Disintegrated Manufacturing

The archetypical Fordist/Chandlerian firm was developed for mass production of standardized final goods. Its organization revolved around a logic of hierarchy, role specialization, and control: Product development and design were strictly separated from manufacturing, while within manufacturing itself conception was separated from the execution of particular tasks. In order to achieve economies of scale, ensure stability of supply, and maximize throughput, firms vertically integrated their operations. Automobile producers in the United States and Europe, for example, typically produced 50–80% of value added inside the firm (Kwon 2005). Resort to outside suppliers generally involved purchase of

---

[2] For a fuller theoretical discussion of this point, see Sabel and Zeitlin (1997, pp. 29–33).

lower value-added parts, specialized equipment (e.g., capital goods such as machine tools), or capacity subcontracting where the blueprints for specific articles were bid out on a short-term basis when in-house facilities for making these items were overstretched. Hierarchy pervaded the chain of development and production. Roles throughout the division of labor were rigidly circumscribed. Authority and leverage were used to control the flow of knowledge and material resources through the production process.[3]

These principles became vulnerable in the new volatile environment because they created rigidity: hierarchy and role specialization undercut communication across locations in the division of labor. A good illustration of how these core Fordist/Chandlerian principles could become quite cumbersome in practice is the product development process in manufacturing. Product life cycles in automobiles during the three decades after World War II, to take a quintessential example, could be as long as ten years or more. Isolated designers developed new models and "threw designs over the wall" to their comparably isolated manufacturing colleagues. Problems encountered with the designs, if discovered, delayed their roll out significantly as manufacturing had to wait for the designers (or its own engineers) to come up with something that could be produced.

The organization of manufacturing itself further exacerbated these delays. Authority ran through layers of management, while shop-floor worker input was de-emphasized. Problems in the flow of production had to be identified from above, and solutions introduced similarly. This occurred again, and again, throughout virtually all the myriad linked component processes and manufacturing stages in complex technologies. Such intra-firm arrangements made the redesign of products, recomposition of manufacturing processes, and reallocation of jobs extremely cumbersome. Change was costly and took a very long time. Yet (roughly), by the beginning of the 1980s, redesign, recomposition, and reallocation were becoming constant and increasingly inescapable for producers. A mismatch existed between the orienting principles of the hierarchical, pillarized, vertically integrated organization and the volatile, unpredictable, and rapidly changing character of the competitive environment.

By contrast, beginning in the 1980s, observers noticed that smaller, more specialized, and/or less bureaucratic organizations showed remarkable flexibility and capacity for innovation in this volatile environment. Observation of successful cases gradually began to generate an alternative set of orienting principles for manufacturing organization. The successful alternative groupings of producers reversed the Fordist/Chandlerian emphasis on the separation of design and manufacture and conception and execution. Less organizational hierarchy and less specialization in the division of labor forced design and manufacturing to collaborate in new product development (Clark and Fujimoto 1991; Clark and Wheelwright 1994). Teams or groups of employees with different functional skills

---

[3] For an analysis of these organizational forms and how they are created from a perspective deeply informed by pragmatist action theory, see Simon (1953).

emerged as core suborganizational units (Schumann et al. 1994; Kochan et al. 1997; Osterman 1999; Appelbaum et al. 2000; Helper et al. 2000). They allowed designers and engineers to solicit the input of manufacturing managers and even generally skilled workers when changes in production were required. Such interaction created greater flexibility and helped shorten product development cycles. In many cases, extensive labor involvement in teams created a form of stakeholderism that fostered internal experimentation and risk taking (Sabel 2005*b*; Doellgast and Greer 2007; Herrigel 2008; Kristensen and Lilja 2009).

These producers were much less vertically integrated than their Fordist/Chandlerian counterparts. Firms or production units specialized on particular technologies and aspects of development and manufacture. They relied on the complementary inputs of other specialists to offer a complete product to their customers. Collaboration across production unit boundaries proved a competitive advantage. Producers benefited from the market and technological knowledge of neighboring specialists. They also did not have to carry the costs in manpower and equipment required to produce such know-how (Sabel 1989; Milgrom and Roberts 1990; Storper 1997; Powell 2001). *Embeddedness* of specialists in myriad repeated exchanges with complementary partners spread the practice as well as the cost of innovation across the networks (Granovetter 1985; Grabher 1993; Uzzi 1996; Uzzi 1997). This made it easier (and less costly) for firms to experiment and take risks on new products and technologies, thereby accelerating change in both areas. In addition, the continuous encounter with outside expertise created the possibility for genuinely new ways of thinking about one's own expertise. In this way, repeated interaction among specialists fostered innovation (Amin and Cohendet 2004, 2005; Maskell and Lorenzen 2004; Smith-Doerr and Powell 2004; Davis 2005; Döring and Schnellenbach 2006).

Governance was also distinctive in the new disintegrated arrangements. Whereas in the Fordist/Chandlerian system, hierarchy and market tended to exhaust the mechanisms governing interpositional and interfirm relations, disintegrated production tended to be governed by a wider array of intermediate forms. Some of these intermediate forms could be quite formal and institutionalized, as in joint ventures, product development projects, development consortia, or supplier upgrading alliances. But in other cases, non-market and non-hierarchical relations among firms were governed either by explicit rules or by informal understandings of trust and mutual purpose. Through a wide array of specific exoskeletal institutional arrangements, these latter governance structures regulated a balance between competition and cooperation among specialists and thereby allowed for (even encouraged) continuous organizational recomposition (Sabel 1989; Grabher and Powell 2004).

In sum, the alternative disintegrated networks of producers avoided the pillarization of narrow role definitions and strong functional boundaries characteristic of Fordist/Chandlerian firms. Sequencing gave way to concurrency in product development and production. Provisional, revisable roles replaced rigidly specialized ones and collectively shared knowledge replaced hierarchical control and fragmentation. Indeed, in this disintegrated context, governance by the polar mechanisms of hierarchy and market gave way to a variety of intermediate mechanisms.

There is widespread agreement in the literature that current conditions are more congenial to the alternative vertically disintegrated, flexible, and networked forms of organization than to old-style hierarchical Fordist/Chandlerian forms. This does not mean that firms have completely abandoned ambitions toward hierarchy, authority, or control. Such powers are relinquished reluctantly, and opportunities to obtain them rarely foregone. Nor have the price mechanism and arm's-length contracting disappeared. The argument is not that such relations or mechanisms no longer exist in the current environment, but rather that hierarchical, role specialized, and vertically integrated organizations are less able to negotiate volatile, uncertain industrial environments than those based on more horizontal, flexible, and decentralized arrangements. There is still considerable debate, as we shall see, about the role of authority, control, hierarchy, and market relations within the alternative more disintegrated interfirm arrangements.

This distinction between the logic of orienting principles and the logic of practice accounts for much of the confusion in academic debates (visible particularly during the 1980s and early 1990s) (Wood 1989; Amin and Robins 1990; Harrison 1994). It also accounts for the peculiar character of the aggregate quantitative literature that has attempted to measure vertical disintegration, collaboration, and the flattening of hierarchies across entire industries or even the entire manufacturing sector. Typically, such studies find that the results, while pointing in the direction of disintegration, are mixed. Vertical disintegration has increased, but integration has not disappeared. Collaboration is diffusing, but arm's-length competition continues to exist (Helper and Sako 1995; Fieten et al. 1997; Helper and Sako 1998). Case-study research tends to show the same thing (Herrigel 2004; Whitford and Zeitlin 2004; Berger 2005; Herrigel and Wittke 2005; Whitford 2006). This should not be surprising. The extreme claims for either pole depended on specific environmental conditions that are not found uniformly in all realms of practice. Actors do not enact orientations blindly; rather they are malleable frameworks or points of reference that actors adapt and recompose as they seek to resolve successive problems in their factories and markets. Moreover, as the discussion of sustained contingent collaboration (SCC) in Chapter 4 showed, many producers pursuing collaborative strategies in uncertain environments systematically enter over time into a heterogeneous array of relations (collaborative, arm's-length, in-house production, capacity subcontracting, etc.), in an effort to avoid becoming entrapped in local, bilateral ties, while scanning the horizon of potential partners for new opportunities for innovation and cost reduction (Helper et al. 2000; Herrigel and Wittke 2005; Sabel 2005).

Predictably, all of this complexity has produced a significant skeptical literature (Lovering 1999; MacLeod 2001; Martin and Sunley 2003; Gertler 2003; Wolfe and Gertler 2004; Martin and Sunley 2006). Even here, however, it is important to recognize that a bar has been crossed since the 1980s. Skepticism is no longer directed at the viability of disintegrated forms of interfirm organization in relation to the Fordist/Chandlerian firm. Instead, skeptics focus on the limits of the diffusion, or the specific conditionality, of the flexible disintegrated forms. Do the alternative forms appear spontaneously and/or inevitably? Are all variants of decentralized organization equally successful? Is it possible to create successful interfirm practices everywhere? Such questions animate debate and make for a very robust research program.

5.1.2. Varieties of Disintegrated Production

Next, however, the alternative disintegrated principles of production need to be parsed a bit more carefully. Though as a generic matter, all forms of flexible disintegrated production share the above-mentioned qualities, there are a wide range of variants of flexible organization identified in the literature (Grabher and Powell 2004; Smith-Doerr and Powell 2004). Within manufacturing, two distinct models of disintegration and flexibility emerged in the wake of the crisis of the Fordist/Chandlerian firm. As with the principles of disintegrated production in general, each of the alternative models of flexible production was rooted in empirical cases of competitive success in the face of volatility. The first is the ID/LPS model and the second is the LP/CSC model. Today, the two models increasingly interpenetrate, but they have distinct origins, both in academic discussion and empirical experience.

The ID/LPS model received a great deal of initial attention in public debate (Brusco 1982; Piore and Sabel 1984; Brusco and Righi 1989; Powell 1990; Pyke et al. 1990). This was surely related to the fact that it very nearly inverts the Fordist/Chandlerian model. In place of giant, hierarchical, integrated firms, industrial districts are geographically localized clusters of small- and medium-sized producers, interrelated by complementary and ever-recombining specialties. Actually existing industrial districts vary widely, and there is significant conceptual debate about how to define them (Whitford 2001; Zeitlin 2007). At one end of the spectrum, we find extremely specialized regions where clusters of interrelated firms produce a single type of product, for example, pottery, bicycles, cutlery, woven textiles, shoes, packaging machinery, etc. At the other end, the clusters are less specialized on particular end products. In such systems, complementary specialists generate a broad and changing array of finished goods and intermediate components, such as industrial machinery, motor vehicles, semiconductors, consumer electronics, software, or biotechnology products (Crouch et al. 2001, 2004).

Whether specialized or diversified in industrial composition, however, the distinctive features of the ID/LPS model, at least initially, were the fluidity of roles among producers and spatial agglomeration. Fluidity or malleability of producer roles within the value chain in ID/LPS regions made for a distinctive mixture of collaboration and competition. Producers played multiple roles (customer, supplier, collaborator, arm's-length price taker, competitor, etc.) in multiple contracts both at the same time and over time. This made it difficult to establish consistent relational hierarchies: assembler, developer, and coordinator roles were unstable, provisional, shifting, and often simply enacted jointly. The spatial element within successful disintegrated regional economies involved, at one level, intense and frequent face-to-face exchange and common cultural understandings among producers. At another level, more importantly, sharing a common geographic space facilitated the creation of a shared extra-firm infrastructure for the provision of collective goods: institutions for training, finance, technical assistance, interest representation, dispute resolution, etc. Without such institutions (however constituted) to govern competition and cooperation, and facilitate continuous recomposition, successful collaboration within ID/LPS regions has generally proven fragile and short-lived (Storper 1997; Bellandi 2001; Crouch et al. 2001, 2004; Bellandi 2006; Zeitlin 2007; Bellandi 2009).

The LP/CSC model traces its genealogy back to the Japanese automobile industry (Cusumano 1985; Nishiguchi 1994; Sabel 1994; Fujimoto 1999). There, producers did not follow the vertically integrated path of Fordist mass production (Womack et al. 1990). Instead, the division of labor in automobile production remained disintegrated with large final assemblers, such as Toyota, directing and collaborating with extended chains of suppliers in the development and manufacture of their final products. Lean production had many striking advantages over traditional hierarchical forms of manufacturing organization. Crucially, it pioneered the radical integration of design and manufacture, known as "simultaneous engineering." Multifunctional teams of customers and suppliers designed a product and developed the techniques for its manufacture simultaneously in iterated rounds of conceptualization and experimentation. This practice radically reduced product development times and shortened product cycles. It also became possible to modify products quickly and add variety (MacDuffie and Helper 1997; Chanaron et al. 1999; Helper et al. 2000; Sako 2004).

In addition, LP/CSC pushed collaborative team organization throughout the entire supply chain (Kochan et al. 1997; Adler et al. 1999; Chanaron et al. 1999). By giving teams self-governing autonomy (their own budgets, production targets, and scheduling responsibility) and by utilizing formal mechanisms for group self-monitoring (mandatory intra-group benchmarking, local quality control, and systematic error detection), LP/CSC made it possible to simultaneously improve production quality and lower total production costs (Helper et al. 2000). In contrast to the Fordist/Chandlerian "push" logic, where production was driven by market forecasts, materials and parts ordered well in advance, and finished product placed in inventory waiting to be sold, LP/CSC followed a "pull" logic. Customer orders prompted downstream teams to mobilize their upstream counterparts, in effect pulling material through production to final assembly. By delegating responsibility for quality and work flow directly to downstream teams, lean producers radically minimized inventory, work-in-progress, waste, and redundancy throughout the production process (Hines et al. 2004).

The LP/CSC model shared many features with the ID/LPS model. Both relied on the continuous blurring of boundaries between design and manufacture and between conception and execution in production. Both were significantly disintegrated, with independent producers collaborating across firm boundaries to exploit complementarities and achieve flexibility. But LP/CSC was distinctive in a number of ways. Unlike ID/LPS, the logic of lean production focused on value chains within industries rather than spatial relations among agglomerations of producers. Although lean production networks were also regionally clustered to some extent, with just-in-time suppliers located close to assembly plants, the linkage logic was not primarily spatial. As a result, collaboration could extend beyond particular regions and continue to be governed by the logic of LP/CSC. Moreover, in classic Japanese LP/CSC interfirm relations, roles were more stable, since suppliers occupied positions in "tiers." The fluidity and ambiguity of roles among firms characteristic of the ID/LPS was much less pronounced in the initial Japanese version of LP/CSC, though even in the latter suppliers could be "promoted" to higher tiers (or demoted to lower ones) based on their relative performance in previous product cycles. Finally, LP/CSC was distinctive in that cross-boundary collaboration, both within and across firms and teams, focused not just on technology and product development, but also on cost reduction. Organizational recomposition through continuous improvement processes—benchmarking, kaizen, self-analysis in error detection, etc.—was a systematic feature of the LP/CSC model. In striking contrast to the flexibility generated by the informal mix of collaboration and competition driving the ID/LPS model, LP/CSC relied on formal procedures that forced producers to evaluate their own practices and forced them to reform in the interest of product innovation, quality improvement, error detection, and/or cost reduction (MacDuffie 1997; MacDuffie and Helper 1997; Sabel 2005*b*).

5.2. THE GLOBALIZATION OF DISINTEGRATED PRODUCTION: OFFSHORING, MULTINATIONALS, AND MULTIPLE LOGICS IN TRANSNATIONAL SUPPLY CHAINS

Soon after disintegrated production emerged in the advanced industrial economies, it began to globalize. The process began in the 1970s with lighter, simpler, labor-intensive products like garments, footwear, and some electronics, but by the late 1990s it had engulfed a wider range of industries, including heavier, more technologically complex, capital-intensive sectors, such as motor vehicles, aerospace, industrial, construction, and agricultural machinery, electrical equipment, steel, and pharmaceuticals (Fröbel et al. 1977; Feenstra 1998; Arndt and Kierzkowski 2001). Globalization both intensified and modified the process of disintegration in production. The internationalization of disintegrated production is animated by two dynamics. Though they are analytically distinct and have separate origins, these dynamics have become increasingly interconnected, with very significant consequences, as will be shown below.

One dynamic is the increasing cost pressure facing customers and suppliers in high-wage regions. Firms are constantly forced to reduce their costs, even as they maintain or even improve the quality and sophistication of their products. These contradictory pressures have driven the trend toward vertical disintegration in production, as firms focus on "core competences" and rely on specialists for everything else. The same pressures are now driving production across borders. Both customer and supplier firms are increasingly establishing production operations (or finding suitable contractors) in lower-wage environments to relieve cost pressure on their product palettes. In this way, production in low-wage environments for delivery to customers in high-wage regions can be understood as a kind of pressure-release valve (in German, a *Ventile*).

The other dynamic driving the offshoring of production is the pursuit of access to foreign markets. Lead firms move to developing countries (especially large ones like China, India, or Brazil) to serve the local market more easily—in particular by adapting designs to local needs and even developing unique products for those markets (Berggren 2003; Buckley and Ghauri 2004; Ghemawat 2007). Suppliers follow lead firms to these new production locations in order to retain their key customers. Lead firms want the reliability of veteran collaborators as they attempt to produce in offshore markets. They also want the flexibility that more global suppliers are believed to provide. Global suppliers, on this view, can draw on know-how and capacity from around the world; they can also use scale as a means of exerting leverage with their own suppliers to achieve lower costs.

Taken separately, these two dynamics generate considerable complexity in the division of labor between high- and low-wage regions. Their interaction not only generates even greater complexity, but also very surprising, and even counterintuitive results. Where globalization strategies are succeeding, production becomes more sophisticated in lower-wage environments and more secure in high-wage ones.

How this is possible will gradually become apparent as the analysis proceeds through three steps. First, it is necessary to look at the strong claims for the emergence of a new production paradigm and a new global division of labor advanced by proponents of the M/CM approach to supply chain restructuring. Their arguments for a radical break between design and manufacture and the emergence of a stable hierarchy between developed and developing regions will be shown to be sharply limited. Not only is this logic circumscribed even in those industries where actors self-consciously pursue modularity, but it does not apply to many manufacturing sectors, which continue to be characterized by "integral" rather than modular product architectures (Ulrich 1995). Second, we examine the progress of offshoring within integral architecture sectors such as motor vehicles and other complex mechanical engineering products from the perspective of firms seeking to reduce their costs. A distinctive feature of this process is the continuing interpenetration of design and manufacture throughout the supply chain. The complex dynamic between developed and developing countries that has emerged from this dimension of the offshoring process appears to be destabilizing what was once considered a stable hierarchy between developed and developing regions. A third step shows that this emergent complexity and uncertain hierarchy of relations between regions and players within the manufacturing supply chain is further exacerbated by the second driver of offshoring noted above: lead firms' efforts to enter new markets and the resultant imperative for suppliers to follow their customers. Each of these offshoring dynamics creates complex spatial and organizational allocations of competence and capacity; together they generate an intriguing multiplicity of firm strategies and resource allocation logics. The rest of this section focuses primarily on the strategies of large multinational lead firms and their suppliers. Section 5.3 considers the strategies high-wage SMEs and the regions that support them are pursuing to cope with these same pressures of globalization.

5.2.1. Separation of Design and Manufacture, Cost-Driven Disintegration, and Offshoring: The Limits of Modularity

Within the dialectic of innovation and cost reduction driving productive disintegration, it was a logical step for firms to look to offshore locations with lower labor costs as a way to achieve quick cost reductions. Much of the initial literature on transnational supply chains focused on the apparel and consumer electronics sectors, where firms seemed to have had dramatic success in leveraging offshore cost differences in production (Gereffi and Korzeniewicz 1994; Borrus et al. 2000; Lüthje et al. 2002; Sturgeon 2002; Bair 2005). Those studying the sectors claimed that a distinctive new dynamic was emerging around the possibilities for reorganizing the global division of labor in production. Indeed, several authors argued that the dynamics in these sectors pointed to the emergence of a new model for manufacturing as a whole. Call this the Modularity/Contract Manufacturing (M/CM) model (Sturgeon 2002; Garud et al. 2003; Langlois 2007).

Distinctive about the sectors in which the M/CM model was pioneered is that large lead firms drove disintegration in the division of labor while at the same time maintaining a rigid divide between design and manufacture. This eliminated the need for the collaborative and recombinatory relations characteristic of the disintegrated model described in Section 5.1.2. Relations between designing customers and manufacturing suppliers were based on a clear and extreme division of roles which, at the limit, could be governed through arm's-length market exchange. This, it was claimed, created the possibility for dramatic spatial separation of design and production. Design and value added, according to this view, tended to concentrate in high-wage environments, while manufacturing, as a low value-added activity, gravitated to locations where labor and other costs were also lower.[4]

---

[4] Though as we will see immediately, control over manufacturing operations in those regions very frequently stayed under the control of independent developed country multinationals.

The key to this strategy, particularly in electronics, was the creation of modular product architectures, based on standard technical interfaces between the overall design and its constituent components or subsystems (Baldwin and Clark 2000; Langlois 2003; Schilling 2003). By developing products with stable, codified interfaces between internal functional elements, lead firms could focus on design and hand off production of standardized components to independent suppliers. Those supplier firms (so-called contract manufacturers), in turn, were responsible for organizing production on behalf of the lead firm, seeking out the cheapest locations and coordinating the flow of components around the world (including final assembly in some cases). Such contract manufacturers worked with multiple lead design firms at the same time, filling their capacity by producing high volumes of differently designed but standardized modules in locations where labor costs were extremely low. Sturgeon's ideal type of these "modular production networks" was concentrated in what he called "product-level electronics" (televisions, computers, cell phones, personal digital assistants, etc.). But similarly sharp divisions between design and manufacture could also be observed in other sectors as well, particularly apparel, footwear, and bicycles. There, in addition to modularity (bicycles), the manufacturing process was labor-intensive and the product simple enough (apparel) to allow for the separation between design and manufacture (Ulrich et al. 1998; Gavin and Morkel 2001; Sturgeon and Lester 2001; Bair 2005; Gereffi 2005).

The M/CM perspective (Humphrey and Schmitz 2002; Bair 2005; Gereffi et al. 2005) envisages an emerging global hierarchy in which lead firms in rich countries increasingly abandon manufacturing for the exclusive control of knowledge, design, and marketing. For their part, developing regions struggle to lure footloose contract manufacturers in order to "upgrade" their infrastructures of physical and human capital, and gain access to know-how and value added that will one day permit them to generate their own contract manufacturing operations. The clear boundary between design knowledge (and brand value) on the one hand and manufacturing know-how and expertise on the other, establishes a fixed hierarchy among stages of the value chain, even as producers, regions, and economies are able to upgrade within it.

In this literature, Taiwan, Israel, and Ireland have emerged as leapfrog cases, political economies capable of springing over the barriers dividing developed and developing regions through adroit state intervention. But such barrier hopping does not change the underlying spatial logic of relative costs relating design to manufacture. Once the Taiwanese, for example, hopped over the design barrier, on this view, they began shifting their own manufacturing to contract manufacturers in lower-cost regions in China (Breznitz 2007). Design and manufacture map onto a specific conception of what it means to be developed and not yet developed. In the M/CM perspective, such hierarchy is a natural and inescapable feature of capitalism. Countries advance their position along a know-how and value hierarchy until they reach a point where it is possible to abandon manufacturing entirely.

These hierarchical lead firm/contract manufacturer arrangements have become a significant feature of global production (Feenstra 1998; Arndt and Kierzkowski 2001; Kenney and Florida 2004; Berger 2005; Gereffi 2005). There has also been significant manufacturing job loss in high-wage regions, some of which can be traced to offshoring (Bronfenbrenner and Luce 2004; Geishecker 2005; Marchant and Kumar 2005; Boulhol and Fontagne 2006; Mankiw and Swagel 2006). For all of that, however, M/CM does not seem to be becoming the dominant model for global disintegrated production as its early scholarly proponents claimed. Manufacturing and design remain mutually dependent among producers in both high- and low-wage contexts (Brusoni et al. 2001; Sabel and Zeitlin 2004; Brusoni et al. 2005; Whitford 2006; Herrigel 2009).

Regarding modularity, firms appear to be acutely aware that the separation of design from manufacturing can lead to so-called modularity traps, where irreversible commitments to a specific product architecture and set of technical interface standards results in a loss of system-level knowledge and capacity to participate in the development of the next new architecture on the part of component specialists (Chesbrough 2005; Fixon and Park 2007; Lenfle and Baldwin 2007). Thus, even within electronics, only a relatively small percentage of products have a genuinely modular character: Estimates of contract manufacturers' share of the global cost of goods sold in this sector range from 13% to 17% (Sturgeon 2002; Berger 2005). In the rest of electronics, the characteristic inter-firm collaboration of the disintegrated model plays an important role and the customer/supplier division of labor between design and manufacture is more complex. Indeed, the turbulence and rapidity of change in product markets and technologies seems to have undercut producers' capacity in these supposedly modular sectors to achieve stable codification systems (Berggren and Bengtsson 2004; Ernst 2005; Voskamp 2005). Sturgeon himself now acknowledges that "as contractors seek new sources of revenue by providing additional inputs to lead firm design and business processes, and new circuit-board assembly technologies appear on the scene . . . the hand-off of design specifications is becoming more complex and less standardized," thereby requiring "closer collaboration in the realm of product design" between customers and suppliers (Gereffi et al. 2005).

More importantly, there appear to be many sectors within manufacturing where the technical capacity of lead firms to design modular product architectures is extremely limited. This is true of many complex metalworking sectors, such as automobiles, construction machinery, agricultural equipment, and virtually the whole vast capital goods area of the machinery industry (Herrigel 2004; Whitford and Zeitlin 2004; Whitford 2006). In such "integral" architecture products (Ulrich 1995), technical subsystems interpenetrate and their interfaces cannot be easily standardized, either from model generation to model generation, or across a palette of common product offerings (MacDuffie 2007). Lead firms in these sectors typically do not seek to break products down into fixed modules defined by a one-to-one mapping between a function and the physical devices that embody it. Instead, they engage in a process of iterated codesign with component suppliers, in which complex wholes are provisionally parsed into parts whose subsequent development then suggests modifications of the initial overall design, which are then provisionally parsed again, and so on. At any given moment, suppliers may be engaged in manufacturing "black box" parts defined by the interfaces of a particular product architecture, but the most capable (and best remunerated) are also expected to assist their customers in redefining those interfaces for cost reduction and performance improvement in the next design iteration (Sabel and Zeitlin 2004).

Integral product architectures are no barrier to vertical disintegration or globalization—indeed many of the archetypical cases of disintegrated production described in Section 5.1 were found in these sectors, in both IS/LPS and LP/CSC versions. But if manufacturers of such products want to exploit the cost advantages of offshore production locations, they must do this in ways that take account of the continued indispensability of interfirm collaboration. This has led to a different offshoring dynamic and, ultimately, to a mutually dependent global division of labor between developed and developing regions.

5.2.2. Offshoring, Collaboration, and the Destabilization of Spatial Hierarchy

The offshoring process in integral-architecture manufacturing unfolded in a distinctive sequence. Initially, lead firms and their suppliers sought to purchase simple, standardized components from offshore producers. Developed country suppliers, when they were able to do so, shifted production of their mature components—parts that had already been designed and that went into aftermarket or replacement markets—to offshore locations. These were arm's-length purchases of low value-added components. Such practices resembled the old-style subcontracting of Fordist/Chandlerian firms, except that instead of procuring parts locally, firms now sought out producers in lower-wage countries. But in the more disintegrated context this kind of offshoring represented an urgent effort to relieve cost pressures. For a time, such practices suggested to some that the radical separation of design from production characteristic of the modular technologies might be applicable in these sectors as well (Humphrey 1998; Sturgeon and Florida 2004).

Unremitting cost pressures on both customer and supplier firms coupled with the inescapability of architectural integrality in product development, however, soon overwhelmed such simple arm's-length *Ventile* strategies. More complex strategies to create offshore outlets for cost reduction, involving new and collaboratively developed products, began to emerge (Dicken 2003; Ghemawat and Ghadar 2006; Frigant 2007; Jürgens 2007). The impetus came initially from powerful final assembler firms in the automobile and complex machinery industries, which insisted that their suppliers develop lower-cost offshore production capacity for new codesigned components (Berger 2004; Köhler and Gonzalez

Begega 2007).[5] Larger supplier firms dutifully shifted new and existing production capacity to lower-wage environments in order to retain their customers' business. This did not necessarily involve closing production facilities in high-wage environments. Instead, it meant the creation of new and more sophisticated supplemental capacity offshore. Indeed, many suppliers gradually realized that having a sophisticated "outlet" in a lower-wage region made it possible for them to blend home and offshore production to make lower overall bids on collaborative projects with their customers. Paradoxically, offshoring has thus enabled suppliers to solidify their market position *at home and abroad* as producers of high value-added specialized products (Herrigel 2007).

This shift in the strategic character of offshoring has initiated a dynamic process of capacity and know-how reallocation that appears to be radically redefining the division of labor between high- and low-wage regions. What is emerging is neither the radical spatial separation of design and manufacture forecast by the M/CM school, nor a traditional comparative advantage model of high value-added manufacturing in high-wage locations and lower value-added manufacturing in lower-wage locations. Instead, emergent practice increasingly blends design and manufacture capabilities and high and low value-added processes across global production locations. Different wage levels play an important but not decisive role in this new logic of competence and capacity allocation (Berger 2005).

At one level, there is still hierarchy between regions in these sectors. Product design and initial production ramp up of a component or subsystem are performed in high-wage contexts, along with especially high value-added production runs that can be efficiently automated or that have lower volumes but more value content. Once the large series process is up and running (six months/one year for complex products such as ball bearing units), it is then transplanted to the low-wage location. But at another level, this process of technology transfer has begun to undermine the very hierarchy it presupposes. The transplantation of production processes results in the diffusion of current manufacturing practice to low-wage facilities. Increasingly, the machinery park in the low-wage location converges with that in the high-wage location.[6]

A key additional point of slippage in this new division of labor is the location of development and design capacity. Again, such capacity is still mainly located in high-wage regions, with their concentration of engineering know-how and experience with the recursive integration of development and manufacture. But significant restructuring of these competences has occurred within supplier firms across existing high-wage manufacturing locations. This is easiest to see in the case of bigger multinational suppliers with broader product palettes and

---

[5] Large final assemblers often encouraged their suppliers to set up operations in lower-cost regions because they were themselves doing so with their own component production. General Motors (GM)'s Delphi and Ford's Visteon, for example, had extensive operations in Mexico and central Europe well before the two parent companies spun off their component divisions into independent companies.

[6] Much of the following material is based on interviews conducted by the author and his colleagues in the Global Components research project (www.globalcomponents.org) in the United States, Germany, Central Europe, and China between 2006 and 2008.

multiple divisions, such as the large automobile suppliers Magna, ZF, Kolbensch-midt-Pierburg, Mahle, Schaeffler, or Robert Bosch. Such firms are increasingly locating competence for the development of specific products in distinct plants in specific high-wage locations. For example, a German piston producer concentrates development capacity for different models aimed at different end users (diesel, passenger cars, commercial vehicles, etc.) in different locations (south Germany, north Germany, and France).[7] Such newly specialized locations are called "lead plants" or "centers of competence." Lead plants assume responsibility for developing and ramping up the new generation of product and production technology for their particular type of piston. They are also responsible for transferring the new product and equipment needed to manufacture it to all the low-wage production locations in which the multinational supplier operates (in the piston case, the Czech Republic, Mexico, Brazil, and China). They send know-how and provide ongoing consultation to these offshore plants to help them get up to speed on the new processes and products.

As an initial step, this division of labor places manufacturing capability in the low-wage region, while retaining development and production, in an integrated way, in more specialized high-wage locations. Significantly, however, this hierarchy is not fixed. There is a slippage, resulting from unavoidable functional spill-overs of know-how and competences to new production locations. Transferring new products and processes involves, among other things, training offshore engineers in the lead plant's own special competences in order to enable the latter to optimize production in the offshore location. The existence of a competent and increasingly experienced corps of engineers in low-wage locations also makes the process of "handing off" production more efficient and allows for its subsequent optimization. It is difficult for firms to maintain completely "headless" or "know-how-less" manufacturing-only facilities in offshore locations. Some development capacity is indispensable for the smooth operation of production.

Finally, in most cases, multiple lead plants in high-wage regions maintain relations with the same offshore production facility. Low-wage region production facilities, as a result, have become remarkably diversified, with an array of products that in high-wage locations is increasingly manufactured—at least initially—in separate locations. In the case of the German piston maker, the Brazilian, Czech, and Chinese facilities can produce nearly the entire product range manufactured in all the firm's European plants, while the Mexican facility, although less diversified than the Brazilian, Czech, and Chinese sisters, is still more diversified than any western European production site within the Multinational Corporation (MNC). In this way, benefits of productive diversity historically characteristic of plants in high-wage regions—synergies among seemingly unrelated operations, possibilities for using manufacturing techniques developed in one process on a wholly different product, etc.—are now extended and concentrated in low-wage locations.

---

[7] This example is taken from Global Components research interviews. Interviews were conducted under the promise of strict confidentiality, so the firm must remain anonymous.

5.2.3. Opening New Markets and Following the Customer: Multiple Logics, Multiple Regions, Multiple Plants, Multiple Hierarchies

The division of labor within multinational supplier firms between high-wage "lead plants" with integrated development/production capacities and modern low-wage "high-volume production" locations is one important trend shaping the globalization of disintegrated manufacturing. But it is not the only logic shaping the distribution of production and competences among plants, even within such multinational suppliers. In addition to the logic of cost reduction, the allocation of production capacity within multiproduct and multiplant firms is also driven by pursuit of proximity to customers.

MNCs operating as lead manufacturing firms in complex integral-architecture sectors, such as motor vehicles and machinery, have gradually begun to expand operations into developing regions in an effort to compete more effectively for local market share. These strategic investments have been driven both by the relative saturation of developed country markets and by the rapid emergence of technologically sophisticated demand in developing economies such as Brazil, India, and China, as well as newly capitalist regions such as Central and Eastern Europe (Humphrey 1990; Domanski et al. 2007; Krzywdzinski 2007). Many lead firms in these sectors (e.g., Ford, Caterpillar, John Deere, Volkswagen (VW), BMW, Hyundai, Toyota, PSA, Volvo) had entered such markets in the past following a product life-cycle model (Wells 1972): that is, offering older or mature versions of products developed for and long produced in their home regions. But increasingly they and many other major producers recognize the need to develop products more specifically adapted to the particular needs and demands of emerging market users. This involves the creation of significant production capacity in developing regions, as well as the transfer of technological know-how to local subsidiaries there. Manufacturing MNCs also increasingly need to upgrade the skills and technical capacities of their personnel in developing country locations (Buckley and Ghauri 2004; Depner and Dewald 2004; Ivarsson and Alvstam 2005; Ghemawat 2007).

Lead firm MNCs cannot pursue these globalization strategies without the collaboration of their suppliers. The increasing disintegration of production makes the expertise of home country suppliers indispensable for the competitiveness of their customers. Such expertise, moreover, is not immediately available among indigenous suppliers in developing regions, even rapidly growing ones like India or China. Thus, multinational customer firms have encouraged their suppliers to globalize along with them (Depner and Bathelt 2003; Coe et al. 2004; Depner and Dewald 2004; Voelzkow 2007).

In this way, globalization literally involves the transfer of the collaborative logic of disintegrated production governing interfirm exchanges in developed regions into developing country contexts. This creates a distinct logic of globalization for suppliers, quite different from the cost-reduction logic described in Section 5.2.2. This alternative logic drives multinational producers to enhance the activities of existing offshore operations and/or to add complementary capacity to them in an effort to satisfy the local demands of their customers. Lead firms, for example, find that they can expand capacities and competences in their existing offshore manufacturing operations to service offshore markets as well as to reduce costs in their own home market.[8]

The result is that multiple global divisions of labor are superimposed on the global allocation of work among plant locations within multinational customer and supplier firms. Low-wage production locations are allocated high-volume work across a broad spectrum of the mother firm's product palette, leading them to become highly diversified. Customer demands for local supply likewise tend to expand their production capabilities. In addition to high-volume work, these plants are increasingly able to produce in shorter series and accommodate special requests from their customers. The development capacity that such facilities acquire in order to facilitate the handoff of manufacturing operations from high-wage regions, then becomes extremely valuable in adapting other products to local customer needs.

A similar logic is affecting the structure and capabilities of lead plants in high-wage regions. Each lead plant, at a minimum, has the capacity to develop and ramp up a specific product or range of products to high-volume manufacture (e.g., small pistons for passenger cars). Development and production is highly integrated in such plants, which can engage in experimental, prototype production as well as very small series, customized, and batch-type operations. They also run highly automated high-volume production lines, where the automation plays a significant role in the creation of product value. At the same time, in unsystematic ways, these lead plants retain a more diverse set of competences in order to accommodate local customer demands for the full palette of component types. Thus, for example, a lead plant for small pistons in France may retain some production capacity for larger pistons to accommodate demand from big local customers for the latter. Since the small-piston lead plant has no local development competence for large pistons, it effectively allocates control over some of its own local production capacity to another lead plant (the one with development competence for large pistons). The small-piston plant's non-core large-piston production is then supervised and serviced by the engineers and developers from the lead plant for large pistons. Thus, in order to accommodate the contradictory and unpredictable demands of new product development, fluctuating series size, and customer demands, lead plants in high-wage regions, despite extensive offshoring and concentration on core competences, are also becoming remarkably diversified.[9]

---

[8] Thus, the Audi engine plant in Győr, Hungary, originally established as a low-cost manufacturing location sending engines back to the home assembly facility in Ingolstadt and to sister company VW's assembly plant in Wolfsburg, Germany, has developed new foreign assembly operations to service other local plants (e.g., the Octavia and Taureg assembly works in Mlada Boleslav, Czech Republic, and Bratislava, Slovakia, respectively).

[9] There are of course limits to such diversification: lead plants do not manufacture wholly different products from other divisions of a large firm; thus piston plants do not produce fuel-injection systems.

The image that emerges from this stylized description of the interaction of different logics of global production allocation (cost reduction and new market entry/follow the customer) is that of a delicate multiregional balancing game. Efforts to concentrate technological competence in particular plants, the continuous pursuit of cost reduction, the desire to maximize production runs while accommodating increasing product variety, and the need to respond to often contradictory customer pressures (to produce offshore and produce locally) are all constantly in play and combined in different ways.

The result of these logics and their interaction is to erode rigid hierarchies between developed and developing regions. Competences may be formally concentrated, yet they inevitably spill over and bleed out from one location to another. Capacity is allocated and reallocated, separated and recombined. Hierarchy is not eliminated: there are still "leaders" and "followers" or "supporters" within the intra- and interfirm division of labor. But such hierarchies are now increasingly recomposable, with the same actors occupying different roles in different contexts ("lead plants" both lead and follow). As a result, the major difference between high- and low-wage locations is that the former have larger concentrations of development competence and deeper integration between design, engineering, and production in particular specialized areas. But both types of location exhibit growing integration between development and production, and both operate in support relations with other facilities with greater competence in particular areas. As development competence bleeds out into emergent market locations, high-wage locations are likely to receive know-how from low-wage locations about production areas outside their own core competences. Even now, high-wage plants regularly receive some capacity-balancing work from low-wage sister plants running at full capacity, which are unable completely to fulfill their own customers' orders. In this model, producers and firms do not become "developed" by abandoning manufacturing. Rather, development involves the continuous capacity to integrate and reintegrate design and manufacturing within and across firm and unit boundaries in an environment characterized by chronic uncertainty and urgent pressures for innovation and cost reduction.

5.3. COPING WITH DISINTEGRATED PRODUCTION ON A GLOBAL SCALE: SMEs AND HIGH-WAGE REGIONS

An important undercurrent in this discussion of multiple globalization logics is that, apart from the early enthusiasm for modularity/contract manufacture, none of these logics of the globalization of disintegrated production involve or foresee the elimination of manufacture within high-wage regions. The continued existence of valuable expertise and human capital, proximity to customers, needs for short-term flexibility in the global allocation of capacity within MNCs—all make manufacturing "sticky" in the developed world (Markusen 1996). Regardless of where production and design occur, they retain many of the features of disintegrated production analyzed in Section 5.1. MNC lead firms and large suppliers collaborate on design and manufacture around the world, but they also collaborate with more locally based small- and medium-sized suppliers in each of the regions in which they operate. Uncertainty and the imperatives of innovation and cost reduction exert a centrifugal disintegrating pressure on the division of labor in production both globally and locally. This section focuses on the strategies that SMEs in high-wage regions and the local institutions that govern their relations have adopted to cope with the pressures of globalization.

The activities of MNCs described in Section 5.2 generate a particular kind of market environment for SMEs in high-wage regions. Innovation and cost-reduction capability are the coin of the realm in disintegrated production. Specialized SME suppliers can take advantage of productive disintegration when they are able to bring know-how in these areas to the table. SMEs must be able to contribute value in larger processes of interfirm collaboration. They also must be highly flexible, quick-response producers, capable of meeting short lead times (between finalization of order and delivery of finished parts). Finally, where MNC lead firms and the lead plants of MNC suppliers are interweaving various products in various series sizes from various locations across their production facilities, SME suppliers to these firms must be able to produce a mixture of components in fluctuating volumes. These general market characteristics have given rise to three developments among high-wage SMEs and regional governance institutions that modify the model of disintegrated production outlined in Section 5.1.

5.3.1. Interpenetration of Industrial District/Local Production System and Lean Production/Collaborative Supply Chain Models

With the growing exposure to global logics of competition, innovation, cost reduction, and capacity allocation, the principles of ID/LPS and LP/CSC have begun increasingly to interpenetrate. Most strikingly, the role fluidity and ambiguity characteristic of ID/LPS has begun to mix with the formal self-reflection and attention to both product innovation and cost reduction of LP/SCS (Sabel 2005; Herrigel 2009). The ability to perform a variety of roles has become an indispensible competitive competence within disintegrated production. Even in sectors where tiering still exists—for example, automobiles and complex industrial machinery—producers within the supply chain increasingly occupy a variety of positions over time. Indeed, in entering into a relationship, neither the customer nor the supplier can have a clear idea of how the specific content of their tie will evolve. Will it be an intimate collaboration? Will collaboration fail and the customer ask for some other more arm's-length service? Will other collaborators turn out to be necessary for the successful construction of a component system? Will the initial supplier lead the collaboration, or will the new supplier do so, or will the customer direct it all? These things are increasingly difficult to predict *ex ante*. The character of a tie with even a single customer can vary substantially over time and a series of discrete contracts. As a result, both customers and suppliers must be prepared to play a variety of roles (Kristensen 2008*a*, 2008*b*; Kristensen et al. 2008; Herrigel 2009). This is a core practice in the ID/LPS model of disintegrated production, but marks a departure from the originally more hierarchical LP/CSC model.

At the same time, all collaborators, regardless of their role, find themselves under continuous pressure to reduce their costs and improve the quality and content of their products and services. For this, it is widely recognized that the formal mechanisms of self-observation (kaizen, five-why error detection analysis, benchmarking, etc.) associated with the LP/CSC model of disintegrated production have become indispensable (MacDuffie 1997; Hines et al. 2004; Sabel 2005*b*). Many large customer firms insist that their suppliers develop these capabilities (MacDuffie and Helper 1997; Sako 2004). Indeed, many large customer firms have developed extensive internal supplier development organizations to teach their suppliers how to deploy these mechanisms of self-analysis (SEA 2008). The dissemination of these lean practices has also become an important goal of public institutions in many industrial clusters (Herrigel 2004; Whitford and Zeitlin 2004; Kristensen 2008). Such formal mechanisms facilitate cooperation and help ensure that its trajectory will be cost-effective. These key practices of the LP/CSC model have begun to diffuse broadly, even among SME specialists within industrial districts and regional clusters where they were never central (Fieten et al. 1997; Whitford 2006). Thus, for example, collective benchmarking and training in quality assurance standards and related techniques have been among the most widely demanded services in Italian industrial districts over the past decade (Sabel 2003; Zeitlin 2007).

5.3.2. Cooperative Globalization of SMEs

In the context of dramatic cost competition and the globalization of their customers, SME supplier firms and specialists from high-wage regions have begun to globalize. This process occurs in two main variants. The first involves regional clusters of specialists who collectively produce and assemble all components of a product. Italian industrial districts for shoemaking, ceramic tiles, or packaging machinery, which organize the offshore production of crucial processes or lower value-added products illustrate this trend (Brioschi et al. 2002; Camuffo 2003; Bellandi and Di Tommaso 2005; Camuffo et al. 2005; Cainelli et al. 2006; Bellandi and Caloffi 2008; Bellandi 2009). The other variant is internationalization of SME suppliers to MNC lead firms and suppliers in integral-architecture manufacturing sectors. Typically, in these cases, groupings of firms form an alliance to follow their customers into foreign markets (Herrigel 2007). The reasons for both variants of SME globalization, however, are the same as those that have driven the globalization of larger firms: cost-reduction pressures and customer demands for proximity of key collaborators in new locations.

In many cases, SMEs from high-wage regions seek to relieve cost pressure in their home markets either by identifying suppliers in low-wage regions or by establishing their own production facilities in those places. Such moves follow the trajectory outlined above regarding MNC suppliers: Initially firms outsource offshore the simplest operations, then they establish their own production in low-wage regions, often simply to accommodate customer demands that they develop such capacity.

Either way, such moves are difficult for SMEs and are frequently undertaken in cooperation with external partners. This is particularly the case when it comes to identifying appropriate suppliers or locations in low-wage environments. Often, SMEs use network ties with larger customer firms to identify attractive potential suppliers or joint-venture partners in low-wage regions. Sometimes, SMEs will hire foreign nationals who know the terrain in their home country and can therefore help in setting up the offshore operation and managing the inevitable problems of communication, logistics, and quality assurance. In other cases, a number of non-competitive SMEs in related lines of manufacturing may cooperate in such offshore ventures. The Global Components project found a case of nine very small family-owned American metalworking firms, each with a related but non-competing proprietary product, which pooled their resources to contract with a firm in Shanghai to identify, audit, certify, and monitor appropriate Chinese suppliers for them (Herrigel 2007). In the case of Italian industrial districts, these tasks may be performed by agents of large groups created by SMEs in the district or by public agencies representing the regions (Bellandi and Caloffi 2008). German SMEs frequently work with the offshore branch of the German Chamber of Industry and Commerce to identify appropriate offshore regions and suppliers (Depner and Bathelt 2003).

SMEs from high-wage regions are much more severely challenged when it comes to the second driver of offshoring: following the customer into low-wage markets. Here the SME often simply lacks the financial leverage to establish on its own the higher-volume production facilities in offshore locations that their mostly large MNC customers require. Nonetheless, SMEs feel compelled to globalize for fear that if they did not, they would lose key customers. In order to make such moves, SMEs therefore seek out partners. This can involve outright merger between firms. But in a surprising range of cases, cooperation has taken very interesting alternative forms.

Take the example of the strategy pursued by the small German family-owned manufacturer of industrial springs mentioned at the end of Chapter 4. The company has been a specialist spring producer for over 120 years. In 2005, the company "became part of" a larger group of spring and stamped metal parts producers—all of whom were small- or medium-sized, specialist family-owned firms just like themselves. The participating specialists were not all from the same place, but all came from traditional regions in Germany of specialized SME production (Herrigel 1996). The original spring family owns a proportional interest in the group, which is a limited liability corporation (Gesellschaft mit beschränkter Haftung (GmbH)), not a joint-stock company (Aktiengesellschaft (AG)). The owner family participates with the other families in the development of overall group strategy. The formation of the group has resulted in an internal rationalization of production capacity and competence among member firms. Exchange of information and experience among group members is ongoing and systematic. The group tries to optimize the specialties of its members on an ongoing basis.

In effect, this process has resulted in the creation of a "lead plant" system very similar to the one described above for larger MNC component suppliers, though in this case each lead plant is one of the original SME specialists. The lead plants service jointly established production locations in foreign regions—the Czech Republic, China, the United States, and Latin America. As with the large MNC suppliers described above, each of those foreign locations produces the complete range of products offered by the group. As a result, the foreign locations are far more diversified production facilities than the lead plants in the high-wage regions themselves. And there is continuous know-how spillover between the lead plants in Germany and the subsidiaries abroad. The new collaborative entity is essentially a globalized specialization cartel of SME spring producers and precision metal stampers. The alliance pools the resources and competences of its members in order to provide production and financing leverage to one another at the same time that they are able to exchange technical, customer, and market know-how. The aim of the group is to create open flows of information and know-how about technology, product application, customers, and markets in order to foster new product and new application development among all participating members.

Analogous groups have emerged in Italian industrial districts. They differ from their German counterparts in that the members of the group are regionally concentrated, and may comprise the gamut of specialists needed to produce the end product(s) manufactured in the district (shoes, apparel, ceramic tiles, etc.). These groups leverage the offshoring of production in the district and coordinate the allocation of capacity on a global basis among local members and offshore suppliers. They also play a key role in orchestrating technological innovation, product development and design, and international marketing among participating firms. In comparison to the German cases, Italian groups often have an even looser property structure, though they may be organized by larger "leader firms," which take equity stakes in key suppliers. Depending on the degree of formalization of ownership ties, these ensembles of firms are variously referred to in the Italian literature as "district groups," "pocket multinationals," or "open networks" (Lazerson and Lorenzoni 1999; Brioschi et al. 2002; Colli 2002; Chiarvesio et al. 2006; Corò and Micelli 2006).

SME globalization is also occurring quite extensively in Scandinavia, particularly in Denmark. Indeed, over 50% of the Danish workforce is employed in firms with at least one foreign subsidiary, and over 34% of those workers are employed in firms with fewer than 650 employees (Kristensen et al. 2008). The range of possible variants of SME cooperation on a global scale is thus extremely great. This is a promising area for future research.

5.3.3. Regional Policy for the Globalization of Disintegrated Production

Globalization places great pressure on the regional governance structures that have historically been indispensable for the sustained competitiveness of disintegrated production clusters. Unlike the firms that they serve, the governance institutions and practices in regions where disintegrated production has been embedded cannot easily shift their operations offshore. They must focus on keeping the operations that remain in the high-wage regions competitive and capable of participating in the fluid roles and formal self-monitoring processes of global competition. This has not been an easy adjustment. Several very significant regional clusters of disintegrated production, such as Prato in Italy, or (arguably) the traditional American automobile complex in Michigan, Ohio, and Indiana, have been largely overwhelmed by these globalization processes. They were not able to establish regional governance practices that could facilitate dynamic disintegrated globalization (Ottati 1996; Honeck 1998; Glaeser and Ponzetto 2007; Ro et al. 2008). Globalization of production, finance, and marketing can create asymmetries of access to technology and information, thereby undermining existing mechanisms for containing opportunism and balancing competition and cooperation (Zeitlin 2007). Further, the globalization of disintegrated production generates demands for new public goods among regional and industry producers, which existing institutional infrastructures are unable fully to supply or even anticipate (Sabel 2005; Bellandi 2006). Currently, there is enormous experimentation across Europe and North America around these issues. Failure exists, everywhere it threatens, but there are also intriguing examples of success (cf. also Crouch et al. 2001, 2004).

A central feature of many regional processes of governance adjustment has been the development of public or public–private collaborations for upgrading the manufacturing supply base (mentioned in Section 5.3.1). These kinds of extra-firm efforts aim at enhancing the core skills that SMEs require to participate in contemporary disintegrated production networks: the development of technical know-how, the ability to perform multiple roles, and the capacity to engage in continuous self-analysis for collaboration and cost reduction. A wide variety of institutional arrangements for this purpose already exist in different national and regional settings (Whitford and Zeitlin 2004; Herrigel and Wittke 2005; Kristensen 2008). Yet, efforts to create a proactive, supportive architecture for the globalization of SMEs from high-wage regions remain very incipient. Public and extra-firm efforts trail behind the informal efforts supporting globalization outlined above, such as large multinational lead firms giving their SME suppliers tips on reliable offshore interlocutors and production locations, or SMEs collaborating amongst themselves to accomplish similar tasks. One interesting, but limited, example of public support in this area is the role of the German International Chamber of Commerce in offshore regions. This agency does not identify specific commercial interlocutors for globalizing SMEs, but does provide them with extensive market information about offshore areas. Perhaps most importantly, it helps SMEs deal with foreign bureaucracies when they move offshore.

More elaborate and multidimensional examples of proactive regional support for disintegrated globalization are only now being discovered. Perhaps the best-attested case is Bellandi and Caloffi's (2008) account of recent initiatives in Italian regions, especially Tuscany. They focus on the identification of "cluster to cluster" public goods—common trade protocols (Enterprise Resource Planning (ERPs)), educational facilities, technical languages, and specific business services—between Italian industrial districts and what they call "proto-industrial districts" in China.[10] At the Italian federal level, an intergovernmental body has been created, the *Comitato Governativo Italia-Cina* (Italy–China Committee), which has sponsored an array of trans-territorial projects between the two countries, and there have been several regional-level "China Projects." Bellandi and Caloffi describe one of these, between the tanning and leather district of Santa Croce sull'Arno in Tuscany and an array of shoemaking regions and specialized towns located between Shanghai and Guangdong in China. At home, the Santa Croce district was crucially supported by a leather tanning trade association, the *Associazione Conciatori* (ASCON), which "carries out lobbying activities, represents their associates in several contexts, supports the realization of promotional activities, organizes training courses, promotes the creation of loan consortia, looks after the procurement of raw materials and provides other specialized services" (Bellandi and Caloffi 2008, p. 11). With the support of its members and the regional government, ASCON identified an array of complementarities between its members and Chinese producers—opportunities for the sale of Italian leather as well as for cooperation on key technologies (antipollution and water purification) that were crucial for the creation of transnational supply chains. Extra-firm institutions seeking proactively to exploit opportunities created by globalization thus successfully generated mutual benefits and synergies between the clusters of regional specialists.

Bellandi and Caloffi's examples of proactive support for regional globalization efforts are striking. They represent what Sabel has called the shift in industrial districts from "worlds in a bottle to windows on the world" (Sabel 2003). Yet, the identification of opportunities for high-wage regions created by globalization are still often overshadowed by expressions of anxiety and distress about potential threats. Increasingly, however, similar discussions to those in Italy are occurring in many manufacturing clusters dominated by competitive and dynamically adjusting SMEs. The Wisconsin Manufacturing Extension Partnership, for example, which

---

[10] The authors note that there are also cluster-building policies sponsored by the Italian Federal Government between Italy and Russia: "Task Force Italy-Russia on Industrial Districts and SMEs" (Bellandi and Caloffi 2008).

has played a crucial role in coordinating supplier upgrading and cooperation with large MNC customers, has recently begun discussions about proactively supporting the globalization of regional SMEs (interview). Analogous cooperative efforts have been identified in Norway and Denmark (Moen 2007; Kristensen and Lilja 2009). This is a core area for future research on the governance of interfirm relations as the globalization of disintegrated production continues.

5.4. CONCLUSION

This chapter has provided an overview of the main issues regarding interfirm relations and supply chain dynamics within disintegrated production. It has focused primarily on the changing character of relations among producers and between regions over the past thirty years. Disintegrated production emerged as a dominant alternative orientation to the hierarchical Fordist/Chandlerian model in manufacturing. Its key distinguishing feature is intense and ongoing collaboration between design and manufacture in the context of increasing fragmentation of the division of labor within and across firms. Production units have become smaller, and frequently transformed into separate legal entities. Their relations are continuously recomposed through collaboration and negotiation, rather than market signals or hierarchical directives. Relations among collaborating producers, furthermore, are often governed by an array of extra-firm practices and institutions designed to balance cooperation and competition and facilitate continuous recomposition of roles and capacities. These relations characterize practices within developed and developing contexts as well as those that bridge both milieus.

Both this chapter and Chapter 4 have operated at a very general level of analysis. They have attempted to characterize competitive dynamics and organizational transformations that can be found across individual country cases. Chapters 6 and 7 will break from this level of generality and examine the way in which the general disintegration dynamics are working themselves out among manufacturers, trade unions, and regional authorities in the United States and Germany. Chapter 6 shows how producers in both the United States and Germany are moving toward SCC, yet they are doing so in ways that reflect the distinctive practical and resource inheritance of each location. Chapter 7 then turns to a case study of industrial relations reform in Germany in a effort to explore the ways in which trends toward disintegration are provoking reform of basic governing arrangements in advanced economies.

6

Vertical Disintegration in National Context: Germany and the United States Compared

The heterogeneity of relations in the context of secular vertical disintegration, which was outlined in Chapters 4 and 5, is a global trend.[1] It is occurring in all national manufacturing contexts. Indeed, the uniqueness of the current period is that "best practice" in manufacturing has been nearly entirely decoupled from the particular institutional characteristics of national political economies. Unlike the practice of much of the 1990s when firms looked to producers in the United States, twenty years ago when they looked to Japan, or a hundred years ago when they looked to Britain, today technological sophistication and organizational innovation (and pressure to change) are broadly distributed across the major developed regions of the world. In the process of breaking a new product down into its many subsystems, components, and production processes, product development actors, manufacturing teams, and purchasing managers in both OEMs and suppliers look "beneath" national models, so to speak, to particular mechanisms, techniques, forms of organization, and design developed by their competitors that could enable them to improve their own practices and achieve their goals. In this way, global trends work their way into all national systems in a self-conscious but very local and piecemeal fashion. Moreover, since the process of benchmarking is continuous, no one can rest on their laurels. No national system is spared pressure to change at some level.

This chapter argues that in the context of the global trend toward vertical disintegration and decentralized best practice, producers in both Germany and the United States are struggling to construct and govern the array of relations and strategies that were outlined in Chapters 4 and 5. In particular, this chapter will focus on efforts to construct the modal type from Chapter 4: that is, sustained contingent collaboration (SCC). The claim is that SCC is emerging as the norm in both Germany and the United States. But the difficulties that firms encounter in constructing and governing these relations, while overlapping, are not identical in each country. The institutional and experiential resource base (habitus) for producers is different so the distribution of possibilities, strengths, and weaknesses in capabilities and competences, is different (Dewey 1922; Bourdieu 1977). Sustained contingent collaborations are prevalent in both the German and the US

---

[1] This chapter is taken and modified from Herrigel and Wittke (2005).

political economies, yet they are entwined and enacted quite differently in both societies.

In this sense, the chapter agrees with the institutionalist claim, against neoliberalism, that there is variety or diversity in the forms of capitalism in the contemporary world (Berger and Dore 1996; Hollingsworth and Boyer 1997; Whitley 1999; Hall and Soskice 2001; Yamamura and Streeck 2003). Nonetheless, it is important to see that the argument here departs quite substantially from the claims of a central school of contemporary institutionalism, the Varieties of Capitalism (VoC) approach pioneered by Peter Hall and David Soskice (2001) and their colleagues and collaborators, in two ways.

First, it rejects the strong Hall and Soskice argument that societies are endowed with comparative institutional advantages (Hall and Soskice 2001, pp. 36–44). For Hall and Soskice, successful German OEMs, because they are embedded in the institutional architecture of a "coordinated market economy" (cooperative labor relations, corporate governance with labor participation, patient capital, and regulatory law), are most likely to construct cooperative (non-market) relations with both labor and their suppliers and pursue competitive market strategies that are characterized by product quality and incremental innovation. By contrast, because US OEM producers are embedded in the institutional architecture of a "liberal market economy" (conflictual labor relations, capital-dominated corporate governance, a financial system concerned only with profitable return and strict contract law), their labor and supply chain relations will be distant and arm's length, characterized by conflict, wage, and price pressure, all of which diverts producer attention from gradual improvements and incremental innovation (Casper 1995, 1997, 2000, 2001).

As Section 6.1 will report, however, this is not what the available evidence shows regarding supplier relations. Producers in both the United States and Germany are engaging in cooperation *and* in arm's-length conflict and price struggle. Indeed, producers in both countries are trying to construct forms of governance that enable them to continue to innovate and improve their products at the same time that they help them cope with the pressures generated by sustained contingent collaboration.

Second, the chapter also rejects the related, but not identical, institutionalist claim that national institutional systems change in path-dependent ways: that is, in the absence of a significant exogenous shock such as a war or a terrible economic catastrophe, the coherence of institutional complementarities within a national architecture of institutions encourage actors to seek solutions to governance problems that are compatible with (if not reinforcing of) existing arrangements and constrain them from adopting governance solutions that are "fundamentally" incompatible with those arrangements (Mahoney 2000; Pierson 2004).

The following argues that, at least in the case of the relations emerging out of the vertical disintegration of manufacturing, actors in both the United States and Germany are to a surprising extent neither significantly constrained nor especially enabled by the institutional architecture of the political economy. Indeed, in many ways the institutional architectures in both the United States and Germany, as coherent systems, have been overtaken by events and stand awkwardly by as actors seek to construct new relations and forms of governance alongside them. This is not to say that there are no efforts to reform or adapt existing institutional arrangements to changing circumstances. There are (Boyer 2003; Jürgens 2003; Thelen and Kume 2003). Nor is the claim here that actors are entirely ignorant of the normative dispositions constituting institutional rules. Far from it! In crucial ways, they are guided by these dispositions (especially Dewey 1922, pp. 14–88). Instead, the chapter argues both that actors act independently of institutional incentives and constraints *and* that they try to use institutional mechanisms in new or non-standard ways in order to achieve their governance ends. That is, they *try to change the incentives and constraints* that institutions provide to make them more suitable to the new context.

Stated in a positive way, rather than looking, as institutionalists do, for structural constraints or enablers, the argument here is that the social terrain of the economy in the United States and Germany is peopled by a community of reflexive actors, beset by common problems of their own definition (though not necessarily of their own making), seeking to construct solutions to the problems they encounter in practice. And, rather than looking for institutional complementarities between system parts and greater and less "coherence" for the system as a whole, the argument here conceives of the (very different) institutional architectures of the political economy in the United States and Germany as constituting sets of resources for actors to use, not use, deconstruct, or redefine in their efforts to contend with the problems of industrial transformation that beset them in practice. Institutions represent the resolution of governance problems. If they do not solve (or even address) the problems that actors have, then institutions are either ignored or changed.

At the end of the day, experimentation upon the social terrain of OEM–supplier relations in both the United States and Germany is very widespread. There are many different kinds of "solutions" to the governance problems posed by the new production relations being constructed. The chapter's conclusion shows that this process of experimentation is slowly recomposing the institutional character of the political economies of both Germany and the United States in ways that nonetheless reproduce significant differences between the two political economies.

6.1. SUSTAINED CONTINGENT COLLABORATION IN GERMANY AND THE UNITED STATES

Chapter 4 constructed sustained contingent collaboration as a type based on qualitative observation of supplier–OEM relations in both the United States and Germany, so I am convinced that this type of relation can be found in both countries. But there is no reason to simply take my word for it. Indeed, there is a strong presumption within the VoC camp that relations in the United States and Germany will systematically diverge, with German relations likely to be more cooperative and US relations likely to be more arm's length and market defined. Appeal to some neutral and broadly representative data would therefore seem to be in order.

Numerous quantitative studies have been undertaken over the course of the last decade to determine the extent to which supply relations in manufacturing (particularly in the automobile industry) have become more collaborative and structured by the precepts of "lean manufacturing" (low inventory, low work in process, early supplier involvement in product design, teamwork, transparency on costs between supplier and customer, etc.). Happily for me, most of the evidence is extremely contradictory. Researchers find conflict and collaboration, trust and distrust almost in equal measure in both societies.

Susan Helper, for example, in studying supplier relations in the US automobile industry, has repeatedly found that many US suppliers are asked to engage in product development, are incorporated earlier into the product development process, and have adopted a wide array of cost-reducing and transparency-enhancing arrangements in production (Helper and Sako 1995; Luria 1996a, 1996b; Helper and Sako 1998; Whitford and Zeitlin 2004). In comparison to the conflictual and arm's-length practices of thirty and forty years ago in the United States, there is a remarkable amount of cooperation in contemporary US manufacturing. But Helper also finds that US suppliers have a low level of trust in their customers. Many feel that their relationships with customers involve one-way exchanges of know-how. Customers press supplier margins in the name of mutually beneficial cost reduction. Customers solicit innovative design from their suppliers only to shop those designs around to supplier competitors. And, OEM requests for just-in-time delivery are experienced as inventory shifting rather than inventory-eliminating moves on the part of the OEM (see also Dziczek et al. 2003).

For Helper, the contradictory character of this evidence is viewed as a marker for the incompleteness of the transition to lean production in the United States and above all as an indication of the legacy of arm's-length contracting in US manufacturing for much of the twentieth century (Helper 1991a, 1991b; Helper and Sako 1995, 1998; Whitford and Zeitlin 2004). From the perspective of the VoC school, such contradictory data is evidence for the strength of the market tradition in the United States and the absence (or weakness) of institutions capable of sanctioning self-dealing in nonmarket relations (Casper 2001). From our point of view, however, the contradictory impulses observed in Helper's findings provide evidence for the kind of sustained contingent collaboration relations we believe are being systematically created in today's competitive environment in spite of the institutional arrangements encouraging or discouraging particular forms of behavior in the society (Chapter 4; O'Sullivan 2006; Whitford 2006). The challenge for producers in the United States, we will see, is to create forms of governance that allow them to cope with the contradictory pressures being generated.

Evidence is similarly contradictory in studies of German manufacturing supplier relations. One very extensive study, conducted by three major economic research institutes in Germany at the end of the 1990s of the automobile, electrical, and mechanical engineering industries, found that German suppliers were indeed being asked to participate in product development at much earlier stages than they had been in the past (Fieten et al. 1997). Forty-one percent of automobile suppliers, 44.4% of electromechanical industry suppliers, and 47.1% of mechanical engineering industry suppliers indicated that they were involved in intensive cooperation with other firms (though not all of these collaborative ties were with their direct customers) (Fieten et al. 1997, pp. 232–8, table 235). The survey also indicated that production cycle times were drastically declining across the supply base and that suppliers were adopting production-level procedures (longer machine utilization rates, cross-functional teams, ISO 9000 certification) to create greater cost transparency, improve quality, and lower inventory (Fieten et al. 1997, pp. 152–75).

Yet, at the same time, the survey also showed that over 91% of all surveyed firms in all surveyed industries ranked price pressure from OEMs as the greatest problem for suppliers, 61.1% said that inconsistent delivery terms were a significant problem, and 47.6% said that OEMs were forcing them to hold inventory (rather than seeking to eliminate it from the supply chain) (Fieten et al. 1997, pp. 152ff). Of those firms engaged in collaborative research and development with their customers, 57% said that they were partially compensated (as opposed to fully compensated) for their efforts. Nearly 50% of firms with fewer than 100 employees indicated that they typically received no compensation at all for their research contributions (Fieten et al. 1997, pp. 282–3). In addition, the report notes that 42.9% of all German automobile suppliers complain of customers shopping the supplier's designs around to their competitors (Fieten et al. 1997, p. 289).

As in the American case, the evidence here is strikingly contradictory. German suppliers are engaging in collaborative relations, but there is considerable conflict and struggle among the producers for the rents from the relationship and significant variety in the quality of relations. Seen with the institutionalist lenses of the VoC framework, this kind of contradiction within a coordinated market economy is a sign of systemic distress. The system of constraints and enablers is not functioning in a way that inhibits the diffusion of arm's-length market relations in Germany. Seen with the lenses of SCC, however, this is not so much a sign of crisis in Germany as it is a sign of crisis in the institutionalist analysis of Germany. Indeed, if we take the evidence from above indicating that there is considerable cooperation in the United States where there are no institutional incentives for it, it is unclear that even the *cooperation* observable in German OEM–supplier relations is in any significant way traceable to the "beneficial constraints" of the institutional architecture in the German coordinated market economy (Streeck 1997). The notion of sustained contingent collaboration, however, makes sense of the evidence quite well.

Indeed, judging by the evidence presented, it is clear that both German and American manufacturing supplier relations today have strong elements of both conflict and partnership within them. It is also clear that the institutional architectures in each of the political economies are not only achieving the outcomes they are thought to be able to produce, they are also allowing for the achievement of those that they are not supposed to produce. For us, this is a sign that in order to understand the character of practical, relational, and institutional recomposition in Germany and the United States, one should not start by observing the performance of institutions. Instead, one must begin by looking concretely at the efforts of both suppliers and OEMs to cope with the contradictory character of their situation.

6.2. COPING WITH THE PROBLEM OF SUSTAINED CONTINGENT COLLABORATION IN GERMANY AND THE UNITED STATES

The situation that confronts both US and German suppliers and OEMs in the context of the trend toward vertical disintegration and the emergence of SCC as the modal relationship between OEMs and suppliers is one of continuous change: the character of relations, technology, specific workplace arrangements, skills, markets etc. are continuously changing. Actors (and regions) unable to cope with this kind of environment are unlikely to reproduce themselves. In this context, there are two different governance problems for which actors in both societies have had to devise mechanisms to cope: the problem of initial learning and the problem of cost reduction.

By initial learning, we refer to the processes by which producers acquire information and know-how in order to be able to participate in the new style of relationship. How do firms learn, for example, about new-style production arrangements (teamwork, cellular manufacturing, low work in process, etc.) and services (just-in-time delivery, subassembly, logistics) that are needed to participate competitively in the new supply chains? How are they able to develop the capacity to participate in collaborative design and product development? By cost reduction, we refer to the strategies and procedures suppliers and OEMs use to organize the generation of continuous cost reductions in production. Analysis of both of these problem areas will reveal some commonalities but also significant differences in the way in which producers in the United States and Germany cope with such demands.

6.3. INITIAL LEARNING

Prior to the onset of the trend toward vertical disintegration in the 1980s, suppliers and OEMs in both Germany and the United States were primarily engaged in the Type 1 style relations outlined in Chapter 4: that is, short-term, arm's-length relations in which suppliers either produced standardized commodity products or produced overflow capacity for OEMs during periods of peak demand. On the whole, price was the determining factor for sales in old-style manufacturing supply chains in the United States and Germany. OEMs were very vertically integrated and supplier structures in both countries tended to be divided between a relatively small number of large standard component producers, such as Robert Bosch or Borg Warner in the automobile industry and multitudes of small- and medium-sized contract shops engaged in capacity subcontracting (Helper 1991*b*; Schrader and Sattler 1993; Birou and Fawcett 1994; Kwon 2004; Kwon 2005).

For the bulk of supplier firms in both economies, the trend of vertical disintegration and the shift toward SCC has therefore involved significant pressures to upgrade their technological capabilities, production quality, service delivery capacities, and internal cost management procedures. This has pressed suppliers into large investments in new engineering personnel, to profound recomposition of their manpower usage and training practices, and to the reorganization of the work flow in production, forward to the customer and back to their own suppliers. Mechanisms and methods facilitating this adjustment in both the United States and Germany have been parallel but systematically divergent.

Initially in the United States, OEMs themselves invested significant direct effort and cost in the form of "supplier development" to instruct their suppliers, one by one, in the new techniques (MacDuffie and Helper 1997). This, however, is a mechanism that has begun to disappear. Supplier development was always accompanied and supplemented by consulting services that firms could acquire over the market, and these practices continue (though they are often too expensive for many smaller firms to make extensive use of). Additionally, firms with the resources (and some without them) sought to acquire knowledge of the new techniques, and also new competences in technology and service, through the acquisition of complementary firms and/or rivals in the market. The pressures placed on supplier firms by OEMs to enhance their development capabilities have led to significant mergers and organizational recomposition in the industry, at all levels, as actors have sought to create entities capable of efficiently participating in SCCs.

The market is a traditional mechanism for resolving governance problems in the United States, but it has not been the only one in play in the current adjustment period. There has also been a very broad array of public, private, and cooperative experiments attempting to upgrade the capabilities of the supply base in the areas of production quality, service provision, and cost reduction. The experiments can be categorized as consortial, associational, and corporate. In each case, public support may or may not play an important role.

The Wisconsin Manufacturers Development Consortium (WMDC) is an example of a public–private consortium of large OEM firms, public agencies such as the Wisconsin Manufacturing Extension Partnership (WMEP), and technical colleges devoted to the improvement of the capacity of local component manufacturers to compete at the levels of production quality and cost-reduction capability that the participating manufacturers require (Rickert et al. 2000; Erickson 2002; Klonsinski 2002; Whitford and Zeitlin 2004). Component supplier firms serving the members of the consortium have their participation subsidized by public money and they gain significant access to OEM know-how through participation in consortia-sponsored courses. Similar programs exist in Illinois, Pennsylvania, and other important manufacturing agglomerations in the US Midwest and East Coast.

There are two different examples of associational leadership in the provision of service to firms seeking to learn how to square the circle of quality, service, and low cost that is constitutive of SCC. The first is a program for supplier training directed by the Industrial Training Program (ITP) in Illinois' Department of Commerce and Community Affairs (Kulek 2002). This program provides public funds to a variety of Illinois industry associations with membership structures composed primarily of small- and medium-sized component manufacturers. In the case of the Valley Industrial Association (VIA) (in the Outer Western Suburbs of Chicago) (Whalen 2002) or of Norbic (a membership-based industrial development association on the north side of Chicago serving primarily small- and medium-sized producers), the ITP awards the associations funds and member firms make specific proposals to the association for training subsidies. Fifty percent of an individual firm's training expense is paid for by the program. VIA encourages members to make use of the funds (which they do in large numbers), but does not give advice or assistance as to the types of training that may be necessary. Norbic provides consulting services to its members to help them optimize the kind of training they utilize and then provides grants to firms for the training (Norbic 2009*a*, 2009*b*).

The final variant of governance mechanisms capable of balancing manufacturing quality with continuous cost reduction is a corporate one. Here there are two different kinds of mechanisms: one directed by internal corporate consulting units on operating units that are active as component suppliers; the other directed by OEM firms toward their component suppliers.

The first mechanism can be found among large component and complex subassembly producers such as Emerson Electric, Danaher, GKN, and more specialized component producers such as ITW. These firms operate their own internal organizational consultancies, often through their corporate "Technology Centers." Firms such as Danaher are widely known for their uniformly "lean" production operations and they are able to achieve this across a broad array of operating units and subsidiaries through the use of corporate training programs for operating unit engineers, managers and workers (often run through their corporate university), and technical consultants who benchmark subsidiaries within the conglomerate and disseminate information on successful organizational forms. These corporate institutions broker solutions for independent operating units, bringing knowledge and expertise to a local production level which those local units would not have been able to marshal on their own.[2]

The second mechanism is in many ways a variant on the now increasingly discontinued practice of supplier development, although here the aim is to provide training to groups of suppliers to enable them to reorganize rather than to directly reorganize individual suppliers. Moreover, in the most prominent case, this corporate policy is undertaken with local government subsidy. The same Illinois ITP program mentioned in the discussion of associational initiatives above also makes supplier training money available directly to the three largest manufacturing OEMs in Illinois—Caterpillar, John Deere, and the Ford Motor Company. These firms use the money to train suppliers needing production quality assistance and improved cost-reduction capability. In these cases, the large OEM designs the curriculum and offers training that it believes will enable suppliers to consistently achieve quality and cost-reduction targets that the firm establishes (DeDobbelaere 2002). In effect, the state of Illinois outsources regional industrial policy to the major actors and shapers of industrial practice in the state. The effect, however, is to insure that small- and medium-sized component suppliers cross the initial learning threshold for participation in the new style subcontracting relations.

In sum, the governance of initial learning on the American side is characterized by processes of merger and firm recomposition guided by the market as well as by an array of non-market experiments: associational, consortial, and corporate. Some of the mechanisms that have been set up (in particular the state-sponsored corporate programs in Illinois) have the traditional character of firm-led or arm's-length incentive creating industrial policy for which the United States has long been known. But others are more path-breaking: the consortial and associational programs in Wisconsin, Illinois, and Pennsylvania and some of the intra-corporate consulting agencies are interesting because they are deliberative. They involve systematic contact for information and experience exchange among the principle parties (OEM, supplier, association, state agency) in both the conception and execution of policy. The difficulty that all struggle with is how to accommodate local initiative and adaptability to central benchmarking and direction.

In Germany, efforts to help producers develop the capability to participate in the new subcontracting arrangements also have been quite varied. Different mechanisms have been in play (market, corporate, and associational) and the use and impact of the different mechanisms has been different in different regions. In some ways, the mechanisms observed are quite consistent with the

---

[2] The danger, of course, is that these centralized mechanisms undercut the strengths of the local units in their efforts to impose a unitary idea of best practice. It is safe to say that the best results in these cases come in cases where the center and the local units engage in an open dialogue about possibilities and capabilities. For an extensive discussion and critique of this kind of centralized top-down benchmarking in the context of multinational companies, see Kristensen and Zeitlin (2005, chs. 8–13).

kind of governance that traditionally has existed in industrial Germany, but in other ways the current experiments mark a clear departure from the path.

One traditional mechanism (often underplayed in discussions of Germany) has been the market. Private consultancies, for example, have been very important vehicles for the diffusion of knowledge about the new production and supply relations in Germany (Jürgens 2003). Mergers have also been very prominent in the component supplier market, again at all levels. In Baden-Württemberg alone, the largest region of automobile component production in the country, the number of prominent first tier suppliers to OEMs has been consolidated from somewhere between twenty-five or thirty players to less than ten over the course of the last decade. Plainly, in both the United States and in Germany, many firms have found it easier to acquire new capabilities by merging with actors who possess them (particularly in the technology and development area) than they have to develop them from scratch in-house.

There have been other efforts, however, involving the cooperation of state, associational, firm, and educational entities, that resemble the kinds of governance arrangement that is extensively discussed regarding the German case in the VoC literature. For example, beginning in the mid-1990s, a series of Länder government "supplier initiatives" were created in the automobile industry (after strong lobbying by component industry associations) that brought together large automobile firms, their suppliers, and local technical universities into an informational network. For several years, these initiatives sponsored regular events in which details about the new production arrangements and supplier relations were extensively discussed. Stronger and more enthusiastically attended in some regions than others, such initiatives made information available to those suppliers interested in receiving it. In large part, such efforts stopped at the boundary of the supplier firm, but they facilitated consulting business for the local technical university experts among member firms in the initiative. Finally, the traditional German system of codetermination has also played an effective role in helping to diffuse the workplace and production arrangements of "lean production" (in particular teamwork, continuous improvement procedures, and cellular production) through the issuance of central guidelines for the adoption of the various elements of lean manufacture (Jürgens 1997, 2003; Roth 1997).

Such reactions to the challenge of the new supplier–OEM arrangements constitute a kind of systemic reflex: the German institutional architecture doing what it can to help producers adjust to a new set of conditions. Such reflexes have been significant, but in crucial ways they have not always been enough for producers. The supplier initiatives had very uneven coverage (in many ways their success depended on the interest of the local OEM). Concretely, they facilitated information exchange and created networks for consultants. But this was often either too little information or too expensive (or both) for many firms to benefit from. The industrial relations system had success with problems related to work organization and production flow within firms, but it was crucially inattentive to the elements of the new system that involved interfirm relations—logistics, services, and cooperation in design and product development. As a result, many German supplier firms felt left in the cold by the traditional institutional architecture. This opened up a space for very interesting experiments in governance that depart quite dramatically from the German norm.

One remarkable experiment of this kind has been taking place in the Bergisches Land in Nordrhein Westfalen. This region is the second-largest center of automobile components production in Germany and the largest concentration of small- and medium-sized component producers in that sector. For traditional reasons, public policy for suppliers has been very underdeveloped in the Bergisches Land (Herrigel 1996). Local banks are overwhelmed and cash poor; larger banks are pulling away from the industrial Mittelstand (SMEs); employers' associations are traditionally fractionalized and as a result passive. In this case, the institutions of German-coordinated capitalism are truly in disarray.

As a result, and somewhat ironically, it has been the local IG Metall union, the strongest extra-firm institution in the region, that has stepped into the breach and begun pushing firms to upgrade and embrace not only newer forms of work and production organization, but new production services and logistics as well. IG Metall's involvement in restructuring takes place in one of two ways (Janitz 2002). First, in a significant array of cases, agents from the trade union district office in Wuppertal act directly as consultants, offering firms advice on how to restructure their product palette, their labor and production arrangements, and their finances in order to be able to achieve the quality and cost targets demanded by large automobile industry OEMs. Second, and more often, the union acts as an intermediary between the firm and consultants who come in, audit the company, and provide advice and consulting on how to restructure the firm to be competitive.

Typically, the union becomes involved (in either of the above ways) because it is asked to do so, first by the works council in a troubled firm (either in bankruptcy or in financial trouble) and then by the management itself. The union establishes a set of conditions with the firm on restructuring—that is, they will help with connections and line up consultants as long as the firm agrees to certain parameters (in the interest of IG Metall members) in the restructuring process. With agreement, the union then goes ahead and lines up the consultant. There are a number of very skilled local consultants who have had success in local restructuring. They know the firms, know the regional culture, know the industry, etc. But the union also uses its position to pressure the works council (to the extent it is resistant) to adopt practices in the long-term interest of the competitiveness of the firm (cells, teams, continuous monitoring, benchmarking of best practices in the industry, etc.).

In these ways, IG Metall is playing a pivotal role in the management of small- and medium-sized firm adjustment in the region. The union is simultaneously a broker and a conveyor of specialized knowledge. IG Metall mediates consultants who help troubled firms restructure; it establishes guidelines for the general restructuring process with the firm before the consultants are deployed; it engages itself in the internal restructuring discussion and is typically given access to the firms' books. Moreover, due to the structure of the German Federal Works

Constitution Act, the union is in a remarkably good position to be able to evaluate the performance of the various actors it engages and sets into action in the restructuring process. Union officials from the local district office sit on the supervisory boards of important mega-suppliers (core customers of local SME firms) and hence are privy to very intimate information on the mega-supplier's practices and strategies—worldwide. IG Metall knows what the customers of local firms want and is in a position to helpfully convey that information to its clients and critically evaluate management suggestions and the performance of consultants.

It is important to emphasize that this kind of intervention constitutes a dramatic departure from traditional practice for IG Metall. It is improvisation in the context of a failure of the traditional system to provide for area firms. In one sense, the union's actions have a very traditional interest: to protect jobs in the region by enhancing the competitiveness of the firms that are located there. But in order to achieve this goal the union has had to break from the traditional confines of union activity within the German system. In effect, they are constructing a system of collaborative management within local firms where the trade union and works council deliberate on strategic questions regarding the firm's future and its customer relations that go well beyond the relatively circumscribed workplace and labor market arenas demarcated in the system of codetermination and works constitution statutes in German law. At the same time, they are acting as a regional benchmarking agent, distributing information regarding best practice among area firms and even using information about international best practice that they are able to access through other roles they play in the system of codetermination (i.e., sitting on boards of multinational corporations headquartered in the region).

This example for how the process of initial learning is being organized in Wuppertal is dramatic, but there are myriad other forms of departure and innovation occurring across the German industrial landscape as firms and associations seek to cope with the limits of the existing institutional architecture. As in the United States then, the problem of initial learning in Germany is being confronted in ways that both conform with and depart from the traditional path. Crucially, the departures from the path in each case do not converge. Although they perform some of the same services and functions, for example, the Wisconsin supplier consortium and the Wuppertal experiment in union-led restructuring constitute quite distinct and different institutional efforts to cope with initial learning.

6.4. COPING WITH COST-REDUCTION PRESSURES IN THE UNITED STATES AND GERMANY

Cost-reduction pressure in the current environment stems from the permanent pressure that producers feel to be technologically innovative. Firms must allocate increasing amounts of resources to research and development—and moreover, in areas that are not always part of the traditional strengths of the business (e.g., plastics or electronics for automobile producers). In order to be able to do this, they must withdraw resources from other areas—hence the trend toward outsourcing and a focus on core competences. But in addition to these measures, the pressure to remain innovative imposes permanent pressure on in-house operations and on suppliers to continually reduce costs. As indicated in the discussion of SCC in Chapter 4, a firm's facility in cost reduction is a major competitive advantage in dynamically changing relations.

Being able to cope with this continuous pressure is thus a crucial governance issue in manufacturing today (Herrigel 2004). Firms must develop the in-house procedures to be able to continuously generate and identify cost-reduction possibilities. The overarching challenge in achieving continuous cost reduction is to create organization that encourages all actors in the product design, development, and manufacturing processes to reveal to others what they know about their area of preoccupation. Such organizational transparency facilitates the identification of inefficiencies within functions as well as possibilities for improvement in the interfaces between functions. Actors have to abandon the opportunistic impulse to protect information for local advantage and recognize that transparency is in the interest of everyone in the process. There are layers of mechanisms for the realization of this kind of voluntary transparency.

At the level of work and production organization, the core arrangements of lean production (teams, production cells, and kaizen practices) make continuous improvement one of their objectives. Typically, these arrangements encourage actors to reveal to one another what they know by grouping all relevant functions in the creation and production of a product together in a governance structure that directs its production—hence the outcome/reward for each function is dependent on the outcome/reward for all the others. All recognize their common stake in the successful delivery and continuous improvement of the product. Such arrangements seem to have diffused quite broadly in both the United States and Germany at this point, though the transformation continues to be incomplete and the emphases in each political economy differ slightly (Jürgens 2003; Streeck and Yamamura 2003, p. 29).

Cost reduction is also a key component of the search process that all producers in SCC relations engage in. Firms scan the terrain, both through collaborative benchmarking procedures in the product development process and through serial contracting with specialists, not only for technological know-how, but also for organizational innovation and cost-reduction expertise. And, as the discussion in Section 6.3 makes clear, practices in the United States and Germany are remarkably convergent.

Both of these layers of cost-reduction practice are limited, however, in that they tend to be focused on particular projects or parts of the production process. As a result, they lack a sense of the overarching situation of multiple projects and multiple production processes in the enterprise as a whole. But it is precisely at this level that much of the "waltz" of cost reduction takes place between firms in

SCC relations. Consequently, firms have had to develop internal mechanisms which encourage product-dedicated teams to reveal to superordinate internal scanning actors what they know. This makes it possible for the scanners both to identify cost-reduction possibilities throughout the firm (including projects whose profitability can be sacrificed to achieve a customer's cost-reduction demand in the interest of the extension and development of other very profitable projects) and to help diffuse innovations and practices that product-dedicated teams may be developing. At this level of internal scanning, American and German firms have some similarities, but on the whole they have been developing different sorts of mechanisms.

The similarities can be found in the smallest firms. Here in both countries the superordinate monitoring role is frequently assumed by the principle owner of the firm. In both countries, the effectiveness of this role depends very much on the local balance of power: If the owner acts autocratically, based on what she can observe rather than on what is revealed to her by the various product cells, cost reduction is often a battle over givebacks and wages between production workers and management. This kind of arrangement is less successful, in large part because the top-down structure of governance does not encourage actors in production to truthfully reveal what they know (Böhm and Lücking 2006). If, on the other hand, the owner facilitates exchange between the various parts of his firm and engages in regularized consultation with shop-floor personnel—team leaders, project coordinators, etc.—the results are better. Cost reduction is most successful when it becomes a process of collective self-examination across roles and lines of authority in the firm.

An alternative mechanism, found in small firms in both the United States and Germany, involves the creation of actors with roles in the firm that systematically cross functions and stages in the production process. In one small family-owned component producer in Germany, for example, the owner describes their internal deliberation procedures, in which works councilors and production workers met regularly with management and ownership, as designed to "systematically produce surprises" about plant layout, machine operation, work organization, and material flow, as well as possibilities for new products. The key to the success of this is the existence of toolmakers and set-up personnel who are allowed (expected) to float back and forth between design engineering and machine operators and across product lines. Similarly, one small US deep-draw stamping firm in western Michigan organizes cost-reduction scanning through the construction of dramatically expansive job descriptions for skilled toolmakers in their shop. These skilled workers shepherd projects from beginning design to end manufacture and meet regularly with one another as well as plant management and machine operators to discuss progress. In both the German and US cases, the key to success is that management and work teams both identify their success with the improvement of the product and the cost-reduction process. Skilled workers who are intimately involved at all stages of the production process act as key integrating figures between the shop floor and firm management.

In larger firms, however, the formation of a superordinate internal scanning practice differs between US and German firms. In the United States, two sorts of scanning practices predominate. One is an autocratic role for finance departments in internal deliberations about cost. Because public US firms are required to make costs more transparent to the outside, finance people are able to use the force of accounting and shareholder value arguments to impose particular decisions on multiple projects. The criterion used is purely financial without consideration for the location strategically of particular projects in the historical relationship between the firm and its customer. In this case, the powerful role of finance departments is very much in line with what one would expect from the institutional structure of the US "liberal market economy."

A second mechanism, often conceived of as a counterweight to the force of finance departments, has been to establish ongoing inter- and intra-operating unit cost-reduction conversations among the relevant actors in the production process. Such conversations (organized in the form of weekly meetings or teleconferences between project teams—often including key sub-suppliers) bring together all those responsible for contracts with particular clients to exchange information and discuss collective possibilities for meeting the client's targets. The parties all have an interest in coming up with something to satisfy the client—each recognizes that future business with the client may depend on it. Such meetings tend both to identify best practice within the firm (through self-reporting) and create a forum in which the generalization of such practice can be discussed.

Rather than by hierarchical direction or financial leverage, such deliberative mechanisms turn mutual learning and information exchange to the competitive advantage of the firm as a whole. In many cases, the genesis of these institutionalized conversations has occurred *because* of the unrelenting internal pressure of finance departments in American corporations: The institutional goal of the cross-project and cross-functional conversations is to achieve (or beat) the goals established by finance, but in ways that are consistent with the health of both internal and customer relations as well as long-term efficiency of production within the enterprise. Regardless of how they are generated, the key to their success is that all stakeholders in the products going to a particular client are represented in the conversation. Needless to say, this kind of mutual monitoring and sharing of information, as a form of governance, marks an interesting departure from the "liberal market" practices associated with VoC characterizations of the American production system.

In the German case, the institutional form of the superordinate scanner is different because the inherited relational contour of the firm is different than in the United States. Many large firms, for example, do not have the same kind of external pressure from finance markets that embolden (and strengthen) the hand of the finance department in US corporations. Engineering and production are far stronger within German corporations than in American ones. But cost-reduction pressure, for the reasons given above, is just as intense in Germany, so firms have had to develop alternative mechanisms to identify firm-wide cost-reduction possibilities. Three different kinds of experiments suggest the flavor and range of organizational recomposition that is taking place.

The first, developed at a large first-tier automobile supplier resembles in some ways the internal consulting groups in American corporations that have played such an important role in initial learning. This is a cross-functional team charged with what the firm calls *Leistungsorientiertes Management* (Performance-Oriented Management). The charge is to monitor operations across the firm seeking efficiencies and cost-reduction possibilities that may be neglected by the structure of team projects: for example, material purchases that could be combined, common design possibilities, complementary machine usage rates, etc. These teams are given general cost-reduction targets, but they can only achieve them in consultation with project and production teams. In turn, the production teams, who experience direct pressure from their customers for specific giveback percentages, view the performance-oriented team as a resource.

The second and third mechanisms seek to achieve the kind of continuous conversation among stakeholders described above in the American context. But the conversations are realized via different institutional actors and catalyzing agents. The second mechanism is to redraw the role of logistics departments in extremely expansive ways, such that agents from that department concern themselves with all organizational and product development issues within and across projects. Logistics teams engage with all existing teams, at all stages of the development and production process, in an effort to generate and diffuse continuous cost reduction throughout the product development and production cycle. The logistics departments also concentrate, in conjunction with purchasing, finance, and development departments, in achieving the flexibility to balance varying intensities of cost-reduction pressure across all projects within the firm. In these ways, logistics players have their incentives aligned both with the teams associated with specific projects and with the general cost-reduction targets associated with the department as a whole within the enterprise.

A third kind of experiment, at once the most remarkably German but also perhaps the most at odds with the traditional institutional structure of the German production system, involves the systematic involvement of works councils, in collaboration with plant management, to scan for cost-reduction potential. In the case of one large supplier to the machinery industry, in which the IG Metall is very strongly represented (over 90% workforce organization, including management), the works council pursues an extremely expansive version of German comanagement. Instead of confining their activities to the narrow tasks of workplace training, wages, scheduling, and arbitration, this works council contributes detailed proposals for work, production, and product design reorganization to plant management (in most cases themselves IG Metall members).

Initially, the works council became involved in the presentation of proposals for reorganization in an effort to present management with alternatives to proposals developed by outside management consultants. With time, however, as it became clear that pressure for cost reduction was unremitting, the works council devoted an increasing share of its resources to the problem (devoting two full time members of the works council exclusively to the problem of cost reduction). It has gone so far that the works council has become involved not only in the optimization of organization in the servicing of existing contracts. They have also become actively involved in the way in which the company constructs its bids on new contracts. These activities are in line with the general role of German works councils—to make the employment of its members secure. But it pursues this goal in a very unconventional manner—involving itself with engineering and controlling departments in addition to production-level management in an effort to achieve internal efficiencies that allow the firm to meet existing cost-reduction targets and to win new contracts (see Chapter 7 for an extensive discussion of these general changes in German industrial relations).

As in the case of the new-style logistics departments (and in some ways, the newly defined boundary spanning toolmakers in the small firm examples), the advantage of the works council in the process is that it is, as an actor, both part of the local level in the plant and involved in superordinate scanning. Local players are willing to reveal what they know regarding the strengths and weaknesses of their area because they know that the works council has no incentive to punish them with that information. The result is greater transparency regarding cost throughout the firm.

As we have indicated, in many of these German and American examples there are clear departures from the traditional path. There are no constraints or enabling rules in the institutional system in the United States to create cost-reduction conversations or boundary-crossing toolmakers; nor are the new-style logistics departments or cost-reduction-oriented works councils enacting a logic prescribed by the German institutional architecture. In all these cases, actors are innovating despite the rules of the game. The institutional arrangements are not so much constraints or enablers as they are resources in the creative process of experimentation.

Finally, although these examples constitute departures from the path, it is important to keep in mind that they should be viewed as experiments. There is no reason to conclude that the above illustrations constitute the emergence of a new "system" in either institutional setting. Rather, by outlining an array of experiments, the aim here is to convey the breadth of current experimentation that exists at a local level. Institutional adaptation is occurring through the recomposition of organizational design and the redefinition of roles. Many of the experiments involve departures either from the traditional roles of actors within the institutional architecture of the German and American production systems or from the organizational ecology established by those architectures. All the experiments draw on existing resources, but apply them in new and creative ways.

6.5. CONCLUSION

This discussion of recomposition in German and American manufacturing has been an extended reflection on the limits of contemporary institutional analysis, particularly that of the VoC school, in accounting for the differences that continue to exist in developed political economies. In insisting on the difference between the argument here and the strong convergence claims of contemporary neoliberalism, there is in the first instance agreement with much institutionalist writing on the persistence of differences across advanced political economies in the context of contemporary trends. But, contemporary institutionalism of the VoC variety goes too far in its emphasis on comparative institutional advantage and the path-dependent character of systemic change. In a way that is inconsistent with the VoC characterization of the national institutional advantages in the United States and Germany, this chapter shows that SCC relations are emerging in both societies. Germany does not have a greater preponderance of nor displays any particular advantage in cooperative practices. US firms are neither more invested in arm's-length contracting, nor more capable of radical organizational recomposition than their German counterparts. Instead, conflict and cooperation and institutional recomposition and experimentation characterize actors' strategies in both societies.

Similarly, regarding institutionalist claims about path dependence, the evidence shows that with the diffusion of SCC, actors' efforts to cope with pressures for adjustment are producing a variety of significant departures from the path of action generally thought to be encouraged by either the US or German institutional architectures. The cooperative deliberation within large US firms regarding cost reduction, and the collaborative supplier training consortia in the United States, and trade union-led restructuring and works council-driven cost reduction in Germany all are significant departures from the path. In some cases, actors are guided by traditional conceptions of their institutional roles, yet find it to be necessary to act in unconventional ways to be able to realize those goals (e.g., the IG Metall in Wuppertal or works councils engaging in systematic scanning for cost reduction). But in other cases, actors respond to challenges posed by the competitive environment in ways that appear to be neither systematically constrained nor encouraged by the institutional architecture in which they are embedded. That is, actors respond creatively to their situation (e.g., the expansive role for logistics departments in Germany or the expansive cross-functional role of toolmakers within US and German small firms).

All of this evidence underscores the reflexive character of action within a social economy. Actors are not confined within a rigid institutional system of constraints and incentives, but instead exist within a social system of contingently coupled dispositions and habits (Dewey 1922; Bourdieu 1977). They solve problems through collective self-reflection and experimentation using and recomposing the resources (institutional and otherwise) that they have on hand. The result is not only that actors appear at times to be oblivious to the constraints or incentives provided by their institutional surround. They also recreate institutional difference across political economies as actors creatively recompose and even break from the framework for practice that their institutional context provides.

The final point to underscore here concerns the experimental and ultimately piecemeal character of change in both the German and US political economies. None of the examples of institutional innovation and recomposition in the areas of initial learning and cost reduction constitute a dominant form of adjustment within either the United States or Germany. Adjustment in both societies is extremely fractured and driven by local experimentation. It is not for this reason to be taken less seriously. Instead, the transformation of institutional architectures within contemporary advanced political economies is occurring in precisely this sort of decentralized, local, and piecemeal fashion. Giants are felled by thousands of arrows.

We put to the side the question of whether or not this is a general matter regarding the nature of institutional transformation in all times and all places. But the current character of global competition, characterized as it is by virtually permanent technological change and organizational uncertainty, leads to the following boundedly general consideration. Much of the literature on institutional systems, not least the VoC tradition, discusses the historical development of institutional architectures in the imagery of periods of stability marked by dramatic junctures of upheaval and change followed again by a period of stability. One can be critical of this historical imagery as a general matter (Sabel and Zeitlin 1997), but it seems particularly inappropriate to impose narrative expectations of a coming period of institutional stability (equilibrium) on the current situation. In large part this is because what stands out about the experiments that one observes today is their self-consciously provisional character. They have been brought into being because actors perceive common problems that are not being addressed by the traditional institutional instruments available to them for the purpose of addressing such problems. Actors are not willing to describe what they are doing as a new order because they are too acutely aware of the possibility that they will have to change again in the current turbulent environment. The distinctiveness of current problems is that they are never definitively resolved: Innovation and cost reduction, and the institutional tinkering and recomposition that they entail, are continuous processes. Old institutional rules today are not only being broken, but new ones are continually being defined and then redefined.

7

Roles and Rules: Ambiguity, Experimentation, and New Forms of Stakeholderism in Germany

By the middle of the first decade of the twenty-first century, there was widespread agreement in Germany on the need for reform in the central institutions of the "German Model" of political economy: that is, in the systems of industrial relations, vocational training, corporate governance, and finance. Remarkably, despite such broad agreement on the need for change, no workable coalitions or reform programs have emerged that a majority of German citizens find acceptable. Indeed, as a grand coalition fragmented and parties split into ever-hardening positions, perhaps the only consensus about reform that broad groupings of Germans across the political spectrum shared was that they did not want to push their society in the direction of the United States. By this they meant that they did not want crucial questions in their society—how the labor market should work, how relations between employers and employees should be governed, and how corporations should be governed and financed—to be adjudicated exclusively by market processes.

How else these questions *should* be adjudicated, however, has not been settled. Indeed, debate has become nearly immobilized. There is a pervasive sense that the range of possibilities for reform is defined by the following opposition: Either outcomes in these core areas will be negotiated out among the traditional social stakeholders (social cooperation) *or* they will be determined by arm's-length price-taking market relations. The former is considered to be politically desirable and just (and traditionally German), but overly rigid and increasingly unworkable. The latter is viewed as workable but unjust and undesirable. The national stalemate is indicative of the absence of any practical conceptual way to move forward in the face of what many regard as an inescapable zero-sum opposition.

Paralysis at the national level has not meant, however, that there is no change occurring in Germany. Far from it. At the level of firms and regions, as well as within specific functional institutional realms, such as in industrial relations, there has been very remarkable change. Interestingly, the same opposition between stakeholder negotiation and market principles also structures the way that these changes have been understood. Commentators, on both the left and the right, have claimed that much of the local-level change has been the result of "liberalization"; that is, the embrace at the local level of precisely the kind of market principles that the Germans reject at the national level (Lane 2000; Streeck and Hassel 2005; Keller 2006). As at the national level, the consensus is that the old institutional system of social coordination is too rigid to be able to foster competitiveness in the current competitive environment. Markets are coded, even by those who object to their social and political consequences, as the vehicles of contemporary flexibility. They make it possible for firms and social actors to rapidly and capaciously reallocate resources and even embrace new roles. Thus, nearly all local efforts in the workplace, in firms, and in associations to achieve flexibility, that define new roles and move away from the traditional rules of social cooperation have been characterized as "movements toward the market," if not the outright embrace of market mechanisms.

Understandably, this interpretation of events at the local level has been tinged with considerable pessimism, especially on the left, as it suggests that despite national-level resistance to the pressures of neoliberalism, the local institutional foundations of social cooperation are increasingly being undermined (Hassel 1999, 2006; Artus 2001; Streeck 2005; Streeck and Hassel 2005; Artus et al. 2006). Indeed, on this view, processes of negotiation between traditional associational stakeholders in the economy, where they are thought to still exist, are regarded as special cases. Either they are understood as reactionary remnants (heroic holdouts) of an outdated old system, increasingly hollowed out and "eroding" from the acid of market process (Hassel 1999, 2006). Or they are viewed as the expression of special conditions, having to do with technological or idiosyncratic political factors, that insulate processes of negotiation from direct contact with market competition (Artus et al. 2006). On either variant of this view, continued stakeholder governance will last only as long as political will or technological caprice allows. There is, apparently, no positive dynamic contained within the economy that allows for the successful regeneration of stakeholder governance and social cooperation in Germany.

The aim of this chapter is to reframe the current process of adjustment in Germany in a way that rejects the above opposition between an older entrenched tradition of stakeholder cooperation and an insurgent challenge of society-transforming market liberalization. In the first instance, it would be possible to make this kind of argument simply by pointing out that the current opposition between negotiation and markets in the debate is overdrawn. It has always been the case that markets have permeated German society, so it is unclear why the two forms of practice must be understood as antithetical today (see Abelshauser 2003). Although there is nothing to disagree with in that claim, this chapter makes a different argument against the notion that there is an opposition between cooperation and liberalization. If we place the German dilemma in the context of the trends outlined in Chapters 4 and 5, then it is not at all clear that "liberalization" is actually the challenge currently being posed to the Germans (or to Europeans more generally). There is undeniably pressure to become more flexible in many areas of work and organizational life in the political economy. It is therefore accurate to say that traditional forms of social cooperation in German society are undergoing sometimes very radical recomposition. But rather than the embrace of "the market," these pressures have induced widespread experimentation with alternative forms of workplace and firm governance that involve continual and collaborative recomposition of stakeholder roles in and among firms and social actors. In other words, stakeholder governance is not disintegrating in Germany. It is being redefined.

The current debate overlooks the significance of this process of stakeholder redefinition because it reifies markets and social cooperation. They are made into mutually exclusive categories with rigid internal characteristics. At worst, this leaves us with projections of clumsy and unrealistic alternatives of path-dependent rigidity (social cooperation digging in its heels) or past-erasing trans-formation (atomized marketization working like acid in social life) noted above. At best, the reified oppositions allow for the construction of so-called hybrid arrangements in which the opposing principles are "combined" through the dilution of cooperative rigidities with market flexibility (Casper 2000; Lane 2000). But dilution or weakening of cooperative arrangements by the introduction of principles of competitive exchange is quite different than the redefinition of what social cooperation actually involves. Hybridity (at least in that debate) implies demotion, while a focus on redefinition allows for the possibility that the practice can actually be enhanced, made stronger, and made better. The range of possibilities in the political and economic practice is greater than the contem-porary debate is able to recognize.

The analysis here will create a space for thinking about a broader range of alternative modes of stakeholder governance by making creative actors and the dynamic interaction of roles and rules the center of analysis. Here both markets and stakeholder arrangements will be understood not as antipodal mechanisms, but rather as different groupings of rules (institutions) that specific groupings of reflexive actors create to govern particular dimensions of their social process in the economy. Such complexes of rules are highly contingent constructs and are recurrently recomposed. Actors, enacting roles that the rules are designed to govern, continually reflect upon and evaluate the adequacy of both their roles and of the governing rules as they struggle to cope with the challenges and opportunities of their situation. Old roles are modified, new roles emerge, and rules that prove to be inadequate or irrelevant to the emerging situation are either changed or ignored. Those that continue to be effective continue to be embraced—though often in unexpected ways.[1] Such differentiated processes of role and rule evaluation and adjustment involve considerable creativity on the part of actors. All solutions are effectively provisional—pragmatists describe them as experiments—and actors embrace them only when they help solve the problems that have been collectively identified (Joas 1996; Sabel 2005).

---

[1] In this sense, we return to a theme that has been present throughout this book: In contrast to much of institutional analysis, the pragmatic emphasis on creative action and recomposition can account for both stability and change in relational environments.

Seen in this constructed, un-reified way, markets and social cooperation are by no means always in conflict or mutually exclusive. In many cases, rules developed in one area can be embraced for ends held by actors committed to the other, and vice versa. This is not the creation of hybrids. It is simply the adaptation of rules for practical problem solving. The difference in perspectives can perhaps be illustrated by the following example. Many of the new experiments in coordination to be described below aim for the creation of alternative sets of governance structures in which transparency rules traditionally associated with markets— such as the formalization of monitoring procedures and of accounting functions to create greater transparency both within and across the borders of organizations—play central roles in the facilitation of new forms of stakeholder collaboration. If one views markets and social collaboration as antithetical modes of governance, then this appears to be the embrace of market mechanisms. But if one views social collaboration and market practice simply as practical (recomposeable) groupings of rules and roles, then the example illustrates the selective deconstruction of market principles in the interest of constructing an alternative (more effective) set of rules for the governance of collaborative practices (Sabel 2005; Günther and Gonschorek 2006; Herrigel 2007*b*).

The range of this sort of experimentation with rules and roles in Germany today is extremely broad—markets, organizations, stakeholders, and forms of social and political negotiation are all in play, and often in quite unfamiliar and counterintuitive ways. To the extent that it still matters, the old institutional order in the German political economy increasingly is being filled with distinctly untraditional forms of practice. But it is also true that in many cases, the old institutions are a sideshow to new forms of practice. The latter draw selectively on the old institutional mechanisms, but deploy them in new ways, quite independently of their place in the old system, according to different rules. We will see below that in this context, stakeholderism is neither paralyzed nor outmoded in Germany. It is undergoing recomposition.

The argument begins, in Section 7.1, with a brief review of the way in which the relational dynamics in industrial markets have been changing. The aim of the section is to emphasize that developments have created great ambiguity in the roles that actors play in production and in the geographic scale at which production takes place. This, in turn, has given rise to new pressures, problems, and governance dilemmas that the existing array of institutions within the German business system was not designed to address. Section 7.2 will then show how these pressures are giving rise to new kinds of actors that are redefining traditional roles in the political economy and engaging in institutional innovation at a very local level. A core claim in this section is that these innovative, emergent actors are engaged in open experiments with the institutional rules that are supposed to govern their relations. Some of these experiments involve creative interpretation of the existing rules, others involve the assertion of exceptions, while in other cases there is mutual agreement among the parties to place the existing rules aside. The German industrial relations system will be used as the primary empirical illustration of these dynamics. The argument concludes (Section 7.3) with reflections on the possible national-level implications of this ongoing experimentation at the local level in the economy.

7.1. CURRENT ADJUSTMENT PRESSURES IN THE MANUFACTURING ECONOMY

As we saw in Chapters 4 and 5, vertical disintegration is the central dynamic in many industrial markets today. This is particularly true of the traditional manufacturing industries that form the core German economy (automobiles, machinery, electrical equipment, etc.). Manufacturing firms are to a large extent breaking their production operations up, focusing their own activities on the most profitable and most innovative dimensions of their business, and shifting both development and production of other operations on to suppliers. This process has had two seemingly contradictory, but nonetheless intense and unremitting drivers: (*a*) a continuous pressure to innovate, improve technology and production organization, and bring out new products more quickly, and (*b*) an equally as unrelenting pressure to reduce production costs.

The former pressure stems from intense global competition among producers and is driven by the shortening of product life cycles and the desire of competing firms to identify, exploit, and redefine dynamic and plastic consumer tastes. The pressure for cost reduction, in part, grows out of the intensifying pressure for innovation, as the development of new technology is expensive and places strains on firm resources. In order to learn about and develop new technologies and applications for their products, firms must divert resources from routine production activities into research and development areas. Internal departments are benchmarked against outside specialists, and if they cannot produce with the same quality and at as low a cost, then the operations are shifted outside and the savings directed toward innovation. Suppliers are also benchmarked against other suppliers, always on the basis of quality and cost, and the winner is always the one with the net lowest costs. In this way, pressures for innovation and cost-reduction structure the entire, increasingly disintegrated, supply chain.

This dynamic of vertical disintegration has affected the character of relations within and between firms in the supply chain in two very distinctive ways. The first is the emergence of ineradicable role ambiguity. Because the value chain has been disintegrated, customer and supplier relations dominate contemporary manufacturing. But the character of relations between customers and suppliers, in particular the specific role that the customer and supplier will play in their relation, is always ex ante highly uncertain. This is true for three reasons.

First, larger customers look to suppliers for innovation in areas that the customer firm no longer specializes in and suppliers look to customers as sophisticated users of their technologies who will push them, even help them, to devise new applications for their products. In other words, both customer and supplier look to one another for innovation and for learning. Second, because both customer and supplier are under constant pressure to innovate, both have an incentive to limit the extent to which bilateral relations with particular customers/suppliers become exclusive. Exclusivity can lead to myopia and blindness to possibilities. As a result, even firms benefiting from intimate collaborative, mutual learning exchanges, seek to limit those relations in order to be able to scan their relevant technological landscapes for customers or suppliers with whom they can learn something new. In this way, one can think of collaboration as having a cost that both suppliers and customers need to minimize. Third, both the customer and the supplier are under extreme cost-reduction pressures, so the customer would like to pay as little for the supplier's product as possible, while the supplier would like to earn as much from the relationship as possible. Both will seek to exploit weaknesses in the other's position in the interest of cost reduction and margin protection (see Chapter 4) (Herrigel 2007, Sabel 2005; Whitford and Zeitlin 2004).

These three logics enter into the constitution of every relationship in the supply chain. As a result, up front, it is never clear to either party precisely what kind of relationship the two are entering into. Neither knows for certain the role they will ultimately play: Will it be a collaborative relationship in which mutual learning is paramount? Will it be an arm's-length relationship in which cost reduction and margin protection is the primary game? There are many possibilities for how relationships can be established. And then, significantly, once established at a single point in time, those relations can then change over time. Past roles are not determining factors for the role one will play in the future. Often a supplier will enjoy and benefit from a collaborative tie with a customer and yet decide to devote its resources to establishing a substantial collaborative relation with one of the customer's competitors because that competitor has know-how that the supplier would like to have access to. Rather than simply abandon the old customer, the supplier can decide, for the sake of the relationship in the future, to provide the customer with some production capacity at cost so that the customer can achieve desired cost-reduction targets. Alternatively, a customer and supplier may enter into what both hope will be a collaborative relation, but then after a short time discover that either the supplier or the customer will not be able to deliver their end of the bargain within specified cost parameters. When the supplier is the disappointer in such cases, the customer will take jointly developed plans and seek bids on them from competitors of the supplier that developed them. Indeed, the supplier could even find itself bidding on its own designs! Customers and supplier at any point can be collaborators in design and production, arm's-length producers, developers without production, producers without design—and all and none of the above. This is sustained contingent collaboration (SCC, see Chapter 4) (also Wittke 2007).

The point is that relations are extremely dynamic and heterogeneous in contemporary manufacturing, both within firms and between firms. The role of customers and suppliers in any given bidding round is fundamentally ambiguous, even to themselves. The division of roles only becomes clear through repeated interaction and reciprocal efforts to define the possibilities and limits of a jointly defined project. And even then, it is merely provisional: Stable, and clear only until the end of the project and the beginning of another bargaining round.

7.1.1. Role Ambiguity Versus Institutional Frameworks Presupposing Unambiguous Roles

Role ambiguity is currently constitutive of industrial practice across the world's industrial economies. Continuous pressure for innovation and cost reduction is the driver of this ambiguity and a vertically disintegrated supply and value chain with highly volatile and heterogeneous relations are its manifestation. The emergence of these kinds of relations in industry has generated tremendous pressure for change on all the institutions that constitute national business systems—in industrial relations, vocational training, finance, welfare provision, and regional industrial policy. By and large, most of those institutions' governing rules were created under conditions that differ significantly from those currently shaping play. Above all, nearly all of those institutions presuppose the existence of relatively unambiguous, not to say fixed, roles among industrial players. As a result, they are oriented toward the protection of rights and positions, rather than to their continual redefinition and recomposition (Kristensen and Rocha 2006). At best, these old institutional arrangements can only partially and often only accidentally address the kinds of problems that actors in industries characterized by SCC encounter and generate. At worst, those institutions constitute barriers to solutions to those problems.

Unsurprisingly, actors on the ground have been energetically engaged in efforts to provide solutions for the kinds of problems contemporary industrial practice generates. As will be shown below, these efforts have neither involved wholesale abandonment of the existing cooperative institutions nor the aggressive embrace of something like unfettered market mechanisms. Rather, current efforts to find reasonable governance structures for the problems generated by role ambiguity all involve experimentation around and with the existing systems of institutional rules governing cooperation. As the character of social cooperation on the ground changes, institutions are being recomposed and reinvented to support it. In this process, old institutional actors are adopting new roles and redefining rules at the same time that new roles and new rules are being created. This is not a process of liberalization. Indeed, far from being a victim, cast aside by the process of change, stakeholder cooperation is quite central to it. But the kind of stakeholderism that is currently emerging is very different than the traditional understanding of corporatist governance that has long defined the German political economy.

7.2. HOW IS THIS EXPERIMENTATION TAKING PLACE?

The main mechanism driving transformation in the institutional framework of the German political economy today is rule breaking—or, at least, experimentation with and around existing rules in ways that do not always involve following the rules. Rules can be "broken" in a variety of ways—many of these ways are not in and of themselves necessarily threatening to the existing system of rules. Some may even be useful for the preservation of the existing rules—secondary or informal sectors in economies often emerge due to rigidities in core sector practices, for example. Other kinds of actions are simply exceptions to the rules, as when one has to break one rule in order to comply with another. There also can be important new action that occurs in areas where the existing set of rules simply do not apply. Finally, since rule following itself is a repetitive activity that involves constant interpretation and reinterpretation as one attempts to apply the general prescriptions of a rule to the peculiar and particular facts of a case, actors constantly change rules (or redefine them) even as they follow them.[2]

All of these forms of normal "rule breaking" can be found in abundance in Germany today. But in crucial cases, it is also true that rules are simply not being applied in areas in which they are intended to govern or they are self-consciously being applied in ways that undermine the end to which they were originally devised. Call this rule breaking by mutual consent or coordination to act in ways that are not proscribed or intended by the existing rules. The crucial occasion for all of the examples of experimentation around rules to be described below is that the traditional rules, and the proscribed roles for actors within those rules, no longer address the dynamics and governance problems that actors in industry confront.

The chapter uses the industrial relations system as a case study of this kind of creative action around rules and roles. The reason for this is that examples of experimentation with rules and roles are especially clear in this area. Moreover, the industrial relations system in Germany has received a great deal of international attention and its changes have elicited much debate about the compatibility of "coordinated capitalism" in the labor market with increasing liberalization. This chapter's view is that industrial relations change in Germany is not rightly understood as a process of liberalization. Rather it is one in which principles of markets and social cooperation are just so many rules for the governance of roles, and in particular in which stakeholder coordination is being redefined.

---

[2] In thinking about the plasticity of rules, I have found the following to be very helpful (Mayo 1954; Miller 1956; Bourdieu 1977; Edgerton 1985; Lewis 1988; Melmberg 1990; Taylor 1999; Ortmann 2003).

7.2.1. Industrial Relations Literature and Contemporary Change in Industrial Relations

There is much hand-wringing in the literature on the current state of the German system of industrial relations (Grahl and Teague 2004). Most analyses, even when there are disagreements on the long-term implications, agree that the traditional dual system of industrial relations, in which trade unions negotiate industry-wide collective agreements with organized employers that are then subsequently implemented within individual firms through negotiation between works councils and plant management, has been destabilized. Most importantly, the crucial informal solidarity linking industrial unions with plant-level works councils has been broken.[3] As firms and plants seek to cope with the constant turbulence generated by the ambiguity of roles in the value chain, they seek greater local flexibility and chafe at the restrictions placed on their ability to organize work time and wage payment placed on them by industry-wide collective agreements. Alliances for adjustment and employment between plant management and works councils have proliferated that systematically implement arrangements locally that depart from the industry-wide benchmarks established by the unions and organized employers (Rehder 2003; Seifert and Massa-Wirth 2005; Williams and Geppert 2006).

This kind of *Verbetrieblichung* (segmentation/atomization) in the industrial relations system has been further exacerbated by the proliferation of so-called variable pay regimes in which workers are paid individually for their performance rather than according to more general hourly metrics calculated on the basis of fixed positions in the division of labor. Finally, and most distressingly, there has been a growing exodous of employers out of employers associations and hence a growing population of firms and workers that do not directly participate in the construction of industry-wide wage agreements at all—although they often remain oriented toward broad industry agreements (Artus 2006). Small- and medium-sized supplier firms, as well as many firms of all types in eastern Germany, and also many so-called new economy firms in emergent high-technology sectors, find participation in the traditional industrial relations system to be disadvantageous, overly costly, and in many cases irrelevant to the pressures they face in their competitive markets (Artus 2001; Artus et al. 2006).

The literature describing these developments has two clear preoccupations. First, most analyses are primarily concerned with whether or not the above developments constitute "liberalization." Evidence is mixed for arguments both for and against. For example, while the segmentation and atomization of bargaining has been interpreted as a kind of liberalization of the system, the segmenting and atomizing has been negotiated out by unions and employers associations

---

[3] See Thelen (1991) for a lucid description of the way in which the informal tie between plant-based works councils and union-based wage bargaining used to work. In the work by Artus (2001) there is an excellent discussion of the breakdown of this tie in the 1990s.

(largely through the innovation of "opening clauses" in industry-wide contracts that allow for local-level deviations, so long as they are necessary for the survival of the firm). Moreover, the individual bargaining units that engage in deviations are themselves governed very intensely by stakeholder principles and the local deviations are all negotiated out between management and works councils. The force and authority of industry-wide agreements have undoubtedly been weakened, but if that is "liberalization," it is still highly mediated by social cooperation. Second, the literature focuses on forms of institutional change that do not involve either rule breaking or even experimentation. Instead, the focus is on forms of practice that result from very explicit decisions on the part of negotiating parties to create new rules that allow for new forms of practice within the framework of the old system. One of the strongest overviews of these sets of changes describes the current situation as "change within continuity" (Streeck and Rehder 2003).

While there is much value in this framing of the situation in the industrial relations system, its weakness is that the preoccupation with the specter of liberalization turns the eye away from widespread experimentation with the character of social cooperation and stakeholderism itself. Moreover, attention to developments that result from formal and explicit rule changes results in the neglect of widespread experimentation with rules and roles.

Section 7.2.2 shows that this is particularly true of developments on the firm and interfirm side of the dual system, though there are also some interesting experiments on the union/employer association side of the now destabilized system. The breakdown of the informal tie between associational collective bargainers and firm-based stakeholders has given rise to very uneven processes of role and rule experimentation. The associations appear to be more conservative than actors within the firms. The following describes a range of experiments with roles and rules currently being undertaken within and between German firms that recast the nature of stakeholder governance. In Section 7.3 I will speculate on potential consequences of these developments for the system of industrial relations as a whole.

7.2.2. Experimentation in Contemporary German Industrial Relations

There are several examples of experimentation with rules and roles involving Volkswagen (VW), the VW works council, and the IG Metall. The first shows actors creatively adapting rules to be able to engage in roles that are explicitly prevented by other rules. In collaboration with the City of Wolfsburg, and with the consent of IG Metall, VW has arranged for the construction of a research and development facility that allows the company to do something that German law technically prevents: that is, to incorporate its suppliers into its development and production processes in a way that facilitates the iterated and role-defining process of design refinement and production organization, known in the industry as "simultaneous engineering." In German law, it is illegal to have suppliers working on a customer's product in plants or facilities that are owned by a customer. This is a law that was designed to prevent companies from hiring workers on short-term contracts under different terms than those specified in the local collective bargaining agreement covering the rest of the workforce at the company (*Arbeitnehmeruberlassungsgesetz*). The existence of this law, a big victory for the union movement and the social democratic party back in the day, has been a major obstacle for German firms in their efforts generally to adopt the collaborative and decentralized principles in the Japanese or Toyota production system, including simultaneous engineering. In other words, it is a barrier to the integration of suppliers as stakeholders in production.

To get around the fact that it was illegal for VW to engage in simultaneous engineering on its own premises, the company persuaded the city government of Wolfsburg to agree to form a joint-stock company, Wolfsburg AG.[4] The city and company shared ownership in the new enterprise equally. This independent company was then made the legal owner of production and design facilities in which VW (and its suppliers) then proceeded to, as legal tenants, engage in simultaneous engineering. Here the market is being used to facilitate collaboration and rules are being used to conflate rules as actors redefine their roles in production. The next step (not yet taken) is to allow VW employees and supplier employees to jointly assemble cars on Wolfsburg AG-owned assembly lines. As auto suppliers come from a variety of industries, governed by a variety of collective agreements with different unions (and in some cases by no collective agreement), this could potentially create the possibility for one assembly line in one plant to be governed by several collective agreements—a very un-German prospect. Yet it is one that creative actors in the supply chain are pursuing in order to be able to construct organizational practices that allow them to cope with the dual pressures of innovation and cost reduction.

Another VW example is a case where the stakeholders involved (VW, the Employers Association in Lower Saxony, the IG Metall, and the VW All Corporate Works Council), with the consent of the regional government, agreed to place all the existing rules of collective bargaining aside. The stakeholders then constructed an entirely new VW car model in a separate VW-owned facility next to the main assembly complex in Wolfsburg. Known as the Auto 5000 experiment, the project built a new minivan model using a workforce composed entirely of formerly unemployed workers in Lower Saxony. The new workers were paid wages set at the regionally bargained minimum rate, rather than the much higher rate that the traditional "Haus" collective agreement between IG Metall and VW traditionally established. In addition, VW and IG Metall agreed to experiment with new forms of work organization, in particular multifunctional team organization in which teams were responsible for their own costs and in which workers

---

[4] For a description of Wolfsburg AG, see: http://www.wolfsburg-ag.com/sixcms/detail.php?template=wob_master&lang=de&sv[id]=25584&nav1=25585.

were rewarded for both product-improvement and cost-reduction suggestions. The latter were practices that VW had awkwardly and haltingly introduced in other German factories—though they were more common in VW facilities outside of Germany. The rationale for this mutually agreed project of rule breaking was that the existing system of rules, and the roles in production that they organized, were both too expensive and too rigid to allow for the continuous redefinition of roles that the twin pressures of constant innovation and systematic cost reduction encouraged. In order to be able to achieve both goals simultaneously one needed to have the alternative, cross-functional, and self-optimizing structures that the Auto 5000 project experimented with (Schumann et al. 2006).[5]

More broadly in the German manufacturing economy, works councils constitute a broad area of experimentation with both roles and rules. Our interviews revealed countless efforts to transform them from specialists for workplace scheduling, training, job retention, and the processing of grievances to "co-managing" units participating with other functional departments within the firm in interrelated discussions on product design, process optimization, and cost in the plant.[6] This represents an expansion/redefinition of the role given to works councils in the Works Constitution Act. In the new role, works councils continue to be responsible for the activities that are legally defined for them. But now in addition, the works council engages as a worker representative in whole firm deliberations about cost reduction and innovation. By drawing on their presence in all workshops and departments in a plant, works councils have the unique capacity to accumulate information (if they choose to collect it) about work flow, inventory, work in process, the efficiency of work organization, and other dimensions of the production process. Such information, particularly as it cuts across the entire plant, is indispensable for the achievement of cost reduction—as well as for the identification of possibilities for both technical design improvements and organizational innovation. Such activities can result in the reallocation of jobs and assignments as well as the elimination of jobs. But it can also ensure that more traditional management departments also engaged in the identification of cost-reduction possibilities expand their attention beyond making savings on labor costs alone (Klitzke et al. 2000; Minssen and Riese 2005).

It is important to emphasize that such experiments in co-management do not simply or even necessarily amount to the self-rationalization of labor.[7] In many cases, the expanding role of the works council involves systematic expansion of its

---

[5] Thanks to Michael Schumann and Hans Joachim Sperling for extensive discussions of their empirical work on the Auto 5000 experiment.

[6] I use the term "co-management" loosely to describe a broad range of efforts on the part of works councils to engage in a variety of "purely" managerial activities, including the identification of possibilities for cost reduction in production and materials flow, as well as the optimization of logistics, product development, and financial costing procedures within the firm. The usage here overlaps with but is not identical to the way in which "co-management" is defined in the industrial relations and trade union discussions of the term. For the latter, see Klitzke et al. (2000).

[7] For that argument, and the legitimation problems thought to emerge from that role, see Rehder (2006).

technical and design capabilities—hiring additional staff with engineering know-how, upgrading the skills of existing works councilors, etc. The reason for this has to do with the linkage between innovation pressure and cost reduction. On the one hand, in order to devote resources to innovation, production processes and work flows constantly need to be rationalized so that costs are minimized. On the other hand, the optimization of production and work flow very often can be achieved through innovation in product design. Because progress on both ends is always desirable and often interrelated, it makes little sense for participants in the process to be specialized in only one aspect. At one Wuppertal-based bearing manufacturing facility, for example, this has prompted the works council to draw additional technically trained employees into its staff. The works council actively seeks to develop innovative product design ideas that can be achieved within desirable cost parameters (interview).

Co-management, at least in the form described, represents an embrace by the works council of a qualitatively different stakeholder role in the firm. It is crucial to see that its efforts to embrace this role are provoked by the pervasive and constant role ambiguity in production that the firm's efforts to cope with the twin pressures of constant innovation and constant cost reduction generate. By simply acting within the confines of its traditional role, works councilors recognize that they forfeit a genuine opportunity to have stakeholder input in the continuous process of recomposition in contemporary production. They need to be involved in the process of recomposition in order to be able to influence it. In order to be able to do that, they need to expand their capacities and collect and share more information about the production process with other "stakeholders" within the firm.

Traditionally, works councils understood stakeholder representation in a narrowly distributive sense: how to maximize employee security and wages relative to the interests of management and ownership. This understanding presupposed a static divide between management and employees and clear and stable roles for each within the production process. At bottom, it provided the works councils with a defensive and rights-defending role in the firm (cf. Kristensen and Rocha 2006). The new works council role, at least in the best and most successful cases we have seen in automobile and machinery industry producers and the suppliers along their supply chains, recasts stakeholderism in a way that maximizes the contribution that employees make to the firm's capacity to successfully innovate and reduce costs. It presupposes—indeed it helps to create—a fluid and continuously self-recomposing distribution of roles within production. In this sense, it is proactive and rights-creating. What this new works council role shares with the old role, interestingly, is the sense that stakeholders have power within the organization. That power is enacted differently—arguably with a more extensive impact on the ongoing organization of design and manufacturing with the firm—but the insistence on mutual recognition among stakeholding parties is the same.

Crucially, works councils, and firms with works councils, are not the only actors in Germany currently experimenting with ways in which traditional modes of cooperative stakeholderism can be redefined. There are many examples of firms that are legally entitled to form works councils, but yet exercise their right not to adopt one. They exercise a rule that allows them to leave the rules in abeyance. And the range of outcomes in these areas is very interesting. It is not all simple management domination (though there is some of that).[8] There are many examples of worker–management coordination on matters relevant to the competitiveness of the firm, in particular regarding reconciling the twin pressures of constant innovation and cost reduction. In these cases, employees view the workplace representation organizations made available to them by law to be inadequate to the collective tasks of innovation and cost reduction that they are confronted with. In the previous example, already existing works councils entered upon new terrain and redefined their role in order to be able to participate in cross-functional plant-wide organizations designed to address issues of innovation and cost reduction. In these latter instances, participatory cross-functional and cross-plant organizations are created that facilitate simultaneous and constant monitoring of costs and search for possible innovative improvements in the technology and production process. In such cases, employees do not bother to set up the traditional, and to them apparently unnecessary (irrelevant?) works council structures. They are relevantly involved in the governance of the firm in an alternative way.

Indeed, in many *Betriebe ohne Betriebsräte* (Artus et al. 2006) in what are provocatively called the "codetermination free zones" of the economy, the ability of employees to participate in in-plant monitoring organizations at various levels that involve multiple departments is at least as great as it is in codetermined plants with formal works councils. In the codetermined arenas, works councils have extra burdens that codetermination free plants do not have: Works councils must struggle to redefine their roles and gain management and cross-departmental acknowledgment and participation in the monitoring of cost-reduction possibilities. Such structures in the codetermination free plants, however, are created for that purpose. It is the difference between having an actor with a traditional role acquire new roles versus the creation of new actors with new roles.

Critics point to the fact that, unlike the formal works councils, the new codetermination free organizations are not explicitly devoted to workplace democracy and the representation of worker interests against those of owners (Böhm and Lücking 2006; Keller 2006). The new representation structures do not have the same continuity that works councils have, in that they tend to be project oriented. The structures of representation and the actors involved in self-representation change and recompose with the change and recomposition of the roles in the firm. The divide between workers and owners is obscured in the new structures, as no side of the ledger reliably contributes more to cost reduction or

---

[8] For a useful typology of governance types in firms without works councils, which includes both mutual cooperation between management and alternatively organized employees and asymmetrical relations of managerial exploitation, see Böhm and Lücking (2006).

innovation than the other. Indeed, both are becoming aware of their increasing mutual dependence. Critics worry that continuous recomposition of participatory arrangements could produce atomization, making individuals vulnerable while at the same time reducing solidarity among stakeholders. But there is just as much reason to believe that the more recomposition is successful, the more it will create an organization-wide feeling of mutual dependence and hence of an intensified sense of the legitimacy of stakeholder entitlement.

This is not to say that there are no difficulties in the new-style organizations. Self-exploitation (working long hours, not taking vacations, etc.) is a dimension of such team organizations. The possibility exists that people get caught up in the challenge of their collective work projects and extend themselves in illegal and unhealthy ways. Worse, co-workers can be intimidated into not taking what is their due because of fear of group reprisal. There are also questions, especially in small family or single-owner entrepreneurial enterprises of arbitrary authority in the last instance by owners. In such cases, collaboration and recomposition occur at the discretion of the owner and are limited by her authority. These are very difficult questions and there are many examples of good and bad process to deal with them. But the key point is that such questions are just as relevant to works councilors engaging in a new co-management role as it is for those actors simply engaging in the new role. Works councils, in their new role, can enthusiastically participate in a culture of self-exploitation, and they can also decide not to invoke their right to challenge entrepreneurial authority in an area that has not tradi- tionally been considered to be within their bailiwick. These are governance and accountability questions concerning a role that is outside the current system of workplace governance. Works councils find themselves upon uncharted terrain in the same way that codetermination-free self-governing project teams do.[9]

In any case, the nostalgic political yearnings of critics for a world of clear boundaries and relatively fixed roles among stakeholders seem to have little currency among participants in the new-style arrangements in firms that for one reason or another have no existing tradition of works council representation. Instead of choosing to adopt an institution, only then to have to redefine what it does in a way that is consistent with contemporary demands, workers in firms without works councils seem to be deciding simply to participate in the con- struction of participatory arrangements that reflect their own, constantly chang- ing and self-recomposing work experience.

Whatever the reason, the facts are that the majority of firms in the eastern part of Germany, increasing numbers of suppliers in manufacturing supply chains, as well as most new start-ups in newer areas of the industrial economy, as in

---

[9] Interestingly, the Dresden group's survey of the degree to which small- and medium-sized firms have adopted "value-accounting" techniques—which facilitate intra-firm information exchange among collaborating stakeholders—shows that the (nearly) pervasive adoption is not regarded by the adopting owners and top managers to be in tension with their "social" commitments to stake- holders within the firm. The majority of adopters have retained the strong social commitments that they held prior to the adoption (Günther and Gonschorek 2006).

software, biotech, and other "new economy" sectors, have decided to exercise their legal right *not* to form a works council. Numbers without works councils are significantly greater in those areas, sectors, and firms where the tradition of codetermination is weak or has been dislodged (Ellguth 2006).

Another kind of remarkable role transformation is taking place in Wuppertal (see also Chapter 6). Unlike all the previous examples, this is a case of rule and role experimentation on the extra-firm, union/employer association side of the German dual system. The Wuppertal IG Metall administrative office is redefining its role to act as a kind of regional restructuring agency. In this case, as in the case of co-managing works councils, the union adds a new role to its traditional one within the rules of the existing system of industrial relations. On the one hand, it bargains with the local employers' association and monitors firms to ensure that they are abiding by the terms of existing collective agreements in a completely traditional way. Yet, on the other hand, the union is now also being called into firms, often by the management of the firm itself, to help with internal restructuring and with the reformulation of product and market strategies. There are no rules that govern the latter form of activity. It is not a traditional activity proscribed in the Works Constitution Act. Nor has it evolved in a common law fashion as the way in which the traditional system works. Instead, it is an entirely new role for the union. Remarkably, the newly created role has grown to dominate the activities of the Wuppertal office. So much so, in fact, the union complains that it would actually be to its advantage if the employers association became involved in the restructuring activities—a partner in crime, so to speak, to share the workload and broaden the experience of the consultants (interview).

To be clear, Wuppertal is not actually a case of rule breaking. There are no rules that apply to the activities of trade unions as restructuring consultants. But in a concrete sense, the fact that it has adopted a role as restructuring consultant has given it the legitimacy to press works councils to embrace the new roles (co-management) described above. Not only that, the union teaches works councils how to participate in the construction of new forms of work organization that enhance the firm's capacity to engage in continuous cost reduction and innovation scanning.[10] Successful cases, such as the Wuppertal bearing manufacturer mentioned above, help to draw other works councils into the embrace of new roles and rules that they previously had not been willing or trusting enough to consider. At the same time, the union can push employers to accept the new role for works councils and in general to turn their eyes in the direction of organizational change that aims at whole organizational analyses of cost reduction, rather than simply focusing on the contribution of labor to costs. In this sense, the embrace of a new role for the trade union has induced players within firms to give up their attachments to the formal and informal rules and practices that had traditionally governed production and engage in practices that constitute new roles for both stakeholders.

---

[10] Monitoring work in progress, reduction of inventory, cellular organization, cross-functional exchanges, etc.

7.3. WHAT TO MAKE OF THESE EXAMPLES: THE RECOMPOSITION OF STAKEHOLDERISM IN GERMAN MANUFACTURING?

These are all experiments around rules and roles. They sometimes involve rule breaking. Other times they are simply examples of cases in which the rules do not apply (and where no one suggests that they should). In other cases, they are expressions of very creative use of existing rules. In many instances, actions seem to be motivated or bound up with the existence of role ambiguity. They involve the creation of new roles. Finally, all of the above industrial relations examples are local experiments that allow employees and managers in firms to cope with the twin pressures of innovation and cost reduction. None are "macro" experiments. Indeed, for the most part they are taking place underneath national-level institutions that are changing much less radically, if at all.

The examples I have presented are also selective in that they address the central dilemma in industry today: how to cope with the twin pressures of innovation and cost reduction under conditions of continuously recurring role ambiguity. To be sure, there are other kinds of experiments in the contemporary German system of industrial relations. For example, there are efforts on the part of management to eliminate employee participation entirely and reimpose a kind of Taylorist control over the workplace. Here the idea is to achieve constant cost reduction through the radical separation of employees from the innovation process within the firm (Springer 1999). There are also (still) examples of the old system in place, where skilled labor, traditional works councils and management, all with very clear roles, informally collaborate in ways that seek to improve the quality of the firm's product and achieve a position in the market that is insulated from cost competition. The problem with both of these kinds of contemporary practice, however, is that, in contrast to the examples above, they focus only on one of the twin pressures facing firms, either cost reduction or innovation. They do not possess the capacity to continuously achieve both simultaneously. It may be that such alternative practices will be able to reproduce themselves in the current environment. Yet by seeking to keep the twin pressures of innovation and cost reduction separate from one another, they impose limits on the range of possibilities available to solve both. This is not true of the examples presented.

It is unclear what will happen with any of these examples of experimentation. In particular, there is no obvious link between the firm- and interfirm-based experiments in stakeholder governance and the union and associational side of the dual industrial relations system. As such, the implications of the redefinition of stakeholderism throughout the German economy for the industrial relations system as a whole are unclear. The examples of rule and role experimentation highlighted in this chapter, however, show very clearly that the recomposition of relations and governance structures in German manufacturing is by no means reducible to a simple process of marketization or liberalization. Social cooperation among stakeholders continues to be a central dimension of industrial practice, though in increasingly different and new forms. All caveats regarding the lack of obvious linkages between these local-level changes and macro transformation acknowledged, the examples provided suggest some intriguing possibilities for further, even macro-level, change. The most dramatic possibilities stem from the fact that the process of experimental change is slowly both creating new social actors in the economy and transforming the notion of what a stakeholder is. What it means to have stakeholder governance, in other words, could potentially be radically redefined.

The examples above show that new actors are emerging as substitutes for, competitors of, or simply as additions to the traditional role-players in the German economy. Works councils engaging systematically in collaborative cost reduction and rationalization or local unions that restructure local firms are incidences of traditional kinds of actors embracing wholly new roles. Their actions do not so much break the existing rules as they ignore them in an effort to solve pressing problems in ways that are consistent with larger normative ends that define the actors. In both cases, the *end in view* for the innovative actors is to keep production in the location, and ultimately, thereby, to save jobs. The means by which the new stakeholder arrangements seek to achieve their ends are in tension with existing rules and role definitions. Nonetheless they are consistent with some (higher-order) understanding of what the ends of union and works councils should be. By retaining and invoking principles of stakeholder legitimacy in governance, but in new roles, these experiments are slowly redefining the stakes that employees hold in firms (and communities). And they are creating new forms of stakeholder participation in firm and community governance.

In many ways, the new stakeholder forms are much more expansively collaborative than the old. They transgress old adversarial divides between labor and capital and unions and employer associations. Rather than attempting to demarcate a realm of distinct employee rights, for example, the alternative stakeholder arrangements attempt to empower those they represent by collaborating with other stakeholders to make the firm (or community) more successful. The irony in this is that in committing themselves to cooperative stakeholderism, the groups facilitate the continuous recomposition of roles and relations in the production process that results in the continual redefinition and realignment of stakes in the enterprise. Who the stakeholders are, in other words, is continuously redefined as relations within and between firms are recomposed over time.

The cases of new forms of participation in codetermination-free zones represent a very different way to arrive at a similar end. Here, old actors are not seeking to define new roles for themselves. Instead, new stakeholder positions and stakeholder conceptions are emerging without (and sometimes against) the old institutions. Rather than a labor/capital divide, the new participatory arrangements are (in the best cases) generating an underlying culture of mutual dependence. In these new arrangements, stakeholderism, in an alternative form, is indispensable for the ability of the firm to be competitive. The more successful the arrangements are at facilitating productive recombination, the more indispensable they become. Moreover, since the constitution of cross-functional projects often involves the participation of actors from both customer and supplier firms, new-style principles of stakeholderism are diffusing along the supply chain. In many cases, they actually govern the supply chain.

The interesting thing about these two distinct processes of change is that they converge. The old institutions redefining their roles (works councils and local unions) increasingly act in ways that are similar to new arrangements that have sometimes constituted themselves in explicit opposition to what they took to be old institutional practice. Irony aside, the convergence of different institutional actors around the principles of collaborative stakeholderism at a local level inescapably poses the question of how such arrangements will be treated by existing national-level stakeholder institutions (trade unions and employers associations). Until now, both national-level associations have shown little interest in redefining their roles or their conceptions of stakeholder governance. Current versions of national unions and employers associations were created on the basis of a perceived divide between labor and capital that presumes a continuity of roles and interest alignments within firms and within the society. In this older view, the principle of stakeholderism is tied to the reproduction of relatively stable stakeholder role positions and identities in the society and economy. They are focused on the protection of rights and entitlements ascribed to role positions. How can such a view of stakeholderism cope with the emergent alternative in which the link between stakeholder governance and stable role positions has been broken?

This is a question that has really yet to be posed in Germany today, at least not in this form. But, without suggesting which is the more likely, plausible, or desirable outcome, it is easy to see that there are at least three possible ways in which the relationship between the old stakeholder institutions can relate to the newly emergent ones.

First, the national organizations could seek to defend their own conception of stakeholderism and block the diffusion of the emergent alternative. They could use their leverage in resources to punish local experiments and ally with actors at local levels that are still committed to the traditional stakeholder conceptions and its institutional roles. This, obviously, would do very little to stanch the already significant centrifugal pressures that currently plague the dual system. Confronted with unsympathetic central associational representatives, stakeholder groupings within firms already pursuing their own independent course are likely to continue to do so. Acting defensively thus, at best, merely exacerbates decay of central institutional power. At worst, by seeking to undermine the construction of collaborative processes within firms that facilitate continuous self-recomposition, a reactionary move by the associations could have disastrous consequences for the competitiveness of German industry. One could, however, imagine this strategy finding successes in niches of the industrial economy. By establishing allies within, for example, re-Taylorizing firms as well as the handful of insulated producers still producing in traditional ways, associational actors hostile to the new forms of stakeholderism could conceivably create a rearguard place within the institutional landscape of the economy in which traditional class-based and rigid forms of stakeholderism continued to exist.

A second possibility would be for actors committed to the emergent alternative stakeholder governance arrangements to construct an alternative national (or supra-firm and supra-regional) system. This alternative system could avoid the existing stakeholder organizations, much in the way the new stakeholder arrangements have emerged in the codetermination free zones at the local level. Aside from invariable opposition to such efforts from the existing stakeholder organizations, it will be crucial for the new players to reconcile the alternative stakeholder forms that involve (redefined) works councils and local unions with those alternative forms that exclude and are opposed to those organizations. The latter need to be disabused of their view that the traditional institutions are irrelevant, while the former need to be disabused of the view that the codetermination-free zones are operating according to different, unaccountable, principles. Far from being far-fetched as a scenario, one could easily imagine gradual processes of experimentation and organizational redefinition at increasingly higher levels of territorial and organizational complexity in response to emergent problems and opportunities for stakeholder actors at lower levels.

For example, a significant problem confronting both forms of new stakeholderism in the context of continuous role redefinition is that all employees may not always be needed in every iteration of production process recomposition. New-style stakeholders do not want to dismiss colleagues, however, for two reasons. First, they feel solidarity and a commitment to providing employment to those with whom they regularly collaborate with on the shop floor. Second, they realize that though not needed in this round, a dismissed employee's expertise may be needed in a subsequent round. The inhibiting fear is that once let go, a valuable skilled employee is difficult to get back. Not letting an unneeded colleague go, however, can add to costs and hurt the competitiveness of the company. Firms and new-style stakeholder groups, therefore, have an interest in creating a system that lessens the disadvantages of dismissal and governs labor circulation among firms in local and regional labor markets in ways that are beneficial for firms and employees.

In Denmark, such problems have led to the transformation of the vocational training system and the way in which both local employers and trade unions are involved in it. Rather than seeking to retain employees within firms, the new extra-firm stakeholder system seeks to support and train workers let go. New training makes the dismissed colleague capable of reentering the process of recomposition within the same or other firms with enhanced skills and capacities. By creating arrangements outside the firm that support worker mobility, the system actually enhances the capacity of stakeholding actors within firms to creatively tackle the challenges posed by constant pressure for innovation and cost reduction (Madsen 2006; Kristensen et al. 2008). The argument here is not to advocate the embrace of the Danish solution to this problem. The aim is only to point out that there are problems generated by the new forms of stakeholder practice within firms that could be addressed with new forms of stakeholder practice at the extra-firm level. Bootstrapping experimentation combined with prudential comparative benchmarking of systems that solve the problems they face could lead stakeholders to create new arrangements at higher levels of social and economic governance.

The third possibility is for the traditional extra-firm stakeholder organizations, trade unions, and employers associations to change. They could embrace the alternative conception of stakeholder governance that is emerging through experimentation at the local level. Here, national unions and employers associations would identify (or respond to the lower-level identification of) public good problems of the sort noted in the previous paragraph. Even better, the national organizations could take it as their charge to continuously monitor lower-level arrangements, facilitate benchmarking processes (that are interregional and international), and help to diffuse best practice across a range of relevant functional problem areas.

In this way, national-level stakeholder organizations would change their role from defenders of social divisions to facilitators of lower-level social and economic recomposition in the interest of greater economic success for all. The specific temporal identity of social stakeholders would in this way be short lived. Who was who and who had what stake would be continuously redefined. But the principle of stakeholder governance would be entrenched from top to bottom in the society. Ironically, the kind of flexibility and continuous recomposition that in the current debate is thought to be the province of liberalization and the diffusion of market processes, would in this alternative case become the systematic objective of social cooperation.

Conclusion

Changing Business Systems, Power, and the Science of Manufacturing Possibilities

There are limits to how much speculation of the kind provided at the end of Chapter 7 can achieve. Ultimately, what emerges in the German system of industrial relations will be the outcome of prolonged political struggles among creative and reflexive social actors under conditions that are not always of their own making. Indeed, one can say this generally about national-level governance reforms (in finance, health care, labor markets, corporate governance, education, etc.) across the advanced political economies. This book's aim, however, is not to predict the future. It is rather to characterize the manner in which manufacturing change, at all levels, is currently taking place. The chapters repeatedly show that actors are creative and that change is recompositional. Far from being paralyzed by seemingly contradictory oppositions, such as those between stakeholder cooperation and liberalization, or coordination and market exchange, creative actors interweave principles from each pole as they collectively resolve practical challenges. As a result, new kinds of social actors, new conceptions of governance, and new understandings of stakeholding are emerging in the United States, Germany, and Japan. This is true despite the existence of widespread political pessimism and scientific skepticism about the possibility for successful reform. Perhaps incumbent national-level actors and institutionalist and neoliberal social scientists should reconsider the degree to which (ultimately only analytical) oppositions are actually constraining in practice. If they understood change as a continuous process of creative experimentation with roles and rules, their sense of paralysis and pessimism would lessen. The range of palatable possibilities for reform would seem greater.

In any case, in this concluding chapter, I would like to reflect on a number of themes and problems that this book's analysis inevitably raises. First, I will compare the theoretical perspective of creative action and recomposition presented here with the main theoretical positions on business system transformation in the academic literature. Second, I will consider the relational and non-structural understanding of power that underlines the analysis in this book. Finally, I will consider the analytical implications of this book's pragmatic perspective for social analysis of the economy.

8.1. SOME THEORETICAL CONSIDERATIONS ON
THE REFORM OF BUSINESS SYSTEMS

The question of how business systems reform themselves has been a major focus of concern for debates in political economy, economic sociology, and historical institutionalism for at least the last decade. The framing of the problem, however, has been evolving over time. Initially, there was a straightforward convergence versus path-dependence framing. The former view claimed that increasing openness to market pressures would give rise to increasingly similar institutional arrangements. The latter indicated that the existence of tightly coupled and complementary institutional arrangements, solidified by mutually reinforcing feedback dynamics, made wholesale adoption of alternative institutional arrangements highly unlikely (Pierson 2004). This framing was then refined by the Varieties of Capitalism (VoC) literature (and its cousins) (Whitley 1999; Hall and Soskice 2001; Amable 2003). They suggested that the convergence of systems was unlikely because different systems did different things well. In particular, coordinated market economies excelled in areas where gradual and continuous innovation was advantageous, while liberal market economies excelled at radical innovation.

Recently, further refinement has been introduced. It has become clear that the polarities of convergence versus path dependence, and gradual versus radical innovation, do not capture the range of possible adjustment paths in advanced industrial states. Institutional systems are neither converging nor simply reproducing themselves in stable path-dependent ways. Moreover, actors in liberal market economies can be found collaborating and gradually innovating while those in coordinated market economies struggle with brutal price competition and radical redefinitions of terrain (Chapters 2–6). The accumulation of deviant cases within institutional systems is all the more surprising in that there are few cases, regardless of institutional system type, in which significant macro- or whole-system-level institutional realignment has occurred. Actors today very often seem to be doing what their institutional contexts do not encourage (Crouch 2005; Deeg and Jackson 2007; Herrmann 2008; Lange 2009).

The institutionalist literature, which dominates discussions of business system transformation, is unclear to date on what to make of this kind of deviant evidence. Sociological institutionalists view institutions as norms that are enacted routinely by unreflective actors (DiMaggio and Powell 1991; March and Olsen 2004, 2005). For them, deviant examples of the kind described here are either marginal noise that can always be found within stable institutional and organizational systems, or evidence for the emergence of an alternative legitimate system (in this case, neoliberalism) (cf. Campbell and Pedersen 2001; Campbell 2004; Somers 2008). For the sociologists, the current situation can be clarified in two ways. One strategy is to measure the diffusion of alternative normative frameworks in the business system (Fourcade-Gourinchas and Babb 2002; Fourcade and Savelsberg 2006; Prasad 2006; Mudge 2008). The other strategy is to absorb the deviant evidence through the construction of ornate catalogs of institutional mechanisms for change (Clemens and Cook 1999; Schneiberg and Clemens 2006).

Rational choice institutionalists, for their part, view institutions as systems of rules that represent equilibria among alignments of interests (Knight 1992; Greif and Laitin 2004; Greif 2006). Thus, they take the deviant data to represent the beginning of a crisis in the institutional system that is likely only to become more severe. It is a sign that working within the institutional arrangements is not in the interest of particular parties. If Bayesian optimization processes among the strategizing parties do not slake emergent interest dissention, new alignments are likely to jettison the old system and replace it with a new, or rationally recast, set of supporting arrangements. Thus, in this view, the core project is to identify the interests of actors with regard to the existing arrangement of institutional rules.

A third perspective, associated with historical institutionalism, is inclined to view cases of deviant action as indications that the institutional architecture is undergoing piecemeal modification. Streeck and Thelen (2005), for example, suggest that the logic driving such changes is that actors are creative, rules are ambiguous, and change is expensive. Confronted with new, turbulent, or uncertain conditions, actors must exercise creativity in applying the rules that bind them. In part this is because rules are general and situations are specific. But Streeck and Thelen also emphasize that actors' interests change over time. Institutional rules must be bent or reinterpreted to conform to new sets of ends. Thus, unlike the sociologists, Streeck and Thelen take deviance seriously. But unlike the rational choice institutionalists, they do not view institutional arrangements simply as a momentary equilibrium of interest alignments, to be scrapped as soon as interests gravitate into misalignment. Instead, they emphasize that despite the creativity of agents and the ambiguity (and hence plasticity) of rules, change is primarily gradual. Sanctioning authorities defend rules and punish those that act rashly. This threat of sanction generates respect for the existing rules, even among those who would change them. Institutions, at the end of the day, are systems of constraint. The result is that change is purchased with considerable institutional continuity.

An alternative variant of this view, pursued more by Thelen than by Streeck (Mahoney and Thelen 2008; Hall and Thelen 2009; Thelen 2010) is to substitute socioeconomic power imbalances for the capacity to sanction as the arbitrating constraint in institutional transformation. In this move, the creativity and ambiguity of actors within institutions is circumscribed by the apparently transparently given exogenous interests provided to actors from their position within the economic structure. Struggles between economic interests, in the last instance, guide institutional reform processes. Exogenous power and leverage arbitrate proposals for institutional change and ensure that arrangements traditionally favoring particular economic interests are reformed in ways that continue to do so. As power alignments change only gradually, so does institutional reform.

In my view, none of these institutionalist frameworks can account well for the kind of experimentation and pervasive recomposition that the chapters in this book have described. The sociological institutionalists' focus on unreflectively held norms misses the collective reflexivity that is central to current experimental social action. The examples here show that actors are continuously experimenting with rules and roles in ways that recompose practice by both rejecting and embracing old and new conceptions of legitimacy in their environment. Central players in this book, such as the Minimill producers, the United Steelworkers of America (USWA), IG Metall, and globalizing small- and medium-sized enterprise (SME) suppliers are not guided so much by norms of legitimacy as they are by a desire to solve dilemmas in their immediate field of practice that are not well addressed by the existing arrangement of rules and practices. As a result, they embark on strategies that depart substantially from the traditional norm for what a steel producer, trade union, or family-run firm is thought to be.

The rational choice view of institutions as equilibria of interests recognizes that rules are there to solve problems. But their perspective can only be awkwardly applied to the current situation because the view presupposes that actors have clear *ex ante* identities and interests. A central dimension of creative action today, as we have seen, is that actor's roles are very ambiguous and their interests emerge only through deliberative, interactive processes of rule and role redefinition. The players in Chapter 3 who recomposed steel companies in the Chapter 11 bankruptcy process, for example, were not so much individually maximizing as they were collectively creating a relational arrangement that would allow them to strategize. Moreover, rules do not represent equilibria among interests. Rather they are provisional guidelines for action that are embraced only so long as they allow collective actors to overcome problems they have identified in their mutual interactions.

Finally, it might seem that the historical institutionalist view of institutions as systems of constraints, upheld by sanctioning capacity or economic leverage, holds somewhat stronger theoretical cards. They emphasize very centrally the importance of piecemeal change and recomposition. The difficulty for them, however, is that in moments of disruption actors embrace roles and invent forms of practice and governance that are not constrained by the existing system of order and sanction. Indeed, sanctioners are often themselves involved in rule breaking: Recall the Wolfsburg City Government's collusion with Volkswagen (VW) to circumvent the *Arbeitnehmerueberlassungsgesetz* (Chapter 7), or the US military government's vetting of indigenous German and Japanese versions of democratic pluralism that strayed considerably from the way those ideals were realized in the United States (Chapter 1). The chapters also repeatedly show that exogenous economic interest is frequently exceedingly ambiguous: Contemporary manufacturing supply chains, for example, are remarkable precisely because the players are not at all sure, *ex ante*, what role they will be playing in the relationship (Chapters 4–7). How is interest clear, when the situation for action itself is ambiguous?

Ultimately, historical institutionalists are trapped in a view of institutions as systems of constraining and enabling rules and relations, protected by sanction or power. This emphasis not only causes them to underestimate the degree to which actors can be creative in reinterpreting "constraints." It also causes them to be unreflective about the conceptual understandings of roles that underpin the institutional systems that are changing. Thus, for example, Streeck and Rehder (2003) present a trenchant analysis of the way in which the old system of German industrial relations is being changed through the addition of seemingly contradictory rules at the firm level regarding retirement, local alliances, and wage payment. Yet they either pass over the emergence of the new stakeholder arrangements outlined in Chapter 7 in relative silence, or they criticize them as crass deformations of the notion of stakeholderism in a neoliberal age (see also Streeck 2005). Their conceptual commitments to the idea that institutions should be constraining/enabling makes it difficult even for new-style historical institutionalists to appreciate the possibilities in contemporary manufacturing practices. Players in the new practices, as Chapters 4–7 show, view all constraints as provisional, experimental, and subject to recomposition and redefinition as roles are redefined.

This book departs from all the institutionalist perspectives above by treating actors and institutions as mutually constituting through processes of collective reflexivity. It does not view institutions as systems of rules that constrain already formed actors from acting in certain ways and encourage them to act in others (with the threat of sanction for deviance). Rather, it takes institutions to be historically recomposed groupings of rules that represent provisional solutions to collectively defined problems. Actors' roles, their identities, the definition of interest, and behavior governing rules are all constituted simultaneously through deliberative interaction and struggle. Action in this view is not understood as the choice among a range of strategic options available to actors within specific role locations in the institutional (or socioeconomic) structure. Rather it is a social process that recomposes actors and the institutional structure itself.

Collective problems typically destabilize affected (habitual) self-understandings. They render relevant roles, identities, and interests—including those associated with the levying of sanctions—ambiguous. Solutions to collective problems reflect and often transform identities, recast interest distributions, and recompose governance arrangements. All of the latter, moreover, are mutually dependent on one another. Such "solutions," in general, but especially in the present context, are effectively provisional. Experiments in identity and governance occur at various levels and rarely simultaneously. Solutions are continuously revised and recomposed as the environment in which social groupings find themselves develops and changes. In my view, such a perspective allows us to understand continuity and change as integrated processes. Recomposition is continuous, but it is historically rooted and always partial, not total. All dimensions of social life are never called into question all at once. The pragmatic perspective identifies possibilities for contemporary political and institutional transformation by highlighting how creative action in specific problem contexts redefines oppositions and overcomes constraint.

8.2. THINKING OF POWER CONTEXTUALLY RATHER THAN STRUCTURALLY

A common worry about a non-structural view that emphasizes creative actors continuously overcoming constraint is that it understates the importance of power relations in social life. This worry is misplaced. The view here does not undervalue power, it conceives of it in a particular way. The pragmatic view has a relational and contextual view of power, rather than a structural one. This can be very clearly illustrated in the case of manufacturing supply chains discussed in Chapters 4–7. The view in those chapters is that the chronic uncertainty and resultant fluidity of relations in disintegrated production destabilizes power imbalances across the community of producers. This is contrasted to the older Fordist/Chandlerian subcontracting world where the context yielded a relatively stable set of power relations. For years, suppliers were a community of proximate producers dependent on one or a few local vertically integrated customers for work. Such large manufacturing customers, in turn, viewed themselves as privileged princes capable of producing prosperity for their underling suppliers, but ever conscious of the need to do so with a firm and strict hand (Kwon 2004; Whitford and Enrietti 2005). Under those very specific and historically contingent conditions, positions were stable and the location of social, economic, and political leverage was clear.

In the present historical context, it is still possible to find isolated moments in the flow of industrial action where power relations resemble the older Chandlerian alignments—especially in cases where role definition is relatively clear *ex ante* and/or arm's-length ties are in play. But even in the latter cases, there is the crucial difference that neither the customer nor the supplier views their power advantage as stable or secure: Leverage is contextually defined and constantly shifting in both local and foreign contexts as roles and strategies are redefined. Where roles are ambiguous and ties are collaborative, power in the sense of asymmetric leverage is still more elusive. Iterative codesign of innovative products and joint definition of competences create mutual dependence that increases switching costs and stimulates commitment to joint problem solving and dispute resolution.[1] The new mixture of close collaboration and open networks in the disintegrated supply chain does not so much eliminate as it chronically destabilizes power imbalances within the community of producers.[2]

---

[1] For an important recent synthesis, see Gilson et al. (2009).

[2] There are also governance problems that emerge within the new serially collaborative relations. For a discussion, see Sabel (2004), Whitford and Zeitlin (2004), and Kristensen and Zeitlin (2005).

The one certainty about power from a pragmatic perspective is that if habitual action is disrupted and collective reflection is induced to resolve a commonly defined problem, then power will be, to some degree, unstable and inconsistent. If there is stability and habitual action, there will be stable power relations. The chapters in this book show that this is true on all levels of socioeconomic life. It is true of relations in the workplace, in the labor market, among producers in an industry and among stakeholders in a national political economy. It is true of interfirm relations along the supply chain. And it is true of relations between developed and developing regions. Over time, roles and relationships, both global and local, are in a recurrently recompositional process. In situations of heightened and chronic disruption, such as those that characterize contemporary manufacturing conditions, actors, firms, and regions that have developed proactive strategies and supporting arrangements for participating in processes of continuous reorganization are most likely to succeed.

8.3. SCIENCE FOR POSSIBILITY RATHER THAN CONSTRAINT

This book has focused on creative actors overcoming constraint and recasting the conditions under which they interact. At the same time, the book has repeatedly criticized arguments for both market and structural/institutional constraint. In particular, it rejects neoliberal arguments for market rationality's leveling power and institutionalist, especially VoC, arguments for the action-shaping effects of complementary institutional arrangements within national model typologies. The book's basic counterposition is that such views direct the eye away from possibility. It is perhaps worthwhile, in closing, to point out that the critique that I have been offering of both of these alternative frameworks does not amount to an argument for more attention to "contingency" at the limits of those other more "properly" causally determining frameworks. On the contrary, pragmatic social theory has its own conception of social explanation. This conception, moreover, has specific implications for the way that one approaches research.

First of all, pragmatism rejects the traditional antimony between causal determination and contingency. Pragmatists believe that there is causality, yet in the case of human social action it is overdetermined (Dewey 1929 [1988], 1988). Too many factors flow into action for it to be possible to reliably (or usefully) isolate a limited number of "determining" ones. Actors themselves construct understandings of their world that do not mirror that world, but rather enable them to serviceably act within it (Peirce 1991a, 1991b). When action is disrupted, they reflect and negotiate until they are able to arrive at an orientation toward the world that once again facilitates successful action. Neither determination nor contingency are relevant notions within this framing. Both presuppose the possibility for causal understandings of the observed actions. To be sure, both causal analysis and pragmatic action deploy techniques of experimentation and falsification. Yet in traditional social science, one thinks that one has identified real causal determination until one discovers that one has not. For pragmatists, one moves forward with a serviceable orientation toward the world until one discovers that it does not work anymore. In the latter orientation, causal determination and contingent deviations are irrelevant to action. The main point is what is working and what is not (Dewey 1929 [1988], 1988; Dewey and Bentley 1949). This understanding applies to all actors, including the work of social scientists analyzing action.

The rejection of the opposition between causal determination and contingency has consequences for research design. The pragmatic eye is turned toward actors and action, rather than to the historically specific constellations of rules and institutional constraint in which they act. When analyzing processes of social change, for example, pragmatists do not ask, as institutionalists and economists would: How are the institutions or incentives within the political economy changing? Instead, pragmatists ask: How are people in the political economy acting and interacting? What are their relations, how do they govern themselves, and how is action and governance changing? Indeed, if one embraces the pragmatic view that disrupted habit engenders reflection, experimentation, and creativity, then one has to approach the empirical terrain of complex societies with an eye toward broad open-ended excavations of actors' normative and practical ambitions. Research should focus on uncovering, across relevant comparative contexts in both the past and the present, a wide range of relational and governance experiments. What seems to work in the contexts that actors define? What does not work? What has worked in similar situations in other places? How fungible are the experiments? Rather than blending out "deviant" or "marginal" practices in the present and the past through the imposition of leveling market logic or abstract typologies of complementary institutional constraint, the analytical eye should be cast very broadly across the range of social practice looking for possibility.

Societies are rich assemblages of historically accumulated creativity and re-composition, not coherent complexes of incentives or complementary (and constraining) institutions. It should be the role of social science to bring that to light. It is itself a form of creative action to identify interesting areas of experimentation and attempt to understand the genealogy of resources that actors might bring to bear in their problem solving. The aim of pragmatic inquiry and theory construction is to foster experimentation by pointing to possibilities that are emerging within actors' experiences.

Finally, pragmatic inquiry is interested social science. One surveys the terrain of action with an eye for promising experiments. This is neither an omniscient nor an objective process of observation. There are many experiments that one cannot uncover and there can be multiple solutions to given habitual crises. Generally, pragmatism wants to uncover those experiments that enhance the capacity of social actors to continuously solve their problems. Mead and Dewey were both great positive democrats in this regard. They believed the more that arrangements allowed for open, capacious social participation in reflection on the possibilities for the resolution of collective problems, the more robust and capable of future recomposition solutions would be. Inclusive collective problem solving—democracy—yields robust but open-ended social development. The pragmatically informed search for possibility involves deep commitment to inclusive self-governance and creative social action.

Bibliography

1949–50. Executive Sessions of the Senate Foreign Relations Committee (Historical Series). *Senate Foreign Relations Committee/Eighty-First Congress*. Washington, DC, United States Publishing Office: 184 & *passim*.

Abegglen, J. C. (1958). *The Japanese Factory*. Glencoe, IL, Free Press.

—— (1973). *Management and Worker: The Japanese Solution*. Tokyo, Sophia University Press.

Abelshauser, W. (2003). *Kulturkampf: der deutsche Weg in die Neue Wirtschaft und die amerikanische Herausforderung*. Berlin, Kulturverlag Kadmos.

Abraham, K. G. and S. K. Taylor (1996). "Firm's Use of Outside Contractors: Theory and Evidence." *Journal of Labor Economics* 14(1996): 394–424.

Acemoglu, D., P. Aghion, et al. (2005). Vertical Integration and Technology: Theory and Evidence. Unpublished Manuscript, Cambridge, MA, MIT.

—— K. Bimpikis, et al. (2006). *Price and Capacity Competition*. Cambridge, MA, MIT: 37.

Acemoglu, D., S. Johnson, et al. (2007). *Determinants of Vertical Integration: Financial Development and Contracting Costs*. Cambridge, MA, MIT/NBER.

Acino, H. (1958). "Zehn Jahre Antimonopolgesetz in Japan." *Internationales Handbuch der Kartelpolitik*. G. Jahn and K. Junckerstorff, Eds. Berlin, Duncker & Humblodt: 307–26.

Adams, W. and J. B. Dirlam (1967). "Big Steel, Invention and Innovation: Reply." *Journal of Economics* 81(3): 475–82.

Adler, P., M. Fruin, et al., Eds. (1999). *Remade in America: Transforming and Transplanting Japanese Management Systems*. New York, Oxford University Press.

Ahearn, L. M. (2001). "Language and Agency." *Annual Review of Anthropology* 30: 109–37.

Allen, G. C. (1946). *A Short Economic History of Modern Japan, 1867–1937*. London, Allen & Unwin.

Amable, B. (2003). *The Diversity of Modern Capitalism*. Oxford, UK, Oxford University Press.

Ambrosia, J. (1994). Sharing Managerial Power with the Worker. *New Steel*, February 1994.

American-Embassy-Bonn (1993). Germany–Steel Industry Profile. *National Trade Data Bank Market Reports*.

Amin, A. (1998b). "Durch Spass mit Menschen zum Erfolg." *Süddeutsche Zeitung*, September 29, 1998.

—— (1999). "Global Strategies and Financing for European Steel." *Steel Times* 227, February, 1999. c2f.

—— (2001). "Germany's Steel Industry." *Steel Times* 229, issue 1.

Amin, A. and P. Cohendet (2004). *Architectures of Knowledge. Firms, Capabilities, and Communities*. Oxford, UK, Oxford University Press.

—— —— (2005). "Geographies of Knowledge Formation in Firms." *Industry and Innovation* 12(4): 465–86.

—— and K. Robins (1990). Industrial Districts and Regional Development: Limits and Possibilities. *Industrial Districts and Interfirm Cooperation in Italy*. F. Pyke, G. Becattini, and W. Sengenberger. Geneva, International Institute for Labor Studies: 185–219.

Anon (1967a). "Korf baut jetzt ein Elektrostahlwerk." *Frankfurter Allgemeine Zeitung*, November 16, 1967.

—— (1967*b*). "Korf Industrie-und Handel GmbH & Co. KG: Grosses Investitionsprogramm-neues Kapital." *Industriekurier.* Dusseldorf, November 16, 1967.

—— (1968). "Korf Industrie-und Handel GmbH & Co. KG: Die ergeizigen Pläne eines 'Aussenseiters in Stahl'." *Industriekurier.* Dusseldorf, November 23, 1968.

—— (1970). "Korfs Ministahlwerk in Amerika: ' "Das Beispiel soll noch öfter wiederholt werden'." *Industriekurier.* Dusseldorf, April 25, 1970.

—— (1974). "Die Korf-Gruppe wächst mit der Direktreduktion." *Frankfurter Allgemeine Zeitung,* June 26, 1994.

—— (1976). "Mister Midrex kommt." *Der Spiegel,* January 12, 1976.

—— (1977). "Korf rechnet mit negativem Ergebnis im Stahlbereich." *Rohstoff-Rundschau.* München-Gräfeling, September 20, 1977.

—— (1980*a*). "Willy Korf: Akquisiteur eigener Ideen." *Wirtschaftswoche.* Düsseldorf, August 27, 1980.

—— (1980*b*). "25 Jahre Korf-Gruppe: Führen heisst dienen und verantworten." *Handelsblatt,* November 21, 1980.

—— (1981*a*). "Korf-Stahl AG: Für 1981 werden deutliche Einbuzzen bei Absatz und Ertrag erwartet." *Handelsblatt,* August 24, 1981.

—— (1981*b*). "Handelsblatt-Gespräch mit Willy Korf: Importstahl kann zu einer Gefahr werden." *Handelsblatt,* October 9, 1981.

—— (1982*a*). "Korf glaubt nicht an das Ende der 'Subventionismus'." *Frankfurter Allgemeine Zeitung,* August 31, 1982.

—— (1982*b*). "Die Stahlkrise beutelt auch Korf." *Süddeutsche Zeitung,* August 31, 1982.

—— (1982*c*). "Willy Korf will stärker in die Weiterverarbeitung." *Handelsblatt,* September 6, 1982.

—— (1983*a*). "Die Korf-Gruppe sucht ein neues Konzept." *Frankfurter Allgemeine Zeitung,* January 5, 1983.

—— (1983*b*). "Willy Korf: Auch zwei neue Grosskonzerne werden die Stahlprobleme nicht lösen." *Handelsblatt,* January 6, 1983.

—— (1983*c*). "Willy Korf: Ich bleibe weiter Vortsitzender des Vorstandes." *Handelsblatt,* January 6, 1983.

—— (1983*d*). "Appel an den Kanzler." *Wirtschaftswoche,* January 7, 1983.

—— (1983*e*). "Willy Korf: Am Ende doch besiegt." *Wirtschaftswoche,* January 14, 1983.

—— (1983*f*). "Korf is Forced to Join the Steel Club." *Business Week,* January 24, 1983.

—— (1983*g*). "Das Korf-Imperium hat sich in seine Einzelteile aufgelöst." *Frankfurter Allgemeine Zeitung,* August 30, 1983.

—— (1983*h*). "Einfach geweigert." *Der Spiegel,* December 5, 1983.

—— (1986). "Korfsche Sparbüchse." *Wirtschaftswoche,* November 14, 1986.

—— (1991*a*). "Schliff nach Drehbuch." *Manager Magazine,* June, 1991.

—— (1991*b*). "Besonderes Verhältnis." *Manager Magazine,* February, 1991.

—— (1991*c*). "Der Name Korf lebt unter dem MG-Dach fort." *Börsen Zeitung,* April 18, 1991.

—— (1993*a*). "Die Vision vom eigenen Unternehmen." *Manager Magazine,* October, 1993.

—— (1993*b*). "Ehrgeiziger Investor für Edelstahl GmbH." *Die Welt.* Hamburg, February 5, 1993.

—— (1994). "Neue Edelstahl-Technologie soll Betrieb retten." *Handelsblatt,* September 8, 1994.

—— (1995). "Als Mittelständler hat die Georgsmarienhütte wieder Erfolg." *Frankfurter Allgemeine Zeitung,* November 9, 1995.

—— (1997*a*). "On a Roll." *The Economist* **354**: issue 8038, 74–5.

—— (1997*b*). "Die Georgsmarienhütte sucht eine breitere Basis." *Frankfurter Allgemeine Zeitung*, August 29, 1997.

—— (1998*a*). "Georgsmarienhütte/ Stahlgruppe wächst stürmisch. Favorit für Neue Maxhütte." *Handelsblatt*, December 17, 1998.

Ansell, C. 2009. "A Pragmatist Institutionalism." Unpublished manuscript, Berkeley, CA, Department of Political Science, University of California-Berkeley: 38 pages.

Aoki, M. (1987). The Japanese Firm in Transition. *The Political Economy of Japan. Volume 1: The Domestic Transformation.* K. Yamamura and Y. Yasuba, Eds. Stanford, CA, Stanford University Press.

Appelbaum, E., T. Bailey, et al. (2000). *Manufacturing Advantage: Why High-Performance Work Systems Pay Off.* Ithaca, New York, Cornell University Press.

Apter, A. (2007). *Beyond Words. Discourse and Critical Agency in Africa.* Chicago, IL, University of Chicago Press.

Argyres, N. (1996). "Capabilities, Technological Diversification, and Divisionalization." *Strategoic Management Journal* **17**: 395–410.

Armour, J. and D. A. Skeel (2006). "Who Writes the Rules for Hostile Takeovers, and Why? The Peculiar Divergence of US and UK Takeover Regulation." *Centre for Business Research Working Paper.* Cambridge, UK, University of Cambridge.

Arndt, M. (2003). "Up From the Scrap Heap." *Business Week.* New York, McGraw-Hill, July 21, 2003: 42–7.

Arndt, S. W. and H. Kierzkowski, Eds. (2001). *Fragmentation: New Production Patterns in the World Economy.* Oxford, UK, Oxford University Press.

Arnold, T. (1940). *The Bottlenecks of Business.* New York, Reynal & Hitchcock.

Arnsdorfer, J. (2001). "Labor's Changing Accent." *Crains Chicago Business.*

Arthur, J. B. (1992). "The Link Between Business Strategy and Industrial Relations Systems in American Steel Mills." *Industrial and Labor Relations Review* **45**(3): 488–506.

Artus, I. (2001). *Krise des deutschen Tarifsystems. Die Erosion des Flächentarifvertrags in Ost und West.* Wiesbaden, Germany, Westdeutscher Verlag.

—— (2006). "Im Schatten des dualen Systems: Zur Bedeutung tariflicher Normen in Betrieben ohne Betriebsrat." *Betriebe ohne Betriebsrat. Informelle Interessenvertretuung in Unternehmen.* I. Artus, S. Böhm, Lücking, and R. Tinczek, Eds. Frankfurt, Germany, Campus Verlag: 141–70.

—— S. Böhm, et al., Eds. (2006). *Betriebe ohne Betriebsrat. Informelle Interessenvertretung in Unternehmen.* Frankfurt, Germany, Campus Verlag.

Aston, A., M. Arndt, et al. (2004). A New Goliath in Big Steel. *Business Week*: November 8, 2004, 47–8.

Baare, G. (1965). *Ausmass und Ursachen der Unternehmungskonzentration der deutschen Stahlindustrie im Rahmen der Montanunion, ein internationaler Vergleich.* Volkswirtschaftslehre. Tübingen, Germany, Universität Tübingen. PhD dissertation.

Bailey, D. and K. Soyouing (2009). "GE's Immelt says US Economy Needs Industrial Renewal." *yahoo!.news*, June 26, 2009, 1.22pm.

Bair, J. (2005). "Global Capitalism and Commodity Chains: Looking Back, Going Forward." *Competition and Change* **9**(2): 153–80.

Baldwin, C. Y. (2007). "Frameworks for Thinking about Modularity, Industry Architecture, and Evolution." *Sloan Industry Studies Conference—2007.* Boston, MA.

—— and K. B. Clark (2000). *Design Rules. The Power of Modularity.* Cambridge, MA, The MIT Press.

Barenberg, M. (1993). "The Political Economy of the Wagner Act: Power, Symbol and Workplace Cooperation." *Harvard Law Review* **106**(7): 1379–496.

Barnet, D. F. and L. Schorsch (1983). *Steel. Upheaval in a Basic Industry.* Cambridge MA, Ballinger.

Beamer, G. (2007). "Sustaining the Rust Belt: A Retrospective Analysis of the Employee Purchase of Weirton Steel." *Labor History* **48**(3): 277–99.

—— and D. E. Lewis (2003). "The Irrational Escalation of Commitment and the Ironic Labor Politics of the Rust Belt." *Enterprise and Society* **4**(4): 676–706.

Beckers, L. (1969). *Die Struktur der Stahlindustrie der Bundesrepublik Deutschland im vergleich mit den übrigen Montanunionländer, den USA, Grossbritannien und Japan.* Rechts, Wirtschafts und Sozialwissenschaftlichen Fakultät, Freiberg, Universität Freiberg in der Schweiz. PhD dissertation.

Belanger, J., C. Berggren, et al., Eds. (1999). *Being Local Worldwide. ABB and the Challenge of Global Management.* Ithaca, NY, Cornell University Press.

Bellandi, M. (2001). "Local Development and Embedded Large Firms." *Entrepreneurship and Regional Development* **13**(3): 188–216.

—— (2006). "A Perspective on Clusters, Localities, and Specific Public Goods." *Clusters and Globalisation: The Development of Urban and Regional Economies.* C. Pitelis, R. Sugden, and J. R. Wilson, Eds. Cheltenham, UK, Edward Elgar: 96–113.

—— (2009). "The Governance of Cluster Progressive Reactions to International Competitive Challenges." *Networks, Governance and Economic Development: Bridging Disciplinary Frontiers.* M. J. Aranguren, C. Iturrioz, and J. R. Wilson, Eds. Cheltenham, UK, Edward Elgar.

—— and A. Caloffi (2008). "District Internationalization and Trans-local Development." *Entrepreneurship and Regional Development* **20**: 517–32.

—— and M. R. Di Tommaso (2005). "The Case of Specialized Towns in Guangdong China." *European Planning Studies* **13**(5): 707–29.

Bendix, R. (1956). *Work and Authority in Industry.* Berkeley, CA, University of California Press.

Bensman, D. and R. Lynch (1987). *Rusted Dreams. Hard Times in a Steel Community.* New York, McGraw-Hill.

Benz, W. (1978). "Amerikanische Besatzungsherrschaft in Japan 1945–1947." *Vierteljahreschrift für Zeitgeschichte* **26**: 331.

Berg, F. (1966). *Die Westdeutsche Wirtschaft in der Bewährung. Ausgewählte Reden aus den Jahren 1950 bis 1965.* Hagen, Germany, Linnepe Verlagsgesellschaft KG.

Berg, P. (1999). "The Effects of High Performance Work Practices on Job Satisfaction in the United States Steel Industry." *Relations Industrielles* **54**(1): 111–34.

Berger, R. (2004). "The Odyssey of the Auto Industry. Suppliers Changing Manufacturing Footprint." *SAE World Congress.* Detroit, MI, Roland Berger Strategy Consultants: 16.

Berger, S. (2005). *How We Compete: What Companies Around the World Are Doing to Make It In Today's Global Economy.* New York, Currency/Doubleday.

—— and R. Dore (1996). *National Diversity and Global Capitalism.* Ithaca, NY, Cornell University Press.

Berggren, C. (2003). "Mergers, MNEs and Innovation–The Need for New Research Approaches." *Scandinavian Journal of Management* **19**(2): 173–91.

—— and L. Bengtsson (2004). "Rethinking Outsourcing in Manufacturing: A Tale of Two Telecom Firms." *European Management Journal* **22**(2): 211–23.

Berghahn, V. (1985). *Unternehmer und Politik in der Bundesrepublik.* Frankfurt, Germany, Suhrkamp.

Berghahn, V. (1995). "West German Reconstruction and American Industrial Culture, 1945–1960." *The American Impact on Postwar Germany.* R. Pommerin, Ed. Oxford, UK, Berghahn Books: 65–82.

Berk, G. and P. Galvin (2008). "How People Experience and Change Institutions: A Field Guide to Creative Syncretism." Unpublished manusript, Eugene, OR, University of Oregon.

Berry, B. (1993a). "An Identity Crisis at Big Steel." *New Steel*: December, 1993: 1216.

—— (1993b). "Big Steel vs Mini Steel." *New Steel*: December, 1993: 18–24.

—— (1994a). "Minimill Roundtable. Maximum Flexibility, Minimum Cost." *New Steel*: April, 1994: 39–45.

—— (1994b). "Minimill Roundtable. Operating Efficiencies. Smart Workers, Smart Machines." *New Steel*: August, 1994.

—— (1995). "Minimill Roundtable. The Challenge of Success." *New Steel*: April, 1995: 48–56.

—— (1998). "Minimill Roundtable. Strong Markets, Higher Margins, Good Pay." *New Steel*: April, 1998.

—— (1999). "Minimill Roundtable: Operating Efficiencies. The Changing Dynamics of Steelmaking." *New Steel*: August, 1999.

—— (2000). "Automotive Roundtable: Improving Conductivity Through e-Commerce." *New Steel*: May, 2000.

—— and P. Ninneman (1997). "Automotive Roundtable. Opportunities for Growth in Automotive Steel." *New Steel*: June, 1997.

Bethusy-Huc, V. G. v. (1962). *Demokratie und Interessenpolitik.* Wiesbaden, Germany, Franz Steiner.

Birou, L. M. and S. E. Fawcett (1994). "Supplier Involvement in Integrated Product Development: A Comparison of US and European Practices." *International Journal of Physical Distribution and Logistics Management* 24(5): 4–14.

Bisson, T. A. (1945). *Japan's War Economy.* New York, Macmillan.

—— (1954). *Zaibatsu Dissolution in Japan.* Berkeley, CA, University of California Press.

Blumer, H. (1986[1969]). *Symbolic Interactionism: Perspective and Method.* Berkeley, CA, University of California Press.

Böhm, S. and S. Lücking (2006). Orientierungsmuster des Managements in betriebsratslosen Betrieben—Zwischen Willkürherrschaft und Human Resource Management. *Betriebe ohne Betriebsrat. Informelle Interessenvertretuung in Unternehmen.* I. Artus, S. Böhm, S. Lücking, and R. Tinczek, Eds. Frankfurt, Germany, Campus Verlag: 107–40.

Borkin, J. and C. Welsh (1943). *Germany's Master Plan: The Story of an Industrial Offensive.* New York, Duell, Sloane and Pearce.

Borrus, M., D. Ernst, et al., Eds. (2000). *International Production Networks in Asia.* London, Routledge.

—— and J. Zysman (1997). "Globalization with Borders: The Rise of Wintelism as the Future of Global Competition." *Industry and Innovation* 4(2): 141–66.

Boulhol, H. and L. Fontagne (2006). "Deindustrialization and the Fear of Relocations in Industry." *CEPII, Working Papers.* Paris, Centre d'etudes prospectives et d'informations internationales.

Bourdieu, P. (1977). *Outline of a Theory of Practice.* New York, Cambridge University Press.

Boyer, R. (2003). "The Embedded Innovation Systems of Germany and Japan: Distinctive Features and Futures." *The End of Diversity? Prospects for German and Japanese Capitalism.* K. Yamamura and W. Streeck, Eds. Ithaca, NY, Cornell University Press: 147–82.

Bradach, J. and R. Eccles (1989). "Price, Authority and Trust: From Ideal Types to Plural Forms." *Annual Review of Sociology* **15**: 97–118.

Bratton, W. (1989). "The New Economic Theory of the Firm: Critical Perspectives From History." *Stanford Law Review* **41**: 1471ff.

Brenner, R. (2006). *The Economics of Global Turbulence*. London, Verso.

Breznitz, D. (2007). *Innovation and the State: Political Choice and Strategies for Growth in Israel, Taiwan, and Ireland*. New Haven, CT, Yale University Press.

Brinkley, A. (1989). "The New Deal and the Idea of the State." *The Rise and Fall of the New Deal Order, 1930–1980*. S. Fraser and G. Gerstle, Eds. Princeton, NJ, Princeton Univesity Press.

Brioschi, F., M. S. Brioschi, et al. (2002). "From Industrial District to the District Group: An Insight into the Evolution of Local Capitalism in Italy." *Regional Studies* **36**(9): 1037–52.

Bronfenbrenner, K. and S. Luce (2004). *The Changing Nature of Corporate Global Restructuring: The Impact of Production Shifts on Jobs in the US, China, and Around the Globe*, Final Report, US-China Economic and Security Review Commission: 88p.

Brooks, R. R. R. (1940). *As Steel Goes*. New Haven, CT, Yale University Press.

Bruno, R. (2005). "USWA-Bargained and State-Oriented Responses to the Recurrent Steel Crisis." *Labor Studies Journal* **30**(1): 67–91.

Brusco, S. (1982). "The Emilian Model: Productive Decentralisation and Social Integration." *Cambridge Journal of Economics* **6**: 167–84.

—— and E. Righi (1989). "Industrial Policy and Social Consensus: The Case of Modena (Italy)." *Economy and Society* **18**: 405–23.

Brusoni, S. and A. Prencipe et al. (2001). "Knowledge Specialization, Organizational Coupling, and the Boundaries of the Firm: Why Do Firms Know More Than They Make?" *Administrative Science Quarterly* **46**: 597–621.

Buckley, P. J. and P. N. Ghauri (2004). "Globalization, Economic Geography and the Strategy of Multinational Enterprises." *Journal of International Business Studies* **35**(2): 81–98.

Budros, A. (2002). "The Mean and Lean Firm and Downsizing: Causes of Involuntary and Voluntary Downsizing Strategies." *Sociological Forum* **17**(2): 307–42.

Burgert, P. (1998). "Ispat's Growth in Europe." *New Steel*: March, 1998.

—— (1998). "European Steelmakers Embracing EF Technology." Electric Furnace Supplement *American Metal Market*, February 5, 1998.

Burke, J., G. Epstein, et al. (2004). "Rising Foreign Outsourcing and Employment Losses in US Manufacturing, 1987–2002." *PERI Working Papers*. Amherst, MA, Political Economy Research Institute, University of Massachusetts: 17p.

Burn, D. (1961). *The Steel Industry 1939–1959*. Cambridge, UK, Cambridge University Press.

Byrnes, N., I. Moon, et al. (2003). "Is Wilbur Ross Crazy?" *Business Week*: December 22, 2003: 74–80.

Cainelli, G., D. Iacobucci, et al. (2006). "Spatial Agglomeration and Business Groups: New Evidence from Italian Industrial Districts." *Regional Studies* **40**(5): 507–18.

Calder, K. (1986). *Crisis and Compensation. Public Policy and Political Stability in Japan*. Princeton, NJ, Princeton University Press.

Callon, M. (1998a). "Introduction: The Embeddedness of Economic Markets in Economics." *The Laws of the Markets*. M. Callon, Ed. Oxford, UK, Blackwell Publishers: 1–57.

Callon, M. (1998*b*). "An Essay on Framing and Overflowing: Economic Externalities Revisted by Sociology." *The Laws of the Markets.* M. Callon, Ed. Oxford, UK, Blackwell Publishers: 244–69.

Campbell, J. L. (2004). *Institutional Change and Globalization.* Princeton, NJ, Princeton University Press.

—— and O. K. Pedersen, Eds. (2001). *The Rise of Neoliberalism and Institutional Analysis.* Princeton, NJ, Princeton University Press.

Camuffo, A. (2003). "Transforming Industrial Districts: Large Firms and Small Business Networks in the Italian Eyewear Industry." *Industry and Innovation* **10**(4): 377–401.

—— A. Furlan, et al. (2005). Customer-Supplier Integration in the Italian High Precision Air Conditioning Industry. *IPC Working Paper Series.* Cambridge, MA, MIT-Industrial Performance Center: 42.

Carbaugh, R. and J. Olienyk (2004). "US Steelmakers in Continuing Crisis." *Challenge* **47**(1): 86–106.

Carr, C. (2005). "Are German, Japanese and Anglo-Saxon Strategic Decision Styles Still Divergent in the Context of Globalization?" *Journal of Management Studies* **42**(6): 1155–88.

Carruthers, B. G. and T. Haliday (1998). *Rescuing Business. The Making of Corporate Bankruptcy Law in England and the United States.* Oxford, UK, Oxford University Press.

Casper, S. (1995). How Public Law Influences Decentralized Supplier Network Organization in Germany. The Cases of BMW and Audi. *WZB Discussion Papers.* Berlin, Wissenschaftszentrum.

—— (1997). Nationale Institutionengefüge und innovative Industrieorganisation: Zulieferbeziehungen in Deutschland. *Ökonomische Leistungsfähigkeit und institutionelle Innovation: Das deutsche Productions-und Politikregime in globalen Wettbewerb.* F. Naschhold, D. Soskice, B. Hancke, and U. Jürgens. Berlin, WZB Jahrbuch.

—— (2000). "Institutional Adaptiveness, Technology Policy, and the Diffusion of New Business Models: The Case of German Biotechnology." *Organization Studies* **21**(5): 887–914.

—— (2001). The Legal Framework for Corporate Governance: The Influence of Contract Law on Company Strategies in Germany and the United States. *Varieties of Capitalism.* P. Hall and D. Soskice. New York, Oxford University Press.

—— (2009). "Can New Technology Firms Succeed in Coordinated Market Economies? A Response to Herrmann and Lange." *Socio-Economic Review* **7**(2): 209–15.

Chanaron, J.-J., Y. Lung, et al., Eds. (1999). *Coping with Variety: Flexible Productive Systems for Product Variety in the Auto Industry.* Aldershot, UK, Ashgate.

Chandler, A. (1962). *Strategy and Structure.* Cambridge, MA, MIT Press.

—— (1990). *Scale and Scope. The Dynamics of Industrial Capitalism.* Cambridge, MA, Harvard University Press [Belknap].

Chen, Y. (2005). "Vertical Disintegration." *Journal of Economics and Management Strategy* **14**(1): 209–29.

Chesbrough, H. (2005). Towards a Dynamics of Modularity. A Cyclical Model of Technical Advance. *The Business of Systems Integration.* A. Prencipe, A. Davies, and M. Hobday, Eds., Oxford, UK, Oxford University Press: 174–98.

Chesbrough, H. W. (1999). "The Organizational Impact of Technological Change: A Comparative Theory of National Institutional Factors." *Industrial and Corporate Change* **8**(3): 447–85.

Chiarvesio, M., E. Di Maria, et al. (2006). "Global Value Chains and Open Networks: The Case of Italian Industrial Districts". *Annual Meeting of the Society for the Advancement of Socio-Economics*. Trier, Germany: University of Trier.

Chimerine, L., A. Tonelson, et al. (1994). *Can the Phoenix Survive? The Fall and Rise of the American Steel Industry*. Washington, DC, Economic Strategy Institute.

CIA (2009). *World Fact Book*. Germany, Japan. https://www.cia.gov/library/publications/the-world-fact-book/geas/gm.html.

Clark, G. L. (1991). "Regulating Restructuring of the US Steel Industry: Chapter 11 of the Bankruptcy Code and Pension Obligations." *Regional Studies* 25(2): 135–53.

Clark, K. B. and T. Fujimoto (1991). *Product Development Performance. Strategy, Organization, and Management in the World Auto Industry*. Boston, MA, Harvard Business School Press.

—— and S. C. Wheelwright, Eds. (1994). *The Product Development Challenge. Competing Through Speed, Quality, and Creativity*. A Harvard Business Review Book. Boston, MA, Harvard Business School Press.

Clark, P. F., P. Gottlieb, et al. (1987). *Forging a Union of Steel: Philip Murray, SWOC, and the United Steel Workers*. Ithaca, NY, Cornell University, ILR Press.

Clay, L. (1950). *Decision in Germany*. Garden City, New york, Doubleday & Co.

Clemens, E. and J. Cook (1999). "Politics and Institutionalism: Explaining Durability and Change." *Annual Review of Sociology* 25: 441–66.

Coe, N. M., M. Hess, et al. (2004). "Globalizing Regional Development: A Global Production Networks Perspective." *Transactions of the Institute of British Geographers* 29(4): 468–84.

Cohen, J. (1949). *Japan's Economy in War and Reconstruction*. Minneapolis, MN, University of Minnesota Press.

Cohen, M. (1914). "Rule Versus Discretion." *The Journal of Psychology and Scientific Methods* 11(8): 208–15.

Cohen, T. (1987). *Remaking Japan. The American Occupation as New Deal*. New York, Free Press.

Colli, A. (2002). *Il quarto capitalismo: Un profilo italiano*. Venice, Marsilio.

Comaroff, J. and J. Comaroff (1991). *Of Revelation and Revolution. Christianity, Colonialism and Consciousness in South Africa, Vol 1*. Chicago, IL, University of Chicago Press.

—— —— (2001). "Revelations upon Revelation: Aftershocks, Afterthoughts." *Interventions* 3(1): 100–27.

Commons, J. R. (1934). *Institutional Economics: Its Place in Political Economy*. New York, The Macmillan Company.

Conkin, P. K. (1968). *Puritans and Pragmatists. Eight Eminent American Thinkers*. New York, Dodd, Mead & Company.

Coro, G. and S. Micelli (2006). *I nuovi distretti produttivi: Innovazione, internazionalizzazione e competitita dei territori*. Venice, Marisilio.

Crawcour, E. S. (1997). Economic Change in the Nineteenth Century. *The Economic Emergence of Modern Japan*. K. Yamamura, Ed. New York, Cambridge University Press: 1–49.

Crouch, C. (2005). *Capitalist Diversity and Change. Recombinant Governance and Institutional Entrepreneurs*. Oxford, UK, Oxford University Press.

—— P. Le Gales, et al., Eds.(2001). *Local Production Systems in Europe. Rise or Demise?* Oxford, UK, Oxford University Press.

—— —— et al., Eds. (2004). *Changing Governance of Local Economies. Responses of European Local Production Systems*. Oxford, UK, Oxford University Press.

Cusumano, M. A. (1985). *The Japanese Automobile Industry. Technology and Management at Nissan and Toyota.* Cambridge, MA, Harvard University Press.

Czada, R. (1998). "'Modell Deutschland' am Scheideweg: Die verarbeitende Industrie." *Transformationspfade in Ostdeutschland.* R. Czada and G. Lehmbruck, Eds. Frankfurt, Germany, Campus Verlag: 365–410.

D'Costa, A. (1999). *The Global Restructuring of the Steel Industry. Innovations, Institutions and Industrial Change.* London, Routledge.

Dahrendorf, R. (1964). *Society and Democracy in Germany.* New York, Norton.

Davis, G. F. (2005). Firms and Environments. *The Handbook of Economic Sociology, Second Edition.* N. Smelser and R. Swedberg. Princeton, NJ, Princeton University Press: 478–502.

—— and D. McAdam (2000). "Corporations, Classes and Social Movements After Managerialism." *Research in Organizational Behavior* **22**: 195–238.

—— K. A. Diekmann, et al. (1994). "The Decline and Fall of the Conglomerate Firm in the 1980s: The Deinstitutionalization of an Organizational Form." *American Sociological Review* **59**(4): 547–70.

DeDobbelaere, D. R. (2002). John Deere: Global Learning and Development. *Conference on Supply Chain Governance and Regional Development in the Global Economy.* Madison, WI, University of Wisconsin-Madison, AMP/COWS.

Deeg, R. and G. Jackson (2007). "Toward a More Dynamic Theory of Capitalist Variety." *Socio-Economic Review* **5**(1): 149–79.

Deitz, R. and J. Orr (2006). "A Leaner, More Skilled US Manufacturing Workforce." *Current Issues in Economics and Finance (Federal Reserve Bank of New York)* **12**(2): 1–7.

Dennison, S. R. (1939). "Vertical Integration in the Steel Industry." *The Economic Journal* **49**(194): 244–58.

Depleteau, F. (2008). "Relational Thinking: A Critique of Co-deterministic Theories of Structure and Agency." *Sociological Theory* **26**(1): 50–73.

Depner, H. and H. Bathelt (2003). "Cluster Growth and Institutional Barriers: The Development of the Automobile Industry Cluster in Shanghai, P.R. China." *SPACES.* Marburg, Germany, Philipps-University of Marburg: 38p.

—— and U. Dewald (2004). Globale Netzwerke und lokale Partner: Deutsche Automobilzulieferer und der Wachstumsmarkt China. *SPACES.* Marburg, Germany, Philipps-University of Marburg: 35p.

Dewey, J. (1916). *Democracy and Education. An Introduction to the Philosophy of Education.* New York, Free Press.

—— (1920). *Reconstruction in Philosophy.* Boston, MA, Beacon Press.

—— (1922). *Human Nature and Conduct.* Carbondale, IL, Southern Illinois University Press.

—— (1929[1988]). *The Quest for Certainty.* Carbondale, IL, Southern Illinois University Press.

—— (1940). "The Vanishing Subject in the Psychology of William James." *The Journal of Philosophy* **37**(22): 589–99.

—— (1988*a*). A Theory of Valuation. *The Later Works of John Dewey, 1925–1953 (Volume 13: 1938–39).* J. Boydston. Carbondale, IL, Southern Illinois University Press: 13.

—— (1988*b*). Corporate Personality. *John Dewey. The Later Works, 1925–1954, Volume 2: 1925–1927. Essays, Reviews, Miscellany and the Public and its Problems.* J. Boydston. Carbondale IL, Southern Illinois University Press: 22–43.

—— and A. F. Bentley (1949). *Knowing and the Known.* Boston, MA, Beacon Press.

Dicken, P. (2003). "Global Production Networks in Europe and East Asia: The Automobile Components Industries." *GPN Working Paper*, ESRC Research Project: Making the Connections: Global Production Networks in Europe and East Asia: 62p.

—— P. F. Kelly, et al. (2001). "Chains and Networks, Territories and Scales: Towards a Relational Framework for Analysing the Global Economy." *Global Networks* 1(2): 89–112.

DiMaggio, P., Ed. (2001). *The Twenty-First-Century Firm. Changing Economic Organization in International Perspective.* Princeton, NJ, Princeton University Press.

—— and W. W. Powell (1991). Introduction. *The New Institutionalism in Organizational Analysis.* P. DiMaggio and W. W. Powell, Eds. Chicago, IL, University of Chicago Press: 1–40.

DiMaria, E. and S. Micelli (2006). "District Leaders as Open Networks: Emerging Business Strategies in Italian Districts." *Global Value Chains Workshop: Industrial Upgrading, Offshore Production, and Labor.* Durham, NC, Duke University.

Dimicco, D. R. (2005). "The Steel Industry. Changing the Global Trading Landscape." Speech delivered to the Southern Growth Policies Board Conference, Point Clear, Alabama, Vital Speeches of the Day, June 15, 2005; 71 ABI/INFORM 535–8.

Doellgast, M. and I. Greer (2007). "Vertical Disintegration and the Disorganization of German Industrial Relations." *British Journal of Industrial Relations* 45(1): 55–76.

Domanski, B., R. Guzik, et al. (2007). "Competence Development and Relocation Dangers in the Automotive Industry in Poland." *Workshop on the Relocation and the Changing Relations Between High Wage and Low Wage Countries in the Auto Industry.* Berlin, WZB-Berlin: 23p.

Domansky-Davidsohn, E. (1980). Der Grossbetrieb als Organizationsproblem des Deutschen Metallarbeiter-Verbandes vor dem Ersten Weltkrieg. *Arbeiterbewegung und industrieller Wandel. Studien zu gewerkschaftlichen Organisationsproblemen im Reich und an der Ruhr.* H. Mommsen, Ed. Wuppertal, Germany, Peter Hammer: 95–116.

Dore, R. (1973). *British Factory/Japanese Factory. The Origins of National Diversity in Industrial Relations.* Berkeley, CA, University of California Press.

Döring, T. and J. Schnellenbach (2006). "What Do We Know About Geographical Knowledge Spillovers and Regional Growth?: A Survey of the Literature." *Regional Studies* 40(3): 375–95.

Duffy, H. (1981). An Entrepreneur Who Builds Small But Thinks Big. *The Financial Times,* August 3, 1981.

Dyer, J., D. S. Cho, et al. (1998). "Strategic Supplier Segmentation: The Next 'Best Practice' in Supply Chain Management." *California Managment Review* 40(2): 57–77.

Dziczek, K., D. Luria, et al. (2003). "Critical Relationships in Manufacturing." Special supplement, *Performance Benchmarking.* Ann Arbor, MI: Michigan Manufacturing Technology Center.

Eckart, K. (1988). *Die Eisen- und Stahlindustrie in den beiden Deutschen Staaten.* Stuttgart, Germany, Franz Steiner Verlag.

Edgerton, R. (1985). *Rules, Exceptions and Social Order.* Berkeley, CA, University of California Press.

Eglau, H. O. (1973). Stahlindustrie: Korf statt Koks. *Die Zeit,* May 1, 1973.

Elkmann, G.-H. (1970). *Möglichkeiten und Grenzen der Konzentration in der Eisen- und Stahlindustrie.* Wirtschafts- und Sozialwissenschaften. St Gallen, Switzerland, Hochschule St Gallen. PhD dissertation.

Ellguth, P. (2006). "Betriebe ohne Betriebsrat-Verbreitung und Charakeristika–unter Berücksichtigung betriebsspezifischer Formen der Mitarbeitervertretung." *Betriebe ohne Betriebsrat. Informelle Interessenvertretuung in Unternehmen.* I. Artus, S. Böhm, S. Lücking, and R. Tranczek, Eds. Frankfurt, Germany, Campus Verlag: 43–80.

Emirbayer, M. and Mischke (1998). "What Is Agency." *American Journal of Sociology* **103**(4): 962–1023.

Erickson, P. (2002). "OEM Leveraged Economic Development." Conference on *Supply Chain Governance and Regional Development in the Global Economy.* Madison, WI, University of Wisconsin-Madison, AMP/COWS.

Ernst, D. (1997). "From Partial to Systematic Globalization. International Production Networks in the Electronics Industry." *Brie Working Paper.* Berkley, CA, Berkley Round-table on International Economics: 113.

—— (2005). "Limits to Modularity: Reflections on Recent Developments in Chip Design." *Industry and Innovation* **12**(3): 303–35.

—— and K. Linsu (2002). "Global Production Networks, Knowledge Diffusion, and Local Capability Formation." *Research Policy* **31**: 1417–29.

Esser, J. and W. Väth (1986). "Overcoming the Steel Crisis in the Federal Republic of Germany, 1974–1984." *The Politics of Steel: Western Europe and the Steel Industry in the Crisis Years, 1974–1984.* Y. Meny and V. Wright, Eds. Berlin, Walter de Gruyter: 623–91.

Essletzbichler, J. (2003). "From Mass Production to Flexible Specialization: The Sectoral and Geographical Extent of Contract Work in US Manufacturing, 1963–1997." *Regional Studies* **37**(8): 753–71.

ETA/Business-Relations-Group (2005). *Advanced Manufacturing Industry: Addressing the Workforce Challenges of America's Advanced Manufacturing Workforce.* Department of Labor. Washington, DC, Department of Labor: 37p.

Farrell, D. (2004). *Can Germany Win from Offshoring?* Washington, DC, McKinsey Global Institute, McKinsey & Company.

Feenstra, R. C. (1998). "Integration of Trade and Disintegration of Production in the Global Economy." *The Journal of Economic Perspectives* **12**(4): 31–50.

Feldenkirchen, W. (1982). *Die Eisen- und Stahlindustrie des Ruhrgebiets, 1879–1914.* Stuttgart, Germany, Franz Steiner Wiesbaden.

Feldman, G. (1977). *Iron and Steel in the German Inflation, 1916–1923.* Princeton, NJ, Princeton University Press.

Fichter, M. (1993). "Hicog and the Unions in West Germany. A Study of Hicog's Labor Policy toward the Deutscher Gewerkschaftsbund, 1949–1952." *American Policy and the Reconstruction of West Germany.* J. M. Diefendorf, A. Frohn, and H.-J. Rupieper, Eds. New York, Cambridge University Press: 257–80.

Fieten, R., W. Friedrich, et al. (1997). *Globalisierung der Märkte—Herausforderung und Optionen für kleine und mittlere Unternehmen insbesondere für Zulieferer, Gutachten im Auftrag des Bundesministeriums für Wirtschaft.* Schriften zur Mittelstandsforschung. Stuttgart, Germany, Verlag Schäffer-Poeschel.

Fine, C. (1998). *Clockspeed.* Reading, MA, Perseus Books.

Finn, R. B. (1992). *Winners in Peace. MacArthur, Yoshida and Postwar Japan* Berkeley, CA, University of California Press.

Fixon, S. K. and J.-K. Park (2007). "The Power of Integrality: Linkages Between Product Architecture, Innovation, and Industry Structure." *MIT Sloan Working Paper.* Cambridge, MA, MIT Sloan School of Management: 56.

Fleming, S. (1983). "Troubled Korf Steel Group Calls on Bonn for Financial Support." *The Financial Times*, January 5, 1983.

Fligstein, N. (1996). "Markets as Politics: A Political-Cultural Approach to Market Institutions." *American Sociological Review* **61**: 656–73.

Florida, R. and M. Kenney (1993). *Beyond Mass Production: The Japanese System and Its Transfer to the US*. New York, Oxford University Press.

Follis, M. and A. Enrietti (1998). "Training Actions to Improve Performances at the Second Tier of the Supply Chain for Automotive Components." Unpublished Manuscript, Turin, Italy, University of Turin.

Fourcade, M. (2006). "The Construction of a Global Profession: The Transnationalization of Economics." *American Journal of Sociology* 112(1): 145–94.

—— and J. J. Savelsberg (2006). "Global Processes, National Institutions, Local Bricolage: Shaping Law in an Era of Globalization." *Law & Social Inquiry* 31(3): 513–19.

Fourcade-Gourinchas, M. and S. L. Babb (2002). "The Rebirth of the Liberal Creed: Paths to Neoliberalism in Four Countries." *American Journal of Sociology* 108(3): 533–79.

Frigant, V. (2007). "Is the French Auto Industry Really Threatened by the Low Wage Countries?" *Workshop on the Relocation and the Changing Relations Between High Wage and Low Wage Countries in the Auto Industry*. Berlin, WZB-Berlin: 38p.

Fröbel, F., J. Heinrichs, et al. (1977). *Die neue internationale Arbeitsteilung: strukturelle Arbeitslosigkeit in der Industrieländern und der Industrialisierung der Entwicklungsländer*. Reinbek bei Hamburg, Rowohlt.

Fujimoto, T. (1999). *The Evolution of a Manufacturing System at Toyota*. Oxford, UK, Oxford University Press.

—— (2000). "Why Product Architectures Matter." *Focus Japan* November, 10–13.

—— (2001). "The Japanese Automobile Parts Supplier System: The Triplet of Effective Inter-firm Routines." *International Journal of Automotive Technology and Management* 1(1): 1–34.

—— and A. Takeishi (2001). "Automobiles: Strategy Based on Lean Production System." *CIRJE Discussion Paper*. Tokyo, University of Tokyo.

Furukawa, T. (2001). "A Marketplace Battle for Tokyo Steel." *New Steel*. 17. March, 2001: 26f.

Fusfeld, D. (1958). "Joint Subsidiaries in the Iron and Steel Industry." *American Economic Review* 48(2): 578–87.

Gao, B. (1994). "Arisawa Hiromi and His Theory for a Managed Economy." *Journal of Japanese Studies* 20(1): 115–53.

—— (1997). *Economic Ideology and Japanese Industrial Policy. Developmentalism from 1931–1965*. New York, Cambridge University Press.

Garding, C. (1995). "Stahl: Heiss auf High Tech." *Focus Magazin*, February 6, 1995.

Garud, R., A. Kumaraswamy, et al., Eds. (2003). *Managing in the Modular Age. Architectures, Networks, and Organizations*. Oxford, UK, Blackwell Publishing.

Gavin, P. and A. Morkel (2001). "The Effect of Product Modulatity on Industry Structure: The Case of the World Bicycle Industry." *Industry and Innovation* 8(1): 31–47.

Geary, D. (1983). "The Industrial Elite and the Nazis." *The Nazi Machergreifung*. P. D. Stachura, Ed. London, Allen & Unwin: 85–100.

Gehlhoff, J. (1977). "Stahl-Erfolg mit kleinen Kapazität." *Die Welt*. Hamburg, March 21, 1977.

—— (1981). "Unverdrossene Zuversicht für das Stahlgeschäft." *Die Welt*. Hamburg, August 22, 1981.

—— (1983). "Ein trauriges Exempel." *Die Welt*. Hamburg, January 6, 1983.

Geishecker, I. (2005). "International Outsourcing and German Wages." *Schmollers Jahrbuch* 125(2005): 87–95.

Gereffi, G. (2005a). The Global Economy: Organization, Governance, Development. *The Handbook of Economic Sociology, Second Edition.* N. Smelser and R. Swedberg, Eds. Princeton NJ, Princeton University Press: 160–82.

—— (2005b). The New Offshoring of Jobs and Global Development. *ILO Social Policy Lectures.* I. I. f. L. Studies. Jamaica, International Labour Office-Geneva.

—— J. Humphrey, et al. (2005). "The Governance of Global Value Chains." *Review of International Political Economy* **12**(1): 78–104.

—— and Korzeniewicz, Eds. (1994). *Commodity Chains and Global Capitalism.* Studies in the Political Economy of the World System. Westport, CT, Greenwood Press.

Gertler, M. S. (2003). "Tacit Knowledge and the Economic Geography of Context, or The Indefinable Tacitness of Being (There)." *Journal of Economic Geography* **3**: 75–99.

Ghemawat, P. (2007). *Redefining Global Strategy. Crossing Borders in a World Where Differences Still Matter.* Boston, MA, Harvard Business School Press.

—— and F. Ghadar (2006). "Global Integration ≠ Global Concentration." *Industrial and Corporate Change* **15**(4): 595–623.

Giarratani, F., G. Gruever, et al. (2002). "A Comparative Analysis of Interindustry Linkages Based on the Clustering Activity Associated with Steel Minimills." *Center for Industry Studies Research.* Pittsburgh, PA: University of Pittsburgh.

—— —— et al. (2005). Agglomeration and Market Entry in the U.S. Steel Industry: Empirical Evidence Based on the Advent of Slab Casting by U.S. Steel Minimills. *Center for Industry Studies Research.* Pittsburgh, PA, University of Pittsburgh.

—— —— et al. (2006). "Plant Location and the Advent of Slab Casting by US Steel Minimills: An Observation-Based Analysis." *Economic Geography* **82**(4): 401–19.

Gilson, R. J., R. Scott, et al. (2009). "Contracting for Innovation: Vertical Disintergration and Interfirm Collaboration." *Columbia Law Review* **109**(3).

Glaeser, E. and G. Ponzetto (2007). "Did the Death of Distance Hurt Detroit and Help New York?" *Kennedy School of Government Working Papers.* Cambridge, MA, Harvard University: 46p.

Gold, B., W. Peirce, et al. (1970). "Diffusion of Major Technological Innovations in US Iron and Steel Manufacturing." *Journal of Industrial Economics* **18**(3): 218–41.

—— —— et al. (1984). *Technological Progress and Industrial Leadership.* Lexington, MA, D.C. Heath & Co.

Gomory, R. (2009). Manufacturing and the Limits of Comparative Advantage. *The Huffington Post,* July 8, 2009.

Gordon, A. (1985). *The Evolution of Labor Relations in Japan. Heavy Industry, 1853–1955.* Cambridge, MA, Harvard University Press.

—— (1993). "Contests for the Workplace." *Postwar Japan as History.* A. Gordon, Ed. Berkeley, CA, University of California Press.

—— (1996). "Conditions for the Disappearance of the Japanese Working Class Movement." *Putting Class in its Place. Worker Identities in East Asia.* E. Perry, Ed. Berkeley, CA, University of California Press.

—— (1998). *The Wages of Affluence. Labor and Management in Postwar Japan.* Cambridge, MA, Harvard University Press.

Grabher, G. (1993). The Weakness of Strong Ties: The Lock-in of Regional Development in the Ruhr Area. *The Embedded Firm: On the Socioeconomics of Interfirm Relations.* G. Grabher, Ed. London, Routledge: 255–78.

—— and W. W. Powell (2004). Introduction. *Critical Studies of Economic Institutions: Networks.* G. Grabher and W. W. Powell, Eds. Cheltenham, UK, Edward Elgar: 1.

Grahl, J. and P. Teague (2004). "The German Model in Danger." *Industrial Relations Journal* **35**(6): 557–73.

Granovetter, M. (1985). "Economic Action and Social Structure. The Problem of Embeddedness." *American Journal of Sociology* **91**(3): 481–510.

Gregor, N. (1998). *Daimler Benz in the Third Reich.* New Haven, CT, Yale University Press.

Greif, A. (2005). Commitment, Coercion and Markets: The Nature and Dynamics of Institutions Supporting Exchange. *Handbook of New Institutional Economics.* C. Menard and M. Shirly, Eds. Berlin, Springer Verlag: 727–86.

—— (2006). *Institutions and the Path to the Modern Economy.* New York, Cambridge University Press.

—— and D. D. Laitin (2004). "A Theory of Endogenous Institututional Change." *American Political Science Review* **98**(4): 633–52.

Grossman, G. and E. Helpman (2002). "Outsourcing in a Global Economy." *NBER Working Papers.* Cambridge MA, National Bureau of Economic Research: 56p.

—— —— (2002). "Integration Versus Outsourcing in Industry Equilibrium." *The Quarterly Journal of Economics* **117**(February): 85–120.

Gulati, R. and M. Sytch (2005). "Exploring the Role of Organizational Interdependence on Performance: The Role of Embeddedness and Power." Unpublished Manuscript, Evanston, IL, Kellogg School of Management, Northwestern University: 73p.

Günther, E. (1951). "Entwurf eines Gesetzes gegen Wettbewerbsbeschränkungen." *Wirtschaft und Wettbewerb* **1**(1): 17–40.

Günther, T. and T. Gonschorek (2006). Wert(e)orientierte Unternehmensführung im Mittelstand-Erste Ergebnisse einer empirischen Untersuchung. *Dresdner Beiträge zur Betriebswirtschaftslehre. Nr* **114**.

Hadley, E. (1970). *Anti-trust in Japan.* Princeton, Princeton University Press.

Haley, J. O. (1991). *Authority Without Power.* New York, Oxford University Press.

Hall, C. G. L. (1997). *Steel Phoenix. The Fall and Rise of the US Steel Industry.* London, Macmillan.

Hall, P. and D. Soskice, Eds. (2001*a*). *Varieties of Capitalism. The Institutional Foundations of Comparative Advantage.* Oxford, UK, Oxford University Press.

—— —— (2001*b*). Introduction to Varieties of Capitalism. *Varieties of Capitalism. The Institutional Foundations of Comparative Advantage.* P. Hall and D. Soskice, Eds. Oxford, UK, Oxford University Press: 1–70.

—— and K. Thelen (2009). "Institutional Change in Varieties of Capitalism." *Socio-Economic Review* **7**(1): 7–34.

Hall, P. A. (1996). "Political Science and the Three New Institutionalisms." *Political Studies* **XLIV**: 936.

Hansmann, H. B. and R. Kraakman (2001). "The End of History in Corporate Law." *Georgetown Law Journal* **89**: 439–68.

Hanson, G. H., R. J. Mataloni, Jr, et al. (2003). *Vertical Production Networks in Multinational Firms. NBER Working Paper Series.* Cambridge MA, National Bureau of Economic Research: 40.

Harrison, B. (1994). *Lean and Mean: The Changing Landscape of Corporate Power in the Age of Flexibility.* New York, Basic Books.

Hart, J. A. (1994). "A Comparative Analysis of America's Relative Economic Decline." *Understanding American Economic Decline.* M. A. Bernstein and D. E. Adler, Eds. New York, Cambridge University Press: 199–240.

Harvey, D. (1989). *The Condition of Post-modernity.* Oxford, UK, Blackwell.

—— (2005). *A Brief History of Neoliberalism.* New York, Oxford University Press.

Hashimoto, J. (1996). "How and Why Japanese Economic Enterprise Systems Were Formed." *Japanese Yearbook on Business History* **13**: 5–27.

Hassel, A. (1999). "The Erosion of the German System of Industrial Relations." *British Journal of Industrial Relations* **37**(3): 483–505.

—— (2006). "Die Schwächen des deutschen Kapitalismus." *Gibt es einen deutschen Kapitalismus?" Die soziale Marktwirtschaft im Weltsystem.* V. Berghahn and S. Vitols, Eds. Frankfurt, Germany, Campus Verlag.

Hayes, P. (1987). *Industry and Ideology. IG Farben in the Nazi Era.* New York, Cambridge University Press.

Helmer, W. (1996). "Wer nichts riskiert, riskiert alles." *Frankfurter Allgemeine Zeitung*, November 25, 1996.

Helper, S. (1991*a*). "How Much Has Really Changed Between US Automakers and Their Suppliers?" *Sloan Management Review* **32**(4): 15–28.

—— (1991*b*). "Strategy and Irreversibility in Supplier Relations: The Case of the US Automobile Industry." *Business History Review* **65**(4): 781–824.

—— and J. P. MacDuffie (1999). "Creating Lean Suppliers: Diffusing Lean Production through the Supply Chain." *Remade in America. Transplanting and Transforming Japanese Management Systems.* J. Liker, M. W. Fruin, and P. Adler, Eds. New York, Oxford University Press.

—— and M. Sako (1995). "Supplier Relations in Japan and the United States. Are they Converging?" *Sloan Management Review* **36**(3): 77–84.

—— —— (1998). "Determinants of Trust in Supplier Relations. Evidence from the Automotive Industry in Japan and the United States." *Journal of Economic Behaviour and Organization* **34**: 387–417.

—— J. P. MacDuffie, et al. (2000). "Pragmatic Collaborations: Advancing Knowledge While Controlling Opportunism." *Industrial and Corporate Change* **9**(3): 443–83.

Henderson, R. M. and K. B. Clark (1990). "Architectual Innovation: The Reconfiguration of Existing Product Technologies and the Failure of Established Firms." *Administrative Science Quarterly* **35**: 9.

Hennes, M. (1993). "Stahlindustrie. Verdammt hart. Ein Manager schmeisst seinen Top-Job, um die marode Georgsmarienhütte zu sanieren." *Wirtschaftswoche*, September 24, 1993.

Herchenröder, K. H., J. Schäfer, et al. (1953). *Die Nachfolger der Ruhrkonzerne. Die Neuordunung der Montanindustrie.* Düsseldorf, Econ Verlag.

Herling, J. (1972). *Right to Challenge. People and Power in the Steelworkers Union.* New York, Harper & Row.

Herrigel, G. (1996). *Industrial Constructions. The Sources of German Industrial Power.* New York, Cambridge University Press.

—— (2004). "Emerging Strategies and Forms of Governance in High-Wage Component Manufacturing Regions." *Industry and Innovation* **11**(1/2): 45–79.

—— (2007*a*). Interim Report on the Global Components Project. *Global Components Project Working Paper.* Chicago, IL, University of Chicago.

—— (2007*b*). Flexibility and Formalization: New Forms of Governance in Firms and Regions. *Globalization and the Experience of Small and Medium Sized Firms in Europe.* K. Bluhm and R. Schmidt, Eds. Basingstoke, UK, Palgrave Macmillan.

—— (2008). "Roles and Rules: Ambiguity, Experimentation and New Forms of Stakeholderism in Germany." *Industrielle Beziehungen* **15**(2): 111–32.

—— and V. Wittke (2005). "Varieties of Vertical Disintegration: The Global Trend Toward Heterogeneous Supply relatins and the Reproduction of Difference in US and German

Manufacturing." *Changing Capitalisms: Internationalization, Institutional Change and Systems of Economic Organization*. G. Morgan, E. Moen, and R. Whitley, Eds. Oxford, UK, Oxford Unversity Press.

Herrmann, A. M. (2008). "Rethinking the Link Between Labour Market Flexibility and Corporate Competitiveness: A Critique of the Institutionalist Literature." *Socio-Economic Review* 6: 637–69.

Hessen, R. (1975). *Steel Titan. The Life of Charles M Schwab*. Pittsburgh, PA, Universitiy of Pittsburgh Press.

Hideo, O. (1987). "The Zaikai under the Occupation: The Formation and Transformation of Managerial Councils." *Democratizing Japan*. R. E. Ward and Y. Yoshikazu, Eds. Honolulu, HI: University of Hawaii Press: 366–91.

High, S. (2003). *Industrial Sunset. The Making of North America's Rust Belt 1969–1984*. Toronto, University of Toronto Press.

Hill, C. and R. Hoskisson (1987). "Strategy and Structure in the Multiproduct Firm." *Academy of Management Review* 12: 331–41.

Hines, P., M. Holweg, et al. (2004). "Learning to Evolve: A Review of Contemporary Lean Thinking." *International Journal of Operations and Production Management* 24(10): 994–1011.

Hirsch, F. (1962). *Die Absatwege bei Walzwerkserzeugnissen und ihre Organizationsformen. Ein internationaler Vergleich zwischen den USA, der BRD, Frankreich und Belgien*. Wirtschafts Fakultät. München, Ludwig-Maximilians Universität z München. PhD dissertation.

Hirsch, P. and M. Lounsbury (1997). "Ending the Family Quarrel. Toward a Reconciliation of "Old" and "New" Institutionalisms." *The American Behavioral Scientist* 40(4): 406–18.

Hirschmeier, J. (1964). *The Origins of Entrepreneurship in Meiji Japan*. Cambridge MA, Harvard University Press.

—— and T. Yui (1981). *The Development of Japanese Business, 1600–1980*. London, Allen & Unwin.

Hirst, P. and J. Zeitlin (1991). "Flexible Specialization Versus Post-Fordism: Theory, Evidence and Policy Implications." *Economy and Society* 20(1): 1–55.

Hoerr, J. (1988). *And the Wolf Finally Came. The Decline of the American Steel Industry*. Pittsburgh, PA, University of Pittsburgh Press.

Hogan, W. T. (1987). *Minimills and Integrated Mills. A Comparison of Steelmaking in the United States*. Lexington MA, Lexington Books.

—— (1994). *Steel in the 21st Century. Competition Forges a New Order*. Lexington, MA, Lexington Books.

Hollingsworth, J. R. and R. Boyer, Eds. (1997). *Contemporary Capitalism*. New York, Oxford University Press.

Honeck, J. P. (1998). *Industrial Policy in Older Industrial Regions: A Comparison of Ohio and the Basque Region*. Political Science. Madison, WI, University of Wisconsin. PhD dissertation.

Horowitz, M. (1992). *The Transformation of American Law, 1870–1960*. New York, Oxford University Press.

Hoshi, T. and A. Kashyap (2001). *Financing and Governance in Japan. The Road to the Future*. Cambridge, MA, MIT.

Hoskisson, R. (1987). "Multidivisional Structure and Performance: The Contingency of Diversification Strategy." *Academy of Management Journal* 30: 625–44.

Hovenkamp, H. (1991). *Enterprise and American Law 1836–1937*. Cambridge, MA, Harvard University Press.

Hufbauer, G. C. and B. Goodrich (2002). "Time for a Grand Bargain in Steel?" *International Economic Policy Briefs* **2**(1).

Huffschmid, B. (1965). *Das Stahlzeitalter beginnt erst*. München, Verlag Moderne Industrie.

Hughes, E. C.(1993).*The Sociological Eye: Selected Papers*. New Brunswick, NJ, Transaction Press.

Humphrey, J. (1990). "Globalization and Supply Chain Networks: The Automobile Industry in Brazil and India." *Global Networks* **3**(2): 121–41.

—— (1998). Assembler-Supplier Relations in the Auto Industry: Globalization and National Development. *Institute of Development Studies*. Brighton, UK, University of Sussex.

—— and H. Schmitz (2002). "How Does Insertion in Global Value Chains Affect Upgrading in Industrial Clusters." *Regional Studies* **36**(9): 1017–27.

Hurst, J. W. (1970). *The Legitimacy of the Business Corporation in the Law of the United States, 1780–1970*. Charlottesville, VA, The University of Virginia Press.

Hwang, S.-C. (1968). *Das Japanische Anti-monopolgesetz im Lichte des deutschen Kartellrechts*. Rechts Fakultät. Heidelberg, Ruprecht-Karl Universität, Heidelberg, PhD dissertation.

Ivarsson, I. and C. G. Alvstam (2005). "Technology Transfer from TNCs to Local Suppliers in Developing Countries: A Study of AB Volvo's Truck and Bus Plants in Brazil, China, India and Mexico." *World Development* **33**(8): 1325–44.

Iwase, N. (2000). "Poor Prices May Stifle Japan's Increase in Output." *Steel Times International* **24**(6): 42–3.

—— (2001). "Ready to Play the Global Game!—The Consolidation of NKK and Kawasaki." *Steel Times International* **25**: 46–8.

—— (2002). "Japan's EAF Mills Enter the Twilight Hours." *Steel Times International*: 1.

Iyori, J. H. (1967). *Das japanische Kartelrecht. Entwicklungsgeschichte, Grundprinzipien und Praxis*. Köln, Germany, Carl Heymans Verlag.

—— (1990). "A Comparative Analysis on Japanese Competition Law: An Attempt to Identify German and American Influences." *Die Japnisierung des westlichen Rechts*. H. Coing, Ed. Tübingen, Germany, JCB Mohr (Paul Siebeck): 227–54.

Jackson, G. (2003). "Corporate Governance in Germany and Japan: Liberalzation Pressures and Responses During the 1990s." *The End of Diversity? Prospects for German and Japanese Capitalism*. K. Yamamura and W. Streeck, Eds. Ithaca, NY, Cornell University Press: 261–306.

James, W. (1897 (1956)). *The Will To Believe and Other Essays in Popular Philosophy/ Human Immortality*. New York, Dover Publicagtions.

—— (1996 [1912]). *Essays in Radical Empiricism*. Lincoln, NE, University of Nebraska Press/Bison Books.

Janitz, F. (2002). Union Led Firm Restructuring Practices. *Conference on Supply Chain Governance and Regional Development in the Global Economy*. Madison, WI, University of Wisconsin-Madison, AMP/COWS.

Japanese Iron and Steel Industry Federation (1952). *The Iron and Steel Industry and Fabricated Products, 1952*. Tokyo, Tokyo Liason and Translation Service.

—— (1998) *Japan's Iron and Steel Industry*. Tokyo, Japanese Iron and Steel Federation.

Jaspert, W. (1996). "Jürgen Grossman hat es geschafft." *Süddeutsche Zeitung*, April 4, 1996.

JILPT (2009). JILPT Data Book of International Labour Statistics 2009. *Statistics*, JILPT.

Joas, H. (1992). *Pragmatismus und Gesellschaftstheorie*. Frankfurt, Germany, Suhrkamp.

—— (1996). *The Creativity of Action*. Chicago, IL, University of Chicago Press.

—— and J. Beckert (2001). "Action Theory." *Handbook of Sociological Theory*. J. Turner. New York, Plenum: 269–85.

—— and W. Knöbl (2004). *Sozialtheorie. Zwanzig einführende Vorlesungen*. Frankfurt, Germany, Suhrkamp.

Johnson, C. (1975). "Japan: Who Governs? An Essay on Official Bureaucracy." *Journal of Japanese Studies* **2**(1): 16.

—— (1981). *MITI and the Japanese Miracle*. Palo Alto, CA, Stanford University Press.

Johnson, S. B. (2000). "From Concurrency to Phased Planning: An Episode in the History of Systems Management." *Systems, Experts, and Computers*. A. C. Hughes and T. P. Hughes, Eds. Cambridge, MA, The MIT Press: 93–112.

Jösten, J. (1948). *Germany: What Now?* Chicago, IL, Ziff-Davis Publishing Co.

Jürgenhake, U., P. Schnittfeld, et al. (1997). "The End of Dinosaurs? The Social Consequences of the Transition from Integrated Steel Production Towards Electric Steel Production." *Beiträge aus der Forschung*. Dortmund, sfs: Sozialforschungsstelle.

Jürgens, U. (1997). "Germany: Implementing Lean Production." *After Lean Production. Evolving Employment Practices in the World Automobile Industry*. T. Kochen, R. Lansbury, and J. P. MacDuffie, Eds. Ithaca, NY, Cornell University Press: 109–36.

—— (2003). "Transformatoin and Interaction: Japnese, US and German Production Models in the 1990s." *The End of Diversity? Prospects for German and Japanese Capitalism*. K. Yamamura and W. Streeck, Eds. Ithaca, NY, Cornell University Press: 212–39.

—— (2004). "An Elusive Model-Diversified Quality Production and the Transformation of the German Automobile Industry." *Competition and Change* **8**(4): 411–23.

—— (2007). "High-Wage and Low-Wage Countries in Production Networks of the Automobile Industry: Relocation, Development Changes and Risks and the Consequences for Work and Employment." *Workshop on the Relocation and the Changing Relations Between High Wage and Low Wage Countries in the Auto Industry*. Berlin, WZB-Berlin: 12.

Kalagnanam, J. R., M. W. Dawande, et al. (1998). "Inventory Matching Problems in the Steel Industry." *IBM Research Report*. Yorktown Heights, NY, IBM Research Division.

Kato, T. (2000). "The Recent Transformation of Participatory Employment Practices in Japan." Research Report, New York, *Columbia University Center on Japanese Economy and Business*.

Katzenstein, P. J. (1987). *Policy and Politics in West Germany. The Growth of a Semisovereign State*. Philadelphia, PA, Temple University Press.

Kaufman, A. and E. J. Englander (1993). "Kohlberg Kravis Roberts & Co. and the Restructuring of American Capitalism." *The Business History Review* **67**(1): 52–97.

—— and L. Zacharias (1992). "From Trust to Contract: The Legal Language of Managerial Ideology, 1920–1980." *The Business History Review* **66**(3): 523–72.

Kawahito, K. (1972). *The Japanese Steel Industry*. New York, Praeger.

Kawai, K. (1960). *Japan's American Interlude*. Chicago, IL, University of Chicago Press.

Kaysen, C. (1957). "The Social Significance of the Modern Corporation." *The American Economic Review* **47**(2): 311–19.

—— (1965). "Another View of Corporate Capitalism." *The Quarterly Journal of Economics* **79**(1): 41–51.

Keller, B. (2006). "Die nicht mehr so schleichende Abschied vom "dualen" System—und einige seiner Konsequenzen." *Betriebe ohne Betriebsrat. Informelle Interessenvertretung im Unternehmen*. I. Artus, S. Böhm, S. Lücking, and R. Tranczek, Eds. Frankfurt, Germany, Campus Verlag: 425–38.

Kelly, M. A. (1949*a*). "Reconstitution of the German Trade Union Movement." *Political Science Quarterly* **64**(1949): 24–49.

—— (1949*b*). "Labor Relations in American-Occupied Germany." *Labor in Postwar America*. C. E. Warne, Ed. Brooklyn, NY, Remsen Press: 607–21.

Kenney, M., Ed. (2000). *Understanding Silicon Valley. The Anatomy of an Entrepreneurial Region*. Stanford, CA, Stanford University Press.

—— and R. Florida, Eds. (2004). *Locating Global Advantage. Industry Dynamics in the International Economy. Innovation and Technology in the World Economy*. Stanford, CA, Stanford University Press.

Kerr, C. (1954). "The Trade Union Movement and the Redistribution of Power in Postwar Germany." *Quarterly Journal of Economics* **LXVIII**(4): 553–4.

Kerr, J. (1985). "Diversification Strategies and Managerial Rewards: An Empirical Study." *Academy of Management Journal* **28**: 155–79.

King, A. (1999). "Against Structure: A Critique of Morphogenetic Social Theory." *The Sociological Review* **47**(2): 199–227.

Kivinen, O. and T. Piiroinen (2006). "On the Limits of a Realist Conception of Knowledge: A Pragmatist Critique of Archerian Realism." *The Sociological Review* **54**(2): 224–41.

Klass, G. v. (1954). *Krupps*. London, Sidgewick and Jackson.

Kleinschmidt, C. (1993). *Rationalisierung als Unternehmenstrategie. Die Eisen- und Stahlindustrie des Ruhrgebiets zwischen Jahrhundertwende und Weltwirtschaftskrise*. Essen, Germany, Klartext.

Klitzke, U., H. Betz, et al., Eds. (2000). *Vom Klassenkampf zum Co-Management? Perspektiven gewerkschaftlicher Betriebspolitik*. Hamburg, Germany, VSA.

Klonsinski, M. (2002). "Targeting Supply Chains as Economic Development Policy: Lessons from the WMDC." *Conference on Supply Chain Governance and Regional Development in the Global Economy*. Madison, WI, University of Wisconsin-Madison, AMP/COWS.

Knight, C. F. and D. Dyer (2005). *Performance Without Compromise: How Emerson Consistently Achieves Winning Results*. Boston, MA, Harvard Business School Press.

Knight, J. (1992). *Institutions and Social Conflict*. New York, Cambridge University Press.

—— and J. Johnson (1996). "Political Consequences of Pragmatism." *Political Theory* **24**(1): 68–96.

Kobayakawa, Y. (1996). "Problems of Technology Choice Faced by the Private-Sector Steel Industry in Prewar Japan. Nippon Steel Pipe's Steel Manufacturing Integration and the Introduction of Converters." *Japanese Yearbook of Business History* **13**: 53–71.

Kochan, T. A., R. D. Lansbury, et al., Eds. (1997). *After Lean Production: Evolving Employment Practices in the World Auto Industry*. Ithaca, NY, Cornell University Press.

Köhler, H. (1969). *Die Walzstahlkontore*. Düsseldorf, Verlag Stahleisen MBH.

Köhler, H.-D. and S. Gonzalez Begega (2007). "Relocation, Follow Sourcing, Clustering— The Iberian Automotive Supplier Industry." *Workshop on the Relocation and the Changing Relations Between High Wage and Low Wage Countries in the Auto Industry*. Berlin, WZB-Berlin: 28.

Köhler, H. W. (1971). *Das Kontornachfolgekonzept: Vier Rationalisierungsgruppen*. Düsseldorf, Verlag Stahleisen mbH.

Konzelmann, S. and W. Barnes (1999). *The Fragility of Functional Work Systems in American Steel*, ESRC Centre for Business Research. Cambridge, University of Cambridge.

Kotkin, J. (2009). "We Must Remember Manufacturing." *Forbes*, April 21, 2009.

Kraut, R. (1990). "Varieties of Pragmatism." *Mind* **99**(394): 157–83.

Krippner, G. R. (2005). "The Financialization of the American Economy." *Socio-Economic Review* 3(2): 173–208.

Kristensen, P. H. (1992). Industrial Districts in West Jutland, Denmark. *Industrial Districts and Local Economic Regeneration.* F. Pyke and W. Sengenberger. Geneva, International Institute for Labor Studies: 122–73.

—— (2005). *Business Systems in the Age of the New Economy. Denmark Facing the Challenge.* Copenhagen, Copenhagen Business School.

—— and R. Rocha (2006). "Unions at a Crossroad: Protectors of Achieved Rights or Active Co-Constructors of the Future?" International Center for Business and Politics Working Papers. Copenhagen, Copenhagen Business School.

—— and C. F. Sabel (1997). "The Small Holder Economy in Denmark: The Exception as Variation." *World of Possibilities: Flexibility and Mass Production in Western Industrialization.* C. F. Sabel and J. Zeitlin. Cambridge, Cambridge University Press.

—— and J. Zeitlin (2005). *Local Players in Global Games.* Oxford, UK, Oxford University Press.

—— M. Lotz, et al. (2008). The Danish Case: Complementarities of Local and National Dynamics. *Translearn.* Copenhagen, Copenhagen Business School: 61.

—— and Kari Lillja, Eds (2009). *New Modes of Globalizing: Experimentalist forms of Economic Organization and Enabling Welfare Institutions. Lessons from the Nordic Countries and Slovenia.* Copenhagen: EU funded 6 Framework Program, Translearn.

Krzywdzinski, M. (2007). German Companies in Central Eastern Europe: Relocation and "Model Flight"? *Workshop on the Relocation and the Changing Relations Between High Wage and Low Wage Countries in the Auto Industry.* Berlin, WZB-Berlin: 14.

Kulek, C. (2002). "State of Illinois, Department of Commerce and Community Affairs, Industrial Training Program." *Conference on Supply Chain Governance and Regional Development in the Global Economy.* Madison, WI, University of Wisconsin Press, AMP/COWS.

Kume, I. (1998). *Disparaged Success. Labor Politics in Postwar Japan.* Ithaca, NY, Cornell University Press.

Kuster, T. (1995). "Labor: The USWA's Battle for the Minimills." *New Steel*, May, 1995.

Kwon, H.-K. (2004). *Fairness and Division of Labor in Market Societies: Comparison of U.S. and German Automotive Industries.* New York/Oxford, UK, Berghahn Books.

—— (2005). "National Model Under Globalization: The Japanese Model and Its Internationalization." *Politics and Society* 33(2): 234–52.

Lammert, F. (1960). *Das Verhältnis zwischen der Eisen schaffenden und der Eisen verarbeitenden Industrie seit dem ersten Weltkrieg.* Wirtschafts- und Socialwissenschaftlichen Fakultät, Universität Köln, PhD dissertation.

Landes, D. (1965). "Japan and Europe: Contrasts in Industrialization." *State and Economic Enterprise in Japan.* W. Lockwood, Ed. Princeton, NJ, Princeton Universitiy Press.

Lane, C. (2000). "Globalization and the German Model of Capitalism—Erosion or Survival?" *British Journal of Sociology* 51(2): 207–34.

Lange, K. (2009). "Institutional Embeddedness and the Strategic Leeway of Actors: The Case of the German Therapeutical Biotech Industry." *Socio-Economic Review* 7(2): 181–207.

Langlois, R. N. (2003). "The Vanishing Hand: The Changing Dynamics of Industrial Capitalism." *Industrial and Corporate Change* 12(2): 351–85.

—— (2007). *The Dynamics of Industrial Capitalism. Schumpeter, Chandler and the New Economy.* Abington, UK, Routledge.

Latour, B. (2005). *Reassembling the Social: An Introduction to Actor-Network Theory.* Oxford, UK, Oxford University Press.

—— (2007). "How to Think Like a State." Conference paper, Anniversary of the WRR.

Lazerson, M. H. and G. Lorenzoni (1999). "The Firms that Feed Industrial Districts: A Return to the Italian Source." *Industrial and Corporate Change* **8**(2): 235–66.

Leachman, R. C. and C. H. Leachman (2004). "Globalization of Semi-conductors: Do Real Men Have Fabs or Virtual Fabs?" *Locating Global Advantage. Industry Dynamics in the International Economy.* M. Kenney and R. Florida. Stanford, CA, Stanford University Press: 203–31.

Lee, J. C. (1990). *Frachtbasissystem bei standardisierten Produkten. Theoretische Analyse und empirische Reflexion am Beispiel der Stahlindustrie.* Bochum, Germany, Universitätsverlag Dr. N. Brockmeyer.

Lenfle, S. and C. Y. Baldwin (2007). "From Manufacturing to Design: An Essay on the Work of Kim B. Clark." *Harvard Business School Working Papers.* Boston, MA, Harvard Business School: 54.

Lewis, A. (1988). "Wittgenstein and Rule Scepticism." *The Philosophical Quarterly* **38**(152): 280–304.

Liebman, B. H. (2006). "Safeguards, China, and the Price of Steel." *Review of World Economics* **142**(2): 354–73.

—— and K. M. Tomlin (2007). "Steel Safeguards and the Welfare of the US Steel Firms and Downstream Consumers of Steel: A Shareholder Wealth Perspective." *Canadian Economics Association* **40**(3): 812–42.

Lieberman, J. (2004). *Offshore Outsourcing and America's Competitive Edge: Losing Out in the High Technology R&D and Service Sectors,* Washington, DC, United States Senate: 42p.

Lieberman, M. B. and D. R. Johnson (1999). "Comparative Productivity of Japanese and US Steel Producers, 1958–1993." *Japan and the World Economy* **11**: 1–27.

Liker, J., M. w. Fruin, et al., Eds. (1999). *Remade in America: Transplanting and Transforming Japanese Management Systems.* New York, Oxford University Press.

Lipietz, A. (1987). *Mirages and Miracles: The Crises of Global Fordism.* London, Verso.

Lipset, S. M. (1963). *Political Man: The Social Bases of Politics.* New York, Anchor/Doubleday.

Lockwood, W. (1968). *The Economic Development of Japan.* Princeton, NJ, Princeton University Press.

Lorenzoni, G. and A. Lipparini (1999). "The Leveraging of Interfirm Relationships as a Distinctive Organizational Capability: A Longitudinal Study." *Strategic Management Journal* **20**(4): 317–38.

Lovering, J. (1999). "'Theory Led by Policy: The Inadequacies of the 'New Regionalism' (Illustrated from the Case of Wales)." *International Journal of Urban and Regional Research* **23**: 379–96.

Lung, Y. (2002). "The Changing Geography of Automobile Production." *International Journal of Urban and Regional Research* **26**(4): 737–41.

Luria, D. (1996a). "Why Markets Tolerate Mediocre Manufacturing." *Challenge* **39**(4): 11–16.

—— (1996b). "Toward Lean or Rich? What Performance Benchmarking Tells Us About SME Performance, and Some Implications for Extension Center Services and Mission." *Conference on Manufacturing Modernization: Learning from Evaluation Practices and Results.* Atlanta, GA.

Lüthje, B. (2001). *Standort Silicon Valley. Oekonomie und Politik der vernetzten Massenproduktion.* Frankfurt, Germany, Campus Verlag.

—— (2002). "Electronics Contract Manufacturing: Global Production and the International Division of Labor in the Age of the Internet." *Industry and Innovation* **9**(3): 227–47.

—— W. Schumm, et al. (2002). *Contract Manufacturing. Transnationale Produktion und Industriearbeit in der IT-Branche.* Frankfurt, Germany, Campus Verlag.

Lutz, B. (1975). *Krise des Lohnanreizes. Ein empirisch historischer Beitrag zum Wandel der Formen betrieblicher Herrschaft am Beispiel der deutschen Stahlindustrie.* Frankfurt, Germany, Europäische Verlagsanstalt.

Lynn, L. H. (1982). *How Japan Innovates: A Comparison with the United States in the Case of Oxygen Steelmaking.* Boulder, CO, Westview.

—— and T. J. McKeown (1988). *Organizing Business: Trade Associations in America and Japan.* Washington, DC, American Enterprise Institute.

Maasoumi, E. and D. J. Slottje (2003). "Dynamics of Market Power and Concentration Profiles." *Econometric Reviews* **22**(2): 155–77.

MacDuffie, J. P. (1997). "The Road to 'Root Cause': Shop-Floor Problem-Solving at Three Auto Assembly Plants." *Management Science* **43**(4): 479–501.

—— (2007). "Modularity and the Geography of Innovation." *Sloan Industry Studies Conference.* Cambridge, MA.

—— and S. Helper (1997). "Creating Lean Suppliers: The Honda Way." *California Management Review* **39**(4): 118–51.

MacLeod, G. (2001). "New Regionalism Reconsidered: Globalization and the Remaking of Political Economic Space." *International Journal of Urban and Regional Research* **25**(4): 804–29.

Maddala, G. S. and P. T. Knight (1967). "International Diffusion of Technical Change-A Case Study of the Oxygen Steel Making Process." *The Economic Journal* **77**(307): 531–58.

Maddison, A. (1999). "Perspective on Global Economic Progress and Human Development. Economic Progress: The Last Half Century in Historical Perspective." *Annual Symposium 1999,* Academy of Social Sciences, Canberra, Australia.

Madsen, P. K. (2006). How Can It Possibly Fly? The Paradox of a Dynamic Labour Market in a Scandinavian Welfare State. *National Identity and A Variety of Capitalism.* J. L. Campbell, J. A. Hall, and O. K. Pedersen. Montreal, Canada, McGill University Press.

Mahmood, S. (2001). "Feminist Theory, Embodiement, and the Docile Agent: Some Reflections on the Egyptian Islamic Rival." *Cultural Anthropology* **16**(2): 202–36.

—— (2005). *Politics of Piety. The Islamic Revival and the Feminist Subject.* Princeton, NJ, Princeton University Press.

Mahnke, V. (2001). "The Process of Vertical Dis-Integration: An Evolutionary Perspective on Outsourcing." *Journal of Management and Governance* **5**: 353–79.

Mahoney, J. (2000). "Path Dependence in Historical Sociology." *Theory and Society* **29**: 507–48.

—— and K. Thelen (2008). "A Theory of Gradual Institutional Change." Unpublished Manuscript, Evanston, IL, Northwestern University.

Manager Magazine (1973). *Manager Magazine.* **12**: 30–4.

—— (1975). *Manager Magazine.* **11**: 27–34.

Manchester, W. (1968). *The Arms of Krupp.* New York, Bantam Books.

Mangum, G. I. and R. S. McNabb (1997). *The Rise, Fall, and Replacement of Industrywide Bargaining in the Basic Steel Industry* Armonk, NY, M.E. Sharpe.

Mankiw, N. G. and P. Swagel (2006). "The Politics and Economics of Offshoring Outsourcing." Unpublished Manuscript, Cambridge, MA, Harvard University: 51.

March, J. G. and J. Olsen, P. (2004). "The Logic of Appropriateness." Unpublished Manuscript, Oslo, Norway Centre for European Studies, University of Oslo.

—— —— (2005). "Elaborating on the 'New Institutionalism'." Unpublished Manuscript, Oslo, Norway, Centre for European Studies, University of Oslo.

Marchant, M. and S. Kumar (2005). "An Overview of US Foreign Direct Investment and Outsourcing." *Review of Agricultural Economics* **27**(3): 379–86.

Marcus, M. (1994). *Truman and the Steel Seizure Case. The Limits of Presidential Power.* Durham, NC, Duke University Press.

Mark, G. A. (1987). "The Personification of the Business Corporation in American Law." *The University of Chicago Law Review* **54**(4): 1441–83.

—— (1998). The Court and the Corporation: Jurisprudence, Localism and Federalism. *The Supreme Court Review, 1997.* D. Hutchinson, D. Strauss, and G. Stone. Chicago, IL, University of Chicago Press: 403–37.

Markovits, A. (1986). *The Politics of West German Trade Unions.* New York, Cambridge University Press.

Markusen, A. (1996). "Sticky Places in Slippery Space: A Typology of Industrial Districts." *Economic Geography* **72**(3): 293–313.

Marshall, J. (2005). "Inside a Steel Deal." *Financial Executive*, Financial Executives International: 29–30.

Martin, J. D. (1950). *All Honorable Men.* Boston, MA, Little Brown.

Martin, R. and P. Sunley (2003). "Deconstructing Clusters: Chaotic Concept or Policy Panacea?" *Journal of Economic Geography* **3**(2003): 5–35.

—— and P. Sunley (2006). "Path Dependence and Regional Economic Evolution." *Journal of Economic Geography* **6**: 395–437.

Maskell, P. and M. Lorenzen (2004). "The Cluster as Market Organization." *Urban Studies* **41**(5/6): 991–1009.

Mayer, D. and M. Kenney (2004). "Economic Action Does Not Take Place in a Vacuum: Understanding Cisco's Acquisition and Development Strategy." *Industry and Innovation* **11**(4): 299–325.

Mayo, B. (1954). "Rule Making and Rule Breaking." *Analysis* **15**(1): 16–23.

McAdams, A. K. (1967). "Big Steel, Invention and Innovation: Reconsidered." *Quarterly Journal of Economics* **81**(3).

McAlinden, S. P., B. C. Smith, et al. (1999). The Future of Automotive Systems: Where Are the Economic Efficiences in the Modular Assembly Concept? *Michigan Automotive Partnership, Research Memorandum No. 1, Office for the Study of Automotive Transportation.* M. A. Partnership. Ann Arbor, MI , University of Michigan Transport Research Institute.

McConnell, G. (1963). *Steel and the Presidency–1962.* New York, Norton.

McCormack, R., Ed. (2009). *Manufacturing A Better Future for America.* Washington, DC, Alliance for American Manufacturing.

McGilvary, E. A. (2000). "Five Myths About Pragmatism, Or, Against a Second Pragmatic Acquiescence." *Political Theory* **28**(4): 480–508.

McKendrick, D., R. Doner, et al. (2000). *From Silicon Valley to Singapore. Location and Competitive Advantage in the Hard Disk Drive Industry.* Stanford, CA, Stanford University Press.

McManus, G. (1985). "Steel's Agony. How Management Is Coping." *Iron Age*, May 17, 1985: 19–31.

Mead, G. H. (1932). *The Philosophy of the Present.* Chicago, IL, University of Chicago Press.

—— (1934). *Mind Self and Society from the Standpoint of a Social Behaviorist*. Chicago, IL, University of Chicago Press.

Mehta, M. (2001*a*). "US Steel Industry Profit From Import Fines." *Steel Times International*, September 56f.

—— (2001*b*). "Section 201—The US Review." *Steel Times International*, July: 41f.

Meissner, H. R. (2007). "East Germany's Auto Industry: In a Sandwich Position?" *Workshop on the Relocation and the Changing Relations Between High Wage and Low Wage Countries in the Auto Industry*. Berlin, WZB-Berlin: 15.

Melmberg, A. (1990). "Repetition (in the Kierkegaardian Sense of the Term)." *Diacritics* **20**(3): 71–87.

Menges, D. W. v. (1976). *Unternehmens-Entscheide. Ein Leben für die Wirtschaft* Düsseldorf, Econ Verlag.

MERB (1936). *Japanese Trade and Industry*. London, Macmillan.

Mesquita, L. and T. Brush(2002). "Relationship Management in Vertical Manufacturing Alliances, Supplier Development and Supplier Performance." *Krannert School of Management Working Paper*. West Lafayette, IN, Purdue University.

Mestmäcker, E.-J. (1978). *Recht und ökonomisches Gesetz. Über die Grenzen von Staat, Gesellschaft und Privatautonomie*. Baden-Baden, Germany, Nomos Verlag.

—— (1983). *Europäische Kartelpolitik auf dem Stahlmarkt*. Baden-Baden, Germany, Nomos Verlagsgesellschaft.

Milberg, W. (2008). "Shifting sources and uses of profits: sustaining US financialization with global value chains." *Economy and Society* **37**(3): 420–51.

—— and D. Schöller (2008). *Globalization, Offshoring and Economic Insecurity in Industrialized Countries*. New York, New School for Social Research.

Milgrom, P. and J. Roberts (1990). "The Economics of Modern Manufacturing: Technology, Strategy, and Organization." *American Economic Review* **80**(3): 511–28.

Miller, L. (1956). "Rules and Exceptions." *Ethics* **66**(4): 262–70.

Mills, C. W. (1940). "Situated Actions and Vocabularies of Motive." *American Sociological Review* **5**(6).

—— (1964). *Sociology and Pragmatism. The Higher Learning in America*. New York, Oxford University Press.

Minssen, H. and C. Riese (2005). "Der Co-Manager und seine Arbeitsweise. Die interne Arbeitsorganisation von Betriebsräten im Oeffentlishen Personennverkehr." *Industrielle Beziehungen* **12**(4): 367–92.

Misa, T. J. (1995). *A Nation of Steel. The Making of Modern America, 1865–1925*. Baltimore, MD, Johns Hopkins University Press.

Moen, E. (2007). Kongsberg—A Small Player in Global Super Games: How Peripheral Actors Can Gain Competitive Leverage. *Transnational Learning Through Local Experimenting: The Creation of Dynamic Complementarities Between Economy and Society*. Helsinki, Translearn: 30.

Mollin, G. (1988). *Montankonzerne und "Drittes Reich."* Göttingen, Germany, Vandenhoeck & Ruprecht.

Montgomery, J. D. (1957). *Forced to Be Free: The Artificial Revolution in Germany and Japan*. Chicago, IL, University of Chicago Press.

Moore, J. (1983). *Japanese Workers and the Struggle for Power, 1945–1947*. Madison, WI, University of Wisconsin Press.

Morgan, G., E. Moen, et al., Eds. (2005). *Changing Capitalisms? Internationalization, Institutional Change and Systems of Economic Organization*. Oxford, UK, Oxford University Press.

Morgan, G., J. Campbell, et al., Eds. (2010). *The Oxford Handbook of Comparative Institutional Analysis*. Oxford, UK, Oxford University Press.

Morgan, K. (2004). "The Exaggerated Death of Geography: Learning, Proximity and Territorial Innovation Systems." *Journal of Economic Geography* **4**: 3–21.

Morikawa, H. (1970). "The Organizatoinal Structure of Misubishi and Mitsui Zaibatsu, 1868–1922: A Comparative Study." *Business History Review* **44**(Spring): 62–83.

—— (1982). *The Zaibatsu in the Japanese Iron and Steel Industry*. Köln, Germany, Zeitschrift für Unternehmensgeschichte.

Morris, J. A. (1954). "The Concept of Steel Capacity." *The Journal of Industrial Economics* **3**(1): 47–59.

Morris-Suzuki, T. (1994). *The Technological Transformation of Japan*. New York, Cambridge University Press.

Mudge, S. (2008). "What Is Neo-liberalism." *Socio-Economic Review* **6**(4): 703–31.

Mueller, H. (1999*a*). "Global Steel Marches Unsteadily into the New Millenium." *Steel Times International*. **23**, May: 30f.

—— (1999*b*). "Steel Survival Strategies, a Sequel." *Steel Times International*. **23**, September: 41f.

—— (2000). "Mills of the New Millenium." *Steel Times International*. **24**, January: 39f.

—— (2002). "Steel Mill Poker: Bluffs, Realities and Strategies." *Steel Times International*. July/August: 46–8.

Müller, G. (1987). *Mitbestimmung in der Nachkriegszeit. Britische Besatzungsmacht-Unternehmer-Gewerkschaften*. Düsseldorf, Schwann.

—— (1991). *Strukturwandel und Arbeitnehmerrechte. Die wirtschaftliche Mitbestimmung in der Eisen- und Stahlindustrie, 1945–1975*. Essen, Klartext Verlag.

Nair, A. (1997). *Evolution of Technology Groups and Their Influence on Member Behavior and Performance: Evidence from the US and Japanese Steel Industries*. Management. New York, Stern School of Business, New York University. PhD.

—— and L. Filer (2003). "Cointegration of Firm Strategies Within Groups: A Long-Run Analysis of Firm Behavior in the Japanese Steel Industry." *Strategic Managment Journal* **24**(2): 145–59.

National Association of Manufacturers (NAM) (2006). *The Facts About Modern Manufacturing*. Washington, DC, The Manufacturing Institute.

Neebe, R. (1981). *Grossindustrie, Staat und NSDAP, 1930–1933*. Göttingen, Germany, Vandenkoeck & Ruprecht.

Negrelli, S. (2002). The Outsourcing Prince: Models of Supply Chain Governance in Italian Automobile Districts (in Italian). *Conference on Supply Chain Governance and Regional Development in the Global Economy*. Madison, WI, University of Wisconsin-Madison.

Nicholls, A. J. (1994). *Freedom With Responsibility. The Social Market Economy in Germany, 1918–1963*. Oxford, UK, Oxford University Press.

Nill, J. (2003). Technological Competition, Time, and Windows of Opportunity—the Case of Iron and Steel Production Technologies. *IÖW Discussion Paper*. Berlin, Institute for Ecological Economy Research.

Ninneman, P. (1997). Clearer Skies at Georgsmarienhütte. *New Steel*, 13.

Nishiguchi, T. (1994). *Strategic Industrial Sourcing: The Japanese Advantage*. New York, Oxford University Press.

—— and J. Brookfield (1997). "The Evolution of Japanese Subcontracting." *MIT Sloan Management Review* **39**(1).

Norbic (2009*a*). "Activities." from http://www.norbic.org/.

—— (2009*b*). "Industrial Training Grants." from http://www.norbic.org/industrial_training_program.htm.

Novak, S. and S. Eppinger (2001). "Sourcing by Design: Product Complexity and the Supply Chain." *Management Science* **47**(1): 189–204.

O'Brien, P. (1992). "Industry Structure as a Competitive Advantage: The History of Japan's Post-war Steel Industry." *Business History* **34**: 128–59.

—— (1994). Governance Systems in Steel: The American and Japanese Experience. *Governing Capitalist Economies. Performance and Control of Economic Sectors.* J. R. Hollingsworth, P. Schmitter, and W. Streeck. New York, Oxford University Press: 43–71.

O'Sullivan, A. (2006). "Why Tense, Unstable, and Diverse Relations Are Inherent in Co-designing with Suppliers: An Aerospace Case Study." *Industrial and Corporate Change* **15**(2): 221–50.

O'Sullivan, M. A. (2000). *Contests for Corporate Control. Corporate Governance and Economic Performance in the United States and Germany.* Oxford, UK, Oxford University Press.

Ojode, L. (2004). "The Impact of Horizontal Strategic Alliances on the US Steel Industry." *Journal of Business Strategies* **21**(2): 149–78.

Okasaki, T. (1994). The Japanese Firm Under Wartime Planned Economy. *The Japanese Firm. Sources of Competitive Strength.* M. Aoki and R. Dore. New York, Oxford University Press: 350–78.

Ondracek, J. and A. Bauerschmidt (1998). "Willy Korf—German Entrepreneur: Case A and Case B." *Entrepreneurship: Theory and Practice* **23**(2): 49–71.

Orr, M. S., Ed. (1990). *Iron and Steel in the Automotive Industry.* Hamilton, Canada.

Ortmann, G. (2003). *Regel und Ausnahme. Paradoxien sozialer Ordnung.* Frankfurt, Germany, Suhrkamp.

Ortner, S. (2006). *Anthropology and Social Theory.* Durham, NC, Duke University Press.

Ortner, S. B. (2001). "Commentary: Practice, Power and the Past." *Journal of Social Archeaology* **1**(2): 271.

—— (2001). "Specifying Agency: The Comaroffs and Their Critics." *Interventions* **3**(1).

Osterman, P. (1999). *Securing Prosperity. The American Labor Market: How It Has Changed and What to Do About it.* Princeton, NJ, Princeton University Press.

Ottati, G. D. (2003). "Exit, Voice and the Evolution of Industrial Districts: The Case of the Post-World War II Economic Development of Prato." *Cambridge Journal of Economics* **27**: 501–22.

—— (1996). "Economic Changes in the District of Prato in the 1980s: Towards a More Conscious and Organized Industrial District." *European Planning Studies* **4**(1): 35–52.

Overy, R. J. (1994). *War and Economy in the Third Reich.* New York, Oxford University Press.

Packer, G. (2008). The Hardest Vote. The Disaffection of Ohio's Working Class. *The New Yorker.* New York, Conde Nast, October 13, 2008.

Panzar, J. and R. Willig (1981). "Economies of Scope." *American Economic Review* **71**: 268–72.

Parrish, J. B. (1956). "Iron and Steel in the Balance of World Power." *Journal of Political Economy* **LXIV** (October 5): 369–88.

Peirce, C. S.(1991*a*). The Fixation of Belief. *Peirce on Signs: Writings on Semiotics by Charles Sanders Peirce.* J. Hoopes. Chapel Hill, NC, University of North Carolina Press: 144–59.

—— (1991*b*). How to Make Our Ideas Clear. *Peirce on Signs: Writings on Semiotics by Charles Sanders Peirce.* J. Hoopes. Chapel Hill, NC, University of North Carolina Press: 160–79.

Pells, R. (1989). *The Liberal Mind in a Conservative Age. American Intellectuals in the 1940s and 1950s.* Middletown, Wesleyan University Press.

Peritz, R. J. (1996). *Competition Policy in America, 1888–1992.* New York, Oxford University Press.

—— (1990). "Frontiers of Legal Thought I: A Counter-History of Anti-Trust Law." *Duke Law Journal,* p. 263–320.

Petersen, D. (1997). Die Sanierung von Firmen als exklusives Hobby. *Handelsblatt,* August 29, 1997.

Phelps, D. H. (2005). US & World Steel Conditions 2005. *Institute for Supply Management Steel Buyers Forum—Spring Session,* American Institute for International Steel, Inc.

Phillips, D. C. (1971). "James, Dewey and the Reflex-Arc." *Journal of the History of Ideas* **32**(4): 555–68.

Pierson, P. (2000). "Increasing Returns, Path Dependence and the Study of Politics." *American Political Science Review* **94**(2): 251–68.

Pierson, P. (2004). *Politics in Time. History, Institutions and Political Analysis.* Princeton, NJ, Princeton University Press.

Piore, M. and C. F. Sabel (1984). *The Second Industrial Divide.* New York, Basic Books.

Pirker, T. (1979). *Die blinde Macht. Die Gewerkschaftsbewegung in Westdeutschland.: vom Ende des Kapitalismus zur Zähmung der Gewerkschaften.* Berlin, Olle & Wolter.

Plumpe, G. (1990). *Die IG Farbenindustrie AG. Wirtschaft, Technik und Politik, 1904–1945.* Berlin, Duncker & Humblodt.

Porter, E. (2005). Reinventing the Mill. *The New York Times.* New York, The New York Times Company, October 22, 2005.

Pounds, N. J. G. (1952). *The Ruhr. A Study in Historical and Economic Geography.* Bloomington, IN, Indiana University Press.

Powell, W. W. (1990). "Neither Market Nor Hierarchy: Network Forms of Organization." *Research in Organizational Behavior* **12**: 295–336.

—— (2001). The Capitalist Firm in the Twenty-First-Century: Emerging Patterns in Western Enterprise. *The Twenty-First-Century-Firm. Changing Economic Organization in International Perspective.* P. DiMaggio. Princeton, NJ, Princeton University Press: 33–68.

Prahalad, C. K. and G. Hamel (1990). "The Core Competence of the Corporation." *Harvard Business Review* **66**(May/June).

Prasad, M. (2006). *The Politics of Free Markets. The Rise of Neoliberal Economic Policies in Britain, France, Germany, and the United States.* Chicago, IL, University of Chicago Press.

Prechel, H. (1990). "Steel and the State: Industry Politics and Business Policy Formation, 1940–1989." *American Sociological Review* **55**(5).

Preston, R. (1991). *American Steel.* New York, Avon Books.

Pritzkoleit, K. (1960). *Männer, Mächte, Monopole Hinter den Türen er westdeutschen Wirtschaft.* Düsseldorf, Germany, Karl Rauch.

Prouvost, S. and J. Wagner-Ferrari (1999). Europe: Mergers, Acquisitions Reshape Steel Industry. *American Metal Market: AMM Flat-Rolled and Galvanized Steel Supplement,* September 19, 1999.

Prowe, D. (1993). German Democratization as Conservative Restabilization: The Impact of American Policy. *American Policy and the Reconstruction of Germany.* J. M. Diefendorf, A. Frohn, and H.-J. Rupieper, Eds. New York, Cambridge University Press: 307–30.

Pyke, F., G. Becattini, et al., Eds. (1990). *Industrial Districts and Interfirm Cooperation in Italy.* Geneva, International Institute for Labor Studies.

Radzio, H. (1991). Als Erbe bleibt nur herzlich wenig. *Handelsblatt,* April 18, 1991.

Rajan, R. and L. Zingales (2004). *Saving Capitalism from the Capitalists: Unleashing the Power of Financial Markets to Create Wealth and Spread Opportunity.* Princeton, NJ, Princeton University Press.

—— and J. Wulf (2003). "The Flattening Firm: Evidence from Panel Data on the Changing Nature of Corporate Hierarchy." Unpublished Manuscript, Chicago, IL, Graduate School of Business, University of Chicago: 31.

Ramanujam, V. and P. Varadarajan (1989). "Research on Corporate Diversification: A Synthesis." *Strategic Management Journal* **10**(6): 523–51.

Ranieri, R. and J. Aylen, Eds. (1998). *The Steel Industry in the New Millennium.* London, IOM Communications.

Ranis, G. (1955). "The Community Centered Entrepreneur in Japanese Development." *Explorations in Economic History* **VIII**(2): 80–98.

Rapp, W. V. (1999*a*). "Steel: Tokyo Steel, K.K., Gaining and Sustaining Long-Term Advantage Through Information Technology." Kyoto, Japan, *The College of International Relations.*

—— (1999*b*). "Steel: Nippon Steel, K.K. Gaining and Sustaining Advantage Through Information Technology." *Columbia University Project: Use of Software to Achieve Competitive Advantage.* New York Columbia University.

Reed, S. and M. Arndt (2004). The Raja of Steel. *Business Week:* 50–2, December 20, 2004.

Rehder, B. (2003). *Betriebliche Bündnisse für Arbeit in Deutschland. Mitbestimmung und Flächentarif im Wandel.* Frankfurt, Germany, Campus Verlag.

Rehder, B. (2006). "Legitimitätsdefizite des Co-Managements. Betriebliche Bündnisse als Konfliktfeld zwischen Arbeitnehmern und betrieblicher Interessenvertretung." *Zeitschrift für Soziologie* **35**(3): 227–42.

Reich, R. (2009). The Future of Manufacturing, GM and American Workers (Parts 1,2 &3). *Robert Reich's Blog.* R. Reich. Berkeley, CA http://robertreich.blogspot.com//search2q= American+.manufacturing.

Relations-Secretariat, I. o. P., Ed. (1941). *Industrial Japan. Aspects of Recent Economic Changes as Viewed by Japanese Writers.* New York, Institute of Pacific Relations.

Reutersberg, B. (1985). *Logistik als Instrument zur Steigerung der Markleistungsfähigkeit von Stahlhandlungen.* Göttingen, Germany, Vandenhoeck & Ruprecht.

Rickert, J., J. Zeitlin, et al. (2000). "Common Problems and Collaborative Solutions: OEM-Supplier Relationships and the Wisconsin Manufacturing Partnership's Supplier Training Consortium." Unpublished manuscript, Madison, WI, Center on Wisconsin Strategy.

Ringleb, G. (1982). Korf senkt Preise bei Walzdraht. *Handelsblatt,* October 6, 1982.

—— (1983). Willy Korf's Höhen- und Tieflüge. Von kühnen Wunschträumen und der harten Realität. *Handelsblatt,* January 10, 1983.

Ro, Y. K., J. K. Liker, et al. (2008). "Evolving Models of Supplier Involvement in Design: The Deterioration of the Japanese Model in US Auto." *IEEE Transactions of Engineering Management* **55**(2): 359–77.

Robert, R. (1976). *Konzentrationspolitik in der Bundesrepublik–Das Beispiel der Entstehung des Gesetzes gegen Wettbewerbsbeschränkung.* Berlin, Duncker & Humblot.

Robertson, A. (2001). "Mobilizing for War, Engineering the Peace: The State, the Shop Floor and the Engineer in Japan, 1935–1960." *Enterprise and Society* **2**: 680–6.

Robertson, S. (2007). Steel's New Heat on Wall Street. *American Metal Market, Metal Bulletin, PLC*: April 23, 2007, pages 4–6.

Roe, M. J. (1996). From Anti-trust to Corporate Governance? The Corporation and the Law, 1959–1994. *The American Corporation Today*. C. Kaysen, Ed. New York, Oxford University Press: 102–27.

Rogers, R. P. (1993). "The Minimum Optimal Steel Plant and the Survivor Technique of Cost Estimation." *Atlantic Economic Journal* **21**(3).

Röper, B., Ed. (1974). *Rationaisierungseffekte der Walzstahlkontore und der Rationalisierungsgruppen*. Berlin, Duncker & Humblot.

Rose, J. D. (1998). "The Struggle over Management Rights at US Steel, 1946–1960: A Reassessment of Section 2-B of the Collective Bargaining Contract." *Business History Review* **72**: 446–77.

—— (2002). "Big Steel: The First Century of the United States Steel Corporation, 1901–2001." *Business History Review* **76**(2): 389ff.

Roth, S. (1997). Germany: Labor's Perspective on Lean Production. *After Lean Production. Evolving Employment Practices in the World Auto Industry*. T. Kochen, R. Lansbury, and J. P. MacDuffie, Eds. Ithaca, NY, Cornell University Press: 109–36.

Rumelt, R. P. (1974). *Strategy, Structure, and Economic Performance*. Cambridge, MA, Harvard University Press.

—— (1982). "Diversification Strategy and Profitability." *Strategic Management Journal* **3**(4): 359–69.

Sabel, C. F. (1989). "Flexible Specialisation and the Re-emergence of Regional Economies." *Reversing Industrial Decline? Industry Structure and Policy in Britain and Her Competitors*. P. Hirst and J. Zeitlin, Eds. Oxford, UK, Berg: 17–70.

—— (1994). "Learning by Monitoring: the Institutions of Economic Development." *The Handbook of Economic Sociology, First Edition*. N. Smelser and R. Swedberg, Eds. Princeton, NJ, Princeton University Press: 137–65.

—— (2001). "Diversity, Not Specialization: The Ties that Bind the (New) Industrial District." *Complexity and Industrial Clusters: Dynamics and Models in Theory and Practice*. Milan, Italy, Accademia Nazionale dei Lincei: 43.

—— (2003). "The World in a Bottle or Window on the World. Open Questions About Industrial Districts in the Spirit of Sebastiano Brusco." Special Issue on Clusters, Industrial Districts and Firms: The Challenge of Globalization. In Honor of Sebastiano Brusco. Modena, Italy, *Stato e Mercato*: 18.

—— (2004). "Pragmatic Collaborations in Practice: A Reply to Herrigel, Whitford and Zeitlin." *Industry and Innovation* **11**(1/2): 81–8.

—— (2005a). "Globalisation, New Public Services, Local Democracy: What's the Connection?" *Local Governance and the Drivers of Growth*. OECD. Paris, OECD: 111–31.

—— (2005b). "A Real Time Revolution in Routines." *The Firm as a Collaborative Community*. C. Heckscher and P. Adler, Eds. Oxford, UK, Oxford University Press: 105–56.

—— and M. Dorf (1998). "A Constitution of Democratic Experimentalism." *Columbia Law Review* **98**.

—— and J. Zeitlin (1985). "Historical Alternatives to Mass Production. Politics, Markets and Technology in Nineteenth Century Industrialization." *Past and Present* **108**(August 1985): 133–76.

—— —— (1997). Stories, Strategies, Structures: Rethinking Historical Alternatives to Mass Production. *Worlds of Possibilities. Flexibility and Mass Production in Western Industrialization*. C. F. Sabel and J. Zeitlin, Eds. Cambridge, UK, Campridge University Press: 1–36.

—— —— (2004). "Neither Modularity Nor Relational Contracting: Inter-Firm Collaboration in the New Economy." *Enterprise and Society* 5(3): 388–403.

Safford, S. (2009). *Why the Garden Club Couldn't Save Youngstown. The Transformation of the Rust-Belt.* Cambridge, MA, Harvard University Press.

Sako, M. (1997). "Shunto: The Role of Employer and Union Coordination at the Industry and Inter-sectoral Levels." *Japanese Labor and Management in Transition.* M. Sako and H. Sato, Eds. London, Routledge: 236–64.

—— (2005). Modularity and Outsourcing: The Nature of Co-Evolution of Product Architecture and Organization Architecture in the Global Automotive Industry. *The Business of Systems Integration.* A. Prencipe, A. Davis, and M. Hobday, Eds. Oxford, UK, Oxford University Press.

—— (2004). "Supplier Development at Honda, Nissan and Toyota: comparative Case Studies of Organizational Capability Enhancement." *Industrial and Corporate Change* 13(2): 281–308.

—— (2006). *Shifting Boundaries of the Firm: Japanese Company—Japanese Labor.* Oxford, UK, Oxford University Press.

—— and F. Murray (1999). "Modular Strategies in Cars and Computers." Survey: Mastering Strategy Part II *Financial Times.* London, Pearson, June 12.

—— and M. Wharburton (1999). *MIT International Motor Vehicle Programme Modulariation and Outsourcing Project Interim Report of the European Research Team.* IMVP Annual Forum. Boston, MA.

Samuels, R. (1987). *The Business of the Japanese State: Energy Markets in Comparative and Historical Perspective.* Ithaca, NY, Cornell University Press.

Saxenian, A. (1994). *Regional Advantage: Culture and Competition in Silicon Valley and Route 128,* Cambridge, MA, Harvard University Press.

Schäfer, W. (1983). Korf-Probleme: Nach dem Sündenfall. *Handelsblatt,* January 6, 1983.

Schatzki, T. R. (2001). *The Practice Turn in Contemporary Theory.* London, Routledge.

Scheppach, W. (1972). *Die japanische Stahlindustrie.* Hamburg, Germany, Mitteilungen des Instituts für Asienkunde.

Scherrer, C. (1988). "Mini-Mills: A New Growth Path for the U.S. Steel Industry?" *Journal of Economic Issues* 22(4).

Schilling, M. A. and H. K. Steensma (2001). Toward a General Modular Systems Theory and Its Application to Interfirm Product Modularity. *Managing in the Modular Age. Architectures, Networks, and Organizations* R. Garud, A. Kumaraswamy, and R. N. Langlois, Eds. Oxford, UK, Blackwell: 172–216.

—— and H. K. Steensma (2001). "The Use of Modular Organizational Forms: An Industry-Level Analysis." *The Academy of Management Journal* 44(6): 1149–68.

Schinkel, W. (2007). "Sociological discourse of the relational: the cases of Bourdieu and Latour." *The Sociological Review* 55(4): 707–29.

Schmidt, E. (1970). *Die Verhinderte Neuordnung.* Frankfurt, Germany, EVA.

Schmidt, J. (1968). *Strukturwandlung des Eisenhandels in der Bundesrepublik als Folge veränderter Markverhältnisse.* Staatswissenschaftlichen Fakultät. München, Ludwig-Maximilians Universität z München. PhD dissertation.

Schmitz, H. (2004). *Local Enterprises in the Global Economy. Issues of Governance and Upgrading.* Cheltenham, UK, Edward Elgar.

Schneiberg, M. and E. Clemens (2006). "The Typical Tools for the Job: Research Strategies in Institutional Analysis." *Sociological Theory* 24(3): 195–227.

Schneider, B. R. (2008). "Comparing Capitalisms: Liberal, Coordinated, Networked and Hierarchical varieties." Unpublished Manuscript Evanston, IL, Northwestern University: 1–36.

Schorsch, L. (2005). "The Industry, the Company, the Acquisition: Introducing Mittal Steel." Chicago, IL, Public Address *SBB Steel Market Conference*: 1–9.

—— and S. Ueyama (1993). "New Game, New Rules." *McKinsey Quarterly* (2): 135–53.

Schorsch, L. L. (2005). *The Industry, the Company, the Acquisitor: Introducing Mittal Steel*, Mittal Steel Publication.

Schrader, S. and H. Sattler (1993). "Zwischenbetriebliche Kooperation: Informaler Infomationsaustausch in den USA und Deutschland." *Die Betriebswirtschaft (DBW)* **53**(5).

Schreiber, P. W. (1978). *IG Farben. Die unschuldige Kriegsplaner.* Stuttgart, Germany, Neuer Weg.

Schröder, E. (1952). Die Westdeutsche Montanindustrie heute. *Der Volkswirt.* **1952**, issue **44**: 27–32.

Schumann, K. (1969). "Korf-stahlhart. Ein Vorwärts-Gespräch mit Willy Korf." *Vorwärts.* Bonn, Germany, April 17, 1969.

Schumann, M., V. Baethke-Kinsky, et al. (1994). *Trendreport Rationalisierung. Automobil Industrie, Werkzeugmaschinenbau, Chemische Industrie.* Berlin, edition Sigma.

—— M. Kuhlmann, et al., Eds. (2006). *Auto 5000: ein neues Produktionskonzept. Die deutsche Antwort auf den Toyota-Weg?*. Hamburg, Germany, VSA-Verlag.

Schumpeter, E. B. (1940). *The Industrialization of Japan and Mauchukuo, 1930–1940.* New York, Macmillan Company.

SEA (2008). "Supplier Excellence Alliance." from http://www.seaonline.org/.

Seebald, C. P. (1992). "Life After the Voluntary Restraint Agreements: The Future of the US Steel Industry." *The George Washington Journal of Law and Economics* **25**(3): 875–905.

Segrestin, B. (2005). "Partnering to Explore: The Renault-Nissan Alliance as a Forerunner of the New Cooperative Patterns." *Research Policy* **34**: 657–72.

Seifert, H. and H. Massa-Wirth (2005). "Pacts for Employment and Competitiveness in Germany." *Industrial Relations Journal* **36**(3): 217–40.

Selznick, P. (1996). "Institutionalism 'Old' and 'New'." *Administrative Science Quarterly* **41**(2).

Sheridan, J. H. (1998). "Steelmaker Nucor Keeps its Workers Razor-Sharp." *Human Resource Management International Digest* **6**(6).

Shimamura, K. (2005). "Three Japanese Steel Makers Enter Production Pact." *The Wall Street Journal.* New York, NY.

Shimokawa, K. (2000). "Reorganization of the Global Automobile Industry and Structural Change of the Automobile Components Industry." *MIT-IMVP Paper.* Cambridge, MA, Massachusetts Institute of Technology-International Motor Vehicle Project.

Shishido, Z. (2000). "Japanese Corporate Governance: The Hidden Problems of Corporate Law and Their Solutions." *Delaware Journal of Corporate Law* **25**(189).

Shusterman, R. (1992). "Pragmatism and Perspectivism on Organic Wholes." *The Journal of Aesthetics and Art Criticism* **50**(1): 56–8.

—— (1994). "Pragmatism and Liberalism Between Dewey and Rorty." *Political Theory* **22**(3): 391–413.

Simon, H. A. (1953). *Administrative Behaviour: A study of decision-making processes in administrative organisation.* New York, Macmillan.

—— (1962). "The Architecture of Complexity." *Proceedings of the American Philosophical Society* **106**(6).

Smelser, N. and R. Swedberg, Eds. (2005). *The Handbook of Economic Sociology.* Princeton, NJ, Princeton University Press.

Smith, S. K. (1995). "Internal Cooperation and Competitive Success: The Case of the US Minimill Sector." *Cambridge Journal of Economics* **19**: 277–304.

Smith, T. C. (1988). *Native Sources of Japanese Industrialization, 1750–1920.* Berkeley, CA, University of California Press.

Smith-Doerr, L. and W. W. Powell (2004). Networks and Economic Life. *The Handbook of Economic Sociology, Second Edition.* N. Smelser and R. Swedberg, Eds. Princeton, NJ, Princeton University Press.

Smitka, M. (1991). *Competitive Ties.* New York, Columbia University Press.

Somers, M. R. (2008). *Genealogies of Citizenship: Markets, Statelessness, and the Right to Have Rights.* New York, Cambridge University Press.

Spies, F. (1978). Beim Stahl kommt Koks ausser mode. *Süddeutsche Zeitung,* November 28, 1978.

—— (1980). Der Aussenseiter rutscht auf die Trainerbank. *Süddeutsche Zeitung,* September 13, 1980.

Springer, R. (1999). *Rückkehr zum Taylorismus? Arbeitspolitik in der Automobilindustrie am Scheideweg.* Frankfurt, Germany, Campus Verlag.

Stahltreuhändervereinigung (1954). *Die Neuordnung der Eisen und Stahlindustrie im Gebiet der Bundesrepublik Deutschland.* München, C. H. Beck'sche Verlagsbuchhandlung.

Stein, J. (1998). *Running Steel, Running America. Race, Economic Policy and the Decline of Liberalism.* Chapel Hill, NC, University of North Carolina Press.

Stokes, R. (1988). *Divide and Prosper: The Heirs of I.G. Farben under Allied Authority.* Berkeley, CA, University of California Press.

Stolper, G. (1948). *German Realities.* New York, Reynal & Hitchcock.

Storper, M. (1997). *The Regional World: Territorial Development in a Global Economy.* New York, The Guilford Press.

—— and R. Salais (1997). *Worlds of Production. The Action Frameworks of the Economy.* Cambridge, MA, Harvard University Press.

Streeck, W. (1992). *Social Institutions and Economic Performance: Studies of Industrial Relations in Advanced Capitalist Economies.* London, Sage.

—— (1997). "Beneficial Constraints: On the Economic Limits of Relational Voluntarism." *Contemporary Capitalism.* J. R. Hollingsworth and R. Boyer, Eds. New York, Oxford University Press.

—— (2005). "Nach dem Korporatismus: Neue Eliten, neue Konflikte." *MPIfG Working Papers.* Köln, Max Planck Institute for the Study of Socieites.

—— and A. Hassel (2005). "The Crumbling Pillars of Social Partnership." *MPIfG Working Papers.* Köln, Max Planck Institute for the Study of Societies.

—— and B. Rehder (2003). "Die Flächentraifvertrag: Krise, Stabilität und Wandel." *Industrielle Beziehungen* **10**(3): 341–62.

—— and K. Thelen, Eds. (2005). *Beyond Continuity. Institutional Change in Advanced Political Economies.* Oxford, UK, Oxford University Press.

—— and K. Thelen (2005). "Introduction: Institutional Change in Advanced Political Economies." *Beyond Continuity: Institutional Change in Advanced Political Economies.* W. Streeck and K. Thelen, Eds. Oxford, UK, Oxford University Press: 1–39.

—— and K. Yamamura (2003). "Introduction: Convergence or Diversity? Stability and Change in German and Japanese Capitalism." *The End of Diversity? Prospects for German and Japanese Capitalism.* K. Yamamura and W. Streeck, Eds. Ithaca, NY, Cornell University Press: 1–50.

Stumpfeldt, B. v. (1995). "Der neue Elektrolichtbogenofen läuft befriedigend." *Handels-blatt,* February 15, 1995.

Sturgeon, T. J. (2002). "Modular Production Networks: A New American Model of Industrial Organization." *Industrial and Corporate Change* **11**(3): 451–96.

—— (2003). "What Really Goes on in Silicon Valley? Spatial Clustering and Dispersal in Modular Production Networks." *Journal of Economic Geography* **3**(2003): 199–225.

—— (2006). "Modular Production's Impact on Japan's Electronics Industry." *IPC Working Paper Series.* Cambridge, MA, MIT-Industrial Performance Center: 28.

—— (2007). "How Globalization Drives Institutional Diversity." *Journal of East Asian Studies* **7**(1): 1–34.

—— and R. Florida (2004). "Globalization, Deverticalization, and Employment in the Motor Vehicle Industry." *Locating Global Advantage. Industry Dynamics in the International Economy.* M. Kenney and R. Florida, Eds. Stanford, CA, Stanford University Press: 52–81.

—— and J.-R. Lee (2001). Industry Co-Evolution and the Rise of a Shared Supply-Base for Electronics Manufacturing. *Industrial Performance Center Working Papers.* Cambridge, MA, MIT-IPC.

—— and R. K. Lester (2001*a*). "The New Global Supply-Base: New Challenges for Local Suppliers in East Asia." *Industrial Performance Center Working Paper Series.* Cambridge, MA, MIT: 55.

—— and R. Lester (2001*b*). "Upgrading East Asian Industries: New Challenges for Local Suppliers." *MIT IPC Working Paper.* Cambridge, MA, Massachusetts Institute of Technology-Industrial Performance Center: 70.

—— J. Van Biesebroeck, et al. (2008). "Value Chains, Networks, and Clusters: Reframing the Global Automotive Industry." *MIT Industrial Performance Center Working Paper.* Cambridge, MA, MIT: 33.

Sturm, N. (1983). "Korf pokert um Bürgschaften." *Süddeutsche Zeitung,* January 7, 1983.

Suri, R. (1998). *Quick Response Manufacturing. A Companywide Approach to Reducing Lead Times.* Portland, OR, Productivity Press.

Suzuki, A. (1997). *The Polarization of the Union Movement in Post War Japan: Politics in the Unions of Steel and Railway Workers.* Department of Sociology. Madison, WI, University of Wisconsin-Madison. PhD dissertation.

Taylor, C. (1999). "To Follow a Rule." *Bourdieu. A Critical Reader.* R. Schusterman, Ed. Oxford, UK, Blackwell.

Taylor, G. D. (1979). "The Rise and Fall of Anti-Trust in Occupied Germany, 1945–48." *Prologue* **11**(1): 22–39.

Teece, D. (1980). "The Economics of Scope and the Scope of Enterprise." *Journal of Economic Behavior and Organization*(1): 223–47.

Teuteberg, H. J. (1961). *Geschichte der industriellen Mitbestimmung in Deutschland.* Tübingen, Germany, JCB Mohr (Paul Siebeck).

Thatcher, M. (2007). *Internationalization and Economic Institutions. Comparing European Experiences.* Oxford, UK, Oxford University Press.

Thelen, K. (1991). *Union of Parts.* Ithaca, NY, Cornell University Press.

—— (1999). "Historical Institutionalism in Comparative Politics." *Annual Review of Political Science* **2**: 369–404.

—— (2004). *How Institutions Evolve. The Political Economy of Skills in Germany, Britain, the United States and Japan.* New York, Cambridge University Press.

—— (2010). "Beyond Comparative Statics: Historical Institutional Approaches to Stability and Change in the Political Economy of Labor." *Oxford Handbook of Comparative*

Institutional Analysis. Glenn Morgan, J. Campbell, C. Crouch, O. K. Pedersen, and R. Whitley, Eds. Oxford, UK, Oxford University Press.

Thelen, K. and I. Kume (2003). "The Future of Nationally Embedded Capitalism: Industrial Relations in Germany and Japan." *The End of Diversity?* K. Yamamura and W. Streeck, Eds. Ithaca, NY, Cornell University Press: 183–212.

Tiffany, P. A. (1988). *The Decline of American Steel. How Management, Labor and Government Went Wrong*. New York, Oxford University Press.

Tilton, M. (1996). *Restricted Trade. Cartels in Japan's Basic Materials Industries*. Ithaca, NY, Cornell University Press.

—— (1998). "Anti-trust Policy and Japan's International Steel Trade." *The Changing Japanese Firm*. New York, Center on Japanese Economy and Business, Columbia University.

—— (2005). "Industrial Policy and Self-Regulation in the Steel Industry." Conference paper, Chicago, IL, Association of Asian Studies.

Treado, C. (2004). "Imports, Technology and the Success of the American Steel Industry." *Sloan Industry Studies Working Paper Series*. Pittsburgh, PA, University of Pittsburgh Sloan Steel Industry Center.

Turner, H. A. (1985). *German Big Business and the Rise of Hitler*. New York, Oxford University Press.

Turner, I., Ed. (1989). *Reconstruction in Post-war Germany: British Occupation Policy and the Western Zones, 1945–55*. Oxford, UK, Berg.

Tylecote, A. and Y. D. Cho (1998). "National Technological Styles Explained in Terms of Stakeholding Patterns, Enfranchisement . . . " *Technology Analysis and Strategic Management* **10**(4): 423ff.

Uebbing, H. (1982). "Gegen Subventionen kein Geld verplempern." *Frankfurter Allgemeine Zeitung*, September 10, 1982.

—— (1983). "Ein Aussenseiter brauchelt. Wie Korf in die Krise geriet." *Frankfurter Allgemeine Zeitung*, January 8, 1983.

Ulrich, K. (1995). "The Role of Product Architecture in the Manufacturing Firm." *Research Policy* **24**: 419–40.

—— T. Randall, et al. (1998). "Managing Product Variety: A Study of the Bicycle Industry." *Managing Product Variety*. T. Ho and C. Tang, Eds. Dordrecht, Kluwer.

Unger, R. M. (2007). *The Self Awakened. Pragmatism Unbound*. Cambridge, MA, Harvard University Press.

Uriu, R. M. (1989). *The Political Economy of Adjustment: The Case of Japanese Minimills, 1970–1988*. Canberra, Research School of Pacific Studies, Australian National University.

—— (1996). *Troubled Industries: Confronting Economic Change in Japan*. Ithaca, NY, Cornell University Press.

Uzzi, B. (1996). "The Sources and Consequences of Embeddedness for the Economic Performance of Organizations: The Network Effect." *American Sociological Review* **61** (August): 674–98.

—— (1997). "Social Structure and Competition in Interfirm Networks: The Paradox of Embeddedness." *Administrative Science Quarterly* **42**(1): 35–67.

Veblen, T. (1904 (1978)). *The Theory of the Business Enterprise*. New Brunswick, NJ, Transaction Books.

—— (1914). *The Instinct of Workmanship and the State of the Industrial Arts*. New York, Macmillan.

Vestal, J. E. (1993). *Planning for Change. Industrial Policy and Japanese Economic Development, 1945–1990*. New York, Oxford University Press.

Vitols, S. (1995). *Corporate Governance Versus Economic Governance: Banks and Industrial Restructuring in the U.S. and Germany.* WZB Discussion Papers. Berlin, Wissenschaftszentrum: 51.

—— (1999). "The Origins of Bank-Based and Market-Based Financial Systems: Germany, Japan, the United States." Unpublished Manuscript, Social Science Research Center, Berlin.

—— (2003). "From Banks to Markets: The Political Economy of Liberalization of the German and Japanese Financial Systems." *The End of Diversity? Prospects for German and Japanese Capitalism.* K. Yamamura and W. Streeck, Eds. Ithaca, NY, Cornell University Press: 240–61.

Voack, N. (1962). *Die japanische Zaibatsu und die Konzentration wirtschaftlicher Macht in ihren Händen.* Volkswirtschaftslehre. Erlangen, Germany, Universität Erlangen-Nürnberg. PhD dissertation.

Voelzkow, H. (2007). *Jeneseits nationaler Produktionsmodelle? Die Governance regionaler Wirtschaftscluster. International vergleichende Analysen.* Marburg, Germany, Metropolis Verlag.

Vogel, S. (2006). *Japan Remodeled: How Government and Industry Are Reforming Japanese Capitalism.* Ithaca, NY, Cornell University Press.

Voskamp, U. (2005). "Grenzen der Modularität-Chancen für Hochlohnstandorte in globalen Produktions- und Innovationsnetzwerken." *SOFI-Mitteilungen* 33: 115–30.

Wagner, S. M. and C. Buko (2005). "An Empirical Investigation of Knowledge-Sharing in Networks." *The Journal of Supply Chain Management* 41: 17–31.

Waller, S. W. (1998). "Prosecution by Regulation: The Changing Nature of Anti-trust Enforcement." *Oregon Law Review* 77: 1383–449.

Wantuck, K. (1989). *Just in Time For America. A Common Sense Production Strategy.* Southfield, MI, KWA Media.

Ward, R. E. and Y. Sakamoto Eds. (1987). *Democratizing Japan. The Allied Occupation* Honolulu, HI, University of Hawaii Press.

Warner, I. (1989). "Allied-German Negotiation on the Deconcentration of the Steel Industry." *Reconstruction in Post-War Germany. British Occupation Policy and Western Zones.* I. Turner, Ed. Oxford, UK, Berg 185F.

—— (1996). *Steel and Sovereignty. The Deconcentration of the West German Steel Industry, 1949–1954.* Mainz, Germany, Verlag Philipp von Zabern.

Warren, K. (1973). *The American Steel Industry 1850–1970. A Geographical Interpretation.* Pittsburgh, PA, University of Pittsburgh Press.

Weder, D. (1968). *Die 200 Grössten deutschen Aktiengesellschaften 1913–1962 Beziehungen zwischen Grösse, Lebensdauer und Wettbewerbschancen von Unternehmen.* Wirtschaftslehre. Frankfurt, Germany, Goethe Universitat Frankfurt. PhD dissertation.

Weil, P. (1970). *Wirtschaftsgeschichte des Ruhrgebietes.* Essen, Germany, Siedlungsverband Ruhrkohlenbezirk Essen.

Weinert, H. (1995). "Perspektiven cler Stahlindustrie in hochentwickelten Ländern." *RUFIS: Ruhr-Forschungsinstitut für Innovations- und strukturpolitik e.V.* Bochum, Germany, Ruhr-Rorschungsinstitut für Innovations- und Strukturpolitik e.V. 2.

—— (1997). "Die Wettbewerbsintensitaet der Stahlmärkte—eine theoretische und empirische Analyse." *RUFIS: Ruhr-Forschungsinstitut für Innovations- und Strukturpolitik e. V.* Bochum, Germany, RUFIS: Ruhr-Forschungsinstitut für Innovations- und Strukturpolitik e.V. 2.

Weiss, H. (2001). "Welcome to the Technology of SMS Demag." *Steel Times*, September, 2001, pp. 285–286.

Welch, M. M. (2002). "The Social Production of Insecurity: An Examination of the Cultural Production of the United States' Steel Industry as a Matter of National Security." Department of Political Science. Chicago, IL, University of Chicago. BA paper: 42p.

Wellhöner, V. (1989). *Grossbanken und Grossindustrie im Kaiserreich.* Göttingen, Germany, Vandenhoeck & Ruprecht.

Wells, L. T., Ed. (1972). *The Product Life Cycle and International Trade.* Boston, MA, Harvard Business School Division of Research.

Wengenroth, U. (1986). *Unternehmensstrategien und technischer Fortschritt. Die deutsche und die britische Stahlindustrie, 1865–1895.* Göttingen, Germany, Vandenhoeck & Ruprecht.

Whalen, J. (2002). "Valley Industrial Association: Multi-Training Grant." *Conference on Supply Chain Governance and Regional Development in the Global Economy.* AMP/COWS. Madison, WI, University of Wisconsin-Madison.

Whitford, J. (2001). "The Decline of a Model? Challenge and Response in the Italian Industrial Districts." *Economy and Society* **30**(1): 38–65.

—— (2002). "Pragmatism and the Untenable Dualism of Means and Ends: Why Rational Choice Theory Does Not Deserve Paradigmatic Privilege." *Theory and Society* **31**(3): 325–63.

—— (2006). *The New Old Economy: Networks, Institutions, and the Organizational Transformation of American Manufacturing.* New York, Oxford University Press.

—— and A. Enrietti (2005). "Surviving the Fall of a King: The Regional Institutional Implications of Crisis at Fiat Auto." *International Journal of Urban and Regional Research* **29**: 771–95.

—— and C. Potter (2007). "Regional Economies, Open Networks and the Spatial Fragmentation of Production." *Socio-Economic Review* **5**(3): 497–526.

—— and J. Zeitlin (2004). "Governing Decentralized Production: Institutions, Public Policy, and the Prospects for Inter-firm Collaboration in US Manufacturing." *Industry and Innovation* **11**(1/2): 11–44.

Whitley, R. (1999). *Divergent Capitalisms. The Social Structuring and Change of Business Systems.* Oxford, UK, Oxford University Press.

—— (2000). "The Institutional Structuring of Innovation Strategies: Business Systems, Firm Types, and Patterns of Technical Change in Different Market Economies." *Organization Studies* **21**(5): 855–86.

—— (2002). "Developing Innovative Competencies: The Role of Institutional Frameworks." *Industrial and Corporate Change* **11**(3): 497–528.

Wilkins, B. T. (1959). "Pragmatism as a Theory of Historical Knowledge: John Dewey on the Nature of Historical Inquiry." *The American Historical Review* **64**(4): 878–90.

Williams, K. and M. Geppert (2006). "The German Model of Employee Relations on Trial: Negotiated and Unilaterally Imposed Change in Multi-national Companies." *Industrial Relations Journal* **37**(1): 48–63.

Wintermann, J. H. (1998). "GM-Hütte im Subventions-Clinch." *Die Welt,* December 17, 1998.

Wirtschaftswoche (1972). *Wirtschaftswoche.* **2**: January 18, 1972, 62–3.

Wittke, V. (2007). "Weder Chandler noch Wintelismus. Zu neuen Formen industrieller Governance." *Arbeitspolitik im Wandel-Entwicklung und Perspecktiven der Arbeitspolitik.* E. Hildebrandt, U. Jürgens, M. Oppen, and C. Teipen, Eds. Berlin, edition sigma: 153–64.

Wolf, M. (2008). *Fixing Global Finance.* Baltimore, MD, Johns Hopkins University Press.

Wolfe, D. A. and M. S. Gertler (2004). "Clusters from the Inside and Out: Local Dynamics and Global Linkages." *Urban Studies* **41**(5/6): 1071–93.

Womack, J., D. T. Jones, et al. (1990). *The Machine That Changed the World*. New York, HarperCollins.

Wood, S., Ed. (1989). *The Transformation of Work?: Skill, Flexibility, and the Labour Process*. London, Unwin Hyman.

Wulff, H. H. (1958). *Der Preiswettbewerb auf dem gemeinsamen Market für Stahl*. Rechts und Staatswissenschaftlichen Fakultät. Marburg, Philipps-Universität Marburg. PhD dissertation.

Wypijewski, J. (2002). Whose Steel? *The Nation*, July 15, 2002.

Wysocki, B., K. Maher, et al. (2007). "New Clout—A Labor Union's Power: Blocking Takeover Bids; Steel-Company Buyers Learn They Must Get USW on their Side". *The Wall Street Journal*. New York, Dow Jones, May 9, 2007: A1.

Yamamura, K. (1967). *Economic Policy in Postwar Japan. Growth Versus Economic Democracy*. Berkeley, CA, University of California Press.

—— (1995). "The Role of Government in Japan's 'Catch-up' Industrialization: A Neo-institutionalist Perspective." *The Japanese Civil Service and Economic Development*. H. K. Kim, M. Muramatsu, and T. J. Pempel, Ed. New York, Oxford University Press: 103–32.

—— (1997). "Entrepreneurship, Ownership, and Management in Japan." *The Economic Emergence of Modern Japan*. K. Yamamura, Ed. New York, Cambridge University Press: 294–352.

—— and W. Streeck, Eds. (2003). *The End of Diversity? Prospects for German and Japanese Capitalism*. Ithaca, NY, Cornell University Press.

Yonekura, S. (1991). "The Post-War Japanese Iron and Steel Industry: Continuity and Discontinuity." *Changing Patterns of International Rivalry*. E. Abe and Y. Suzuki, Eds. Tokyo, University of Tokyo Press: 193–241.

—— (1993). "Postwar Reform in Management and Labor: The Case of the Steel Industry." *The Japanese Experience of Economic Reforms*. J. Teranishi and Y. Kosai, Eds. London, St Martin's Press: 205–40.

—— (1994). *The Japanese Iron and Steel Industry: Continuity and Discontinuity*. New York, St. Martin's Press.

—— (1996). "Industrial Associations as Interactive Knowledge Creation. The Essence of Japanese Industrial Policy Creation." *Japanese Yearbook on Business History* **13**: 27–51.

Zeitlin, J. (2007). Industrial Districts and Regional Clusters. *The Oxford Handbook of Business History*. G. Jones and J. Zeitlin, Eds. Oxford, UK, Oxford University Press: 219–43.

Zenger, T. R. and W. S. Hesterly (1997). "The Disaggregation of Corporations: Selective Intervention, High-Powered Incentives, and Molecular Units." *Organization Science* **8**(3): 209–22.

Ziegler, J. N. (2000). "Corporate Governance and the Politics of Property Rights in Germany." *Politics and Society* **28**(2): 195–221.

Zizalova, P. (2007). "Foreign Direct Investment and Czech Automotive Industry: TPCA Case Study." *Workshop on the Relocation and the Changing Relations Between High Wage and Low Wage Countries in the Auto Industry*. Berlin: WZB-Berlin: 26.

Index